Milton and the Tangles of Neaera's Hair

Milton
and the
Tangles of
Neaera's
Hair

The Making of
the 1645 *Poems*

Stella P. Revard

University of Missouri Press *Columbia and London*

Copyright © 1997 by
The Curators of the University of Missouri
University of Missouri Press, Columbia, Missouri 65201
Printed and bound in the United States of America
All rights reserved
5   4   3   2   1   01   00   99   98   97

Library of Congress Cataloging-in-Publication Data

Revard, Stella Purce.
    Milton and the tangles of Neaera's hair : the making of the 1645
Poems / Stella P. Revard.
        p.   cm.
    Includes bibliographical references (p.) and index.
    ISBN 0-8262-1100-3 (alk. paper)
    1. Milton, John, 1608–1674—Knowledge—Mythology.   2. Milton,
John, 1608–1674—Knowledge—Literature.   3. Classical poetry—
Appreciation—England.   4. Mythology, Classical, in literature.
5. English poetry—Classical influences.   I. Title.
PR3592.M96R48   1997
821'.4—dc21   97-360
                                                                                      CIP

♾™ This paper meets the requirements of the
American National Standard for Permanence of Paper
for Printed Library Materials, Z39.48, 1984.

Designer: Stephanie Foley
Typesetter: BOOKCOMP
Printer and binder: Thomson-Shore, Inc.
Typefaces: Garamond and Medici Script

The University of Missouri Press gratefully acknowledges the support of these individuals and divisions of Southern Illinois University at Edwardsville: Steven Hansen of the
Graduate School; Alice Petry, Chair of the English Department; and Sharon Hahs, Dean
of the College of Arts and Sciences.

For credits, see page 299.

In Memory of

Irene Samuel
and
Gertrude C. Drake

Contents

Preface

In 1991 in the beautiful sculpture hall of the Ny Carlsberg Glyptotek in Copenhagen, I had the privilege of delivering the plenary address for the Congress of the International Assocation for Neo-Latin Studies. The lecture bore the future title of this book: "The Tangles of Neaera's Hair" and dealt with the influence of the classical and neo-Latin tradition on Milton. As I looked about me in that sculpture hall and saw in marble the statues of Athene, Bacchus, Aphrodite, Apollo, the Muses and the Graces, I had visual testimony of how the tradition that shaped Milton was also shaping my work on him. I am grateful to the Huntington Library for a fellowship in Spring 1991 that helped me begin work on this project, to the National Endowment of the Humanities for support in 1993 and 1994, and to the Folger Shakespeare Libarary for a fellowship in the Fall of 1994 that enabled me to revise and complete the study. I wish to thank those who offered encouragement and wrote letters in support: Richard Schoeck, Michael Lieb, Louis Martz, Julia Gaisser, Carl Conrad, John Roberts, Paul Sellin, and Mario Di Cesare. I am also grateful to the Provost of Southern Illinois University, David Werner, and to the Graduate School, the School of Humanities, and the Department of English for research grants and released time for research. My thanks, also, to those individuals at Southern Illinois University who particularly helped the process: Isaiah Smithson, Carol Keene, Jean Kittrell, Rosemary Archangel, and Steven Hansen. I wish to thank David Butler and the School of Humanities for purchasing computing equipment that much facilitated my work. I appreciate the comments and suggestions of the readers for University of Missouri Press—Stephen Honeygosky and John Roberts—and a third anonymous reader. I also wish to thank Beverly Jarrett, the Editor-in-Chief of the University of Missouri Press, for her solid support of the book, and Jane Lago, the Managing Editor.

I am particularly grateful to Louis Martz who asked me to deliver the address, "The Nativity Ode: Apollo and the Flight of the Pagan Gods," for the Milton Society of America in 1992. The address first appeared as part of an essay on "Apollo and Christ in Seventeenth-Century Religious Lyric," in John Roberts's collection, *New Perspectives on the Seventeenth-Century English Religious Lyric* (Columbia: University of Missouri Press, 1994), and has now been reworked once again as Chapter 3 of this book. Other chapters contain material that first appeared in the following articles and essays: " 'L'Allegro' and 'Il Penseroso': Classical Tradition and Renaissance Mythography," *PMLA,* 101 (May 1986), 338–50; "The Tangles of Neaera's Hair: Milton and Neo-Latin Ode," *Acta Conventus Neo-Latini Hafniensis,* (Binghamton: MRTS, 1994), 75–96; "Alpheus, Arethusa, and the Pindaric Pursuit in 'Lycidas,' " *Of Poetry and Politics: New Essays on Milton and His World,* ed. Paul Stanwood (Binghamton: MRTS, 1994); "Ad Joannem Rousium: Elegiac Wit and Pindaric Mode," *The Urbane Milton,* ed. James Freeman and Anthony Low (Pittsburgh: University of Pittsburgh Press, 1984). I am grateful to the University of Missouri Press, to Medieval and Renaissance Texts and Studies, to the University of Pittsburgh Press, and to the Publications of the Modern Language Association for permission to reprint.

The book is dedicated to two extraordinary scholars who influenced my work on Milton and on classical and neo-Latin studies. They did not know one another, but they both studied with a third extraordinary scholar, Lane Cooper. Irene Samuel was my teacher at Hunter College; Gertrude Drake my colleague at Southern Illinois University. Irene taught me what I know about Milton; Gertrude insisted that I work on my Latin and that I learn Greek. She also took me to my first neo-Latin Congress in Tours in 1976.

Much of the pleasure of this book has been its delightful and sometimes tangled path from concept to composition to publication. I have enjoyed the company of other scholars as I searched for phoenixes at the Huntington, for Muses as the Bodleian, for Apollo at the Vatican, for Cyrene at the British Museum, and for Graces everywhere. Another pleasure has been delivering various parts of this book at conferences from Vancouver to Bangor, from Southern California to Cambridge. My thanks to those who listened with sympathy and understanding.

Oxford
October 8, 1996

Milton and the Tangles of Neaera's Hair

Introduction

Milton's 1645 *Poems,* his first published volume of poetry, is a double book, comprising an opening volume of English poems followed by a volume of Latin poemata with its own separate title page, preface, and set of dedicatory poems. Scholars have long recognized that the first English volume is a precisely ordered book that carefully presents a portrait of an aspiring young poet even as it arranges in sequence the poems that introduce him to the world. The title page of the English volume with its Latin epigraph and facing portrait above a Greek epigram advertises the future *vates,* as Milton calls himself. In the English volume Milton has carefully placed his coming-of-age poem—the Nativity ode— first and placed last his most mature English works: "Lycidas," followed by the *Mask at Ludlow,* the work that had won him praise from English readers. He takes care to showcase himself as a poet in these first and last selections and at the same time to build his poetic reputation along the way by skillful positioning of poems such as "L'Allegro" and "Il Penseroso." Louis L. Martz and most recently C. W. R. D. Moseley have examined the way in which the English sequence is arranged and developed.[1] Although scholars have recognized that the Latin sequence of the second book is also comparably arranged, it has not received comparable attention. But the Latin sequence not only tells its own story with the unfolding of each of the poems in its collection, it also balances and speaks to the English collection. Both English and Latin sections follow a roughly

1. See Louis L. Martz, "The Rising Poet," in *The Lyric and Dramatic Milton,* 3–33. Gale Carrithers also argues that the order of both English and Latin poems constitutes a meaningful sequence; while he only examines the English poem, he notes that the order of the Latin poems deserves to be just as closely examined. See Gale H. Carrithers Jr., "*Poems* (1645): On Growing Up," in *MS* 15. Also see C. W. R. D. Moseley, *The Poetic Birth: Milton's Poems of 1645.* Although Moseley devotes his primary attention to the English poems, he briefly discusses most of the Latin poems and even appends a translation of them to his text.

chronological order of presentation. The first Latin poems introduce us to a younger schoolboy Milton and the last Latin poems, however, present us with a more mature Milton who has already composed most of the English poems of the book. Both English and Latin poems are concerned with self-presenting, but the Latin poems more often speak intimately of the poet's hopes and aspirations. Understanding how the second volume relates to the first—reading the Latin poems in tandem with the English— considerably enhances our understanding both of the English poems and their Latin counterparts. To ignore the Latin section of the double book and confine our attention only to the well-known English works upsets the careful balance of the book that Milton published and ignores the intentions of its author. The sections of this double book work together, much as Milton's famous twin poems, "L'Allegro" and "Il Penseroso" do. For example, "Lycidas" and "Epitaphium Damonis," though composed in different languages, are Milton's penultimate and ultimate works in each volume, his only pastoral laments, and should be read together, since together they each close a poetic book and a stage of his poetic life. The anonymity of "Lycidas" falls away, however, in "Epitaphium Damonis" when Milton takes on the person of the classical Thyrsis and pours his heart out—in Latin. Thus it completes "Lycidas" and advances beyond it. "L'Allegro" and "Il Penseroso" not only balance one another, but they are in turn balanced by Latin poems such as "Elegia 1" and "Elegia 6," which deal with much of the same material. When we consider the making of Milton's 1645 volume, it is necessary to consider both English and Latin parts.

Both the English and the Latin volumes are miscellaneous collections, organized not just by chronology but also by generic type.[2] The English volume collects a wide range of genres: it begins with odes—brief and extended—and with psalms (the Hebraic equivalent to the ode); it groups English and Italian sonnets; it includes an epitaph and two pastoral masks. The Latin collection—no less miscellaneous and experimental— comprises elegies and odes and epigrams, funera, and a pastoral epitaph, as well as commendatory and philosophical verse, and a brief "epic" in Latin hexameters. The Latin volume, like many neo-Latin books, is divided into two parts, both also organized metrically and chronologically. The first is a book of seven elegies *(Elegiarum Liber)*, followed by a set of epigrams, also, like them, in elegiac couplets. The second—a book of *sylvae* or miscellaneous poems *(Sylvarum Liber)*—comprises works in other meters—odes, iambics, hexameters—and also includes two poems in

---

2. Critics have remarked upon the diversity of types among Milton's poems in both the number of genres they represent as well as their metrical types. See Martz and Moseley.

Greek. An even more miscellaneous collection, its title *sylvae,* or "woods," makes us recall that Ben Jonson's "Underwoods" and "Forest" are just such miscellaneous collections. Each book of the Latin poems, like its English counterpart, progresses from the earliest work of the poet to the most mature poems. The book of elegies contains elegies and epigrams composed during his Cambridge years but closes with the mature epigrams to Leonora Baroni that Milton wrote during the Italian voyage. The sylvae move from the Cambridge years to a final Latin group, most of which were composed in Italy in the late 1630s. Except for the few English sonnets of the 1640s included with the sonnet group of the first volume, the Latin sylvae represent the final poems composed—Milton's last thoughts as a young developing poet.

The publication of English and Latin works together is not unusual for a seventeenth-century poet. Contemporaries of Milton were accustomed to publishing their Latin poems with their English—and poetry in Latin was highly prized and admired. During James I's reign there was an efflorescence of Latin poetry, particularly among Scottish poets—John Barclay, John Leech, John Scotus, David Hume, Arthur Johnston, and William Alexander—all of whom followed the example of their most famous neo-Latin compatriot of the sixteenth century, George Buchanan. Their counterparts exist in English with the Fletchers and many others who composed Latin verse. We have only to point out how Alexander Gil, the son of Milton's schoolmaster at St Paul's School and ten years Milton's senior, published his Latin *Parerga* in 1632. Besides that, there was the outpouring of Latin verse in the 1610s, 20s, and 30s from university volumes that came forth regularly for official occasions—weddings and funerals and returns of the king and the prince from abroad. The university collection for Edward King, in which "Lycidas" is published, is only one of these—a double book, like Milton's *Poems,* with a first volume of Latin poems followed by a second of English. When he published his own double book, Milton reversed that order, giving priority to his English verse. But for Milton the Latin poems were not an afterthought to be consigned to an index.

While Milton's continental reputation as a Latinist was based on his prose and on his official position as Latin secretary, it was also supported by these Latin poems. When Milton went to Italy in 1638 and 1639, he was hailed as the writer of the elegies and odes of the *Poemata,* not as the writer of the *Mask at Ludlow* and "Lycidas" for which he had attained comparatively lesser fame in England.[3] Contemporary Italian writers wrote extravagant

---

3. See J. Milton French, ed., *The Life Records of John Milton,* 1.389, 408, 409. French has consulted the records of the academy of the Svogliati in Florence that mark occasions on which Milton read Latin poems.

testimonia for this verse and for Milton as a future Homer or Vergil or Tasso. Accordingly he affixed these testimonia to the *Poemata* in recognition of his contemporaries' tribute to him and his own accomplishments in Latin verse. Unless we include Humphrey Moseley's preface advertising the volume and the new poet or Henry Wotton's letter, no comparable testimonia exist for the English poems.[4] Paradoxically, Milton gradually turned away from Latin poetry at the very time that he produced his last and best Latin poems in the late 1630s, for he had already determined to devote himself to the English language. That he records his turn to English poetry in Latin verse is curious. But then his most intimate disclosures both about poetics and his personal life are often recorded in Latin.

That his departure to Italy should trigger a second and more mature phase of Latin composition is not so surprising when we consider that Italy was the cradle of the Renaissance and the Renaissance sparked among the poets of Italy in the fifteenth and sixteenth century a renewed and serious production of Latin poetry. Closely following classical models, the humanist poets from the fifteenth century on strove to produce in Renaissance Latin—that is, in neo-Latin—works that would be the equals of Vergil's or Ovid's or Propertius's or Horace's in Latin and Theocritus's or Pindar's or Callimachus's in Greek. As a humanist poet, Milton shared their aims. Serving an apprenticeship as a neo-Latin poet, he modeled his verse not only on the classical Roman and Greek elegies, odes, and epigrams that he knew so well, but also paid attention to the tradition of Renaissance imitation that lay immediately behind him. As a poet who from his earliest youth produced poetry in Latin, Milton could not escape from the Renaissance Latinity of this tradition that, together with the Latin and Greek classics, had formed him. Even as late as the 1630s, some years after he had finished his formal training at Cambridge, he decided to complete his "education" as a poet by setting aside several years to read both ancient Greek and Latin poetry and the continental scholarship that supported this poetry. While scholars have explored the classical underpinnings of Milton's poetry, many of its neoclassical sources—the rich Renaissance tradition of Latin imitation on the continent—remain undisclosed.

Renaissance Latin and vernacular poets provide a link between the classical and Christian worlds and help us to understand the nature of Milton's classical imitation. Long before Milton undertook his classical imitations,

4. Peter Lindenbaum discusses the context for the publication of the 1645 *Poems* and the relevance of Moseley's preface in the following essays: "John Milton and the Republican Mode of Literary Production," in *YES* 21:121–22, 129–32; "The Poet in the Marketplace: Milton and Samuel Simmons," in *Of Poetry and Politics,* 260–61.

neo-Latin poets were imitating the classical genres of ode, eclogue, and epigram and were transforming these genres, adapting them to their own time and culture. Pontano, Poliziano, Marullo, Flaminio, Crinito, Bembo, Secundus, Amalteo, and Buchanan—to name a few—were immensely popular writers that Milton would have known. All are mentioned by Edward Phillips in his *Theatrum Poetarum* as prominent "modern" poets, and we may safely assume that Milton's nephew would not have given attention to neo-Latin poets of which his schoolmasterly uncle was ignorant. To suppose that Milton only studied Horace's and Catullus's lyrics without knowing Pontano's and Secundus's imitations, that he knew Vergil's eclogues but not Amalteo's or Bembo's, or Martial's epigrams but not Marullo's, is preposterous. Not only were they readily available to him in anthologies and single editions, but also they were of primary importance since Milton was interested in what other poets working in Latin and in the vernaculars had done with classical models. As Richard Schoeck has pointed out, Milton refers to Neaera in "Lycidas" not because he is thinking of the classical mistress of Horace or Tibullus, but because he knows this was the name Pontano, Marullo, Secundus, and countless other neo-Latin poets chose for their mistress. This tradition of classical imitation was vital not just for the Latin, but also for the English poetry. Whether he produced imitations of classical ode, eclogue, elegy, or mask in English or in Latin, Milton was deeply affected by the example of Renaissance Latin poets and often drew on their work as well as on ancient models. In experimenting in English with different types of ode forms (from the funeral ode to the birth ode to the hymn to the monody), he is trying out different Renaissance adaptations of classical models. Milton's English poems have important classical and neo-Latin referents. Can we imagine "Lycidas" stripped of its classical dress and form? Or "L'Allegro," "Il Penseroso," and the Ludlow *Mask* without their mythological play? Milton's English poems are in a way just as densely classical and neoclassical as his Latin poems. As influenced as he was by the native tradition—by Spenser, Drayton, Shakespeare, and the Fletchers—Milton as often turned to the continent and to the tradition of Latinity that he found very much alive when he visited Italy in 1638 and 1639. Classical poets gave Milton the basic models for his poetry; Renaissance poets showed him what he could do with those models. If one of the aims of this book is to study how Milton's English and Latin poems balance one another, the second aim is to understand how the continental Renaissance shaped Milton's poetry both in English and Latin.

Both the order of presentation and the order of composition are important when we look at Milton's 1645 *Poems*. But if we wish to evaluate Milton's development as a poet, we must replicate in our investigation the order of composition. We cannot simply begin with the English poems, first reading the English book and then turning to the Latin book. We must look first at the earliest Latin poems—primarily those of his Cambridge years. Over half of the Latin poems were composed before the English poems that introduce the first volume. The English works from the Nativity ode to "Lycidas" exist, as it were, between these Latin parameters. After he broke into English at the end of 1629 with his Nativity ode, he composed few—almost no—Latin poems until the eve of his departure for the continent, in 1638, when he returned to Latin verse. Then Latin once more dominated his poetry for the next two years with the Latin poems of the Italian journey and "Epitaphium Damonis," composed after his return from the continent.

Ultimately this is not a book about the English poems or the Latin poems, but about what we can learn about John Milton by looking at both together and by considering the shaping influence of classical and neo-Latin writers. As we shall see in Chapters 1 and 2, Milton was schooled in Latin elegiac forms not just by Ovid and Propertius but by neo-Latin poets such as Secundus, Buchanan, and Pontano. His Latin elegies show us that Milton the elegist might indeed have taken a different turn as a poet, had the time and the circumstances been different. In Chapter 3 we will see how Milton's breakthrough English poem—the Nativity ode—is indebted to Renaissance Latinity even as it strongly proclaims an English voice and English inspiration and even takes an early political stand against continental Catholicism and its encroachment in England. "L'Allegro" and "Il Penseroso" are indebted both to classical hymn and to the hymnic imitations that sixteenth- and seventeenth-century Latin and vernacular poets on the continent were producing. The *Mask at Ludlow* is linked not just to the English masque tradition, but also to the world of the classical and continental pastoral. Sabrina is a close cousin to the nymphs of place celebrated in neo-Latin odes. Similarly, "Lycidas" is indebted to both Renaissance and ancient Latin and Greek pastorals and odes. In order to interpret what it has to say about England in 1637 we must know how it is related to the tradition that the continent had fostered. We cannot underestimate the importance of the final sequence of Latin poems—together with "Ad Joannem Rousium," the ode addressed to the librarian of Bodley in which Milton describes his little book. They tell us more about Milton's views of poetry and his aspirations as an epic poet than the English poems that conclude the comparable section of the "double book."

The Latin poems finish the story of Milton's poetic aspirations that his English odes and his English monody "Lycidas" leave half-told. When he visited the cradle of the Renaissance in Florence, Rome, and Naples and shared his youthful Latin compositions with the academic sodalities in

Florence, he confronted firsthand the Italy to which he owed so much as a poet. The last Latin poems he wrote show him facing both ways as a poet: back to the tradition of classical imitation that had nurtured him, and forward to new fields of poetic imitation as an English epic poet. It is the task of this book to recognize his debt to that tradition.

THE COMING OF SPRING

The Latin Elegies

In December 1629 Milton celebrated his twenty-first birthday, composed the Nativity ode, and proclaimed in "Elegia 6" his coming of age as a vatic poet—a Homer, not a Horace; a Platonic seer, not an Ovidian trifler. Yet despite his protest Milton was in 1629, as his poetic work up to that time amply testifies, more an elegiac than an epic poet. Just that spring in "Elegia 5" he had been rejoicing in Phoebus's inspiration and the result was not a vatic poem, but an elegy on the coming of spring. Milton had a while to go before Penseroso would overshadow Allegro. As the celebratory verses to May, the sonnet to the Nightingale, and the sequence of Italian sonnets to the dark lady—all poems composed during this period—also demonstrate, Milton was entertaining thoughts of Amaryllis and Neaera. He was not yet ready to turn from the protective arms of Lady Elegia or, as the retraction of "Elegia 7" affirms, to forswear love and love poetry.

Young Milton was sporting. It is the exact word—*lusit*—that he used to describe himself and the poetry of this period in the Latin poem he composed for John Rouse to introduce the poetry of that first collection of 1645. His sportiveness, however, did not take the form of mere play but the kind of play that deliberately tries out different roles. He had yet to decide what kind of poet he was to be. If we look at the range of poetic types and poetic subjects that he entertains in the Latin and English poems of the 1645 collection, we witness that diversity as he moves from psalm to love elegy, from sonnet to mini-epic, from sportive ode to serious pastoral lament. Even if we limit ourselves to the elegies that constitute the first section of his Latin *Poemata,* we note that the seven elegies of this first section— the *Elegiarum Liber*—represent the different types of elegiac performance that we might find in most first collections of young neo-Latin poets of the sixteenth or seventeenth century: Three are poetic epistles, two funeral elegies, and two elegies on set topics concerned with popular themes—

the coming of spring and first love.[1] In fact, in order to understand Milton's early performance in elegy, we should look at both the standard elegiac models from ancient Rome—the elegies of Propertius and Ovid—and also the Renaissance elegies composed in imitation of these same Roman poets by neo-Latin poets of the fifteenth and the sixteenth centuries. When Milton remarks in "Lycidas" how he might—"as others use"—have sported "with *Amaryllis* in the shade, / Or with the tangles of *Neaera's* hair," (68–69) he is alluding not just to hypothetical mistresses but also to the career as a neo-Latin elegiac poet that he at first contemplated and for a while followed.[2] The guides along the elegiac pathway were the popular poets of the Continent, many of them from Milton's beloved Italy—Sannazaro, Marullo, Crinito, Navagero, Flaminio—and Joannes Secundus, the young Dutch neo-Latin poet, who imitated these Italians and made their mistress Neaera his own mistress, the lady to whom he dedicated many of his elegies and the celebrated *Basia,* perhaps the most popular neo-Latin book of the sixteenth century. Although the elegiac road turned out for Milton a path not taken, the Latin elegies of the *Elegiarum Liber*—above all, the first, the fifth, and the seventh—mark Milton's exploration of a poetic alternative. They never ripen into the *monobiblos,* the love book in the style of Propertius and his follower Secundus, but they leave a lasting mark on his poetic style and also define his beginnings as a poet.

PRECEPTORS OF LOVE

For Milton as well as for the many Renaissance elegists who imitate them, Ovid and Propertius were the leading classical preceptors of love. The many echoes of these two Latin elegists in Milton's poetry demonstrate, as critics have recognized, his fondness for them and their impact on him. Propertius wrote four books of *Elegies* in which he traces his love affair with Cynthia, the prototypical "dura puella" of Latin literature. The first book of these elegies, called the "monobiblos," both proclaims Propertius's devotion to Cynthia and at the same time seeks to define his calling as a poet.

1. For commentary on Milton's Latin elegies see James Holly Hanford, "The Youth of Milton," in *Studies in Shakespeare, Milton, Donne;* and Walter MacKellar, ed. and trans., *The Latin Poems of John Milton.* Also see Don Cameron Allen, "Milton as a Latin Poet," in *Neo-Latin Poetry of the Sixteenth and Seventeenth Centuries;* John T. Shawcross, "Form and Content in Milton's Latin Elegies," in *HLQ;* John T. Shawcross, *John Milton, The Self and the World;* Ralph W. Condee, "The Latin Poetry of John Milton," in *The Latin Poetry of English Poets;* and John K. Hale, "Milton Playing with Ovid," in *MS* 25; John K. Hale, "Artistry and Originality in Milton's Latin Poems," in *MQ* 27.
2. John Milton, *Complete Poems and Major Prose,* ed. Merritt Y. Hughes. All quotations of Milton (unless noted otherwise) are from this edition.

Propertius's first lines name Cynthia as his love and fix her as the subject of his poetry. She has taken him captive with her eyes—to his everlasting misery—and love, personified as Cupid and symbolizing the poet's own erotic desires, commits him to her service.

> Cynthia prima suis miserum me cepit ocellis
> contactum nullis ante cupidinibus. (1.1.1–2)[3]

> Cynthia first took me (miserable me) captive with
> her eyes, holding me before all other desires.

This is the signature event of Propertius's monobiblos, and many Renaissance poets imitate it, sometimes also adopting, as Ercole Strozzi or Enea Silvio Piccolomini did, a Cynthia for their mistress. Joannes Secundus dedicates his own monobiblos to a Julia and recounts the inception and development of the love for her. Echoing Propertius, Secundus declares that one woman absorbs him and his poetry completely: "Una meas igitur versabit famina curas!" ("Thus one woman keeps my cares in turmoil!" 1.5.1).

Ovid, the other Latin preceptor of love for Renaissance poets, with his *Amores,* the three books of elegies dedicated to that other Roman "dura puella," Corinna, was hardly less influential than Propertius. The signature event of the *Amores* (1.1) is the appearance of Cupid and the capitulation of the unwilling lover to his demands. Secundus echoes Ovid when he announces Cupid has appeared to him commanding service (1.1.6–7).[4] Although the young Joannes Secundus has adopted both Propertius and Ovid as his preceptors, the three books of elegies that he creates are in many ways unlike those of his teachers. First, Julia, the mistress of his monobiblos, is no "dura puella," but an innocent girl whom he briefly loves and soon loses. The other books of his elegies tell how he languishes for her love, searches for other girls to fill her place, and finally encounters Neaera, who fully fits the profile of the "dura puella" and becomes the mistress of Secundus's other love cycle—the *Basia.*

As an elegist Milton has in many ways more in common with Secundus than with the classical love elegists who shaped the tradition and whose precepts he seems to follow. It is certainly true, however, that he persistently echoes Propertian and Ovidian elegy and even alludes to the signature events of both Ovid's and Propertius's opening elegies. Like Propertius, Milton expresses a serious devotion to love, and in his first and seventh

---

3. Propertius, ed. L. Richardson (Norman: University of Oklahoma Press, 1977). All quotations from Propertius are from this edition.
4. Ovid, ed. G. P. Goold (London: Heinemann, 1927). Quotations from Secundus are from *Poetae Tres Elegantissimi* (1582).

elegies he seeks the compelling eyes of a Cynthia that might capture him and make him the servant to love. And in "Elegia 7" he almost finds them. His witty allusions to Cupid and his golden arrows also mark Milton as an Ovidian, and he is certainly following Ovid when he narrates in "Elegia 7" how Cupid demands his service. Also, the major *topoi* of ancient love poetry appear in Milton's elegies. When he tells his friend Diodati in "Elegia 1" that he is fleeing from London before the god Cupid can take him captive, his audience, well-versed in love elegy, knows that he is really flying toward love and love poetry. When he yields to love in "Elegia 7," this same audience will have anticipated this surrender.

While we may suspect that Milton originally planned to create in the "Elegiarum Liber" something like a "mini-monobiblos" in the style of Propertius, we can be sure, I think, that he did not intend to compose merely a pedestrian neo-Latin amatory biography. He entertains in his elegies a range of topics. If he is seeking a would-be mistress, he is seeking one more like Secundus's Julia—an innocent and beautiful girl, no wily seductress. Further, he sometimes seems more interested in defining his thoughts on love than in being captured by Amor or by a mistress's eyes. Moreover, as the themes and events of the "Elegiarum Liber" demonstrate, he is seeking love and a loved one indirectly rather than directly. As we investigate Milton's progress toward love, we find that it is inextricably connected with another event. The signature event for Milton's elegies 1, 5, and 7 is the coming of spring. The proper celebration of the coming of spring had been a challenge to the ingenuity of neo-Latin elegists throughout the preceding centuries and one that affords Milton the opportunity both to follow their lead and to make his own innovations.

Milton's earliest elegy concerns spring, a set of verses he did not publish, "Carmina Elegiaca," found with his Commonplace Book and probably written in 1624 at about age 15. The elegiac verses do not directly concern love, but in saluting dawn and spring, the adolescent Milton lets us read between the lines. In urgent yet tentative tones, he exhorts an unidentified person—perhaps a friend or even himself—to rise and experience the dawn. Not yet does he address an aubade to a woman.

> Surge age surge, leves, iam convenit, exute somnos,
> Lux oritur, tepidi fulcra relinque tori (19–20)[5]

> Arise, come, arise; now is time, put an end to slumber.
> The light rises, leave the foot of the languid bed.

---

5. "Carmina Elegiaca," in *The Works of John Milton*, ed. Frank Allen Patterson et al., 1.326–27.

Milton carefully describes, as he will later in "L'Allegro," the sights, the sounds, and even the scents of a spring morning—the cock's crow, the rising sun that peers out on happy fields, the cessation of the nightingale, the commencement of the lark, the scent of the rose and the violet, the sight of growing grain and fields newly clad in green. The effect is that of a classical or Renaissance catalogue, an effect enhanced by the reference to the sun as Titan and to the nightingale as the Daulian bird (a favorite designation made by classical and neoclassical poets).[6] By the time Milton comes, some five or six years later, to the description of a spring landscape in sonnet 1, there will be a reason to appeal to the nightingale. Here there is not. The bird is only part of the basic catalogue.

What we have here is very restrictive imitation. Framing his elegiac lines on models ancient and modern, Milton might well be echoing lines from the Greek epigrammatist Meleager (*A.P.* ix. 363) or from the Renaissance Hieronymus Baldi, both exponents of what I would call the "basic spring song #1."[7] Such songs celebrate the flight of winter and signs of spring's arrival, carefully marking the growth of green vegetation and the advent of spring's birds, and alluding only indirectly to human love or poetic inspiration. Like Meleager and Baldi, the young Milton views spring as an awakening, a casting off of slumber, sloth, and by implication wintry seclusion. He chooses to focus on the sounds and sights of the season, excluding all but his solitary sensory perceptions. He deliberately refrains from taking the second step forward to "basic spring song #2" that describes human love, procreation, and the waking of poetic inspiration. Shepherds and their sheep he reserves for later poems as well as their songs for Pan or Apollo or for their mistresses. One could argue that such impulses are present—unexpressed. Milton is reticent and cautious as a love poet. He will journey around love, long before he declares it. He will let the nightingale appear long before he will let it sing with full-throated ease. Those impulses that he suppresses here, he expresses gradually in the spring elegies 1, 5, and 7. When his elegiac poet welcomes dawn in "L'Allegro,"

6. Joannes Secundus, for example, regularly mentions the "Daulian bird" when he refers to spring. See "Elegia Solennis 1" and "De Veris Discessu," in Secundus's *Poetae Tres Elegantissimi* (1582), 24r, 126r. (Secundus was first published in Utrecht in 1541, next in Paris in 1561, and with Marullus in 1582. Milton might have known the popular edition published in Leiden in 1619, *Opera quae reperiri potuerunt omnia.*)

7. Meleager moves his eye across the earth as the season smiles and puts forth its first green: "γαῖα δὲ κυανέη χλοερὴν ἐστέψατο ποίην, / καὶ φυτὰ θηλήσαντα νέοις / ἐκόμησε πετήλοις." (The fertile earth puts on green grass, and nature brought forth blooming things with new growth.) (*Anthologia Palatina, The Greek Anthology,* 9.363). Balbi begins his spring song by describing the flight of Winter before the Sun's warming and Zephyr's return and the earth's greening: "Ridet ager, vestitur humus, vestitur & arbos / Induit herbosum terra benigna caput." (The field smiles, the ground and trees are clad, / The mild earth covers her head with grass.) Hieronymus Balbus, "De primo vere," in Ranutius Gherus, ed., *Delitiae CC. Italorum Poetarum* (1608), 1.330.

Milton makes it a part of an unfolding process of poetic discovery. But not until *Paradise Lost* 5 does Milton compose a real aubade: Adam's greeting to the dawn leaves us no doubt about its addressee nor its intent. Dawn and spring waken Adam to love, and he turns to the sleeping Eve to share with her the greening of nature. But the fifteen-year-old Milton is not yet ready to take that step. Yet surely, even then, he must have already known and listened to more seductive voices of spring than those of the Greek epigrammatist or the Renaissance lyricist.

Horace was one of the most melodic of those voices of spring and a later model for Milton. The ancient Roman poet took such basic spring songs as Meleager's and developed them, not only linking spring with the return of greenness and spring birds but also populating his leafy landscapes with nubile nymphs and goddesses that inspire sexual love. In *Carmina* 1.4 Horace may begin by noting how the winter passes when the breath of the West Wind Favonius warms the land. He may remark how the earth brings forth green—myrtle and flowers—that adorn her and create garlands for the heads of celebrating human beings. But he very soon makes clear the point of all this growing foliage: Venus leads on the Graces and the nymphs, teaching a mythic lesson on the fertility of the wakening season, the implication of which Milton would not ignore in "Elegia 5" and still later in *Paradise Lost* 4, where Pan, in Venus's stead, leads on the Graces and the Hours. Moreover, the young shepherd Lycidas makes a first appearance in Horace's ode—a tender youth, not yet a poet, whom young men and women alike burn to love:

> nec tenerum Lycidan mirabere, quo calet iuventus
> nunc omnis et mox virgines tepebunt (1.4.19.20)[8]

> nor wonder at tender Lycidas for whom all our
> young men now burn and virgins will soon warm for.

The growing warmth of the season begins to have another meaning, one Milton would soon also attend to.

"ELEGIA 1": THE BLIND BOY'S INDULGENCE

"Elegia 1," Milton's verse letter written in spring 1626, indirectly contemplates and toys with the central event of the monobiblos—the appearance of Cupid and the poet's unwilling declaration of service to him or to his lady. The elegiac letter is addressed to Charles Diodati, Milton's closest friend,

8. Horace, *Odes and Epodes,* ed. Charles E. Bennett (1984).

his future confidant in the Italian poems as well as in "Elegia 6." The epistle is given the pride of place in the Latin *Poemata* that he reserves for the Nativity ode among the English poems. (In fact, the first and last poems in the Latin volume are addressed to Diodati.) It is not unusual for elegists—Ovid and Propertius and many Renaissance poets—to address poems that concern love to male friends, recounting adventures and confiding hopes and despairs. Even English neo-Latinists follow this practice. Alexander Gil Jr. has a verse epistle in his *Parerga* (1632) addressed to a Cambridge friend in rustication in Northampton that jokes about Cupid's bow, warns of the dangers of devotion to a most beautiful Phyllis, and urges speedy return to Cambridge.[9] Milton, writing from his place of rustication in London, makes similar allusions to love, but does so less overtly. Yet text and subtext testify to the presence of the Roman Amor even before his appearance at line 60. First of all, there is the abundance of lines drawn from Catullus and the Roman elegists.[10] Confiding in Diodati how easy it was to depart from Cambridge, a place bare of soft shades and woods ("molles . . . umbras," 13), his word choice tells us that he has been entertaining in his reading the soft shades of Propertius 3.3.1 or Catullus 66.55, hopeful to find similar shades and leafy groves in London. No love ("amor") held him in Cambridge. In London, however, there are peaceful Muses; innocently he applies the amorous phrase for a loved one—"mea vita"—to his love of books and study.[11] He also refers to the pomp of the curved theater, and his phrase "sinuosi pompa theatri" (drawn from *Ars Amatoria* 1.89) reminds us that Ovid and Propertius recommended Rome's theaters as places for "girl-watching" (see Propertius 4.1.15). In Milton's commendation of ancient comedy and tragedy, there is an amatory subtext, too. His summary of the plots and characters of new comedy emphasizes the joy of their usual protagonists—a love-struck young man who wins his beloved, a young virgin who wonders at the warmth of love, while she scarcely knows what love is ("Saepe novos illic virgo mirata calores / Quod sit amor nescit, dum quoque nescit, amat," 35–36). There is the afterglow of a little Horatian warmth here. Even when he describes tragedy, Milton does not forget love. He draws his phrase, the "sweet pain of tears" ("lacrymis dulcis amaror inest," 40) from Catullus, adapting from love poetry the reaction to tragic loss.[12] Tragedy also focuses upon a young man, here the tragic, rather than the comic protagonist, who dies leaving the joys of love unexperienced—

9. Alexander Gil, *Parerga Sive Poetici Conatus* (1632), 24–26.

10. Both the *Variorum (The Latin and Greek Poems)*, and Walter MacKellar *(The Latin Poems of John Milton)*, cite individual passages that Milton may have imitated. Also see Milton, *Complete Shorter Poems*, ed. John Carey.

11. See Propertius 2.3.23; Pontano, *Carmina* (1948), 395.

12. Catullus 68a.18: "Quae dulcem curis miscet amaritiem."

Milton's first allusion to the death of an unmarried Lycidas or Damon. In this passage on classical drama the flame of love burns unseen, and we might not detect it except for the fact that Milton has drawn descriptive vocabulary and phrases from his favorite elegiac poets. It is the young man in the play—not Milton—who loves; it is the innocent young girl—not his own beloved—who responds. No "dura puella" of Roman elegy enters to spoil the fantasy.

At line 47, however, Milton is placed in a situation where Amor may enter with a capital letter. It is spring; he has wandered from the city, and from the vantage of a shady grove, he sees a crowd of girls—"Virgineas . . . choros" (52). Here Milton begins to exploit the pattern of the more elaborate spring song—a song that not only marks the advent of the season, but also welcomes love. While the Roman elegist could connect the sight of his beloved with the return of the spring, the Renaissance love elegist almost always did. Petrarch set his first meeting with Laura in April, as nature stirs to new life and his heart wakens to the suffering of love (see sonnets 3, 8, and 9). The final lines of Balbi's spring song tell us that his "saeva puella" has made his heart burn at the very moment that the season brings new warmth (1.330). Christoforo Landino concludes his spring song to Xandra (1.3) with love fixing his arrows in his heart. Tito Strozzi reports the same bittersweet experience in his elegy, "On first beginning to love Anthia." Joannes Secundus catches first sight of his Julia in May, and every May thereafter celebrates the commencement of that unhappy love with an anniversary May elegy.[13]

Milton's spring elegy has all the right ingredients for the beginning of a love affair. But the affair does not develop—at least not yet. The poet of "Elegia 1" never becomes more than a spectator who comments on the sighting of a group of beautiful girls. He begins with the noncommittal "videas"—you may see—rather than that committed "video"—I see. While his response to these beauties is warm, his comment is cautious. Such beauty might cure Jove's old age, but it does not spur Milton's youth to committal. The virgins could almost be the maidens .on antique vases, except that the flames—"blandas flammas"—that they shoot forth from their eyes suggest the seductive fires from the eyes of a Cynthia. But he is not captured, as Propertius was. As he gazes, however, the response to female beauty becomes more specific—not that Milton ever singles out one woman, as a Roman elegiac poet would. No, he moves from stupefaction

13. Francesco Petrarca, *Rime, Trionfi e Poesie Latine* (1951), 5, 11; Cristophorus Landinus, *Carmina Omnia* (1939), 3–6; Tito Strozzi, in Gherus, ed., *Delitiae CC. Italorum Poetarum* (1608), 2.990–93; Secundus, "Elegia Solennis 1," *Poetae Tres Elegantissimi* (1582), 24r; also see Basilius Zanchius, "Ver," in Gherus, ed., *Delitiae CC. Italorum Poetarum* (1608), 2.1459–60.

at the miracle of beauty ("forma") to wonder at starry eyes ("lumina") and ivory necks and arms. He does not venture to white breasts, but his allusion to the whiteness of the Milky Way suggests them. Then he retreats very quickly to the safe abode of brows, golden hair, and blushing cheeks. Now Cupid makes his first real appearance—"fallax Amor," who has laid the girls' golden hair as nets to entrap. The hunter Cupid with his nets has been prowling amatory forests since antiquity. We expect him to work his arts, to draw forth an arrow, to address the young poet. Milton has, after all, done his homework in Ovid and Propertius, so he knew what should have happened at this point. But it does not. Instead, having catalogued the features of lovely English girls, he turns now to rival groups—the heroines of ancient literature, the loves of Jove, the girls of Persia, Asia, Greece, Troy, Rome. Here Milton brings specifically into his text the world of Roman elegy—the Roman girls much admired by Ovid and Propertius who visited the theaters and Pompey's colonnade. But Ovid's praise of Roman girls only leads Milton to a patriotic praise of British beauties.

The climax of this passage is curiously oblique. What Milton should praise is one woman from the group—not praise an entire nation. When "the one" appears, however, she is the goddess of love, Venus herself, come not to inspire love, but to declare her preference for London over her Mediterranean dwelling places. From now on Milton's retreat from love is still more determined. The refusal to choose one is followed by a flight from the soft amorous shades of London back to boggy Cambridge, the barren haven. The opening elegy of a monobiblos should conclude with the poet-lover's capitulation—however unwilling—to Cupid. Milton does exactly the opposite. Now alluding a second time to Cupid, the blind boy, who, Milton tells us cryptically, has granted him permission to depart, Milton takes his leave of London and the elegiac form. Is his deferral a deferral of love or of love poetry—the reluctance to become the writer of the monobiblos? At the same time he departs, he depicts love as a Circean bait. Up to this point the poet of "Elegia 1" has looked on love as an innocent pastime for himself, a much desired state for others. What has changed his view? The Circean allusion is interesting in that Propertius at one point in the love affair (3.12.27) compared Cynthia to the sorceress Circe and himself to one doomed because of Cynthia's witchcraft to perish with the herbs of Circe. Without succumbing to the blind boy of Roman elegy, Milton has taken on the attitudes of a Propertius fatally suffering from love. We do not know when Milton translated Horace's fifth ode, but it too celebrates the escape from the golden nets of Cupid, from a "fallax amor" that has claimed the life of another. "Elegia 1" records Milton's fascination with the world of elegy to which as both poet and lover he refuses to commit himself.

"ELEGIA 5": THE COMING OF SPRING

"Elegia 5" takes a different approach both to spring and love. Composed in the spring of 1629, it is a much more ambitious poem than the early personal "Elegia 1." Despite its elegiac couplets, it is hymnic in concept and structure and is in fact organized like a hymn to Apollo on the coming of spring.[14] The "I" of elegiac love poetry has no real role in "Elegia 5," and personal anecdote plays only a small part in the poem. Phoebus Apollo, rather than the poet-narrator, is the central person. It is true that "Elegia 5" employs many of the same motifs of the spring songs that we have been looking at. It opens with the characteristic description of the passing of winter and the greening of the earth that could harken back to any number of Renaissance elegies:

> In se perpetuo Tempus revolubile gyro
>   Iam revocat Zephyros, vere tepente, novos.
> Induiturque brevem Tellus reparata iuventam,
>   Iamque soluta gelu dulce virescit humus. (1–4)

> Time, turning back upon its own tracks in a revolving circle,
>   Is now calling new Zephyrs with the warming spring,
> And Earth recovered is putting on her brief youth,
>   And already the ground is sweetly greening, the ice having dissolved.

Milton, however, interrupts this descriptive passage and begins anew in a different mood. Turning to himself and describing how the warmth of spring regenerates his poetic powers, he changes the focus of the poem from earth and the commencement of its seasonal greening to the poet and the effect that Apollo has on his own reviving poetic powers.[15] Instead of saluting the spring by adopting the persona of a shepherd-singer or rustic poet, he takes on the voice of one of Apollo's poet-priests, who, welcoming the god of poetry and prophecy, falls into a poetic trance.

    With the entrance of the Delian Apollo and the trembling of the laurel, therefore, we have something a bit more powerful than a simple spring song. Milton has deftly combined in "Elegia 5" two traditions—the first is the poet's welcome to spring, the second the poet's response to divine

---

14. It is not unusual for Renaissance poets to use elegiac couplets for classical hymns to gods. See, for example, the hymns to Bacchus by Pontano, Sannazaro, and Flaminio.

15. The connection of spring with the return of poetic inspiration is, of course, also a time-honored topos. In the Greek Anthology Meleager described spring as the time that calls forth the poet's song: "πῶς οὐ χρὴ καὶ ἀοιδὸν ἐν εἴαρι καλὸν ἀεῖσαι." (Is it not fitting for a fine singer to sing in this way in the springtime?) (*Anthologia Palatina*, 9.363, 23.)

inspiration.[16] He derives his model for the second from Callimachus's "Hymn to Apollo," a hymn much imitated in the Renaissance by poets from the neo-Latin poet Michele Marullo to the French Pierre de Ronsard. Milton follows in this line of inspiration, but like the Renaissance poets before him he adapts the hymn to his own devices. Callimachus's hymn involves an epiphany—a revelation of god to man. The poet begins by describing how the devotees to Apollo become frenzied at the approach of the god. As the god knocks at the door of the temple, the Delian palm tree trembles, giving a sign to the young men that they are about to enter into the god's presence. They sound the tortoise-shelled lyre and welcome King Apollo into their midst, commencing a song that describes Apollo's appearance and praises his attributes.[17] Milton's response to Apollo is no less intense, but his is a personal inner encounter, not (as in Callimachus's hymn) a religious initiation experienced in the company of other devotees.[18] We can recognize in this encounter with Apollo, written by the twenty-year-old Milton, the same impulse that later that year would produce the hymnic ode to Christ and that in *Paradise Lost* would move him to address a hymn to another divinity of light: the Holy Light that he hails in the proem to book 3. In both, Milton describes his personal reaction to the deity and couples this reaction with the impulse to compose poetry.

> Castalis ante oculos, bifidumque cacumen oberrat,
>   Et mihi Pyrenen somnia nocte terunt.
> Concitaque arcano fervent mihi pectora motu,
>   Et furor, et sonitus me sacer intus agit.
> Delius ipse venit—video Peneide lauro
>   Implicator crines—Delius ipse venit.
> Iam mihi mens liquidi raptatur in ardua caeli,
>   Perque vagas nubes corpore liber eo.
> Perque umbras, perque antra feror, penetralia vatum;
>   Et mihi fana patent interiora Deum.
> Intuiturque animus toto quid agatur Olympo,
>   Nec fugiunt oculos Tartara caeca meos.
> Quid tam grande sonat distento spiritus ore?
>   Quid parit haec rabies, quid sacer iste furor? (9–22)

16. Le Comte argues that there is a connection between the return of spring and the return of male sexual potency in this elegy. See "Sly Milton," in *Milton Re-viewed, Ten Essays,* 55. Dayton Haskin takes another approach, looking at Milton's use of the word *ingenium* for poetic talent in this elegy and in "Elegia 1" and "Elegia 3." See *Milton's Burden of Interpretation,* 41–42.

17. Callimachus, "Hymn to Apollo," in *Hymns and Epigrams.*

18. Milton's letter to Alexander Gil (May 20, 1628) describes a similar experience and also attributes it to the agency of Apollo. (See French, ed., *The Life Records of John Milton,* 1:158–59). Like Marullo and Ronsard, Milton takes Callimachus' hymn and makes it into a personal statement.

The Castalian fountain and the forked peak swim
    before my eyes, and at night dreams bring Pirene to me.
My soul is deeply stirred and glows with its mysterious impulse,
and poetic frenzy and the sacred sound stirs me within.
Delius himself is coming; I see his hair bound with Penean laurel;
Delius himself comes. Now my mind is whirled up to the heights
of the bright clear sky; freed from my body, I move among the
wandering clouds. I am carried through shadows and caves, the inner
    retreats
of the vates, and the innermost sanctuaries of the gods are open to
    me.
I see in my mind's eye what is going on all over Olympus, and the
    unseen
depths of Tartarus do not escape my eyes. What song is my spirit
    singing
so loudly with an open mouth? What is born of this madness, this
    sacred frenzy? (adapted from John Carey's translation)

With this passage of trancelike response to Apollo, Milton departs for a moment from the classic spring song, and following in the tracks of other Renaissance humanist poets, indulges in something that approaches the cult-hymn to the classical god.

Although humanist poets of the late fifteenth and early sixteenth centuries sometimes modeled their odes to Apollo on Callimachus's "Hymn to Apollo," they also adapted techniques from other ancient hymns and odes to this god—the Homeric hymns to Pythian and Delian Apollo, Orphic hymns, Pindaric ode, and also Neoplatonic ode. The revival of Neoplatonic learning in Florence spurred study of Proclus (c. A.D. 410–485) and his famous Neoplatonic "Hymn to the Sun." Proclus invokes Apollo not only as the son of Zeus or Jupiter, the god of poetry and healing, and the leader of the Muses, but also as a sun god.[19] The Neoplatonic Apollo is not merely the charioteer of day, as he is in late Greek and Roman myth; he is the god whose light is instinctive with first creation—indeed the *protogonos* or "first being" who exists prior to creation and is the agent for the creation of the universe. It is this Apollo, as we shall see further in Chapter 3, that many Renaissance poets adopt and celebrate in their hymns. The fifteenth-century Italian poets Marullo and Pontano view Apollo as a creation deity in their astronomical-astrological poems *Hymni Naturales* and *Urania*. Marullo's sun god inspires the poet with a Callimachean trance very like that Milton

19. Proclus was frequently printed in the Renaissance. See *Poetae Graeci Veteres, Carminis Heroici Scriptores, qui extant, Omnes* (1606). Ficino studied and translated Proclus.

experiences in "Elegia 5."[20] In this introductory passage of "Elegia 5," Apollo becomes for Milton essentially what he was for Renaissance poets before him—a protogonos, who is a sun god, a god of poetry, and the nature deity who brings on the spring. As we shall consider more fully in Chapter 3, the Neoplatonic Apollo can also be a figure very close to the Christian Son of God.

Apollo's role as a nature deity is for Milton and many Renaissance poets simply a logical extension of his function as a cosmic protogonos. As the primal sun god who brings warmth and life to the earth, Apollo sometimes joins with, sometimes displaces, the female gods of procreation and spring—Venus, Ceres, and her daughter Proserpina—who in ancient hymns waken the earth to greenness and animals to procreative functions. The Homeric and Orphic hymns to Aphrodite and Demeter, as well as Lucretius's hymn to Venus-Genetrix at the opening of *De Rerum Natura,* have a profound influence in the Renaissance. Poliziano in his celebrated "Stanze per la Giostra Orfeo" to Lorenzo de' Medici and Botticelli in his "Primavera" (based on these "Stanze") celebrate the power of the generative Venus.[21] In some Renaissance hymns the sun god Apollo appears together with these generating goddesses. Sometimes, as in Bernardo Tasso's hymns to Apollo, he simply assumes their creative functions, creating the world with his light and nurturing it each spring with the returning warmth of his rays, making the earth fertile and causing it to produce fruit and flowers. Hence for Tasso, Apollo is the "Gran Padre de le cose" (18)—the great Father of all Things.[22]

After he has invoked Apollo as the inspiring force for his poetry, Milton returns to his spring song. First, he claims the authority to be a singer of spring by likening his own poetic voice to Philomela's; both he and the nightingale can announce the coming of spring.[23] In the "Carmina Elegiaca," Milton called upon the nightingale and associated her voice with

20. Michele Marullo, "Soli," in *Hymni Naturales, Carmina* (1951); Pontano, "De Sole," *Pontani Opera* (1505); Pontano, "Ad Solem," in *Lyrici Opera* (1518).

21. The Venus that Navagero addresses in "Precatio ad Venerem, ut pertinacem Lalagem molliat" is certainly a love goddess, but Navagero first invokes her to come from heaven to work her generative force on earth. See *Doctissimorum Nostra Aetate Italorum Epigrammata* (1548), 55r and v.

22. Bernardo Tasso, "Ad Apolline," in *Ode di Messer Bernardo Tasso* (1560), 18–19. Also see Tasso, "Al Sole," 27–30; and "Ad Apolline" ("O gran Signor de Delo"), 85–89.

23. Although Milton uses the name *Philomela* to describe the nightingale, he does not here allude either directly or indirectly to any aspects of the mythic story of her rape, mutilation, and transformation. Instead, as in sonnet 1, he identifies her only as the first voice of the spring. In "Il Penseroso" he does almost the same, contrasting her expected song with the silence of the wood: "And the mute Silence hist along, / Less Philomel will deign a song" (55–56). But he also in this instance glances at the original Philomela's tragedy that he "softens," however, by coupling "sweetest" with "saddest plight" (57).

spring, but he neither privileged her above the lark and the cock nor linked her intimately with himself or poetry. In sonnet 1, "To the Nightingale," however, (written perhaps in the same year and spring) Milton clearly looks on the bird both as a presence synonymous with the incipience of spring and the inspirer of poetry and love. Yet he only invokes and does not command her favor. In "Elegia 5" the poet boldly joins forces with the nightingale to sing, blending his voice with hers to welcome the coming of spring and to invoke the sun god who inspires poetry and lovemaking. With this deft transition, Milton returns from his excursus on his own poetic inspiration to focus once more on Phoebus Apollo as the subject of his elegiac hymn. The elegy becomes—as it promised at its beginning—a salute to spring.

Milton's Phoebus, taking on the central role, moves from the sky god, Phoebus Coelius, to the god of nature and pasture and grove, Phoebus Agrestus or Nomios, an almost Pan-like presence.[24] Phoebus also assumes at this point an overtly sexual role as the lover of Tellus (Earth) in what is clearly both a symbolic and a comically realistic love affair. A shepherd, welcoming the returning sun, taunts Phoebus, almost as though he was addressing a tardy lover, telling him to hasten to wake the Earth, since he lacks a "puella" who might detain him in bed. The elegy is full of mythological jokes, but jesting is not alien to classical hymn or Renaissance elegy. Callimachus—after his solemn invocation to Apollo—could assume a joking tone and could pun on Apollo's name and title, as well as address the god familiarly. Milton does the same. His elegy has overtones of dithyramb as well as hymn. Phoebus in his turn taunts Aurora, telling her not to delay because there is no pleasure in bed with the old man Tithonus when the young Cephalus awaits her in the woods. Milton even uses the same word ("surge") that he employed in his "Carmina Elegiaca," but here the insistent command to rise and greet the dawn has definite sexual connotations.

The central section of the elegy is the wedding song of the goddess Earth, who has thrown off her wintry old age to greet the renewed and youthful sun god. Tellus or Earth is a composite deity—mother goddess, genetrix, love goddess; she possesses characteristics both of the Great Mother and Mother Ceres/Demeter, the goddess of the fruitful grain, but she also resembles Ceres' daughter Proserpina, the goddess of the springtime renewal, as well as Venus—the most seductive genetrix of all. Mother Earth actively woos her young lover—Apollo-Sun. This love affair, a turnabout

---

24. See Harold Skulsky's discussion of Milton's mythic debts in this elegy. He too suggests that the elegy partakes of hymnic design ("Milton's Enrichment of Latin Love Poetry," in *Acta Conventus Neo-Latini Lovaniensis* [1973]). Skulsky also comments that Apollo Nomios is not only a god of the fields, but also the god who brings law—*nomos* (605).

from that of the ever-young Aurora with her old husband, has this old mother wooing the young god. Like Venus she breathes Arabian perfumes and the scent of Venus's own Paphian roses. Both ancient and renewed, she binds her hair with roses as a young girl might, indeed, as the girls in Renaissance spring songs do when they entwine flowers in their hair and join in choral celebration.[25] Tellus is a very appealing "female" as she offers her own dowry to Phoebus and sings her own wooing and wedding songs. Milton could have found many models for his Tellus in the Renaissance spring anthology, for again and again Renaissance poets describe Earth as a sexually appealing woman wooed by a young lover. Joannes Secundus, for example, in his springtime elegy creates an amorous relationship between Apollo and Earth. When he smiles and dissolves the frozen waters, she, welcoming him, shakes off her icy mantle and clads herself in grass and bright flowers ("De Vere," *Elegies* 3.6). In Buonamico's spring song, it is Zephyrus, rather than the sun, who warms Earth in his embrace so that she gives birth to grass, leaves, and flowers. Landino gives us still another version of cosmic lovemaking: the Sun is driving his horses, as he gives the signal to Venus, who reclads the earth in foliage and flowers (1.3).[26] Milton clearly has ample precedents both for his description of the amorous Earth and the loving Sun, and in following them, he is bringing a little of the freedom and the sexuality of the Italian Renaissance to England.

While "Elegia 5" is hymnic in structure, its mythic descriptions draw now from hymn, now from love elegy. Milton has no objection to adopting a sportive view of the gods, quite similar to that of the Roman elegist. But he is chary of alluding directly to human analogues, and unlike the Roman elegist, he refrains from applying mythic experience to his own experience in love. It may be that the young "lover" Milton, who so eagerly takes Phoebus as a poetic father, implicitly wishes to share Phoebus's amorous as well as his poetic experiences. But he refrains directly or explicitly from making Phoebus's case his own. Milton the lover is present only indirectly and subliminally in this hymnic elegy. The Roman elegist in contrast is direct. Ovid and Propertius frequently compare their frustrations in love to those one god or another experienced. When Propertius, for example, alludes to Aurora and Tithonus in *Elegies* 2.18, he is drawing an analogy between their love and his and Cynthia's. The dawn goddess is faithful to her husband, even though he is old, but Cynthia, he complains, cannot be

---

25. Bernardo Tasso's ode to Apollo tells the young girls to go to the woods and to bind their hair with flowers (*Ode* [1560], 87–89).

26. Secundus, *Poetae Tres Elegantissimi* (1582), 43r–44r; Lazarus Bonamicus, in Gherus, ed., *Delitiae CC. Italorum Poetarum* (1608), 1.468–69; Landino, *Carmina Omnia* (1939), 4.

faithful even to her young lover. Aurora becomes the faithful stand-in for the faithless Cynthia. Even though Milton has Apollo make a joke at the expense of the old husband Tithonus, Milton does not bring the Aurora-Tithonus-Cephalus triangle down to a personal level. He applies the loves of the gods allegorically, making the sexuality that he alludes to a metaphor for the returning creativity of the spring. A further example from Ovid also illustrates a similar case. Ovid berates Corinna for leaving him to a sexless bed while she goes off to attend a festival for Ceres and Proserpina. Ceres, he points out, is a goddess who makes the seed ripen and ploughed fields sprout; she is not herself above an amorous adventure, for she conceived Proserpina on such an encounter with Jove. What does Ceres have to do with sexless nights? demands Ovid (*Amores* 3.10).[27]

While Milton in "Elegia 5" deliberately declines to draw parallels between Tellus's lovemaking and his own, he does not refrain from multiplying the number of fertility goddesses, who are also preparing for *divine* lovers— Idaean Ops and Sicanan Proserpina join fertile Tellus. No *human* lover intrudes upon the scene. In *Paradise Lost,* however, he makes myth take on human immediacy. Mother Eve is likened to the divinities of the flowering Mother Earth, to the fruitful goddess Pomona, to Ceres, "yet virgin of Proserpina" (9.395–96), and even to the fatal goddess of spring, Proserpina herself. In *Paradise Lost* all nature sings the hymeneal chorus for Eve—and Eve and Adam celebrate with their own sexuality the sexuality of an ever-flowering Eden. Divine and human loves are inextricably connected. Milton no longer refrains from applying the human lesson that mythic loves teach.

Yet, even so, we cannot help remarking in "Elegia 5" on the length to which Milton goes in anthropomorphizing Earth and her lover Sun. He has transferred the overt sexuality of love elegy and applied it to a love scene between Earth and Sun, treating his Earth and Sun as though they were an amorous human couple. The "lasciva" Earth bares her bosom and urges her young lover to bury his bright eyes in her lap. It is true Lucretius tells us that the vernal Earth seeks the embraces of the Sun; but the explicit sexuality of Milton's passage recalls instead some Renaissance elegies in which Sun and Earth are stand-ins for human lovers.[28] The fifteenth-century poet Giovanni Pontano uses celestial myth in one of his warmer love lyrics

---

27. Ovid, *Heroides* and *Amores*. Milton could have found many Renaissance poets who, like Ovid and Propertius, applied myth personally. Giovanni Pontano describes, for example, how Venus woos Adonis (again we have an older goddess and a younger lover). He immediately applies the example, moreover, to a beautiful girl and boy whom he tells to gather the flowers of love (Giovanni Pontano, "Eridanus" 1.37, in *Carmina* [1948], 409–11).

28. See *De Rerum Natura* 1.250–51; 2.992–93; 5.318. See *A Variorum Commentary on the Poems of John Milton, The Latin and Greek Poems,* 1.102.

to urge on human lovemaking. His mistress Stella breathes on him like Zephyr and warms him; she is both sun and moon to him. He compares her to Phoebe whose beams makes the flowers fertile, to Phoebus who lightens and warms the earth. Then he lets the lovers act out their mythic roles.

> Stella mihi sol est, easdem mihi roscida luna
>   hinc fovet et flammis, irrigat hinc et aquis ("Eridanus," 2.27,5–6, in
>   Carmina [1948], 437)

> Stella is the sun to me, at the same time she is the dewy moon;
>   Here she warms me with her flames, there she floods me with her
>   waters.

There is no mistaking the erotic intent of Pontano's celestial allegories. The young Milton is reticent, declining to tell us directly whether we should apply his allegory to our own or his wistful lovemaking. There is more than a little role-playing, however, in the eagerness with which the young male Sun receives the female Earth's advances.

While "Elegia 5" began as a hymn, it definitely concludes as a love elegy—though certainly not a conventional one. Cupid and his amorous mother Venus are almost inevitable presences in both the love elegy or the spring poem. Cupid appears with his mother Venus at the center of Botticelli's "Primavera," often considered an illustration for the spring stanzas of Poliziano's "Stanze per la Giostra Orfeo."[29] When Cupid makes a tardy appearance at line 95, we are neither surprised at his appearance nor at the delayed entry on the scene; both being quite typical strategies in elegy. But we are surprised that Milton does not give Cupid a more extended role. Ovidian, Propertian, and most Renaissance elegies—even Milton's own "Elegia 7"—make the appearance of Cupid the climactic event of the elegy. The Cupid of "Elegia 5" only plays a supporting role to Apollo, having kindled his arrows and renewed his bow in the fire of Apollo's returning sun-chariot. Moreover, instead of directing his arrows at Apollo and Tellus or one of the amorous gods or at the young poet or some other young lover, he goes after the unassailable virgins Diana and Vesta. When Venus appears, moreover, to second his efforts, she is not the amorous Venus of love elegy but the generative goddess of the Renaissance hymn, herself renewed and reborn with Apollo's light and the warmth of the spring. Chaste and subdued, she participates in the rites of spring, but

29. See Edgar Wind, *Pagan Mysteries in the Renaissance,* 116–17. Also see Agnolo Poliziano, "Stanze per la Giostra Orfeo," in *Rime* (1968).

she is a supporting, not a central figure here.[30] Hymen accompanies her and together they provoke young men to sing wedding songs and young women to pray that Venus will grant them the man of their choice.

With the allusion to the young men and women whom Venus and Hymen inspire, at last Milton alludes directly to human love. In "Elegia 1" he had described his own personal celebration of spring and had alluded to a young girl's awakening to love. He tells us there that the virgin in a comedy feels the first warm desires without knowing what they are; here in the later elegy a girl, more knowing, experiences first love and prays to the goddess that her lover may reciprocate her love. The wish motif, particularly when it is connected with love, recurs repeatedly in Milton's early poetry. In "Elegia 7" he, as lover, hopes that Cupid will transfix him and his loved one with arrows that will inspire reciprocal love; in sonnet 1 to the nightingale he hopes that the nightingale will sing first (before the cuckoo) and grant him success in love. Here the young girl's hope for a lover replicates his own unstated wishes. Milton repeatedly expresses the desire that love be reciprocal, but he also depicts love as a natural and fulfilling emotion, one that is warmed by spring winds, inspired by beneficent deities. Love grows pleasurably and innocently with the renewed grass and herbs and flowers. Each creature prays that his or her love may be answered; the wish is universal to all: "votum est tamen omnibus unum" (111). Absent here is the baleful sentiment of Vergil's *Georgics* that the sexual furor in animals and human beings alike is a madness or an evil: "amor omnibus idem" (*Georgics* 3.244).[31] Although human love has a very small part in this elegy, the part it plays is natural.

Having brought love down to human beings, Milton very quickly restores it, however, to the gods. The human beings of the next passage are enjoying the spring, but not making love. Like the poet himself, Phyllis and her shepherd lover are innocently composing spring songs on their reed pipes; the sailor-poet is pleasing the distant stars rather than his mistress, calling up the dolphins to the surface of the water to admire his singing. These are, of course, entirely fitting pastimes for spring. It is also appropriate that an elegy that began with remarking how the spring inspired both the poet and Philomela with song should conclude by once more calling up song. But Milton is not finished with the sexually active Olympians. Jove is sporting on Olympus with his wife, a marital example of sexual activity

---

30. Similarly, in Pietro Crinito's spring song, "De potestate amoris," Venus and her son and Erato introduce the warmth of love into the season. See Petrus Crinitus, *Poematum Libri Duo* (1508), G3v.

31. Vergil, *Opera,* ed. R. A. B. Mynors.

that Milton will not exclude from the garden of Eden when he compares the love of Adam for Eve to that of Jupiter for Juno (*PL* 4.497–502). In the woods below Olympus, however, the sexual pursuit is not so licit—the Satyrs, Silvanus, and Pan are lustfully pursuing Dryads, Oreads, and other nymphs who hide not to escape the attention of their "capering" lovers but to provoke them still more.[32] Milton does not even chide Maenalian Pan whose indiscriminate sexual passion does not even leave mother goddesses such as Ceres and Cybele safe. What is a reader to do—to turn aside with leer malign at this pageant of unbridled sexuality or to accept as allegorical the activities of Pan who, in embracing these earth goddesses, brings fruition to the spring?

When Milton alludes to Pan in *Paradise Lost* he is not the Maenalian Pan pursuing females, but "Universal *Pan* / Knit with the *Graces* and *Hours* in dance," (*PL* 4.266–68). Not otherwise, however, does he change this pageant of the gods of Nature leading on Eternal Spring. Without a blush he celebrates in *Paradise Lost* the sexuality of earth. The pageant of spring that begins with the celebration of the dance of Pan and the nymphs and the lovemaking of Juno and Jupiter leads in *Paradise Lost* to Adam and Eve's bower and the celebration of human lovemaking. In this early elegy Milton already, as it were, has his eyes turned toward Eden. He concludes the elegy with a prayer that the gods continue their presence in human woods and that they let the golden age return.

The very essence of a spring song from classical examples of Meleager and Horace to the songs of Renaissance Latin poets and Milton's own contemporaries is celebration of the passing of winter. The inevitable wish is that spring remain as long as it might. Many Renaissance spring songs include a wish that spring might be eternal, that the golden age might return and resume its reign over the earth. The return of spring inevitably reminds the Renaissance poet Fracastorius that once in the golden age of Saturn springtime was eternal.[33] Conversely, the departure of spring makes the poet Secundus regret that winter will return and wish that spring be eternal. Milton expresses sentiments very similar at the close of "Elegia 5." Addressing his plea to Phoebus, the very god he invoked at the beginning of the elegy, he asks him to drive his swift horses more slowly and let

---

32. John Hale remarks on Milton's adaptation of Ovid in line 122: "Semicaperque Deus, semideusque caper." See Hale, "Artistry and Originality," in *MQ* 27. Hale is particularly helpful in his comments on Milton's metrics in the elegies.

33. See Hieronymus Fracastorius, "Ver," in Gherus, *Delitiae CC. Italorum Poetarum* (1608), 1.1118–19; Secundus, "De veris Discessu," in *Poetae Tres Elegantissimi* (1582): "sic certè Elysiis viuitur in locis, / Vno perpetuo vere vbi perfruens, / Felix turba piorum" (But certainly in the Elysium places a happy crowd of pious ones live, where they enjoy a perpetual spring," 126v).

winter with its long night return late. The hymn to the god concludes, as it began, with a personal prayer.

"ELEGIA 7": "O CHARMING AMATHUSIA"

Milton's "Elegia 7" is both a personal love poem and a salute to May that is intimately linked to the Renaissance May elegy. Among the most accomplished Renaissance composers of May elegies are the Scottish neo-Latin poet George Buchanan (1506–1582) and Joannes Secundus (1511–1536), both assiduous celebrators of May and their mistresses. They did not, of course, invent the May song, since celebrations welcoming the spring went back to antiquity, but they succeeded in bringing the Latin spring elegy into the contemporary world. The May song of the Renaissance was a welcome to spring and love that often urged lovers—as Horace had—to pluck the flowers of the season and of love. Sannazaro's "Calendiae Maii" is one of the earliest Renaissance May songs; it proclaims the beginning of the reign of youth and Cupid, of a time to bind the ivy with the violets and the lilies with the roses. And it also warns how quickly mortal joys pass with death inevitably attending.[34] More innocent is Bernardo Tasso's May song, which, like Milton's "Carmina Elegiaca," is a salute to dawn, to spring, and to the amorous song of the birds.[35]

The May elegies of Joannes Secundus and George Buchanan have affinities not only with "Elegia 7" and the "Carmina Elegiaca," but also with Milton's short English lyric, "On May Morning." Written probably the same year as "Elegia 5," "On May Morning" directly addresses "Flow'ring . . . bounteous *May*," and like the basic spring song welcomes the return of green vegetation and flowers. Although it hints at something more, "Mirth and youth and warm desire!" (5–6), it does not (at ten lines only) develop these themes. Nor does it openly advise, as Sannazaro does, the lover to seize the day. Rather, like George Buchanan's first and briefest May song, "Calendae Maiae," it begins and ends by hailing the season.[36]

34. Jacopo Sannazaro, "Calendae Maii," in "Epigrammaton, Liber Primus," *Opera Omnia Latine Scripta* (1535), 32r.

35. Tasso, *Rime di Messer Bernardo Tasso* (1560), 33.

36. Buchanan's "Calendae Maiae" begins with a Latin salutation—"Salvete sacris deliciis sacrae / Maiae Calendae" and concludes with a second salutation—"salve fugacis gloria saeculi." It also greets, like "L'Allegro," the unreproved pleasures of spring—games, jesting, and the dances of the Graces, the pleasures of youth—all in a delightful landscape revived by spring. See Philip J. Ford, ed., *George Buchanan, Prince of Poets, with and Edition of Miscellaneorum Liber* (1982), 152–53; for Buchanan's longer "Calendae Maiae," see "Elegiarum Liber," in *Poemata* (1687), 301–4.

Buchanan's longer "Maiae Calendae" is a more extended celebration of May and love. Like Milton's "Elegia 5," it describes Venus renewing the earth and Cupid with his arrows inspiring love in crowds of celebrating boys and girls and in shepherds courting their loves. But like Horace and Sannazaro, it recommends, while youth lasts, to pluck the joys of passing life: "Carpite dum fas est fugituae gaudia vitae" (93). While its thematic organization resembles Milton's "Elegia 5," it emphasizes human and not divine love, advising young girls (rather than Mother Earth) to bare their breasts and let down their hair.

> Pandite lacteolas (iussit Cytherea) papillas,
>   Excipiant flauas lactea colla comas (123–24)

> Bare your white breasts, orders Cytherea,
>   And let down your golden hair on your milk-white necks.

Although Buchanan directs his attention to erotic human love, he does not offer his own addresses to his Neaera or to any other another mistress. In this he is unlike Secundus, who addresses two of his three May elegies to Julia, who had been the focus of his monobiblos. He met Julia in the month of May and though he lost her before the end of the year, he devotes each of his solemn elegies to commemoration of the beginning of that love. The solemn elegies are important models for Milton in that they combine an elegiac greeting to May with a hail and farewell to a girl briefly loved and then lost.

Milton's "Elegia 7" opens with a direct address to May and a specific reference to the dawning of its first day:

> Ver erat, et summae radians per culmina villae
>   Attulerat primum lux tibi, Maie, diem (13–14)

> It was spring and the light, radiant
>   Over the rooftops of the city, brought me your first day, May.

The closest of Milton's elegies to Roman elegy and to the Renaissance May song, "Elegia 7" is a recusatio that tells how the poet-scorner of Cupid's arrows comes to be struck by them and, even at the moment he loses his would-be mistress, to submit to love's power. Although the elegy may have been written earlier than "Elegia 5" and "Elegia 6," the elegies that precede it in the 1645 *Poems,* Milton has placed it last in his sequence and has included after it a retraction of the *nequitiae*—worthless trifles—of his youth, a retraction to which we shall return later.[37]

---

37. See the discussion of dating in *Variorum (The Latin and Greek Poems),* 1.127–30.

The poet-speaker of "Elegia 7" adopts the conventional pose of the young man proud that he has so far resisted Cupid and eager to heap ridicule and scorn on the god of love. His denunciation of Cupid and his subsequent meeting with him are clearly modeled upon Ovid's famous encounter in *Amores* 1.1. Like Ovid, the poet-speaker challenges the god:

> "Tu puer imbelles," dixi, "transfige columbas,
> Conveniunt tenero mollia bella duci." (5–6)

> "You boy," I said, "pierce unwarlike
> doves in that soft war as becomes a tender warrior."

The military metaphor is pure Ovid, for Ovid had contrasted the wars of Cupid with the real wars that become a man or soldier. Like Ovid but unlike the elegists Propertius and Secundus who were ready to submit before Cupid could threaten, the poet puts up token resistance. In "Elegia 1" Milton gratefully escaped from Cupid's threats; now he is bolder, all but challenging Cupid, who appears to him in a dream.[38] Far more voluble than the usual elegiac Amor, Milton's Cupid is no playful jesting god, but a wrathful threatener who predicts not just love, but love's agony. The poet-speaker of "Elegia 7," helpless before these threats, joins the company of lovers from Propertius to Petrarch to Secundus who yield first to Cupid and then to a specific lady and then to love's dire distress. Milton indirectly predicts the speaker's capitulation, for, following the strategies of the Roman elegists, he alludes, as they did, to mythic characters who submitted to love: to Phoebus as unsuccessful wooer of Daphne, to Orion, Cephalus, Hercules, Jove—all lovers mentioned by Propertius and Secundus.[39] Hence Cupid's threats only prepare us for Cupid's triumph.

The sequence that follows—where the poet-narrator wanders forth into the fields and sees groups of girls—inevitably reminds us of the springtime scenes of "Elegia 1." While such scenes are commonplace in Renaissance odes and elegies, Milton's sighting of one girl among the crowd recalls particularly one ode by Joannes Secundus. Secundus describes how he saw a very beautiful girl who stood out from a crowd of maidens: "Una inter omnes florida virgines" (*Odes* 1.xi.5). He is so struck as he watches her dancing that he calls the very earth blessed under the touch of her foot. She passes into and out of his life, however, without ever seeing him. Overcome with emotion at her beauty, he cries out that he wishes

---

38. Although Milton compares Cupid to a beautiful youth like Hylas and Ganymede, he is hardly the object of homosexual attention, but more like the youthful Hylas of Propertius (*Elegies* 1.20) whom the nymphs attempt to seize.

39. See, for example, Propertius *Elegies* 1.2; 2.33; 3.15; Secundus *Elegies* 1.8.13–14.

she might walk upon his heart and face and eyes, as she walks upon
the ground.

Both situation and sentiments are very like those Milton depicts in
"Elegia 7," except Milton has coupled the sighting of the girl with the
signature event of love elegy—Cupid's shooting of the golden arrow.[40]
Having first threatened the poet in a vision, Cupid reappears, as we knew
he would, and fixes himself on the girl's eyebrows, mouth, lips, and cheeks.
Milton replays the catalogue of parts from "Elegia 1" with a significant
difference. It is now one girl who inspires the poet's passion—one set of
features that calls forth his praises, not the collective features of the girls
of Britain. Further, the mythological comparisons now line up exactly with
Roman elegy. Just as Propertius had compared Cynthia to Venus and Juno
(2.2; 2.3), so Milton compares his unknown beauty to these goddesses.
The sensation that he describes—"loving, I burn"—is chosen from the
vocabulary of love elegy, perhaps from Buchanan's hendecasyllabics or
Pontano's *Eridanus* (see 1.15.13).[41]

> Hei mihi! mille locis pectus inerme ferit.
> Protinus insoliti subierunt corda furores;
>   Uror amans intus, flamma que totus eram. (72–74)

> He struck my unarmed breast in a million places.
> Immediately unaccustomed furor attacked my heart;
>   Loving I burned internally and I was all aflame.

What is striking here is that Milton the lover suffers the classic symptoms of
the love-elegists' condition—distress and grief and irreparable loss. When
he loses the girl, he even reaches out, as the elegists typically do, for some
mythic examples to which he might compare to his loss. Hephaestus's
loss of heaven and Amphiaraus's demise at the beginning of the Theban
conflict hardly appear appropriate, however, to the circumstances. The
appropriate mythic story—Orpheus's loss of Eurydice—he never alludes
to, even though, as Edward Le Comte has argued, the classic example of
lost love may be implicitly present. Milton inevitably resembles Orpheus as
he sees the loved maiden disappear from his sight.[42] But, like Secundus,
Milton blames the loss on fate, not on the heartlessness of the "dura puella"

---

40. See Anthony Low, "Elegia Septima: The Poet and the Poem," in *Urbane Milton;*
and Brian Striar, "Milton's Elegia Septima: The Poetics of Roman Elegy and a Verse
Translation," in *MQ* 47. Also see J. R. C. Martyn, "Milton's Elegia Septima," in *Acta
Conventus* (1973).

41. See the list of possible echoes in *Variorum (The Latin and Greek Poems)* 1.138.

42. Le Comte, "Miltonic Echoes in Elegia VII," in *Milton Re-viewed,* 119–27.

of Roman elegy. He even entertains the possibility that the lost girl may have responded to his pleas, may have been kind rather than obdurate.

> Forsitan et duro non est adamante creata,
>   Forte nec ad nostras surdeat illa preces. (89–90)

> Perhaps she was not made of hard adamant,
>   Perhaps she would not have been deaf to our prayers.

What is different here from the usual pattern of love elegy is that the affair begins and ends in one episode. Amor appears, the lover expresses resistance, Amor makes the girl appear and transfixes the lover with his arrows, the lover then confesses Amor's power and prays for success. But the history is without the usual sequel; the girl never reappears. Milton's monobiblos opens and closes on the first chapter. Moreover, although he has lost the loved girl, he is not desolate. Like a now convinced "servant" of the god, he prays that the next time Cupid shoots his arrows, he will transfix not one, but two lovers, granting the reciprocal love that he now denies. As in Secundus's ode, we are left with the vivid memory of the unknown girl and her incomparable beauty—a loveliness seen once then lost. The effect is poignant, but not devastating. To complete the cycle, to see how Milton as a poet reacts when he fixes his attention on one girl and she reciprocates his feeling, we must leave Milton's sequence of elegies and turn to the Italian poems—a different experience of love in a different language.

THE ITALIAN POEMS: "GIOVANE PIANO, E SEMPLICETTO AMANTE"

If John Carey is right about the dating of the Italian poems, if they are indeed the poems that Milton refers to at the end of "Elegia 6," then Milton's sequence of sonnets and its single canzone belongs to the year 1629 and completes the sequence of elegies—1, 5, and 7—in which the young poet is experimenting with Continental modes of love poetry. Further, if Milton was ready to send them to Diodati at the beginning of 1630 with the newly composed Nativity ode, their composition antedates that ode and so belongs even more closely to the love elegies.[43] When he was arranging the order of the 1645 volume, however, Milton did not place the Italian poems

---

43. John Carey, "The Date of Milton's Italian Poems," in *RES* 14. Also see John K. Hale, "The Audiences of Milton's Italian Verse," in *RS* 8; *The Sonnets of Milton,* ed. John S. Smart; *Milton's Sonnets,* ed. E. A. J. Honigmann; and Anna Nardo, *Milton's Sonnets and the Ideal Community.* Annabel Patterson has challenged the dating of many of the

with the elegies to which they seem so closely related, but with his English sonnets. He situated the sonnet group after "L'Allegro" and "Il Penseroso" and before *Arcades,* as though they supplied a kind of interlude between the recreational odes and the pastoral mask. Whether he considered them "vernacular" as opposed to "Latin" poetry, their placement links them with the lyric poetry of the English volume and separates them from the Latin elegies where the poet addresses himself—also incognito—to other would-be loves. Yet this separation serves in another way to balance the volume of vernacular and Latin poetry. In the English volume the Italian poems fill the place that the love elegies do in the *Poemata.* Are these Petrarchan poems academic experiments comparable to those love elegies or are they real testaments of a young poet's devotion to an anonymous Italian beauty?

In the 1645 volume Milton's Italian poems are integrated into the sonnet group that begins with the nightingale sonnet and ends with the sonnet to Lady Margaret Ley—the English sonnets, five in number, enclosing five Italian sonnets and the canzone and providing an interior foreign language dialogue on love.[44] In 1673 when the sonnets had swelled in number to nineteen, the English sonnets overwhelm their Italian companions. In 1645, however, the nightingale sonnet introduces the Italian sequence, and the sonnets to the young Lady and to Lady Margaret Ley conclude it, providing examples of courtly respectful address to English women that balance the idealized courtship of the Italian "donna."[45] The vogue for sonnet writing, as John Carey has remarked, had been over in England for almost thirty years, so in terms of English literature, these love poems might appear old-fashioned. Neither Milton's sonnets to the young Lady and Margaret Ley nor his sonnets to the dark lady seek, however, for models in English poetry. Metrically with their Italian octave and sestet they belong to the Petrarchan tradition, and with their formal tone, elegant address, and commendatory style they have a uniquely Continental manner that looks to Italy. As Michael Spiller has commented, Milton's frequent use of apostrophe in the sonnets links them to Italian practice and perhaps even to specific Italian poets such as Giovanni Della Casa and Benedetto Varchi, whom we know Milton was studying.[46] Both in his attitude toward his

---

sonnets, including the sonnet to the nightingale. She also offers perceptive rereadings of several sonnets, including that to Lady Margaret Ley. See "That Old Man Eloquent," in *Literary Milton.*

44. Both in the 1645 and 1673 volumes the Italian poems are distinguished from the English by being printed in italics.

45. In his notes to the sonnet Honigmann points out that Milton could have found models for these closing lines on the name of Margaret in sonnets by Dante, Tasso, and Claudio Tolomei. Also see Smart, *The Sonnets of Milton,* 55.

46. Michael R. G. Spiller, " 'Per Chiamare e Per Destare': Apostrophe in Milton's Sonnets," in *Milton in Italy.* Also see F. T. Prince, *The Italian Element in Milton's Verse.*

own lady and toward other ladies and friends, Milton imitates the manners of Italy.

Milton is specific about his admiration for Italian love poets. He purchased his copy of Giovanni Della Casa in 1629, but he clearly knew other Italian vernacular poets well—Benedetto Varchi, whose *Sonetti* were bound in the volume, Pietro Bembo, both Bernardo and Torquato Tasso (father and son), and especially Dante and Petrarch, for whom he expressed particular admiration in a letter he wrote in 1638 to the Italian poet whom he met in Florence—Benedetto Bonmattei.[47] Milton's sequence of Italian poems shows him well schooled in the conventions that Dante and Petrarch had established for sonnet and canzone, but also marks an independence from that tradition. The poet-persona of the sonnets bears a striking resemblance to the poet of the love elegies—young, fresh, hopeful, yet at the same time timid and fearful. Milton's donna, like Dante's and Petrarch's and Della Casa's ladies, is a gentle spirit, beautiful, assuredly, but also possessed of intellectual gifts that he prizes. Unlike the typical golden-haired lady of Petrarch's sonnets and of elegiac tradition, she is dark-haired and, like Sidney's Stella, dark-eyed. But what most separates her from the ladies of Della Casa or Tasso or Varchi is that she is never cruel, never cold, never deliberately unkind.

It is surely significant that Milton chooses to introduce his sequence of Italian poems with an English sonnet that, like the canzone of Pietro Bembo or like the passages in some neo-Latin spring songs, celebrates the amorous and poetic qualities of the nightingale.[48] As he invokes the nightingale, Milton carefully creates a spring scene that resembles the scenes in his own springtime elegies.

> O Nightingale, that on yon bloomy Spray
> Warbl'st at eve, when all the Woods are still,
> Thou with fresh hope the Lover's heart dost fill,
> While the jolly hours lead on propitious *May*
> Thy liquid notes that close the eye of Day . . . (1–5)

47. See French, ed., *The Life Records of John Milton*, 1:205, 382–89. Also see *I Sonetti di M. Benedetto Varchi* (1551). Milton annotated his copy of Della Casa's *Rime, et Prose* (Venice, 1563); see "Marginalia," in *The Works of John Milton* (ed. Patterson), vol. 18. The original copy is in the New York Public Library.

48. *Le Rime di Messer Pietro Bembo* (1562), 18r. Both Smart and Carey suggest that either Bembo's poem or one by another Italian poet is Milton's original. Lazaro Buonamico's verses to spring also describe the nightingale hidden in the forest shades: "Frondosique alta nemoris Philomela sub vmbra / Dulce querens, tenui permulcet gutture siluas" (Bonamicus, *Delitiae CC. Italorum Poetarum* [1608], 1.468–69). In fact, the apostrophe to the nightingale that opens the sonnet could just as well have come out of Milton's own elegies 5 and 7.

Milton suggests simultaneously the sound of the bird, the flowering foliage of springtime woods, still except for her song. Then he sets things in motion—the hours lead on "propitious May." Milton has not capitalized hours, letting the word suggest both the quiet procession of time and season and the classical goddesses, the Hours or Horae, so often associated with the procession of spring, so often directly invoked, as in the elegies or later in *Paradise Lost*. Whereas Milton in the elegies so often overloads a poem with mythological reference, he is sparing here. It is only a nightingale—not Philomela—only the hours—not necessarily the dancing lightly veiled goddesses of springtime. And the hours are jolly, as they enter (as though in a dance), leading on May.

What a youthful word "jolly" is, a word that reminds us of harmless sport and merrymaking, of the "youthful Jollity" who is Mirth's companion in "L'Allegro," one of the twin odes that precedes the sonnets in the 1645 text. May herself enters dancing—"propitious May,"—a close cousin to "Flow'ry May" of Milton's "Song: On May Morning." Echoing audibly with its rhyme the "bloomy Spray" on which Milton's nightingale sits, May seems "almost" to fulfill the nightingale's song. Movement and song work together here, as they do in Milton's "On May Morning." Milton is a very "procession-conscious" poet. His allegorical characters are fond of joining hands with seasons and stars and birds and love itself. In his May song the Morning star enters dancing from the east and leads with her "Flow'ry May." In the sonnet the nightingale incites the procession of the hours and the flowering of May, all of which awaken the desire for love. But the sonnet on the nightingale personalizes love in a way that only "Elegia 7" has done before. Powerful as is the call for spring in the song "On May Morning," it is a collective call for the sports of May that concludes with a collective we—"We welcome thee, and wish thee long." It lacks the sonnet's tentative note of fearful expectation and is a proem, an invocation, a salute, an enthusiastic welcome, but not a call for love.

The sonnet speaks for the individual lover. Milton begins by referring in the third person to the "Lover"; he ends emphatically with the word "I." It is the lover who listens for the nightingale with fear and "with fresh hope"—hope that he will hear the nightingale sing and that her song will "portend success in love"; fear that he will hear first the "shallow Cuckoo's bill" and that it will "foretell my hopeless doom" (6–7). The word "my" does not enter the poem until the second voice is heard—the cuckoo, who joins the nightingale in a baleful duet, canceling fresh hope with hopelessness. But Milton's sonnet is not a "hopeless" Petrarchan exercise. At the end of the sonnet, as at the beginning, neither the nightingale nor the cuckoo has yet been heard. The poet still waits with hope, now appealing to the Muse and Love as the Nightingale's mates ("Both them I serve, and of their train am I."), and in ready attendance for his own "mate."

Yet although there is love in this opening sonnet, there is no lady, no donna to whom the poet declares his dedication. Like the poet-persona of "Elegia 1" he has not yet sighted "the one." Critics have connected the mood of expectation in this sonnet with that in sonnet 7 (written on his twenty-third year). In sonnet 1 he waits for the critical moment—the Greek *kairos*—that will bring him love, in sonnet 7, for the maturation of his poetic talents. As a poet and a lover, Milton's disposition is to wait patiently, unwilling to be impatient and seize the day. Unlike Comus, the wanton protagonist of his Ludlow *Mask* who invites the Lady to anticipate love's sweetness, the poet avoids a coarsely erotic "carpe diem." Milton patiently attends for the time to be ripe.

The Italian love poems are among the few poems devoted completely to love and are a testament to the poet's devotion to the sonnet genre and to love. If the "carpe diem" of the Latin amorist is missing from Milton's elegies, the "dolore" of the Italian sonneteers—Petrarch, Della Casa, Varchi—that he was reading in the late 1620s is missing in his sonnets. It is not, of course, that the poet's experience of love is without pain or tears or disappointment; it is simply that Milton neither creates nor "wallows" in a lover's hell nor, except in a single sonnet (5), makes the lover's suffering the focus of his attention. Yet clearly he is taking pains to follow the Italian love tradition. From the time of Dante and the poets of the *dolce stil nuovo*, sonnets addressed to the lady were often also directed to the audience of poet-friends and ladies who were "knowing" in love; Dante's most famous poem, "Donne ch' avete intelletto d'amore," is one of this type. Milton ostentatiously makes his Italian poems public performances, alluding in the canzone to the young men and ladies who question him about his love. He opens sonnet 4, moreover, by adopting the common practice of Italian poets of addressing a friend by name. Both Della Casa and Varchi do this.[49]

Looking closely at Della Casa's and Varchi's sonnets, we can identify in them certain themes, devices, and techniques, some particular to these poets, some common to the sonnet tradition in general, that reappear in Milton's sonnets. Like many another sonneteer, Della Casa describes his

---

49. Commentary and analysis of sonnets by other poets is another early Renaissance tradition that carried down through the sixteenth century to Della Casa and Varchi. In 1545, for example, Benedetto Varchi published his commentary on a sonnet of Della Casa, "Dura che di timor ti nutri," that analyzed the sonnet's exploitation of the theme of jealousy. As Varchi notes, the sonnet develops from suspicion to fear to torment to frenzy and to madness ("Sospetto, Timore, Martiro, Frenesia, Rabbia," *Lettura di M. Benedetto Varchi* [1545]).

lady as a gentle spirit to whom he dedicates his service. He praises her eyes (sonnets 5, 37); he describes how his hopes renew with the dawn (sonnet 6); he addresses his friend Varchi to tell him of his love (sonnet 49). Della Casa several times uses an extended metaphor to begin a poem (3, 39). He could have suggested to Milton the metaphor of the shepherdess in sonnet 3 and its allusion to the alpine clime. But even if these are traces of Milton's reading of Della Casa and Varchi, Petrarch is probably the strongest influence in Milton's sonnets. Although a sonnet of Varchi's begins "Donna Leggiadra, al cui valor diuino" (95), Milton must have recognized that "leggiadra" was a favorite adjective for sonneteers. Petrarch used it, for example, to describe his lady in sonnet 2.[50] Probably Milton also recognized that Petrarch in his sonnets was extending, rather than rejecting, the Latin elegiac tradition that Milton exploited in his "love" elegies. The Latin god Amor inhabits both Latin elegy and Petrarchan sonnet, for Petrarch was, after all, the man who closely studied Propertius and restored his elegies to the Renaissance. He may even have patterned his own suffering lover on the persona of Propertius's elegies.[51]

The Latin Amor whom Milton invokes in his sonnets is both the Roman god of Ovid and Propertius and the Amor of Petrarch and Italian love sonneteers. It is true that Amor does not make a dramatic appearance in the sonnets, as he does in "Elegia 7," but "Amor," as Milton indicates by capitalizing the word, is both love and the god of love—Amor or Cupid. In sonnet 2, Milton alludes to Love's bow and arrows, which are synonymous with the gracious looks and gifts that Milton's lady, like the conventional lady of the sonnets, possesses. Love's sting, referred to in the very last line of sonnet 6, must be Cupid's dart as well as the lasting effects of Milton's attachment to the lady. In sonnet 4, moreover, when he alludes to his former scorn of love (4.3), he is also alluding to his present submission to the god. All these allusions to love form the very stones and mortar of the conventional love sonnet. Milton's sonnets do not make so elaborate a journey as Petrarch's or Della Casa's, but we can trace from the first to the last sonnet a development from admiration to love to the offer of his heart to the lady.

Sonnet 3 permits Milton to be a bit more adventurous in his dealings with the Petrarchan Amor. It also shows that he is following the Italians only in the end to differ from them. The sonnet begins with an elaborate

50. Della Casa also uses the word *leggiadra* in sonnet 51 to describe Vittoria Colonna. Sannazaro uses it repeatedly; see *Sonetti, e Canzoni del Sannazaro* (1534), 25v, 29r, 28v.

51. Petrarch discovered a manuscript of Propertius when he was in Paris, had it copied, and brought the copy back to Italy. This copy was the earliest known manuscript of Propertius in Italy and thus had enormous influence. See James Butrica, *The Manuscript Tradition of Propertius*, 16–17, 209, 298.

metaphor of a young shepherdess in an alpine clime watering a strange and lovely plant until it puts forth its leaves and flowers. So Amor calls forth from the poet the new flower of foreign speech. While some critics identify the shepherdess as the lady and still others as the poet, we must, if we follow the syntax of the sonnet, identify the shepherdess (despite gender considerations) as Amor itself. The plant that Amor nurtures is the poet, who flourishes at Amor's prompting.[52] Amor is three times repeated in this sonnet. Amor calls forth the poet's foreign song, making him change his Thames for the Arno; Amor also wills that he write ("Amor lo volse") and Amor refuses to be denied since nothing that he wills is in vain ("Amor cosa mai volse indarno," 13–14). In response, the poet—like Dante's Francesca—refuses nothing to Amor's promptings.

In the canzone that follows, love appears both as the god and as the poet's own growing attraction to the lady. Milton has given a situation familiar to love poetry a special turn of his own. Dante in *La Vita Nuova,* for example, had made a public confession of love for Beatrice to a group of friends—young women sympathetic in matters of love. Milton, however, is addressing friends who have made jest of him. They do not ask him—as friends usually ask the sonneteer—why he loves, or why he writes of love, but why he writes of love *in a foreign language.* Milton has added a second turn to his response.[53] The sonneteer usually replies that he writes because love or his lady commands him to do so. Haven't poetic ladies from Propertius's Cynthia to Sidney's Stella commanded the poet's pen? Milton's Italian donna makes a different request—not that he write—but that he write of his love *in Italian* rather than English.

> Dice mia Donna, e'l suo dir è il mio cuore,
> "Questa è lingua di cui si vanta Amore." (14–15)

> So says my Lady, and her word speak to my heart:
> "This is the language in which Love proclaims itself."

52. See Prince, *The Italian Element in Milton's Verse,* for example: "He cultivates the flower of an alien tongue as a 'shepherdess' would carefully foster an exotic plant in an uncongenial climate" (98). Also see Nardo, *Milton's Sonnets and the Ideal Community,* which calls Emilia the young shepherdess who nurtures the poet (34). Certainly, as Carey and Smart note, there is a connection between Milton's sonnet and Petrarch's 165, where the virtue of the lady as she passes through the grass of a meadow makes the meadow renew and flower: "Come 'l candido piè per l'erba fresca / i dolci passi onestamente move, / vertù ch 'ntorno i fiori apra e rinnove. / de la tenere piante sue par ch' esca" (Francesco Petrarca, *Rime, Trionfi e Poesie Latine* [1951] 285).

53. Milton follows the Italian poetic tradition here in not addressing his reply to the ladies and young men who jest, but in including the envoy or *congedo* in which he directly addresses the canzone. See, for example, Della Casa, "Canzone 2," in *Opere* (1937).

Although Milton does not reject in any way the Petrarchanism of his models, adopting both their language and conventions, he is selective about those conventions he wishes to follow and how he uses them. Even in the most conventional sonnet, he achieves effects that are uniquely Miltonic. Both sonnet 4 and sonnet 5 employ the all-too-familiar conceit of the lady's sun-like eyes. While sonnet 5 is entirely conventional in its treatment of this image, making the eyes suns that both light the lover and scorch him as they would the sands of Libya, sonnet 4 is more original in its approach. Even though it depends, as Smart and others have recognized, on Petrarch's sonnet 213, where the lover is caught (as the poet-speaker is here) between the radiance of the lady's eyes and the sound of her voice singing. Milton embraces the paradox and creates another metaphor to deal with it. Even if he could seal up his ears with wax (as Odysseus sealed up his sailors' ears to prevent their hearing the Sirens' song), he could not escape the great fire of her eyes. Thus, it is not the lady's blazing eyes that make this sonnet memorable, but her enthralling song. Is she a Siren, a Circe, one of the Naiades? No. Milton emphasizes the artistry, the intellect that her singing conveys. He turns away from the pert enchantresses of Latin elegy or the entrapping Petrarchan donna. But he is not above using a tried and true classical metaphor from Vergil's eighth eclogue (69) to praise his lady's artistic gifts. So great are her powers, says Milton, that she, like Vergil's shepherd, could draw down the moon from the sky.

All the elements of Milton's sonnets are conventional; united by him in a new way they depict not the lover's suffering, but the overwhelming charm and power of the lady. Even in sonnet 5, the only one of the set that describes the lover's "duole" and consents to deal in sighs and tears and to depict the "rainy" night of the lover's despair, Milton refuses to remain in the posture of the suffering lover. The sonnet concludes with hope—with the dawn that comes brimming over with roses: "Finchè mia Alba rivien colma di rose" (5.14). However much he follows the patterns of other sonneteers, Milton refuses to create a sequence that depicts a lady who is cruel or that celebrates hopeless love.

The final sonnet begins with a recollection of Petrarch's sonnet 234, in which the lover attempts to fly from his own thought.[54] Doubt overwhelms him, for he is young, simple, and inexperienced; doubt is a key word in the Petrarchan experience: "Poichè fuggir me stesso in dubbio sono" (2). Unlike Petrarch, Milton immediately draws back from doubt and humbly offers his heart to his lady, returning to the stance of the devoted lover. No more tears drown his eyes, no more sighs perplex him. In fact, he adopts

54. "Ne pur il mio secreto e 'l mio riposo / Fuggo, ma più me stesso e 'l mio pensero" (234, 9–10).

the heroic rather than the Petrarchan stance in offering his service—he is faithful, intrepid, and constant at the same time he is courteous, gracious, and good. Significant also is the way in which he couples his service to love and his lady with his service to the Muses. It is almost as though he were closing the circle that the opening English sonnet to the nightingale had opened, confirming himself as the servant of the Muse and Love.

The sonnet that follows the Italian poems in the 1645 text—"How soon hath time"—has seemed to some critics a cruel awakening after this devoted sequence on love. I do not think it very different from them. In sonnet 7 the spring metaphor also prevails; the poet regrets that he has not yet put forth bud nor blossom. His spring is late; he longs for his poetic talent to ripen into maturity and fruitful accomplishment. The patience and resolution that concludes sonnet 7 are one with the patient hope of the Italian sonnets and the conviction of sonnet 1 that next time the nightingale will sing for him.

Sonnets 9 and 10 also profit from Milton's sojourn in the camp of the Italian love sonneteers. These sonnets focus on the question that the Italian sonnets entertain but do not fully explore—the why rather than the how of love. Within the Italian sonnets there is a tension between talking of love as an emotion and love as admiration. The Italian sonnets emphasize the former, the sonnets to the young Lady and to Margaret Ley the latter. Milton may begin by speaking of the Italian Lady's beauty, but he ends by praising her grace, her talents, her virtue. Yet he does not free himself of the conventions that rule the praise of beauty. The very struggle there leads to the victory of virtue in the sonnets that follow. Virtue is the beginning point not only of the sonnets Milton wrote for the young Lady and for Margaret Ley, but also of every other sonnet he wrote for an individual—male or female. The whole point of the sonnet to Margaret Ley is that the virtue of the father, "unstained with gold or fee," is living yet in the daughter: "So well your words his noble virtues praise" (12).[55] The focus in the sonnet, "Lady that in the prime of earliest youth" is on the Lady's "growing virtues" (7). Milton speaks not one word of outer beauty.[56] If this is a sonnet to the young Mary Powell, as Leo Miller has argued, then it is all the more remarkable that he focuses entirely on the Lady's choice of laboring up "the Hill of Heav'nly Truth" (4). He is all admiration for this "Virgin wise and pure" (14). We miss a little the poet's engagement with his subject. The "how" of love is now totally absorbed in the "why" of admiration. Perhaps one reason is a disaffection with Petrarchanism, another the natural bent

55. For a fuller reading of this sonnet including the complexities of the praise of virtue, see Patterson, "That Old Man Eloquent," in *Literary Milton*.
56. Leo Miller, "John Milton's 'Lost' Sonnet to Mary Powell," in *MQ* 25.

to praise inner virtue. Yet a third reason may involve a certain change in attitude toward sexual love.

THE RETRACTION OF LOVE

In the 1673 volume of *Poems* the translation of Horace's ode, "Quis multa gracilis," (with Horace's Latin facing Milton's paraphrase) immediately follows Milton's expanded sequence of Italian poems and English sonnets. When does Milton translate this poem and why does he translate it? Its exclusion from the 1645 *Poems* might argue that it was a late poem, but we have no other evidence for a late date of composition. The "lover" of Horace's poem is an experienced man who comments cynically on the experience of a young lover, who is courting the beautiful but faithless Pyrrha. Seeing the young man's credulousness, he enjoys his own "safety"; he has forsworn love and will not be buffeted any longer by its storms. The paraphrase differs in tone from the love elegies of the *Poemata* and from the sonnets it follows, but it resembles in both tone and manner the retraction that Milton appended in 1645 and 1673 to "Elegia 7." Both ode and retraction deny the eager young love that the sonnets and the elegies celebrate, introducing a different mood and a reproving tone. Did Milton hang up his own trophies to the stern god of love at the same time he translated Horace's wry rejection of Amor?

The "retraction" is a puzzle. It directly follows "Elegia 7" in the 1645 and 1673 texts, printed on the same page and separated from the elegy only by a line that extends across the page. It refers to the preceding, using only the word "Haec" (these) to describe these "vain trophies of his nequitia" that he once erected with a perverse purpose. He goes on to deplore the evil error that led his undisciplined youth astray, saying that he has escaped from its yoke and is now devoted to the shady Academy of Socratic discipline. He goes on to affirm that love's flames are extinct and his breast so icy that Venus and Cupid fear to approach him. Does the retraction apply only to "Elegia 7" or collectively to the group of elegies that precede, only three of which, however, deal with the subject of love? Most critics would agree that it cannot refer to the funera or to the epistolary elegy to Thomas Young; he would hardly have called these poems "trifles" or "vain trophies of his nequitia."[57] The motif of escape from Cupid takes us back, moreover, to the conclusion of "Elegia 1." As critics argue, however, we cannot be certain

---

57. For a discussion of Milton's intent in the retraction see J. R. C. Martyn, "Milton's Elegia Septima," 386.

either about the referents of the retraction or about its date of composition. Milton might have penned the retraction at the time he completed the elegies in the late 1620s, or when he dallied with Plato in the mid-1630s, or in 1645 shortly after Mary Milton's return and at the time of the publication of the *Poemata*.

The retraction itself presents other problems. Is the retraction a rejection of love or of a certain kind of love poetry? In describing the preceding poetry as the "vain trophies of his nequitia," what precisely does Milton mean by *nequitia*? Only once in his Latin poetry—here—does he employ the word *nequitia*—a term that appears to be drawn from Roman elegy.[58] Ovid uses the word to accuse and excuse his love poetry: "Ille ego nequitiae Naso poeta meae" (*Amores,* 2.1.2). Propertius uses it to castigate himself for loving Cynthia rather than following a more serious career as poet or politician. Catullus applies it scathingly when he indicts the faithlessness of Lesbia. Horace and Martial use the word sometimes in serious, sometimes in humorous situations.[59] It covers a range of "crimes" from idleness and negligence to wantonness and vice.

We should not, however, confine our consideration only to classical poetry. Perhaps the closest application comes not from Roman elegy but from Secundus's "Elegia Solemnis 2," the second of the May elegies that commemorates the loss of Julia (25r–26r). Secundus repines that Julia took the first *trophies* of his pride: "E fastu referens prima tropaea meo," (18). Now he comes to offer an appropriate sacrifice, to perform annual rites for his nequitia: "annua nequitiae ponere sacra meae" (22). *Nequitia* in Secundus's sense does not describe either wantonness or idleness or vice, but youthful obsession with an affair that caused him suffering and afforded no future security or pleasure. He had "wasted" his time, misplaced his devotion, so he comes to commemorate his humiliation and loss. But at the same time, he neither disclaims Cupid nor his devotion to poetry: "Vates tuus, alme Cupido, / Haec tibi pro miti dedicat imperio" (49–50) (Your poet, gracious Cupid, dedicates to you these things for your mild empire). Both the words *tropaea* and *nequitia,* used in Secundus's elegy, recur in Milton's retraction. His situation at the end of "Elegia 7"—an elegy dedicated to a lost love—is also not very different from Secundus's. Both have lost the girl. Yet while Secundus openly confesses that he has wasted his time, he forswears neither love nor love

58. See Lane Cooper, ed., *A Concordance of the Latin, Greek, and Italian Poems of John Milton* (1923).

59. See MacKellar, *The Latin Poems of John Milton;* and the *Variorum (The Latin and Greek Poems)* 1.141.

poetry. Milton's retraction gives us something different. He says that he is now immune to love, that his breast is frigid alike to Cupid's arrows and Venus's flames. His retraction recalls Secundus's, but at the same time differs from it. He concluded "Elegia 7" with hope that Cupid's arrows might transfix two hearts as one. The retraction appears to revise that statement.[60]

Nothing that follows in the *Poemata* directly contradicts the retraction. "Elegia 7" is the last "love" poem in the Latin collection, although certainly not his last statement on love or his last praise of woman. The epigrams to Leonora Baroni, the Neapolitan Siren, speak of a susceptibility to a different kind of beauty. Only the Italian sonnets tell a different story, and Milton has placed those among his English poems.

But the retraction can have another implication. It can mark the end of Milton's attempts to be a Renaissance Ovid or Propertius. Milton does not forswear love, but he does forswear a career as a Latinate praiser of a Cynthia or a Julia or a Neaera or even this or that nameless beauty. In the second book of his *Elegies,* Joannes Secundus went on from his aborted affair with an innocent fair-haired Julia to a passionate affair with the golden-haired seductive Neaera, who became the mistress of his *Basia.* Even when pining for Julia in "Elegia Solemnis 2," Secundus wishes that some other girl might take her place. His retraction of one kind of nequitia led to his involvement in a more pernicious type. Milton's swain in "Lycidas" confesses that he once was tempted to follow the example of those who sport with Amaryllis and Neaera. To what is Milton referring? I believe that he refers to his youthful attempt to be the writer of a monobiblos, to be perhaps for his century and country the successor to Secundus. Milton the elegist did not go on to write a *Basia;* in Latin poetry at least he remained unkissed. Both the elegies and the Italian sonnets are explorations of genres that he did not continue to cultivate. When he composes sonnets to women in the 1640s and 1650s (now in his native language), he departs from the conceits of the Italian love sonnet to adopt a different idiom of praise. He determined to dally no longer with Cupid's darts or Venus's amorous glances. But was he immune to love? Did he come to dwell only in Plato's shady groves and abjure the society of women? The answer in life and in poetry is no. As a love poet he was also biding his time, resetting his lute until he found a unique voice in *Paradise Lost* to praise both lovers and love. Neither

---

60. The way in which the retraction is printed in both the 1645 and 1673 editions would also lead us to this view. It immediately follows the text of "Elegia 7," separated from it only by a single line that crosses the page. So it appears as a postscript to this elegy rather than as an afterword applying to the complete *Elegiarum Liber.*

spring nor love is missing from Milton's new revised version of the old spring song. The mature poet who was once an eager young lover waits with Adam under a Platonic plane tree. It takes only one glimpse of the golden-haired Eve for the praise of spring and love to begin once more in earnest.

2

THE WINTER ELEGIES

Latin and English Funera

In the plague year of 1625–1626 Milton found himself not once but several times turning to the funerary ode or elegy, a form that he would return to in another plague year over a decade later for "Lycidas." While often dismissed as youthful exercises, the Latin elegies and the funera of the *Poemata* are more than perfunctory epitaphs for the dead. In his Latin "love" elegies Milton staked his claim as a neo-Latin Propertius or Secundus; in the funera he presented his credentials as a neo-Latin elegist who took it on himself to commemorate the passing of some of the important figures of his time. With these sober exercises, addressed to elderly men of honor, he balances and tempers the vision of spring that he addressed to a youthful friend in the opening elegy, employing for them the same Latin tongue but in heavy, weighty, honorable syllables. Writing funera was a natural medium for a young Renaissance Latin poet, one that schoolmasters readily encouraged as a means for the young poet to exercise and establish himself. All of the Latin poems in this group are commemorative pieces, written to or about established men connected in some way with Cambridge University—bishops, a vice-chancellor, a beadle. Yet they are also, like his mature funerary laments, meditations on the meaning of life and the Christian claims for immortality. Curiously enough, the Latin funeral laments occupy a larger section of the *Poemata* than their counterparts in the English *Poems*—the epitaph to the Marchioness of Winchester, the monody to Edward King, and the comic epitaphs for the university carrier Hobson. "On the Death of a Fair Infant Dying of a Cough," the English poem written the same year as the Latin funera and closest in genre to them, Milton withholds from publication until 1673, placing it with the odes (before "The Passion") rather than with the epitaphs in the augmented volume. The Latin funera demand consideration in themselves and for their relationship to their English counterparts.

THE RENAISSANCE FUNERAL ELEGY

In the opening "Elegia 1" to Diodati Milton proves that he is poet of spring and love; in the elegies that follow and in the other *funera,* composed in the same year as winter approached, he demonstrated that he could sing of winter and death. For a young neo-Latin poet the funeral poem was de rigueur. All of the neo-Latin poets of the fifteenth and sixteenth century wrote *funera,* the most popular form of which was either the funeral epitaph or the funeral elegy. When he published his *Parerga,* Milton's friend Alexander Gil Jr. (1597–1642), the son of his master at St. Paul's School, gave pride of place in his volume to the elegy that he had written as a schoolboy on the death of Prince Henry. In composing these four Latin *funera,* Milton recognizes the importance of the Latin funeral piece and models his poems on well-established examples of neo-Latin *funera.* It is not surprising then that these four Latin *funera* are some of the most highly imitative pieces he wrote during this initiation period.

Before examining Milton's *funera,* we must look more closely at the funereal poems of two young neo-Latin poets: Alexander Gil Jr. and Joannes Secundus. Although Gil published his *Parerga* in 1632 when he was—as Milton was in 1645—in his mid-thirties, many of the poems are products of his youth.[1] Unlike Milton's double book, Gil's volume is entirely in Latin and Greek. While not so scrupulously nor so carefully arranged as Milton's *Poemata* there is some sign of organization. Gil ostentatiously dedicates the volume to Charles I and places as the first poems in the volume funeral poems to Charles's brother Prince Henry, to Queen Anne (in Greek), and to James I, followed by a brief epitaph on Arthur Lake, Bishop of Bath and Wells, one of the two bishops who had walked with Charles in his coronation procession. Gil had been in trouble recently with both Charles and Laud for some indiscreet remarks about Buckingham's assassination and, having narrowly escaped having his ears clipped, was openly courting favor. Gil's schoolboy poem on Prince Henry is, like Milton's 1626 *funera,* an ambitious classical exercise with imprecations of the fatal Atropos, allusions to the death of Phaeton, and comparisons of Hecuba's and Priam's grief over Hector to the King and Queen's grief for Prince Henry. Although Gil opens his volume with *funera,* they do not dominate the collection that follows. His, like Milton's, is a miscellaneous collection, mostly comprising verse to friends together with some complimentary poems to eminent seventeenth-century persons.

---

1. Alexander Gil, *Parerga* (1632). For Alexander Gil Jr.'s biography see the DNB. For his relations with Milton, see William Riley Parker, *Milton: A Biography,* 2: 711–12.

In Joannes Secundus's collected works, serious elegies predominate in *Elegies* 2 and 3, and an entire book is devoted to funera (over twenty), a not inconsiderable number for a poet remembered for his love elegies. Secundus recognized the importance of commemorating the death of important contemporaries and so took up elegies and funera at an early age. He was a particularly apt model for the young Milton, who notes on the title page of his *Poemata* that most of his Latin poems were composed by the age of twenty: "Quorum pleraque intra Annum aetatis Vigesimum Conscripsit." Secundus's funera include laments or *querelae,* funeral songs or *naeniae,* a monody, but by far the largest number are epitaphs, written usually in elegiac couplets.[2] Most of the epitaphs are serious, summarizing the deceased's life with a brief expression of grief; some, however, can combine wit with expression of regret.[3] His funeral epitaph "In Mortem Mercurini" (60r-v) plays on the name, Mercurinus, with allusions to the messenger god Mercury, and so looks forward to Milton's banter on the occupations of the Cambridge beadle and on the messenger Hobson.

Most of his naeniae and querelae take their task seriously. The longest of his funera, the querela (56r-60r) that he composed on the death of his father, Nicolas Everardus, is both a personal poem of grief, which offers the tears of a son, and an official lament for his father as president of the Grand Council of the Netherlands at Mecklin and a dignitary important in the court of the Holy Roman Emperor Charles V. Secundus follows the neo-Latin practice of mixing personal references with classical allusion, comparing his mother's and his siblings' sorrow to Niobe's tears and Hecuba's grief for Priam. He also alludes to a classical underworld, to the rivers Lethe and Cocytus, and even to the dog Cerberus. Significantly, he does not imagine his father (a noted jurist) in a Christian heaven, but in the blessed fields of Elysium, where he walks with other jurists—Solon, Lycurgus, Numa, and Ancus. Secundus also evokes scenes in a classical underworld in the naenia for his teacher, Jacobus Volcardus; he reproaches Proserpina for not sparing Volcardus and chastises Phoebus for not saving a fellow physician.[4] As we shall observe in Chapter 6, Secundus can even mount the machinery of classical epic for his ambitious monody on the death of Thomas More. These techniques are not without importance for the neo-Latin English elegist who wrote one hundred years later.

2. For a discussion of types of funeral poetry, see J. W. Binns, *Intellectual Culture in Elizabethan and Jacobean England: The Latin Writings of the Age,* 60–61.

3. Secundus, "Funerum, Liber Unus," in *Opera* (1561). Most of the epitaphs are included in the section on funera; some, however, appear among the epigrammata.

4. His naenia for the female poet, Joanna Fontana, is different in that Secundus adopts a female persona and has Joanna speak the consoling words to her husband.

Milton's early Latin *funera* all date from a short period in the fall of 1626—between late September and early December.[5] Written to commemorate men connected with Cambridge University, the four poems perhaps signal the beginning of a book of *funera* that, like the book of love elegies, never materializes.[6] Milton never lends his pen again to commemorating official persons, as did most of his contemporaries, nor does he ever write poems exactly like these again—either in Latin or English. Yet, even so, these *funera* represent a distinct genre and are important precursors to later elegiac poetry, for Milton will later employ some of the same devices used in them when he composes his English epitaph for the Marchioness of Winchester, his monody for King, his epitaph for Diodati, and even the comic epitaphs for Hobson. He first tries out in these Latin verses various types of apostrophe and digression; he employs mythic interlinking as he will later in "Lycidas." He also makes use of opening *exordia,* closing exhortations, and prayers, as he will later in his English experiments in the hymn-ode. His utilization of first-person narration as well of the odic "I" in the epitaphs for the Bishops of Ely and Winchester is striking.

These poems are both official commemorations for the vice-chancellor, the beadle, and the bishops and are also meditations on death. Although allegorized and apostrophized in all four, Death shows a different face in each, treated wittily or seriously as the occasion and Milton's aim dictates. The elegy on Richard Ridding and the ode on John Gostlin are witty exercises in the funereal mode and have more in common with each other than with the poems with which they are paired in the text.[7] "In obitum Praeconis Academici Cantabrigiensis" ("On the death of the Beadle of Cambridge University") opens with an apostrophe to the beadle, the bearer of the university mace who has fallen prey to the mace-bearing Death, and more concerns the beadle's profession than the man himself. Similarly, "In obitum Procancellarii medici" ("On the Death of the Vice-Chancellor, a Physician") looks at John Gostlin the physician, not the man. Neither elegy nor ode addresses the deceased by name, but uses the familiar *tu.* Both develop a similar controlling paradox, as they consider the

---

5. For the dating of these poems, see French, *The Life Records of John Milton,* 1:120–24. See Clay Daniel's discussion of these *funera* (*Death in Milton's Poetry,* 91–107).

6. When we look at Milton's *funera* on notable men, we should remember them in connection not only with private collections of *funera,* such as Secundus's, but also those university volumes of the Jacobean period that commemorated the death of kings and princes. Only a year before—in 1625—both universities had issued volumes of Latin and Greek poems on James I's death. Milton did not contribute to the Cambridge volume.

7. The elegy and ode for the two Cambridge officials are closely related to each other in tone and technique, although composed in different meters and included, therefore, in different sections of the *Poemata.* Further, the elegy for Andrewes and iambics for Ely are closely related, although also separated in the text for the same reason.

official's death in relationship to his Cambridge office and the Cambridge community. Addressing the beadle directly, Milton asks him how he who was renowned for summoning crowds of undergraduates by virtue of his glittering mace should now be summoned by the ultimate beadle, Death. Also addressing the physician familiarly, Milton questions how he who was skilled in Apollo's healing powers should himself be snatched away by Persephone to her dark realm. If we did not know that such opening addresses, such wit, such contrived paradox were part and parcel of the neo-Latin epigrammatic tradition, we might wonder why a university undergraduate should take such license in his lament for a dead university official. But such paradoxical wit was not only expected—it was much admired. As we have noted, Secundus was exercising elegiac wit when he alluded to Mercury in an epitaph for Mercurinus or remarked that his father, trained in the legal arts, would dwell in Elysium with those famed for law. In these Latin epitaphs, Milton employs not just one, but an accumulation of such apt examples, drawing them, moreover, when he can, from classical or mythic lore. Having opened his elegy on the beadle by remarking on the beadleship of Death, Milton continues to compare the Cambridge beadle to others famous as beadles or heralds or criers—to Mercury who was sent forth by Jove or to Eurybates whom Agamemnon sent to Achilles. Further, he repeats three times, almost in the fashion of a beadle making an official announcement, that Ridding was worthy ("dignus")—worthy to have had his youth restored by harmonious drugs, worthy to have lived as long as Aeson, worthy that Apollo's son should recall him from the Stygian waves.

Milton demonstrates a similar kind of "mythmanship" in the Gostlin ode. The ode opens by commenting that the whole human race, the children of Iapetus, are summoned by Death and remarks sadly that the call is irrevocable. Milton then displays his ingenuity by listing those whom Death overcame in spite of strength, ingenuity, and skill. Paradoxically, the illustrious strong men—Hercules, Hector, Sarpedon—could not defeat Death even though they had conquered many others. Likewise, the skillful enchantresses, Circe and Medea, who were also mistresses of herbal arts, failed to elude Death; finally the physicians—Machaon, Chiron, and Aesculapius—like the physician Gostlin, could not save themselves even though they had saved others.

The reference to Chiron and Aesculapius in this context is noteworthy, for it may indicate Milton's early interest in Pindar. In *Pythian 3*, his consolatory ode to Hieron, Pindar links the two, regretfully conceding that all human beings must face death. He uses the mythic account of Aesculapius's death to prove his point. At his birth Aesculapius wondrously escaped from Death, snatched live from his dead mother's body, only to be executed by Zeus's lightning when he tried to bring another back from the dead. Further, his father Apollo granted him those very powers to heal that ultimately caused his own death. Milton emphasizes the same paradoxes, as he alludes to Aesculapius, using the myth to bring his ode to its climax. Gostlin is the example par excellence of the physician who, like Aesculapius, failed to save himself. Aesculapius's great skill, Milton points out, angered Jove; Gostlin's angered the gods of Hades, namely Proserpina, for he used his medical prowess to rescue the victims of the plague. Milton closes the ode, as he had "Elegia 2," in a conventional way, calling on the gods of the underworld—Aeacus and Aetnean Proserpina— and by invoking peace for the dead in a classical Elysium.

Although the funera for the Bishops of Winchester and Ely, written also in the fall of 1626 at a time of plague, are more serious and personal in tone, they too rely heavily on classical allusion and employ consistently the standard formulas of neo-Latin funera. Both elegy and iambics open with a statement of grief. The elegy for the Bishop of Winchester begins: "moestus eram" (1); "I am grief-stricken"; the poem for the Bishop of Ely reiterates that grief: "My cheeks are still wet and stained with tears." In both, Milton, recreating poetically the moment he learned of the bishop's death, commits himself to commemorating him in an appropriate way. In his antiprelatical tracts, as Thomas Corns had noted, Milton criticizes the office of bishop, even singling Andrewes out specifically. But even then he separates man and bishop. He could accept Andrewes as well as Ridley, Cramner, and Latimer as good Christian men, while refusing to sanctify or approve their office.[8] In these early poems, as in his tracts, Milton refrains from praising either Ely or Winchester in their office; he grieves for them only as pious men who have passed on. It is a significant silence.

The focus of both poems is the meditation on death as the universal human end. In the elegy on Winchester, Milton links the bishop's death with the recent deaths of the aristocrats warring on the Continent, Duke Christian of Brunswick-Wolfenbüttel and his brother, refraining once more from commenting on the political implications of these deaths. (His stance is different from that in "Elegia 4" with its endorsement of the Protestant cause.) In the poem for the Bishop of Ely, Winchester's death is linked with Ely's. Milton's comments possess an intensity quite different from the apt and witty remarks of the Ridding elegy or the Gostlin ode. Angrily indicting

8. See Thomas N. Corns, "Ideology in the *Poemata* (1645)," in *Urbane Milton*. Corns points out that Milton chose to print his poems on the bishops of Winchester and Ely in 1645, even though his view of the bishops had radically changed in the interim. His antiprelatical tracts had criticized the bishops, even naming Andrewes specifically. He speculates that he published these poems as a record of his poetic achievement and as poems that had been received (perhaps) with acclaim by the Italian academies.

Persephone and Pluto, and directly addressing the savage goddess Death
("Mors fera"), he asks if it is not enough that to her fields and oaks and
flowers fall victim but that also human beings must also die. But while the
young poet poses the universal "why" and laments the brevity of human
life, he neither connects the death of the elderly bishop with his own
death, nor cries out in protest, as in "Lycidas," against the "Blind Fury," the
servant of Death, come to sever life at the very moment when its rewards
might be reaped. Nonetheless, this indictment of Death and the gods of the
underworld serves as an anticipation of "Lycidas," but with a difference.

A second anticipation of "Lycidas" occurs in the iambic verses to Ely. The
poet is complaining about the fate of the bishop when a voice answers—as
Phoebus will in "Lycidas"—responding to him and vindicating the ways of
the gods. Death is not an enemy to man but a friend, the voice instructs.
Neither the daughter of Night and Erebus nor one of the Furies, she is,
like the Horae, the daughter of Jove and Themis, sent to release human
beings from their bodies and to bring them into the presence of the eternal
father. Not until the midpoint of the protracted speech does the reader
realize that Ely himself is speaking. Milton retains in "Lycidas" the device
of the speaker who answers the complaining poet. But the speaker is not
the dead Lycidas, but Apollo whose reply is succinct and who, if he refers
to all-judging Jove and the rewards of a classical heaven, leaves to the
reader's imagination exactly what those rewards will be. By the time he
composed "Lycidas" Milton knew the benefits of a lightly classical touch
and less fulsome commentary.

Whereas these poems to Christian bishops offer assurances of immortality that are implicitly Christian, the visions of heaven are classically inspired.
Both adopt the conceit of death as a journey to a quite classical afterlife. Ely
is lifted aloft and carried through the stars and constellations in a dragon-
chariot until he comes to a heavenly Olympus. Winchester's voyage is more
like that to the Isles of the Blessed. Employing strategies not unlike those
that Pindar uses at the end of *Olympian 2* to assure Theron of the beauties
of the blessed isles, Milton conjures up a paradise, like Pindar's, where
all is radiant with light and Favonius blows, and the earth is brilliant with
color.[9] Is it so far-fetched in this context that he borrows a line from Ovid's
Amores 1.5 to describe the delights of this heavenly vision?[10] Even in these

9. In *Olympian 2* Pindar assures Theron of Zeus's ultimate justice toward human
beings,telling him that righteous heroes are brought after death to a paradise where
ocean breezes blow, golden flowers bloom, and flowers crown their heads. To sources
such as Revelation 14.13 and the *Aeneid* 6.644, Pindar's *Olympian 2* and its vision of
the paradise of the righteous should be added.

10. "Proveniant medii sic mihi saepe dies" (*Amores* 1.5,2). Readers and critics have
often been puzzled that Milton should have borrowed a line that described Ovid's

two early *funera*, as also in both "Lycidas" and "Epitaphium Damonis," the heavenly "Olympus" is delightful to the senses. Likewise, in the heaven of *Paradise Lost* Milton does leave behind the intense sensual enjoyment. He continues to endue his visions of heaven and the Christian afterlife with vitality and to portray them with intense colors of classical paradises.

EPITAPHS

For the Renaissance poet the inscriptional epitaph could be and often was a serious commemorative piece, used to honor a friend, a fellow poet, or a man of eminence. Secundus, for example, includes just such a piece on Erasmus among his *funera*, remarking on the great man's wit and his love of virtue, and concluding with Virtue herself joining the Charites and Faith to weep for him. Michael Marullus includes similar pieces among his *epigrammata* to remember the passing of his father or his uncles. But these very same epigrammatists could turn the inscriptional epigram upside down and use it as a form of humor and even ridicule, employing the very same devices that in the serious epigram produced apt and fitting commemoration. Sometimes these epigrams were to actual persons, other times to fictive or historical figures. Secundus writes a mock epitaph for Menelaus, who now lies cold in the ground, having spent his life consecrated to service of lovely Venus (66v). Or he can write a grim little exercise on death itself, addressing his remarks to a physician inept alike in his practice of medicine and surgery:

> Es simul medicus, simul cherurgus:
> Cur? mittis Stygium viros ad Orcum,
> Et manu simul, & simul veneno. (27r)

> You are at the same time a Doctor and a Surgeon
> How so? You send men to Stygian Orcus,
> Both with the hand and with drugs.

Among his serious epitaphs Marullus can include pieces addressed to the ancient hero, Germanicus Caesar, or the modern condottiere, turned Duke of Milan, Francesco Sforza. But at the same time he can berate Hannibal for invading Italy and remark wryly of Alexander the Great that a small tomb must hold the man who tried to conquer the whole world.

---

delight in his dreamlike encounter with Corinna to describe the delight of imagining Bishop Andrewes in paradise. Milton is not making an improper sexual innuendo, but commenting on the vivid experience of the dream state that replicates a would-be reality.

With these epitaphs Renaissance poets are simply extending for comic effect or for criticism the impulse generic to the epigram itself—the impulse to sum up in a pithy and apt manner. Poliziano undoubtedly admires the ancient poet, Ovid, but the epitaph on his exile and death is two-edged.

> Terra tegit vatem, tenderos qui lusit amores
> Barbara, quam gelidis alluit Ister aquis.[11]

> A foreign earth covers the poet, who sported of
> tender loves, he whom the Ister bathes in its cold waters.

This tribute combines poignant feeling with satiric wit; it is difficult to say which prevails. Poliziano both laments Ovid's lonely death in exile and remarks how much the cold waters of that distant place sobered the warm passions of the notorious love poet.

Milton's Latin verses for the beadle, Richard Ridding, are not too distant in kind from his English verses on the university carrier Hobson. In both he laments the loss of a Cambridge "official" while he exercises his wit on Death's outdoing a luckless mortal. His epitaph on Hobson opens with a clever observation: "Here lies old *Hobson,* Death hath broke his girt, / And here, alas, hath laid him in the dirt" (1–2). Only diction and the Latin language dignify and separate Milton's witty observation on the one from that on the other. For Death who has summoned Ridding has also deprived Hobson of his calling. It is true that Milton undoubtedly applies the epigrammatist's license more freely in this affectionate yet irreverent tribute to the university carrier. Milton imagines the elderly carrier waylaid by Death, as though Death were a highwayman who accosted him. Both epitaphs depend on the same concept: the living move, the dead are still. So long as Hobson moved, Death could not intercept him.

> And surely, Death could never have prevail'd,
> Had not his weekly course of carriage fail'd (9–10)

Milton extends the personification of Death further when he makes him the innkeeper who escorts Hobson to his room; the afterlife for the university carrier is supper and a good lodging for the night: "If any ask for him, it shall be said, / '*Hobson* has supt, and 's newly gone to bed'" (17–18). Yet is this so different from the wit in the Latin elegy that has Death as a beadle escorting the beadle Ridding to a classical underworld? Milton's jest in the second epitaph on Hobson becomes almost metaphysical. Milton reiterates

---

11. Fred J. Nichols, ed. and trans., *An Anthology of Neo-Latin Poetry,* 284.

that Hobson would never have died if he had continued to move, making the paradoxical observation: "Rest that gives all men life, gave him his death" (11). Indeed Milton piles paradox on paradox: "too much breathing put him out of breath"; "He died for heaviness that his Cart went light"; "His leisure told him that his time was come" (12, 22, 23).

Milton's epitaphs on Hobson were written some time after 1630, perhaps close to the time when he composed his epitaph for the Marchioness of Winchester or his ode "On Time," both of which also abound in paradox. If the carrier died because Death overtook him when he slackened his pace, the marchioness died (paradoxically) in trying to bring life: "That to give the world increase, / Short'ned hast thy own life's lease" (51–52). Only taste and context modify the paradox and differentiate tragic and comic wit. Allusion to Atropos, the last and fatal Parca, is appropriate in a funeral poem; to sharpen the metaphysical wit, Milton couples Atropos and Lucina, transgressing perhaps the boundaries of modern if not seventeenth-century taste. The marchioness "calls *Lucina* to her throes; / But whether by mischance or blame / *Atropos* for *Lucina* came" (26–28). The wit is further heightened by the epigrammatic rhyme (blame/came) that threatens the pathos aimed at. He does not make the same miscalculation when the blind Fury in "Lycidas" comes in Atropos's place and "slits the thin spun life" (26).

The epitaphs to persons that Milton composed during this period are closely related to the metaphysical ode "On Time." Milton has freed the meditation on Death in "On Time" from specific reference either to a person or persons. We are not reflecting on a slow-footed university carrier or a mace-bearing beadle or a marchioness whose womb becomes a tomb for her baby, but with Time as an abstractly personified figure linked paradoxically with another abstract, Death. Time also flies (how like the university carrier in his prime); but it flies abstractly until its race is run, until it runs out of time: "Fly envious *Time*, till thou run out thy race" (1). Like the marchioness, quick Time has a womb that becomes its own tomb.[12] Time consumes until it is itself consumed: "For when as each thing bad thou has entomb'd, / And last of all, thy greedy self consum'd" (9–10). By eliminating the human subject from this epigrammatic epitaph-ode, Milton has preserved the wit of his elegy on the beadle, the paradoxes of his observations on the marchioness, even the neat aphorism of the Hobson poems without risking either tragic or comic miscalculation. The movement of the ode is, curiously enough, not unlike that in the poems to the bishops, Andrewes and Felton. At the moment when time consumes itself we move

---

12. The more conventional reading of "womb" is as belly or stomach—hence Time "devours" until it is itself devoured.

to a vision of eternity that resembles the dream at the conclusion of Milton's early elegies. But a person does not quit the mortal body; instead human beings as a group quit the concept of Time and take on Eternity.

> And Joy shall overtake us as a flood,
> When every thing that is sincerely good
> And perfectly divine,
> With Truth, and Peace, and Love, shall ever shine
> About the supreme Throne . . . (13–17)

It is not a single but a collective triumph—quit of "Earthy grossness" and "Attir'd with Stars," *we*, Milton says, shall triumph over Death and Chance and Time. From the very personal apotheosis that he dramatizes in the poems to Andrewes and Felton, Milton comes to this universal vision. When he returns in "Lycidas" and in "Epitaphium Damonis" to portraying the individual's triumph over death, Milton will combine the vision of the early elegies with the collective triumph of this ode.

EPIGRAMMATIC WIT

Milton's gunpowder epigrams, composed as was the gunpowder "epic" in the fall of 1626, are yet another outgrowth of the neo-Latin epigram tradition. Their closest relatives are in fact the satiric epitaphs that Italian poets wrote to lampoon Renaissance popes such as Alexander VI and Leo X. Although they refer specifically to an event that might have been the subject for a serious epitaph—the death of James I—they are mock epigrams, sharpened by Milton's nascent political wit.[13] Addressed to Guy Fawkes or to the pope or to the inventor of gunpowder, they exploit the occasion of James's death to rejoice over a long-past poliltical victory over Catholicism—the foiling of the Gunpowder Plot in 1605. Milton's irony is heavy-handed. In the second epigram he asks if the pope and Fawkes and his Catholic co-conspirators were trying to send James to the stars—that is, to heaven—with a blast of gunpowder. If they were, Milton says, they have finally succeeded. King James has gone to heaven, Milton taunts the pope, but without the assistance of gunpowder.

---

13. Milton composes neither an inscriptional epitaph nor a naenia on the death of James. Even the long hexameter narrative poem, "In Quintum Novembris," is not on James's death, although it too seems to have been called forth by the event. Instead it is an anachronistic piece that celebrates James's rescue from the threat of Guy Fawkes's plot and concludes with celebrations that mark James's coming to the throne in 1605.

Ille quidem sine te consortia serus adivit
  Astra, nec inferni pulveris usus ope. ("In eandem," 5–6)

He is the same one who has gone lately to the starry consort,
  Without the help of you or of your infernal powder.

It is a curious epitaph for a newly deceased king. It is still more curious that this epigram, together with the three others that commemorate James's death and taunt his long-dead adversaries, takes as its model that satiric epitaphs from the late fifteenth and early sixteenth century that mocked controversial popes. Paolo Belmesseri composed a comic epitaph for the venal and venereal Borgia pope, Alexander VI, that jibes at the pagan ways of the dead pope now consigned to a pagan underworld:

Quis iacet hic? Sextus. Qui Sextus? Qui mare caelo,
  qui caelum terris, miscuit arte, dolo;
qui nunc Tartareas vexat crudelius umbras; (221)

Who lies here? Sextus? Which Sextus? He who confused the sea with
  heaven,
  Heaven with the earth, with art, with tricks;
He who now more cruelly vexes Tartarean shades.

More witty but equally to the point is Sannazaro's epitaph on Leo X that connects the rumor that he did not receive the final rites of the Church with his notorious selling of indulgences:

Sacra sub extrema, si forte requiritis, hora
  Cur Leo non potuit sumere: vendiderat. (151)

Under the extreme rites, if you strongly require them,
Why could Leo not receive them; he had sold them.[14]

The kind of comic epitaphs that flourished among Catholics on the eve of the Reformation was being revived by Protestants in the seventeenth century. Milton's friend, Alexander Gil Jr. composed several satiric pieces on the death of General Tilly, the leader of the Catholic League, the final piece a mock epitaph. Gil sarcastically remarks that Tilly, who died in 1632 fighting against the Swedish king, Gustavus Adolphus, has gone to dwell in the Stygian shades, a fitting place for someone of his religious

14. Both of these epigrams are contained in *Renaissance Latin Verse, An Anthology,* ed. Alessandro Perosa and John Sparrow. The translations are my own.

persuasion.[15] (No doubt he would have as companions the popes whom earlier epigrammatists had consigned to similar regions.)

Milton's "epitaphs" for James do not, of course, satirize the dead king. They assure us that James has gone to heaven. The mockery, the jests, the satirical wit are directed at Fawkes and the pope, and they are characterized by a strong anti-Catholic invective. Milton ironically asks in one epigram whether the conspirators were trying to provide James with Elijah's chariot but propelling it with sulphurous powder. Was gunpowder, he demands in another, the pope's version of purgatorial fire? These questions indirectly warn that the Catholic conspiracy of 1605 could recur in the England of 1626. Hence, the satire could implicate the new king and his Catholic consort, reminding the son (in the uneasy political climate following Charles's accession) of the Catholics' unsuccessful attempt on his father's life. Although paired in the 1645 text with the complimentary epigrams to Leonora Baroni (written in Italy over ten years later), these ironic epigrams speak a quite different epigrammatical language. Only when Milton in *Paradise Lost* describes a gunpowder conspiracy against heaven's king will the ironic tones first employed here recur in an epic context.

"FAIREST FLOWERS"

Milton did not include "On the Death of a Fair Infant, Dying from a Cough" in the 1645 *English Poems,* but reserved it for the 1673 *Poems* where it occupies a place among the odes. It is his earliest attempt to employ some of the devices of Pindaric ode.[16] But it also imitates neo-Latin elegy and epigram, employing many of the same techniques used in the Latin *funera* composed during this same period. Milton had learned from Renaissance Latin poets that he could mix devices from different genres within an ode. The first stanza of the ode exploits both the compression of Renaissance epigram and the figural development of Pindaric ode. Elaborately describing the flower killed by the winter cold, Milton fulfills exactly the requirement of an extended Pindaric metaphor:

> O fairest flower no sooner blown but blasted,
> Soft silken Primrose fading timelessly,
> Summer's chief honor if thou hadst outlasted

15. Gil, *Parerga* (1632), 90–91.

16. When Ben Jonson composed a Pindaric ode, only a year or so after Milton's "Fair Infant," he opened it with a highly developed allusive figure—the famous figure of the infant of Saguntum who, witnessing the horrors of war, chooses to return to the womb unborn (see the Cary-Morison ode in Jonson, *Works*).

> Bleak winter's force that made thy blossom dry;
> But he being amorous on that lovely dye
> > That did thy cheek envermeil, thought to kiss
> But killed alas, and then bewailed his fatal bliss. (1–7)

Looking closely at this introductory image, however, we observe that it also fulfills the requirements of imagery of other genres. Simply as an image, Milton's "blasted flower" resembles some of the similes which Homer or Sappho employ to describe flowers crushed in the field by passersby. As a conceit, it could have been suggested by the myths in Ovid that describe young men who, dying, are transformed into lovely flowers, one of which—Hyacinthus—Milton alludes to in stanza 4. But in practice this opening figure owes the most to that tradition that was very closely connected with mourning for the dead—the epigram. The Greek Anthology—that collection of miscellaneous epigrammatic pieces so popular in the Renaissance—contains a number of epigrams that mourn the death of young children. None of them, however, employs the conceit of the fading flower. But this very conceit is a favorite with the Renaissance poets who imitated epigrams from the Anthology, particularly Giovanni Pontano, who composed several books of sepulchral epigrams—the *Libri Tumulorum*.[17] Fast-dying violets are the very essence of Pontano's description of a dead girl in "Tumulus Jeselminae" (218). Violets and roses adorn the grave of Pontano's dead wife. In one epigram a dead girl speaks from her grave, identifying with the violets that are yet fragrant in the garden at her tomb. Still another speaks as a fallen rose, a flower that, like the Fair Infant, has been nipped by winter.

> Non aestus, sed te rapuerunt frigora brumae,
> > non aestas, sed te frigora solvit hiems;
> ergo non hiemi flores, non rapta per imbrem
> > frondescis, tumulo sed male rosa rosa es. ("Tumulus Rosae puellae,"
> > lines 6–10)[18]

> Not the heat, but the frost of winter bore you away,
> > Not age, but cold winter killed you;
> There are no flowers in winter, borne away by storms
> > You do not flower, but Rosa sadly in the tomb you are a rose.

Rosa, like the Fair Infant, did not survive cold December.

---

17. Some of Pontano's epigrams from the *Libri Tumulorum* (*Pontani Opera* [1518]) were translated into English and included in *Flowers of Epigrams* (London, 1577).

18. Pontanus, *Carmina* (1948), 211.

Marc-Antonio Flaminio, a later neo-Latin poet influenced by Pontano, imitates Pontano's flower epigrams in an ode on the death of Francesca Sforza, comparing the young woman to a ruby red flower that a winter storm has shattered.

> Sic florem hiantem mollibus
> Telluris almae amplexibus
> Vellens procella turbinis
> Leues in auras dissipat.[19]
>
> Thus the flower, opening in the
> soft embraces of nourishing earth,
> A tempest, uprooting with a whirlwind,
> shatters in the insubstantial air.

Once more we have a figure that could have been a model for Milton's "fairest flower."

Flaminio's naenia, however, like Milton's ode, involves more than the single epigrammatic image of the shattered flower. Specific and universal, personal and impersonal, it develops an extended lament for the young woman's untimely death that is no less extravagant in its expression of grief than Milton's. All Rome—the city itself and its people—mourns for the dead Francesca, insists Flaminio, the waves of the Tiber, its Naiads, and the seven hills joining in the lament. Dead with her in the grave lie Modesty, Beauty, and Grace. Finally, her family mourns for her—her brother and her uncle, all hoping that she lives above in heaven. She becomes finally an allegorical figure for virtue itself. Flaminio has expanded his poem from a single flower image; in this he could have provided an instructive example for Milton. Like Flaminio, Milton does not treat the dead girl as only a girl. Like Flaminio, he idealizes her as Mercy, Youth, and Truth that have left the earth. He imagines her soul hovering above in the Elysian fields. Finally, at the end, as Flaminio had, he offers personal consolation to her mother.

Representative Renaissance laments such as Pontano's and Flaminio's provide the ambitious young Milton with only one strand of influence. Milton's ode, "Fair Infant," was, after all, his first attempt at a classical Pindaric ode, written, like the majority of Renaissance Pindarics, in stanzas and not in so-called Pindaric triads—strophe, antistrophe, and epode. Not

19. Marcus Antonius Flaminius, "Naenia in Mortem Franciscae Sfortiae Sororis Guidi Ascanii Card.," in *Carmina Quinque Illustrium Poetarum* (1558), 61v. The opening comparison "Puella delicatior / Molli columba, pulchior / Rosae rubentis flosculo" is particularly poignant because it echoes a love poem by Pontano: "Puella molli delicatior rosa," (1), "Ad Fanniam," *Parthenopei Libri duo,* in *Carmina* (1948), 69.

until twenty years later (in the Rouse ode) was he to experiment with triadic ode. His occasion—the lament of the death of a child—is quite different from Pindar's, which celebrates an athlete's victory, but Renaissance poets on the Continent had long been adapting Pindaric ode for encomia for the living and funera for the dead. Milton's Pindaric debt is evident not only in his use of the opening figural exordium but also in the extended digression, Pindaric sententia, and in the development of the series of brief exemplary portraits.

With a daring above his years, Milton takes the characterization of the child as a blossom beyond the epigram genre and attempts to develop with it a mini-Pindaric myth. Ignoring probability and decorum, Milton elaborates on the myth of Aquilo's courtship of the Athenian maiden and makes the Fair Infant another "maiden" pursued by an unlikely suitor, here the elderly Winter.

> He thought it toucht his Deity full near,
> If likewise he some fair one wedded not,
> Thereby to wipe away th' infamous blot,
>   Of long-uncoupled bed, and childless eld,
> Which 'mongst the wanton gods a foul reproach was held. (10–14)

Winter mounts in his "icy-pearled car" and wanders through the freezing air until he spies the child; then descending from his chariot, he embraces and unwittingly kills her.

Unlike Pindar, who composed his odes on celebratory occasions to compliment aristocratic families, Milton has composed his ode to lament and not to celebrate. Yet celebratory and consolatory occasions need not be so far apart. In *Olympian 1* Pindar congratulated the Sicilian ruler Hieron on winning a prestigious race and chose the myth of Pelops's victory in a chariot race to compliment him and to assure him of the perpetuation of his family. In addressing a family, distressed by the death of one of its own—its youngest member, Milton therefore inverts the Pindaric myth and uses it to lament the discontinuation of a family, rather than to celebrate its continuance. The story of Pelops in *Olympian 1* concludes with a successful marriage—Pelops's winning of the maiden Hippodamia—and the establishment of a dynasty. Milton's myth of Winter describes exactly the opposite. Winter takes the maiden-flower into his "cold-kind" embrace and "unhouse[s] unawares her Virgin soul" (20–21). Instead of celebrating success with a myth of marriage, Milton by recounting the myth of an abortive marriage marks the tragedy of death. Pindar's myth heightens the celebration, Milton's the mourning. But Milton does not see the Fair Infant's death as the end to the family's hopes. He too can console and promise renewal.

To follow up this first myth, Milton alludes in quick succession to another, recounting how Apollo lost his beloved Hyacinthus whom he transformed into a flower. Here again he employs the odic strategies of Pindar, making the second myth replicate and interlock with the first; the fair flower dies destroyed by Winter's touch, the youth Hyacinthus, the beloved of Apollo, is slain by his "unweeting hand" only to be transformed into a flower at his untimely death. The second myth, however, presents its inverse. Death does not destroy the flower but makes it bloom eternally.

Sixteenth-century Renaissance poets had been quick to adapt Pindaric techniques to their own poetry, and sequential myth is one such technique. We can find sequential myth combined with the flower theme in an ode written by the sixteenth-century Italian Pindarist Benedetto Lampridio to celebrate Pietro Mellini's villa and at the same time to mourn the premature death of his brother Celso. Even before he alludes to Celso's death, Lampridio recounts in sequence three myths on the deaths of young men: first Adonis, then Hylas, and finally Castor. Only after he has told the myths does he refer to Celso's death, mourning it, as he mourned the others, and connecting it to the theme of springtime revival. The flowers will return with the spring, but the spring will not bring back Celso to his mourning brother. But the myths that recount early death also promise return and immortality. Adonis will be restored, as will Hylas, and Pollux will share his immortality with his dead brother Castor. Lampridio finds consolation for Pietro in these mythic accounts that interlock one with another. Similarly, Milton, by alluding to Hyacinthus, seems to promise the restoration of the flower that has been blasted by Winter.

Like the funera of the *Poemata,* Milton's "Fair Infant" is philosophical. What can be said of the Fair Flower that briefly blooms and dies? Does she lie in a "wormy" bed? Is there something in her above mortality? Does her soul hover in the "first-moving Sphere / Or in the Elysian fields" (39–40)? Here the ode attempts to do more than the Renaissance epigram that only laments untimely death, the quick fading of the flower. In fact, it is the very nature of the ode tradition that it attempts to provide answers. For example, in *Olympian 2* Pindar does more than dramatize the tragedies that beset the house of Cadmus, particularly the untimely deaths of Cadmus's daughters, Semele and Ino. From the perspective of earth, he tells us, their deaths were tragic, but from the vantage of heavenly Olympus, they live eternally, Semele having been translated to heaven, Ino to the depths of the sea. Pindar insists on the narrowness of the human perspective alone. Similarly, in his ode, Milton tries to offer some alternatives, engaging in some fast-paced mythic transformations. Who was the Fair Infant, he asks? Was she only a flower killed by Winter's or the plague's ravages? Might she not have been instead a star, shaken from Olympus, a goddess fled after the Gigantomachia, Astraea returned to the hated earth? Or if she was not Astraea, the goddess of Justice, was she perhaps one of Astraea's divine sisters—Peace or Mercy or white-robed Truth, all classical goddesses? To this list of goddesses Milton adds one more possible persona for the Infant—was she an angel, a genius come to earth to show the way back to heaven, a being who now can best perform her offices of "good," having been translated back to heaven? Why is Milton proposing these mythological alternatives?

Human beings cannot be certain of their condition and must endure this uncertainty with hope. Classical myth provides a way of giving transcendent expression to what Christian faith promises. Myth transforms the fragile human being—the fast-dying flower to a classical goddess or to heaven-loved Innocence or to a saving angel. On the one hand, the Fair Infant is killed by the plague that continues to rage after it has taken her life. On the other, she is the heaven-sent present returned to God, the angel who might drive away the slaughtering pestilence. At the end of the ode, he addresses the Infant's mother, urging her to cease to lament, to curb her sorrow, and to render back with patience what God lent. These are conventional Christian consolations in a classically charged ode. Having asked Pindaric questions about human happiness, Milton closes the ode with the conventional Christian wisdom of human acceptance.

The only serious English funeral poem on a female subject that Milton published in the 1645 *Poems* is the "Epitaph on the Death of the Marchioness of Winchester," written some time after 1632 to commemorate the death of Jane Paulet and possibly meant for a Cambridge volume commemorating her death. The death of the marchioness called forth a great many funera from a number of poets, but the hypothetical Cambridge volume to commemorate her was never published.[20] As a funeral elegy or epitaph, the poem to the marchioness is related to the early Latin elegies by its use of certain verse techniques and to "Fair Infant" by the female subject and the references to childbirth.[21] Up to line 12 the poem could almost be a Jonsonian epitaph, a piece like Jonson's "To Elizabeth, L. H."[22] However, Milton is doing more than writing an inscriptional poem, and

20. See William R. Parker, "Milton and the Marchioness of Winchester," in *MLR* 44; and Gayle Edward Wilson, "Decorum and Milton's 'An Epitaph on the Marchioness of Winchester,'" in *MQ* 8.

21. See James Holly Hanford, *John Milton, Englishman*: "The spirit of the poem on a Fair Infant finds an echo in the tenderness with which Milton celebrates the young mother's death in child-bed, but there is a new refinement both of feeling and of language" (43).

22. The use of octosyllabics connects the epitaph with the epigram tradition where octosyllabic couplets were the favorite English equivalent to the classical elegiac couplet, used in this way by Jonson and after him by Herrick.

the epitaph radically changes character, employing, as Milton had in the Latin elegies, a series of interconnected paradoxes. First he alludes to the unlucky wedding, with a virgin choir and a Hymen that summons her from an earthly to a heavenly marriage-feast, and then to a nativity that proves a funeral both for her and for her child.

In reworking the flower imagery of "Fair Infant," Milton refrains from creating an extended myth or from making too many classical allusions to transformed flowers. The countess is untimely plucked by a Death, a thoughtless swain who cuts both the "tender slip / Sav'd with care from Winter's nip" (35–36) and the new flower, killing thus both mother and child. The fair blossom—the mother—hangs its head and weeps, hastening its funeral. Despite a few infelicities, Milton has curbed the figural extravagance of his earlier English ode and the excessive classical allusion of the funera. He moves significantly from classical to biblical reference with the comparison at the close of the epitaph of the countess to the biblical Rachel: "the fair *Syrian* Shepherdess," who bore the highly favored Joseph, dies, as the countess did, by giving birth to her second child. The comparison contains, as Hanford has noted, an imbedded allusion to Dante—*Paradiso* 32.7–10—the description of Rachel seated with Beatrice in the heavenly rose. Milton calls the countess a bright saint and in his closing apostrophe describes her, like Dante's Rachel, throned in glory.

The "Epitaph" is Milton's final exercise in the inscriptional elegy. Later funeral poems venture into different genres—into the pastoral mode with both "Lycidas" and "Epitaphium Damonis" or later into the elegiac sonnet with two poems not published until 1673. In his inscriptional epitaphs and elegies, Milton has learned something that he applies to the sonnet form—how to use apostrophe, classical allusion, and abstract figures. He had also learned the lessons of economy and subtle understatement, moving toward finesse both in imagery and in allusion. The sonnet "On the Religious Memory of Mrs. Catherine Thomason," composed not long after the publication of the 1645 *Poems,* employs the apotheosis of the Latin elegies and the abstract female personifications of "Fair Infant." "Faith" and "Love" are the just soul's handmaids who convey her good deeds before the judge to speak "the truth of [her]" (13). Milton refrains from adding to their number or identifying them with classical goddesses; further he narrates their journey to heaven with an understatement that contrasts with the extravagant voyages that Milton had constructed for his dead bishops. Milton's most famous elegiac sonnet—"Methought I saw my late espoused Saint"—also benefits from understatement. The sonnet depends for its effect on allusion to classical myth. Milton had learned in his 1645 sonnet to the young Lady how to use allusion sparingly. Combining brief allusions to two biblical stories, he commends the Lady's choice as the "better part with *Mary,* and with *Ruth*" and bids her await her reward with the wise virgins who attend the heavenly bridegroom. In the sonnet to his dead wife, Milton also uses allusion sparingly, beginning and ending the sonnet with reference to the same classical story, the myth of Alcestis brought back from the dead and restored to her husband. At the beginning of the sonnet, he compares the apparition of his dead wife in a dream to the revived Alcestis brought from the grave by Hercules, "*Jove's* great Son" who gave her "to her glad Husband" (3). He narrates the myth no further, however, letting it quietly work its effect as he describes the appearance of his returned "saint" and rejoices in the "Love, sweetness, goodness" that "in her person shin'd" (11). He supplies no allegorical stand-ins for these virtues, as he had earlier, summoning no classical goddesses to depict Christian goodness. Moreover, by narrating the Alcestis myth no further, he lets his readers reflect on the irony that his wife, unlike Alcestis, must return to Hades when day brings back the husband's night. He also lets us supply, moreover, another myth of a dying wife, one who, like his own wife, is recovered briefly, to be lost again. If only indirectly, the story of Orpheus's second loss of Eurydice— the unnamed second mythic wife—exerts its influence on this sonnet. As his own wife disappears at the end of the sonnet, however, he allows the unstated allusion to this second myth to convey the poignancy of his loss: "I wak'd, she fled, and day brought back my night" (14).[23] Milton understood in his elegies to the bishops that myth could convey grief more effectively than statements of bereavement. He did not yet know, however, exactly how poetically to let myth tell its own story. His poignant use of mythic allusion in his final sonnet tells us how far the Milton of the 1645 *Poems* had developed.

23. See Anna Nardo's discussion of this sonnet, particularly her comparison with Adam's quest for Eve in *Paradise Lost: Milton's Sonnets and the Ideal Community,* 37.

APOLLO AND THE ROUT
OF THE PAGAN GODS

The Nativity Ode

On the Morning of Christ's Nativity," the first poem of the *English Poems,* holds the place that "Elegia 1" to Charles Diodati occupies in the *Poemata*. In different ways the Nativity ode and the Latin elegies stake Milton's claims to the world as a future poet. It is not "Elegia 1," however, but "Elegia 5"—composed also in 1629—that is closest in generic type to the ode. Both adopt as models literary modes well established in the world of humanist poetry: the Christmastide poem and the spring poem. Both feature the return of a deity to his world, the infant Christ to the world he as creator made, Apollo-Sun to the world of winter he will bring to life with his life-giving rays. "Elegia 5" belongs to the tradition, moreover, of pagan *fasti* that celebrate the seasons of the year, the Nativity ode to the tradition of Christian *fasti* that Renaissance poets such as Baptista Mantuan initiated, which celebrate Christ and the saints and banish the pagan gods that had inhabited Ovid's Roman *Fasti*. Mantuan's December verses on the "Nativity of our Lord" served, moreover, as one of the models for Milton's own Nativity ode.

Yet despite many resemblances in mode, "Elegia 5" and the Nativity ode are quite different poems. The Nativity ode marks Milton's coming of age as a Christian English writer and takes Christ and the heavenly Muse as its patrons just as surely as "Elegia 5" proclaims Milton's stance as a humanist poet who appeals, as his Continental Latin counterparts had, to Apollo and the Muses. As many of his Latin and some of his English poems demonstrate, Milton could inhabit both classical and Christian worlds— sometimes simultaneously. Moreover, the Nativity ode dislodges Apollo from his Delphic shrine as prophet and priest, just as forcefully as "Elegia 5" embraces this same god as a patron to poets. But when Milton banishes

Apollo in the ode and introduces himself as an English Christian poet de-voted to sing of Christ alone and to wait for Christ's kingdom on earth, this announcement has political as well as poetical and religious implications.

CHRIST AND APOLLO

"On the Morning of Christ's Nativity" is the work of an English Christian writer looking forward to a Protestant millennium. It could not have been written, however, without knowledge and use of, indeed reaction to, the tradition of Renaissance Catholic Latin humanism. Now employing, now rejecting that tradition, Milton brings his English ode to birth. The Christ portrayed in the art and poetry of the Continental Renaissance was a syncretic figure—a blazing sun god who, like the classical Apollo, sat at the right hand of his father dispensing light. He is not unlike the Christ that Milton describes in the opening section of his ode: sitting in heaven in "far-beaming blaze of Majesty . . . at Heavn's high Councel-Table . . . [in] the midst of Trinal Unity" (9–11).[1] Milton has endowed his Christ with all the splendor of this pagan deity. Moreover, as Christ descends into the world, he does so as a greater Sun, who displaces the sun of the world, which Apollo traditionally charioted.

> The Sun himself with-held his wonted speed,
> And hid his head for shame,
> As his inferiour flame,
>   The new-enlightn'd world no more should need;
> He saw a greater Sun appear
> Then his bright Throne, or burning Axletree could bear. (79–84)[2]

Even though Milton does not name Apollo as the charioteer of the sun, the language he uses inevitably calls to mind Ovid's description of Apollo's bright throne and burning Axletree.[3] Further, not long afterward, the angels in glittering ranks appear with a burst of light to herald Christ as their newborn Prince of Light. Now that Christ has assumed Apollo's qualities,

1. Whenever possible, I use the reading from the 1645 *Poems*. Otherwise (unless noted) I adopt the reading from Milton, *The Complete Poems and Major Prose,* ed. Merritt Y. Hughes.
2. Milton is perhaps echoing "Elegia 5" with its descriptions of Earth's courtship of Apollo-Sun when he says, "It was no season then for her [Nature] / To wanton with the Sun her lusty Paramour" (35–36).
3. The phrase, however, "burning Axletree," as John Carey points out, is probably from Chapman. See Milton, *Complete Shorter Poems,* 99.

the new god of light can dismiss the old sun god, as Milton does so with dispatch in the final section of the ode.

> *Apollo* from his shrine
> Can no more divine,
>   With hollow shriek the steep of *Delphos* leaving,
> No nightly trance, or breathed spell,
> Inspire's the pale-ey'd Priest from the prophetic cell. (176–180)

What exactly are we to make of Milton's dismissal of Apollo? Of course, we can assume that he is merely embracing a well-known topos, for the exorcism of the pagan gods was conventional in Renaissance nativity poems. On that Christmas morning of 1629 Milton might merely have been remembering passages from poets such as Baptista Mantuan or Torquato Tasso.[4]

Critics usually tell us, moreover, that Apollo's exorcism, together with the rout of the other pagan gods, is nothing more than Milton's affirmation of Christianity's ascendancy over paganism at Christ's birth. But surely that ascendancy over pagan religion was not much in question in December 1629. Something else, I believe, was on Milton's mind that Christmastide than Christ's contest with a paganism long conquered. When he eclipses the light of the Delphian Apollo, Milton is announcing the eclipse of what Phoebus Apollo had come to stand for in his time—a potent symbol in the iconography of the Roman Catholic Church and a political symbol in contemporary Stuart England. As he is affirming himself as the future English Protestant bard, he is dismissing an Apollo that had become the symbol of a threatening Catholic religious movement—a new "paganism" that was holding out against and attempting to conquer English Protestantism.

For Milton as a classics-loving Christian, the impulse to embrace Apollo as a symbol of Christ must have been very compelling, as the first part of the ode demonstrates. The linking of Apollo and Christ—and the Christianization of Apollo, the classical god of light or of the sun—has a long history that goes back to the early centuries of the Christian Church. Both Christian and Neoplatonic writers associated Christ and Apollo as gods of light. The Greek Apollo—as archaic poets such as Pindar describe him—is the son of the highest god Zeus and has a prominent place next to his father in Olympus. As god of poetry he holds the golden lyre and leads the Muses (*Pythian* 1.1–2); he is also a prophet (*Pythian* 4.5–8); the allotter of disease and remedy (*Pythian* 5.60–62), the conqueror of the presumptuous

---

4. John Carey notes that Milton seems to have patterned the Apollo stanza on Tasso's "Nel giorno della Natività" (*Complete Shorter Poems,* 78).

giants (*Pythian* 8.17–18).[5] He is already in the fifth century B.C. a god who could come to stand beside Christ the prophet, Christ the Lord, Christ the physician, and Christ the conqueror of Satan and his presumptuous angels.

Even though the Nativity ode is firmly Christian in subject and concept, classical decorum guides Milton in his structuring of the poem.[6] Like a Greek hymn or ode, the poem opens by setting the scene in the first four introductory strophes, ("This is the Month, and this the happy morn," 1.1), by describing both Father and Son, and by invoking the heavenly Muse. Milton's ode is not merely an ode in honor of Christ, however; it is an ode that celebrates his birth and examines the implications in heaven and on earth of that birth. As such, it is doing what Greek hymns did before it. The Homeric hymn to the Delian Apollo contains a birth account of the god that would influence Renaissance poets who were imitating the classical hymn and later influence Milton himself. This Homeric hymn renders a particularly poetical account of Apollo's birth, telling how the goddess Leto knelt in a soft meadow and, throwing her arms about a palm tree, gave birth to Apollo. Attendant goddesses gave a cry and the Earth rejoiced when Apollo leapt to the light; then the goddesses bathed him and wrapped him in pure garments, and Themis gave him nectar and ambrosia.[7] Milton takes his cue from the Greek hymn as he narrates the opening "hymn" section of his Nativity poem. Nature serves as an attendant goddess and, since it is winter, doffs her gaudy trim and presides at the birth in a saintly veil of maiden snow. Meek-eyed Peace, the personification of order, like the goddess Themis in the Homeric hymn, is also in attendance; and the birds of calm, which sit brooding on the charmed wave, add a sense of pastoral quiet. Instead of goddesses, angels raise the paean to the newborn God and announce to a rustic and almost Greek band of shepherds, that "the mighty *Pan* / Was kindly come to live with them below" (89–90).

However prominent the birth account appears at the beginning of a Greek hymn, the aim of the hymn is not merely to celebrate the birth of the god, but to show in that birth anticipation of the god's future deeds and triumphs. Accordingly, in the Homeric hymn to the Delian Apollo, the god is no sooner born than he displays his powers, pronouncing his mastery over the lyre and the curved bow, shooting afar, and beginning to walk over the wide-pathed earth. In the Homeric hymn to the Pythian

5. Also see *Olympian 14,* where Apollo, seated by the Graces, offers evermore honor in reverence to the Olympian Father (10–12), in Pindar, *Carmina* (1935).

6. See David B. Morris, "Drama and Stasis in Milton's 'Ode on the Morning of Christ's Nativity,'" in *SP,* 68. Morris notes that Pindaric ode provides the form for the Nativity ode (212–13).

7. See the Homeric hymn to Delian Apollo and the Homeric hymn to Pythian Apollo in *Hesiod, the Homeric Hymns, and Homerica.*

Apollo, his attributes as far-shooter, healer, and giver of prophetic oracles are specially featured, and he is named the slayer of the serpent Python. Milton's aim in the Nativity ode is similar, for while he opens and closes the hymn proper in the manger, like his Greek models he alludes to the future powers and achievements of the newborn God, who, as he tells us in the first strophe of the ode, has come to release us from "deadly forfeit" and to "work us a perpetual peace" (6–7). Hence, Milton's ode looks back as far as the Creation and Fall and forward to the Redemption and the Second Coming of Christ. The powers that the Son is to exercise on earth as prophet, priest, and king, moreover, have a peculiar relevance to those very powers that Apollo, son of Zeus, acquired at his birth and which he must relinquish with the birth of a greater "son."

The Greek Apollo of Pindaric ode or Homeric hymn was not yet god of the sun. Later Greek religion added to Apollo's dominion the regency of the sun; he supersedes the Greek Helios and Hyperion as the sun god and takes over their qualities. Then Christ the Sun supersedes him. Like the greater Sun come to earth to make the earthly Sun hide his head in shame, Milton's Christ outshines the resplendent golden-haired Apollo. The musical jubilee he commands at his birth is more sweet and sublime than Apollo, the very god of music, could call forth. Welcomed by the shepherds as their true God "Pan," the Son dispossesses Apollo, the lord of flocks and shepherd god, of an authority he once exercised.[8] Milton's Son takes on also Apollo's attributes of monster-slayer; for as Apollo was extolled in hymn and ode for his great feat of conquering the mighty Python, the Son now limits and straitens "th'old Dragon under ground" (168). Finally, to mark his complete assumption of the Apollonian role, the Son, with his birth, silences the god of prophecy at the oracle Apollo established, and Apollo in defeat departs with a "hollow shriek" (1.178), bequeathing his authority to a new god of prophecy.

Early Christians recognized the resemblance of Christ to Apollo, particularly in his role as a sun god. A fourth-century Christian mosaic found in the tomb of the Julii in the catacombs of the Vatican depicts Christ as a charioteer of the sun, his head encircled with a halo and his hand holding a globe.[9] At the same time, Neoplatonic Christians such as Synesius were

---

8. As critics have recognized, it is the shepherds and not the kings (the magi) who are the central biblical figures in the ode. The poet bids his Muse to hasten and present his ode to the infant Christ before the kings arrive. Moreover, it is the humble shepherds—the common people and not the kings—to whom the angels in Milton's ode (as in the gospel Luke) announce the birth of the Messiah. Milton insists here too on an antiroyalist stance, preferring the laity to kings or priests.

9. James Lees-Milne, *Saint Peter's: The Story of the Saint Peter's Basilica in Rome,* 68–69.

describing Christ's Apollonian qualities and church fathers such as Gregory Nazianzen, Clement of Alexandria, and John of Damascus were describing Christ as the light of lights. In Synesius's hymns the Son is the light from the fountainhead, the founder of the universe, the wisdom of the Father's mind, and the splendor of his beauty.[10] We need only look back to the hymns and odes of Gregory Nazianzen and Clement of Alexandria to find similar descriptive epithets used for Christ. In a choral hymn, Clement addresses Christ as Lord of all, the omnipotent word of the Father, the fountain of wisdom, the perpetual light. In his odes Gregory Nazianzen describes Christ as the word of God, the light from light. John of Damascus's "Hymn to the Theologian" describes the Son as God's sacred word, radiant in light.[11] Correspondingly, the Neoplatonic Proclus in his "Hymn to the Sun" was Christianizing the pagan Helios or Apollo, describing him as the intellective soul and heart of the universe, and the fourth-century emperor Julian named the sovereign Sun a deity.[12] During the Renaissance, both Proclus and Julian were revived and studied, providing humanist poets with assurance that hymns to the pagan god could speak symbolic Christian truth and that hymns to Apollo might also symbolically address Christ.[13]

APOLLO BELVEDERE

It was not until the Renaissance, however, that Apollo was officially, as it were, brought into the Church. When Giuliano Della Rovere was elevated

10. See Synesius, *The Essays and Hymns of Synesius of Cyrene,* 2.372–92. Synesius's account of the generation of the Son (in Hymns 2, 3, 4) especially borrows from Greek religion, Neoplatonism, and Gnosticism. Synesius's hymns were first printed by Aldus in 1499, but were reprinted throughout the sixteenth century, the two most important editions being those of Oporinus in Basel in 1567 and of Stephanus (Henri Estienne) in Geneva in 1568. Henry More translates the hymns of Synesius. See More, *The Complete Poems of Dr. Henry More.* Thomas Stanley translates hymn 1.

11. Clement of Alexandria, *Hymni in Christum;* Gregory Nazianzen in *Poetae Graeci Veteres,* ed. Petrus de la Roviere (1614), 185–89; John of Damascus in *Poetae Graeci Veteres,* 189–91.

12. Proclus (c. A.D. 410–485) was born approximately the year that Synesius died. His philosophical hymns employ the choral formulas of the traditional Greek hymn and although addressing the gods of the Olympic pantheon, they invoke those divine forces symbolized by the gods, rather than the gods themselves. He was a universalist in religion and endeavored to move beyond sectarian boundaries to reach the philosophical principle that he felt was common to all religion, whether Greek, Christian, or Hebraic. Proclus's Helios, addressed in Hymn 1, is neither the ancient Greek sun god, Helios, nor the Romanized Apollo, god of the sun, but the lord of light, the intellectual soul and heart of healing and poetry. As such he has much in common with the Christian lord of light, the divine Son.

13. See Iulianus Caesarus, *In Regem Solem* (1625); Proclus, *Poetae Graeci Veteres, Carminis Heroici Scriptores, qui extant, Omnes* (1606).

in 1503 to papacy and moved as Julius II from the confines of SS. Apostoli's in Rome to the Vatican, he took with him an ancient sculpture—a Roman copy of a Greek original—that had been dug up in a nearby garden and was to become the centerpiece of a vast Vatican courtyard. The Belvedere Apollo is still at the Vatican (in a more modest setting) and is the most famous image of this pagan god. When Julius first installed it in the cortile of the Vatican, it excited an almost religious passion. The son of the ancient god Jove had come to make his home at the ecclesiastical center of Christianity, taking the central place in the courtyard that the very Son of God—Christ himself—was to take at the apse of Julius's temple to the first pope, the Basilica of St. Peter's that was then rising. The adorning of the Vatican under the popes of the fifteenth and sixteenth centuries with newly recovered ancient statuary and with wall paintings that imitated Roman interior design, depicting Christian and pagan mythological scenes in the same tableaux, well illustrates the way in which Christian Rome was enthusiastically embracing its classical past. Renaissance popes espoused in the visual arts a mythological mystique that attempted to unite ancient and modern Rome, and prominent in this mythological mystique was the use of the classical gods as metaphorical stand-ins for the Christian God. In the Vatican's Stanza della Segnatura, Raphael's *School of Athens* faces directly opposite his *Miracle of the Host* with its transformation of the elements into the body and blood of Christ. The third wall of Raphael's celebrated stanza attempts to unite classical and Christian, for on it both ancient and modern poets hail Apollo as their king. So Apollo in a fashion inevitably is linked to Christ. At the beginning of the sixteenth century the Vatican was popularly called the "Hill of Apollo" because of the interest by Popes Sixtus IV, Alexander VI, and Julius II in the cult of Apollo and the Muses.[14] Julius II's installation of the recovered Apollo in the Belvedere Court simply crowned that interest.[15]

When Leo X succeeded Julius II as pope in 1513, humanist poets celebrated the occasion as the coming of the age of Minerva where scholars and poets would thrive.[16] At Rome the statue of Pasquino, clad as the Belvedere Apollo, announced: "At last I am recalled from banishment."[17] Leo himself was depicted by poets both as a new Apollo and as the Augustus who,

14. Elisabeth Schröter, "Der Vatikan als Hügel Apollons und der Musen. Kunst und Panegyric von Nikolaus V bis Julius II," in *Römische Quartalschrift* 74.

15. Deborah Brown, "The Apollo Belvedere and the Garden of Giuliano della Rovere at SS. Apostoli" in *JWCI;* H. H. Brummer, *The Statue Court in the Vatican Belvedere;* A. Michaelis, "Geschichte des Statuenhofes im vatikanischen Belvedere."

16. See Benedetto Lampridio's epigram "De suis temporibus" (composed for Leo's possesso in 1513) in *Carmina Illustrium Poetarum Italorum* (1576), 1.152v

17. See Ludwig Pastor, *The History of the Popes,* 8.185. Also see Julia Haig Gaisser, *Catullus and His Renaissance Readers,* 110.

following Julius, would usher in a "Pax Romana."[18] Neither the Pax Romana nor the Age of Gold were to last long, yet the son of Lorenzo de' Medici fulfilled for a while the promise to support the arts, being the genius who poured the Florentine riches from his papal cornucopia.[19] He founded a college for the study of Greek, brought a Greek printing press to Rome, encouraged the sodalities of poets that were flourishing in Rome, and commissioned artists such as Raphael to adorn the Vatican and his private villa.[20] Not all, however, were pleased with the new Apollonian pope.

Baptista Spagnoli Mantuanus, who had criticized the extravagance and worldliness of the Roman *curia* in the 1580s and 1590s, deplored the return of the age of Apollo. Eclogues 9 and 10 of his *Adulescentia* (published in 1498) were already widely known throughout Europe for their attack on the corruption of the clergy. His earlier work, "De calamitatibus temporum," composed some time after 1478, and his sermon before Innocent VIII in 1488 were also much to same purpose. Having been named by Leo X in 1513 as Prior General of the Carmelite Order, Mantuan undertook to compose a Christian fasti, "De sacris diebus," a calendar in twelve books that celebrated the events of the Christian year; it was published in 1516, the same year as his death, and dedicated to Leo X. The preface of the work was directly addressed to Leo and declared that neither Jupiter nor Saturnian Juno nor Venus would be found in his fasti nor would this calendar celebrate the myths and the places of the pagans—instead Christ, his mother, and the saints would reign unchallenged. Further, in the last book of the work, Mantuan both criticized the "paganism" of Leo's pontificate and banished the pagan gods from Rome. His poem for the birth of Christ, "De Nativitate Domini," not only welcomed the coming of the divine Child to the earth, not only celebrated his glorious presence as our only light, but also put to flight the pagan gods who had usurped his place on earth. Prominent among these gods is Apollo. Mantuan tells "Delphic Apollo" to shut the doors of his false temple, to sink with his tripods into Hades, and to cast his oracle into Stygian darkness.[21] Although the description of the flight of the

18. See Achilles Bocchius's ode to Leo X in *Carmina Illustrium Poetarum Italorum* (1719), 2.344. "Tu verus es Phoebus, tu bonarum / Dulce decus, columenque rerum / O si Camoenas, sancte Pater, meas / non spernis" (You are the true Phoebus, you / the sweet glory of good and the protector / of all things; O, holy Father, / if you do not spurn my Muses.)

19. See Benedetto Lampridio's ode to Leo X in *Carmina* (1550).

20. See Pastor, *History of the Popes,* 8.181–241; 258–62.

21. Baptista Mantuanus, "De Nativitate Domini" in *Fastorum Libri Duodecim* (1518). See particularly the banishment of the pagan gods: "O praeclara dies omni memorabilis aeuo / Ite lares procul inferni discedite templis, / Gloria uestra ruit, ueterem deponite fastum, / Delphice claude fores templi falacis Apollo / Cortinam tripodasque ferens ceruice sub Orcum / Labere, & ad stygias tua fer responsa lacunas. / I Venus in tenebras,

pagan gods had traditionally been part of nativity poems, Mantuan is doing more here than following a tradition. His pastoral eclogues had manifested no animosity to Apollo. Indeed, even in eclogue 10, where Mantuan was deploring the corruptions in the Church in Rome, he could describe his friend Bernardo Bembo, the father of the celebrated humanist cardinal, as the idealized shepherd and servant to Apollo, who had wreathed him in laurel and given him his cithara and plectrum (10.8–10).[22] The banishment of Delphic Apollo in "De sacris diebus" is not an attack on poetry, but on the excesses of the Rome of Leo X and the pope's own espousal of the son of Jove as his symbol.

Milton was familiar with Mantuan's eclogues, even echoing Mantuan's ninth eclogue in his own criticism of the corrupt clergy in "Lycidas."[23] One of the models for his Nativity ode must surely have been Mantuan's nativity hymn from "De sacris diebus"[24] Milton could hardly have been ignorant of the dedication of the Christian fasti to Leo nor of Mantuan's disapproval of Leo's Rome. That Mantuan could dismiss Phoebus Apollo, Leo's alter ego, and inveigh against the corruption of papal Rome even in a book he had dedicated to Leo made it all the easier for Milton to make the dismissal of Apollo in his own Nativity ode into a contemporary protest.

Yet despite protests such as Mantuan's, the exaltation of Apollo-Sun continued unabated in art and in letters. There was indeed a veritable sunburst of activity among the Renaissance poets. The ancient hymn to the sun that both Christian and pagan Neoplatonists had practiced had been revived in the fifteenth century by poets such as Michele Marullo, whose *Hymni Naturales* had immense influence.[25] Writing at the very time that

---

& tu Saturnia Iuno / Cum Ioue, maiestas uobis cum nulla supersit / Amplius in terris, Erebi descendite ad umbras. / Rex uerus sua regna subit, procul ite tyranni, / Ponite personas, & quos rapuistis honores. / Hic Puer, his infans est, qui Titania fecit / Sydera, qui solem docuit consurgere ab ortu . . ." (Liber 12, Av–Aljr).

22. See Baptista (Spagnuoli) Mantuanus, *Adulescentia, The Eclogues of Mantuan* (1989).

23. *The Eclogues of Baptista Mantuan* (1911), 46.

24. Another model was probably the verses on the birth of Christ from *Parthenice Mariana*. Both A. S. Cook and Rosemund Tuve argue for the influence of *Parthenice Mariana* on Milton, pointing out Mantuan's use of imagery in characterizing the nativity—the quiet descent of peace, the snowy landscape, the halcyons, as well as the approach of the Age of Gold. See A. S. Cook, "Two Notes on Milton," in *MLR* 2; Rosemund Tuve, *Images and Themes in Five Poems by Milton;* 39, 56n.

25. With a comprehensive knowledge of Greek and Latin literature, Marullo was a direct link between the Renaissance and the ancient world. His four books of *Hymni Naturales* comprise hymns not only to deities of the Olympic pantheon, but also to Eternity, the Sun, and other heavenly bodies, and to Earth. Celebrating the interaction between the divine and the human, Marullo attempted to incorporate in his hymns elements from cult hymns to the Olympian gods, the Neoplatonic philosophical tradition, and contemporary astronomical poetry and to synthesize all this with Christianity. For

the Vatican was Christianizing the deities of ancient Rome, Marullo makes his gods function as classical cult figures, as planetary influences, and at the same time as allegorical equivalents to the Christian Father, Son, and Holy Spirit. The Hymn to the Sun ("Soli") that opens the third book of the *Hymni* is one of Marullo's richest and most syncretistic poems. Like Synesius and Proclus, Marullo looks on the light of the sun as a creative force. Right at the outset, his hymn celebrates Apollo-Sun as a protogonos, or first being, who, having been generated before the earthly sun, created the universe. Hence he brings light physically and intellectually, and, like Proclus's Apollo-Helios, gives and sustains life as well as promoting order and law.

> Solus inexhausta qui lampade cuncta gubernat,
> Sol pater—unde etiam Solem dixere priores—,
> Et patria longe moderatur imagine mundum,
> Idem rex hominum atque deum, pater omnibus idem . . . (3.1,20–23)[26]

> Who alone governs all things, his torch inextinguishable,
> Sun Father—whence even our ancestors called him the Sun—
> Who from afar controls the earth with his father's image,
> The same king of men and gods, the same father to all . . .

This Apollo is the lord of life, the fountain of living things, creating order and law as he creates life; it is not difficult to see a resemblance between him and the Neoplatonic Christ, also the fountain of light and being.

Marullo's philosophical hymn to the sun is not unique in fifteenth- and sixteenth-century literature. Marullo's contemporary, Giovanni Pontano, celebrates the sun both in his long philosophical poem *Urania* where he describes its place in the universe as the father of all things and in a Sapphic ode, "Ad Solem," where he comments on its function as the orderer of the cycles of days, months, years—the bringer of spring and the renewer of life.[27] He emphasizes the role of the sun god as the bringer of

---

commentary on Marullo's hymns see Philip Ford, "The *Hymni Naturales* of Michael Marullus," in *Acta Conventus* (1985); and Pier Luigi Ciceri, "Michele Marullo e i suoi 'Hymni Naturales,'" in *Giornale Storico 64*.

26. Quotations of Marullo are from *Michaelis Marulli Carmina* (1951), ed. Alessandro Perosa. I have also consulted Renaissance editions, including *Hymni et Epigrammata Marulli* (1497); *Marulli Constantinopolitani Epigrammata & Hymni* (1561); and *Poetae Tres Elegantissimi* (1582).

27. Adopting, like Marullo, concepts from Proclus, from Synesius, and from Orphic religion, Pontano describes the Sun as the sower of souls, the fountain of all, the force necessary for life. His light causes things to grow, to turn green once more and to flower; he controls the return of spring and the regeneration of the earth, bringing form to the animals, and strength to the mind of man. He divides time into years and months and

spring and so influences, as we noted in Chapter 1, Milton's depiction of Apollo in "Elegia 5." Later humanistic poets follow Marullo and Pontano, each one adding to the stature of Apollo as the creator god and lord of life. Joannes Secundus describes the sun as the fountain of all things; Bernardo Tasso calls him the eternal eye of God ("Occhio eterno di Dio").[28] Ippolito Capilupi, Bernardo's friend as well as the Bishop of Fano, describes Apollo as an intellective force, the Mind of the world.[29] This philosophical tradition continues with Ronsard and the poets who followed him, notably Isaac Habert, who celebrated the sun intellectually and scientifically in *Les Trois Livres des Meteores*.[30] Humanist poets of the fifteenth and sixteenth centuries have brought down to the Renaissance a powerful figure in Apollo. More than ruler of the sun, he is the intellective creator of the universe and hence inevitably a Neoplatonic figure to set beside Christ.

APOLLO IN ENGLAND

In "Elegia 5" Milton easily adopts the Renaissance Apollo, making him the symbol for the creative vitality of nature and also of human love. He does not, however, in any way confound him with Christ, nor does he extend his creative aspects to the founding of the world. Milton's Apollo is no protogonos. In the Nativity ode, however, this powerful figure inevitably must be either a symbol for Christ or a rival to him. Milton's response to this humanistic tradition, it would seem, is both—to embrace it as he endows his Christ in the Nativity ode with Apollonian splendor and to reject it as he dismisses Apollo himself.

The Apollo that Milton rejects, however, is not just a humanistic Christianized Apollo. Milton might have succumbed to Renaissance syncretism, had not the Renaissance Apollo had another function. Pope Julius II installed the Apollo Belvedere in the Vatican as a symbol of his power as well as

---

days, fills everything with his holy light, and so controls human fate on the individual and on the societal level. See Giovanni Pontano, "De Sole," in *Pontani Opera (Urania)* (1505), 6r; and "Ad Solem," in "Lyra," *Carmina* (1948), 360–62.

28. See Joannes Secundus, "Ad Solem," *Poetae Tres Elegantissimi* (1582), 11; and Bernardo Tasso, "Ad Apolline," *Ode di M. Bernardo Tasso* (1560), 18–19; also see Tasso, "Al Sole," 19–22.

29. Ippolito thinks of the Sun as the force that regulates the universe; he is the prince of stars, orderer of the nine orbs of planets and also of the sea and the land. In his planetary aspect he is the bringer of day and night, hence the orderer of the diurnal regularity for humankind. Through his mastery of the art of music, he guides the universe in its eternal orbiting, as the lyre guides the feet of the chorus. See Hippolytus Capilupus, "Ad Apollinem," *Capiluporum Carmina* (1590), 23–26.

30. Pierre de Ronsard, *Les Hymnes de Pierre de Ronsard* (1555); Isaac Habert, *Les trois livres des Meteores, avec que autres oeuvres poétiques* (1585).

Impresa of Pope Urban VIII, *Aliusque et Idem,* from Giovanni
Ferro, *Teatro d'Imprese* (Venice 1623), F.4.7. Art, p. 650,
reprinted by permission of the Bodleian Library, University of
Oxford.

his artistic taste. This is an active Apollo, repulsing his enemies, defeating the Python, defending his shrine at Delphi—little suspecting that a young English poet was to eject him from it in a little over one hundred years. The Belvedere symbolized an aggressive Catholicism. It was carried all over Europe in sketches made by visiting artists. Filippino Lippi imitated it; Albrecht Dürer made it the model for his Sol-Apollo; Michelangelo for his Christ. François I had it modeled in bronze for Fontainebleau and so the symbol of the warring pope became a symbol for the warring French king.[31] Philip II of Spain placed Apollo-Sun with his chariot of horses at the center of his impresa.[32] Apollo was also dear to the seventeenth-century pope, Maffeo Barberini, who had ascended to the papacy as Urban VIII in 1623 and was the pope whose influence both Milton and other English Protestants would grow to fear. Like Leo X and Julius II, Urban thought of himself as an Apollonian pope dedicated to the arts; he also boasted himself a poet. One of Urban's imprese was the Apollonian laurel covered with bees; another was the rising sun. His motto "Aliusque et Idem" ("another and the same") was drawn from Horace's *Carmen Saeculare* to Apollo and Diana. Apollo had also been Augustus Caesar's patron god.[33] Both in the Vatican and in the Barberini palaces Apollo and the sun are ubiquitous: in the radiant head of Apollo under the papal arms, in the ancient statue of Apollo in the landing of the palace, in the Apollo head above the fireplace of the salone, as well as the Belvedere Apollo Urban had inherited from Julius. As John Beldon Scott has pointed out, "Urban even had a wall in his apartment at the Vatican painted with a shining sun so that each morning he would be greeted by the light of his own impresa"—the Apollo-Sun.[34]

31. Phyllis Pray Bober and Ruth Rubinstein, *Renaissance Artists and Antique Sculpture: A Handbook of Sources,* 28–29, 71–72.

32. See Girolano Ruscelli, *Le Imprese Illustri con espositioni et discorsi* (1566), illustrated in René Graziani, "Philip II's Impresa and Spenser's Souldan." Graziani points out that Philip II had invented this impresa sometime after 1566, remarking that the motto, "Iam illustrabit Omnia" represented Philip's mission as the champion of Catholicism to convey the light of the Catholic faith to all the nations that the sun illuminated. He argues further that Spenser had satirized Philip's mission by turning his representative, the Souldan, from an Apollo to a Phaeton. My thanks to Peggy Simonds for drawing my attention to this article and the impresa.

33. See Giovanni Ferro, *Teatro d'Imprese* (1623), 650. Also see John Beldon Scott, *Images of Nepotism: The Painted Ceilings of Palazzo Barberini,* 114–15. Urban (Maffeo Barberini), whose *Poemata* had been published in Paris in 1620, had composed an "Ode Hortatoria ad Virtutem" in which he asked Apollo to prophesy and sing: "Sensus recludet Cynthius abditos / Audi canentem" (The Cynthian reveals hidden secrets; hear him singing), 204–6.

34. See Scott, *Images of Nepotism,* 58, 70, 142. The sun was extraordinarily prominent both in Urban's natal chart and in the astrological chart that was drawn for his ascendancy to the papacy on August 6, 1623. Urban said that he was born and elected to rule (Scott, 82). Also see Patricia Waddy, *Seventeenth-Century Roman Palaces.* Waddy notes

Urban was clearly a pope in the style of Julius II, emulating him as he collected antiquities and as he pursued papal wars. With him Apollo was reigning once more in the Vatican.

When Phoebus Apollo comes to England he is the emblem for James I. In Chapman's *The Memorable Masque,* performed before the king at Whitehall in February 1613, priests of the sun address a song to Phoebus-James, "rise rise, O Phoebus, ever rise . . . set set, great Sun, our rising love / Shall ever celebrate thy grace . . . be to earth her only light: All other kings, in thy beams met, / Are clouds and dark effects of night."[35] In poems published in 1617 to celebrate James's return to England, James was described as an Apollo returning to the Muses, a sun god giving light to his kingdom, which was dark in his absence. Even before Charles assumed the throne, he had assumed his father's mythological titles, appearing as a Phoebus scattering night in the poems written in 1623 to welcome him back from Spain to England.[36] So important is the Apollo symbolism to Charles that he commissioned a painting of Apollo and Diana (dated 1628) from Gerrit van Honhorst, a Dutch follower of Caravaggio, directing the artist to give King Apollo his own features and Diana Henrietta Maria's. This Apollo-Charles is enthroned receiving the homage of a Buckingham-Mercury and the Arts and is routing Ignorance and Vice—ironically just as Milton's Christ will rout the pagan gods.[37]

In 1628–1629 Charles had been strengthening his ties with Italy, having just purchased the Gonzaga collection with its superb Titians and Raphaels. Pope Urban was Henrietta Maria's godfather, and there had been arrangements at the time of her marriage to Charles to set up a private chapel in St. James's Palace. The queen, moreover, was to appoint Cardinal Francesco

---

that the Barberini had an ancient torso of Apollo to which they eventually commissioned the sculptor Giorgetti to add a head, arms, and legs. The renewed Apollo was eventually installed in a fountain court at the Barberini palace (257). Also see J. K. Newman, "Empire of the Sun: Lelio Guidiccioni and Pope Urban VIII," in *IJCT.*

35. Chapman, *The Memorable Masque* (1613), 580–81. Also see Jonson's *The Masque of Blackness* (1605), where James rules England like a sun.

36. *Iacobi Ara. Deo Reduci* (1617), and *Carolus Redux* (1623). Also see the later volumes collected for Charles's return from Scotland in 1633, when he is also greeted as an Apollo or a Sun returned to England. See *Rex Redux* (1633), and *Solis Britannici Perigaeum* (1633).

37. See Christopher Lloyd, *The Royal Collection,* 39, 41, 81–84. The painting, on a large canvas, is at Hampton Court Palace and depicts not only Apollo and Diana receiving the homage of Mercury and Grammar (the Duke and Duchess of Buckingham) and the other arts, but also the rout of Ignorance. The painting can be dated precisely since Buckingham was assassinated in 1628. Buckingham visited Cambridge in 1628 and a collection of poems (to which Milton—significantly—did not contribute) marked the visit. The mythological scene of reception and rout that pictures both Charles and Buckingham prominently is an interesting contrast to Milton's ode of advent and rout.

Gerrit van Honthorst, *Apollo and Diana*, from the Royal Collection, reprinted by permission of Her Majesty Queen Elizabeth II.

Barberini, the pope's nephew, to select art for the English court. In art as in life Milton and other Puritans could recognize the encroaching influence of the Vatican "Apollo" on the English court.

At least one reader of the Nativity ode understood quite well the implications of Milton's exorcism of the "Renaissance" Apollo. William Blake's painting of the Apollo stanza of the Nativity ode demonstrates that Blake was an unusually astute interpreter of Milton. That Blake has chosen Apollo Belvedere as his model for Milton's Greek god is hardly accidental. It was not merely that for the Renaissance and for the ages that follow no image of the ancient god was quite so popular. For Blake the Belvedere Apollo with its the perfect (but as he thought perverse) classical beauty symbolized Christianity's enslavement in the Renaissance to the mercantile and imperialistic ethics of classical art. Apollo's bow and quiver represent the militarism of Renaissance kings and popes, a militarism that debases art: "a warlike state," said Blake, "never can produce Art. It will rob & plunder & accumulate into one place & translate & copy & buy & sell, but not make." About the column in Blake's picture a seductive serpent twines—the insidious power to corrupt that this beautiful form possesses. By using the Belvedere statue as his model, Blake is telling us that it is not an ancient pagan Apollo that Milton is exorcising, but the Apollo that the Renaissance revived and revered and made a substitute for the true God. Blake's speaking picture leaves us no doubt exactly who and what Milton was exorcising in his famous stanza.[38]

1629

1629 was an important year for Milton. He was turning 21, was offering a birthday poem to Christ in English as the sign of his poetical maturity, and was also manifesting a growing political consciousness. In March 1629 Charles I had dissolved parliament and those who called attention to the king's misdoings had been sent to the Tower. That Milton vividly remembered these events is attested by his reference to them in the sonnet he wrote some twelve to fourteen years later to Lady Margaret Ley, recalling the "sad breaking of that Parliament" (5). He also describes the events of 1629 in some detail in *Eikonoklastes* when he narrates Charles's successive encounters with parliament, giving particular prominence to the dissolving of the 1629 parliament, which he recognized as a pivotal point in the

---

38. See Raymond Lister, *The Painting of William Blake*, plate 51. Also see Stephen Behrendt, "Blake's Illustrations to Milton's 'Nativity Ode' " in *PQ*.

William Blake, *The Overthrow of Apollo and the Pagan Gods,* watercolor to Milton's "Ode on the Morning of Christ's Nativity," reprinted by permission of the Henry E. Huntington Library and Art Gallery, San Marino, California.

developing political and religious crisis. Is the exorcism of a Charles's alter ego Phoebus Apollo in Milton's Nativity ode a reaction to that crisis?

It has long been recognized that one of the literary models for Milton's Nativity ode, particularly for its central section on the Age of Gold, is Vergil's fourth bucolic, the so-called messianic eclogue. Christians since the age of Constantine looked on the child whose birth was prophesied in the eclogue as Christ and saw him as the restorer of the classical Age of Gold.[39] This very eclogue was revived by Vatican poets of sixteenth-century and seventeenth-century Italy, however, for a different purpose. Pietro Bembo, for example, used it to predict the triumph of Renaissance Pope Julius II, whose function it was to bring back the Age of Gold.[40] One hundred years later poets celebrated Maffeo Barberini's accession to the papacy in a similar way. The Jesuit neo-Latin poet Casimire Sarbiewski proclaimed that Urban had brought peace to the world, had renewed the Age of Saturn, and would make the rivers of Italy flow with milk and honey.[41] Francesco Bracciolini composed twenty-three cantos on Urban's election to the papacy that concluded with Astrea descending to witness Urban's defeat of Envy and the banishment of Error.[42]

This movement in Rome had a political and cultural counterpart in England. In Stuart masques Astrea appears to announce the Age of Gold and to identify James as the Apollo who is to preside over this golden era.[43] In the 1620s Charles had assumed his father's place as ruler of the Age of Gold. But in December 1629 a new ruler was about to appear; the "child" of the Vergilian eclogue was expected, for Henrietta Maria was bearing the heir to the throne—Charles II. In November 1629, there were confident reports of Henrietta Maria's pregnancy; at Christmastide, prayers were offered for a safe pregnancy. Milton could not have failed to know of the coming event.[44] From the very beginning the future Prince Charles was associated with the "child" of the Vergil's messianic eclogue.

When the prince was actually born in May 1630, the event was treated like a "second coming." A midday star was reportedly seen as the king went to give thanks for his son's birth, and the new prince was accordingly

---

39. See Tuve, *Images and Themes,* 39, 54.

40. Petrus Bembus, "Julii Secundi," *Carmina, Quinque Illustrium Poetarum* (1753), 41. Bembo's poem to Julius begins by noting that the god Jove had ordained the end of the Age of Gold, making men languish in the Age of Iron. But now a new "Jove" is to rule on earth, and the Jovian oak revives in the Della Rovere emblem; all other trees yield to the oak—the Apollonian laurel, the Venerean myrtle, the Bacchic ivy. Now the oak has brought back to the earth the Age of Law and probity and faith.

41. See Casimire Sarbiewski, *Lyricorum, Libri Tres* (1625), 187–95. Urban (Maffeo Barberini) himself was a poet whose poetry illustrates his fascination with antiquity. See his "Ode Hortatoria ad Virtutem," *Poemata* (1620), in which Cynthian Apollo appears to reveal secrets. He also addressed Pindaric odes to the Virgin Mary and the Saints.

42. See Scott, *Images of Nepotism,* 172–73.

43. Chapman's *The Memorable Masque* (1613) concludes as Honour confers the "blessing of the golden age" on England.

44. See Elizabeth Hamilton, *Henrietta Maria,* 98; Carola Oman, *Henrietta Maria* (Hodder and Stoughton Ltd., 1936), 66–67. "The prospect of their Papist queen providing England with an heir had been resented by 'mutterers'" (66); also see I. S. MacLaren, "Milton's Nativity Ode: The Function of Poetry and Structures of Response in 1629," in *MS* 15:181–200.

compared to Christ himself. Ben Jonson and other Caroline poets celebrated the queen as a second Mary; the author of the birth-poem *Carolides* announced the arrival of the age of Saturn; Cambridge and Oxford poets in the university collections printed for the occasion wrote royal nativities that welcomed Prince Charles as a Vergilian messiah and, of course, as another Phoebus.[45] Although Charles's birth had not yet taken place when he wrote his Nativity ode, Milton was reacting at Christmas 1629 to claims that the imminent royal birth would establish a Stuart Age of Gold. Milton responded by affirming that only the coming of the "king of kings," only a reestablished Protestantism could bring England her golden age. Christ must be reborn—not another Charles.

For Milton the term *Age of Gold* reverberates with millenarian promise, and he gives it unmistakable prominence in the Nativity ode.[46] "Enwrapt" by the song of the angels, he thinks that "Time will run back, and fetch the age of gold" (135). Then, "speckl'd vanity" will die and "leprous sin" melt away (136–38), and "Truth, and Justice then / Will down return to men" (141–42). "Wisest fate" reminds him, however, that the time is not yet ripe; the Christ child still lies in smiling infancy. But the very mention of the imminence of the golden age creates a sense of double time. In the present tense, in the ode's own time, the millennium seems far closer for the young Protestant poet. Milton would challenge parliament in *Areopagitica*

45. Jonson's poem is on the Queen's lying-in; he compared the two Marys. David Echlin was the Queen's physician; he addressed the *Carolides* (1630) to King Charles. The title page of the work declares that the age of Saturn will return. The poem makes similar claims. The Oxford collection *(Britanniae Natalis)* was published in 1630, the Cambridge collection *(Genethliacum Illustrissimorum Principum Caroli & Mariae)*, which celebrated the birth of Princess Mary also, in 1631. Other collections celebrated the birth of other royal children. Such a volume is *Voces Votivae* (1640), a later university collection, in which Crashaw's poem appears. He describes Charles as a child whose grandsires were a Phoebus-James and a Mars-Henry: "Bright Charles thou sweet dawn of a glorious day!" (503).

Charles retains the identity of Phoebus into the Restoration. In a university collection welcoming him back to England in 1660, he is greeted as a Phoebus returning to take the place of his father *(Sostra sive, Ad Carolum II, reducem*, 1r). Curiously, during the Protectorate, Cromwell was sometimes addressed as Apollo—one title he managed to usurp successfully from Charles I. See, for example, the Oxford volume celebrating the peace with Holland in 1654: *Elaiophoria sive Ob Faedera, Auspiciis serenissimi Oliveri, Reipub. Ang. Scot. & Hiber. Domini Protectoris* (1654).

46. Michael Wilding, *Dragons Teeth: Literature in the English Revolution.* Wilding has argued that the apocalyptic appeals in the Nativity ode manifest an unusual sensitivity even in the prerevolutionary days to the political pressures about to erupt. It was almost as though Milton foresaw, Wilding says, as he described the rout of the pagan deities, "the parade of defeated bishops, clergy, and courtiers" that the Revolution would displace (14). Also see David Norbrook, *Poetry and Politics in the English Renaissance*, 241–44. Norbrook also emphasizes the apocalyptic strain in the Nativity ode as an indication of Milton's political awareness at this time in his poetic career.

to begin to build for that new age and remind Englishmen that they must resist the worst Vatican repression and refuse to enact laws of censorship. He would contrast the true English age of liberty from licensing with the Vatican imposition of imprimaturs. Milton would also specifically indict in *Areopagitica* Popes Martin V and Leo X together with the Council of Trent and the Spanish Inquisition for creating modern censorship. Finally, he would declare that "God is decreeing to begin some new and great period in his Church, even to the reforming of reformation itself."[47] Contrasting England and Italy, Milton proclaims the commencement of a "new and great period"—an Age of Gold, directly opposed to that which Vatican poets and Stuart kings had once proclaimed. The Nativity ode's apostrophe to the Age of Gold is the first blast of the trumpet of prophecy.

When Milton silences Apollo at the beginning of the catalogue of routed deities, it is not Apollo the god of poetry or even Apollo the sun god, but Apollo the prophet that he is specifically thinking of. He is intent on refuting the claims of Catholic Rome and Stuart England, on silencing their prophecies along with their "gods." As the prophet of the new Protestantism, he declares, "The Oracles are dumb." At the same time he predicts that the old dragon—the satanically inspired Catholic Rome—will be "under ground / In straiter limits bound" (168–69) and those gods that Renaissance Rome and Stuart England had so extravagantly revived to adorn their palaces and temples will be extinguished. Together with Apollo go the nymphs that were so popular in Renaissance wall painting and the Roman gods of the hearth, the Lars and Lemurs, revived as Renaissance Italians celebrated their Roman heritage. The Egyptian deities of the catalogue remind us how Egyptology also flourished in the Vatican under the influence of the writings of Annius and Giles of Viterbo, who persuaded Renaissance men that the Egyptian Ammon, Hercules, Isis, and Osiris were counterparts to Hebraic and Christian figures. Pope Alexander VI had celebrated his own "Egyptian" heritage by using the figures of Osiris and Isis in the wall decorations of the Borgia apartments of the Vatican and by making the Egyptian bull his own personal symbol.[48] Milton, however, dismisses the Egyptian pseudo-Christian substitutes with Apollo, connecting them with the false idols of the heathens, with Moloch, Baal, and the crew of deities that misled the Israelites.[49] In asserting the power of prophecy in the new Protestantism, Milton will not leave any of the pagan gods of Rome unrouted.

47. Hughes, ed., *Complete Poetry and Major Prose,* 724, 743 (quotation).
48. See J. W. O'Malley, S.J. "Fulfillment of the Christian Golden Age under Pope Julius II: Text of a discourse of Giles of Viterbo, 1505," in *Traditio;* also see John D'Amico, *Renaissance Humanism in Papal Rome.*
49. See C. W. R. D. Moseley, *The Poetic Birth: Milton's Poems of 1645,* 88. Michael Wilding makes a similar point in *Dragon's Teeth,* 16–17.

"NOR ALL THE GODS BESIDE, / LONGER DARE ABIDE"

C. W. R. D. Moseley has argued that when arranging his poems for publication Milton intentionally placed immediately after the Nativity ode the translations of Psalms 114 and 136 that he did as a schoolboy. These psalms were scripture that English Protestants looked to as celebration of the deliverance of the Reformed Church from the Egyptian or Babylonian captivity of the Roman Catholic Church. He even suggests that "given the political circumstances at the time of the publication of *Poems* (1645), the psalms, to those of Milton's party persuasion, could hardly not seem a triumph-song after Naseby" (88).[50] His argument is persuasive. In 1673 when Milton adds to *Poems* the group of psalms translated in the 1650s, he places these psalms at the end of the English volume. He does not alter, however, the position of Psalms 114 and 136; they appear in 1673, as in 1645, immediately after the Nativity ode. Both psalms are exodus celebrations that praise the power of God as well as the release from captivity. Psalm 114 opens:

> When the blest seed of *Terah's* faithfull Son,
> After long toil their liberty had won,
> And past from *Pharian* fields to *Canaan* Land,
> Led by the strength of the Almighty's hand,
> *Jehovah's* wonders were in *Israel* known,
> His praise and glory were in *Israel* known. (1–6)

Milton exults in this freedom by calling on the earth to shake with apocalyptic premonition and "at his presence be aghast / Of him that ever was, and aye shall last" (15–16).[51] In the Nativity ode with a psalmlike exultation and apocalyptic expectation both heaven and earth resound and the crystal spheres ring out. Psalm 136 follows and praises God's power both in saving his people and in quelling tyrants. As in the Nativity ode the action of the psalm is double. God's might makes the world, causes the "Golden-tressed Sun, / All the day long his course to run" (29–30).[52] God's might also causes the fall of pharaoh, the "Tawny King with all his power," just as in the Nativity ode it puts to flight Apollo and the gods of Egypt.

When Milton translates Psalm 114 again in 1634, this time turning the Hebrew into Greek, he pairs it with the Greek epigram, "Philosophus

---

50. Moseley, *The Poetic Birth*, 88.

51. Milton must surely have known Psalm 114 as the psalm that the saved people of Dante's ship of souls are singing at the beginning of the *Purgatorio* in sign of their deliverance.

52. Just as in the Nativity ode, Milton uses an Apollonian epithet for the sun.

ad regem."[53] The Greek version of Psalm 114 reinforces even further the Protestantism manifest in the 1624 version, now displaying, together with the verses on the philosopher, a growing antiroyalism. As in his 1624 translation, Milton begins by describing the exodus: "When the children of Israel, the holy race of Jacob, left the land of the Egyptians." Lines 3 and 4 of Milton's Greek paraphrase, however, depart both from his early version and from a precise biblical reading. They affirm not only the sanctity of the children of Israel but also that God alone is *the king* of the people:

Δὴ τότε μοῦνον ἔην ὅσιον γένος υἷες Ἰούδα.
Ἐν δὲ θεὸς λαοῖσι μέγα κρείων βασίλευεν. (3–4)

Only surely then were the children of Juda a holy race,
and among the people *God was king* ruling strongly.
(my translation; emphasis mine)

Milton's paraphrase uses the Greek word βασίλευεν to insist on *God's* kingship, not the rule of pharaoh or any other earthly prince. In affirming here the primacy of God as king, Milton moves one step further to challenging the authority of earthly kings. In the Nativity ode Milton had covertly asserted the ascendancy of the godly Protestantism in England by dismissing Apollo-Charles and praising Christ as the new ruler. In the Greek psalm he interpolates a phrase that asserts *God's* kingship over his people—delivering the message that no other ruler is king but God. With a Greek translation of this key "Protestant" psalm, he makes known his views of kingship to those of his persuasion, those, that is, who can read the Greek and understand the subtleties of the translation.[54]

The Greek verses—"Philosophus ad regem"—are dated by some editors in the mid-1620s, by others in the mid-1630s, and still by others in the mid-1640s. The time of composition, however, is not nearly so important as

53. In December 1634 Milton sent his Greek translation of Psalm 114 to Alexander Gil Jr. (See French, *The Life Records of John Milton* 1:289–90). Wilding, in *Dragon's Teeth*, remarks that the Greek psalm too takes on prophetic significance in 1645 (17). In 1673 the two Greek poems were also printed together, joined by Milton's Greek epigram on his effigy (originally printed under Marshall's engraving). The offending picture had been removed.

54. The word "king" is not found either in the English translation of the Geneva Bible or the 1611 Bible or in the Latin Vulgate or in the Greek of the polyglot Bible or in the original Hebrew, which uses the word "dominion"—*mamsheloth*. See *Psalterium, Hebraeum, Graecum, Arabicum, & Chaldaeum, cum tribus latinis interpretionibus & glossis* (1516). The use of Greek here to make a political point is comparable to Milton's use of Greek in 1645 to protest a quite different issue. Under the portrait in the frontispiece of the 1645 *Poems,* he placed a Greek epigram, addressed to his learned friends, that asserted that the image that engraver Marshall has presented of him was not a true image.

Milton's coupling these hexameters in the 1645 text with the Greek psalm; he is not, as some editors have suggested, merely coupling two poems composed in Greek. The second poem takes an even stronger antiroyalist stance, for it reports a wrongly condemned philosopher's words of protest to the king as he is being led to execution. Addressing the king directly, the philosopher advises him, as Socrates advised the Athenian jury that was about to condemn him, that if the king killed him, he would destroy a law-abiding man, who had committed no crime, a man who was (as a philosopher) a renowned safeguard for the city. Linked with Milton's Greek psalm, the verses made a powerful political statement.[55]

Milton's youthful anti-papal Latin poem, "In Quintum Novembris," also supports the Protestantism, the patriotism, and to some extent the millenarianism of the ode. In the English ode Milton is rejecting the symbols of Catholic Rome; in his Latin mini-epic he objects to the idolatry of Rome and its subversive plots against England. He depicts the pope carrying idols or, as Milton calls them, gods made of bread, in procession about Rome; he also compares the chanting of the worshippers in procession to the cries of Bromius in the rites of Bacchus. The pope in "In Quintum Novembris" is both a satanically inspired tyrant and a pagan "god," a Typhoeus, exiled from Olympus.[56] While the mini-epic is strongly anti-papal, it is not antiroyalist; Milton supports James against the papal attempts to unseat him. Its conclusion, however, celebrates the triumph of an English Protestantism over the schemes of papal Rome.

The Latin gunpowder epigrams, as we observed in Chapter 2, also are directed against papal machinations; they recall the same event that "In Quintum Novembris" narrates, James's escape from the Gunpowder Plot of 1605. The composition of these poems on the occasion of James's death demonstrates just how anxious Milton and Protestant England were about the passing of one king and the accession of another. The Protestant James had resisted both Rome's threats and blandishments; would his son do the same? The marriage of Charles I in 1625 to a Catholic princess, whose godfather was Pope Urban VIII, hardly allayed the English Protestants' fears. Milton's gunpowder poems end with celebration of a triumph over Rome. In 1629 on the eve of the birth of a Catholic Mary's son, the English Protestants looked for further assurance. A young Protestant poet gave it to them when he described in the triumphant conclusion of the Nativity ode how the infant Christ routed the pagan gods of a pagan Rome. Just as

55. Some editors connect these verses with Milton's support of Alexander Gil Jr., whom the king and Laud had threatened with punishment and imprisonment for speaking out. See *Variorum (The Latin and Greek Poems)*, 1.259–60.

56. Milton calls the pope's sighs Typhoean. See my article, "Milton's Gunpowder Poems and Satan's Conspiracy," in *MS* 4.

surely as Calvin and Luther and Zwingli had routed paganism in their time, the English Protestants with their reborn Christ would deliver the Church in theirs.

HERCULEAN CHRIST

At the conclusion of the Nativity ode Milton's triumphant Christ, having routed the pagan gods and having assumed the splendor of a new Sun God, takes over the role of another "pagan" figure—Hercules. At his birth Hercules—"Jove's" other son—had performed a miraculous feat in his cradle, strangling the serpents that came to kill him. Milton has placed a reference to this Herculean feat in the Nativity ode at a strategic point, immediately after he has described Christ's routing of the last of the pagan gods—Osiris—and immediately before he describes his control of the snaky Typhon. "He [Osiris] feels from *Juda's* Land / The dreaded Infant's hand, / The rays of *Bethlehem* blind his dusky eyn" (221–23). Osiris is both the Egyptian sun king and the apis or bull figure, who suggests both the calf of gold that the Israelites worshipped and the monstrous bull that Hercules put down as one of his labors. In a passage from *The First Defense of the People of England* that alludes to the slaying of tyrants, Milton refers to Osiris as a tyrannical Egyptian king.[57] As a sun king Osiris was also linked with the Greek Apollo, the god of light whom the new sun Christ will replace. While Milton dismisses these brutish gods of Egypt, he does not include the heroic Hercules in their company; he even allows Christ, the other Son of God, to take over the Herculean role, controlling Typhon as Hercules had the serpents.

> Nor all the gods beside,
> Longer dare abide,
>   Nor *Typhon* huge ending in snaky twine:
> Our Babe to show his Godhead true,
> Can in his swaddling bands control the damned crew. (224–28)

Even though Hercules could have just as many "royal" associations as Apollo, Milton chooses to depict his Hercules-Christ as a liberating hero rather than as a king, performing as his first act the symbolic repulse of the monstrous enemies of humankind.[58]

---

57. See Cartari (1571), 73–4. *Complete Prose Works* (Wolfe), 4.432.

58. On the Continent Hercules was closely connected with the Farnese, with the Medici, and with the kings of France, particularly François I, Henri II, and Henri IV. James I of England also assumed Herculean traits. Charles I, however, seems to have

Milton's readers could not have missed the allusion to this popular story about the infant Hercules and the serpents, for the topos was a popular one. Although found in many sources, it ultimately goes back to the concluding myth of Pindar's *Nemean 1* where Pindar tells the story of the Greek Heracles and the serpents to compliment Chromius, a Nemean victor who claimed descent from Heracles.[59] What links Milton to Pindar is the political purpose that Pindar puts the story to. Chromius was the governor of the new city of Aetna, and Aetna was, of course, the mountain under which Zeus's monstrous enemy Typhon was pinioned.[60] The ode begins by lauding Zeus and ends by lauding Zeus's son Heracles, who like his father is also a queller of monsters. By alluding to Typhon and by telling the story of Heracles and the serpents, Pindar is making a connection between Zeus's and his hero-son's control of monsters and would-be tyrants and the political control that a governor such as Chromius must also exert over enemies.

The Heracles section of Pindar's ode first recounts and then interprets the episode of Heracles' strangling the serpents. Pindar tells us that no sooner was the newborn child swaddled than Hera, stirred up by wrath, sent two serpents to attack him. Lifting up his head, Heracles made his first essay of battle by seizing the serpents by their necks and throttling them. Pindar describes the scene graphically. Heracles' foster-father Amphitryon calls on Teiresias to prophesy the child's future, and Teiresias declares that Heracles is destined to defeat lawless monsters on land and sea and finally to ascend to the seat of bliss, to be glorified by his father Zeus. The child proves his divine birthright even in infancy, by giving a clear sign of the future heroic deeds he was to perform. This victory indicates—as the seer Teiresias prophesies in the ode—that despite adversity Heracles will triumph and achieve the destiny that his divine father ordained for him.

For Milton the story of Heracles has both typological and political significance. First of all, he recognizes Hercules in the Nativity ode, as in "The

---

been more an Apollonian than a Herculean king. Not until Charles II assumes the throne is the king again associated with Hercules. See my article, "The Politics of Milton's Hercules," in *MS* 32.

59. The story of Hercules and the serpents could be found in Ovid as well as in countless other ancient and Renaissance sources, including the usual retellings and interpretations in the myth books. See for example, Natalis Comes, *Mythologiae* (1581), 445; Vincenzo Cartari (1571), 348.

60. The Harvard Pindar (Saumur, 1620) that the Columbia edition of Milton's *Works* identifies as having been purchased by Milton in 1629 cannot be connected with the poet on the basis of the annotations in the book. As Maurice Kelley and S. D. Atkins have demonstrated, Milton's handwriting does not match that in the Harvard Pindar. Having examined the book myself, I concur. See Maurice Kelley and S. D. Atkins, "Milton and the Harvard Pindar," in *SB* 19.

Passion" as a type of Christ, a hero whose trials and triumphs predicted those of the Son of God. It was a familiar Renaissance reading. But, second, he uses the story of the serpents, as Pindar did, to make a political point. By recounting the story of the serpents, Pindar is alluding also to the monster Typhon imprisoned under Aetna and yet threatening. By depicting Heracles as a future monster-slayer, Pindar refers in political terms to Sicily's and specifically Chromius's controlling of the enemies that threaten the Dorian or Heraclean institutions of that island—its rule by Greek law. Chromius had served both Hippocrates, the ruler of Gela, and his sons, Gelon and Hieron, and had been appointed governor of Aetna, a city that was threatened by "monsters" that were more than metaphorical (Etruscans to the north and Carthaginians to the south).[61] Pindar is telling Chromius that he can, like his ancestor Heracles, rule over the "monsters" of sea and land—tyrants who walk in the ways of envy, giants who make war on the plains of Phlegra. These are real, not mythical enemies; the ode to the ruler of Aetna deals with practical politics.

Like Pindar, Milton has given us a vivid picture of an infant "wrestler" overcoming his enemies in a first act of battle and has suggested, moreover, that the act of battle both proves the child's divine heritage and prefigures his future career as a monster-slayer. Heracles, like Jesus—the child of one divine and one human parent—foreshadowed his future role as a monster-slayer with his strangling the serpents. The infant Jesus, like Hercules, displays similar supernatural powers even though he is in swaddling bands. Milton also emphasizes the principle of inherited birthright—Christ proves his divine heritage by controlling the satanic Typhon.[62] Typhon, the huge snake or dragon that he controls, is not just a Heraclean snake, or the

---

61. The tyrants of southern Italy were continually trying to extend their control to Sicilian cities, and the Carthaginians and their Phoenician allies had more than once made war on the Sicilian city-states. Hieron had sent Chromius in 477 B.C., the year before he became governor of Aetna, to assist the Locri in northern Sicily against Anaxilas of Rhegium, who was trying to take over that city. For commentary on Pindar's views of Sicilian politics, see M. I. Finley, *Ancient Sicily;* and C. M. Bowra, "Echoes of Politics," in *Pindar.*

62. Milton undoubtedly also remembered that many of the tyrant-monsters of the later books of *The Faerie Queene* are descended from Typhon and are figures for the papacy, for Spain, and for Catholic tyrants in Europe. In book 5 of *The Faerie Queene,* moreover, Artegall is cast in the mold of the Herculean hero who goes out to conquer the "monsters" of Europe that were threatening the allies of the Faerie Queene. Spenser specifically tells his readers that all the monsters of modern Europe are descended from those that Hercules first grappled with, son-monsters who, after the death of their fathers, simply fled into new abodes to assert their tyranny there. The Belge episode in canto 10 of book 5 is particularly to the point, for there Artegall must conquer the monster Geryoneo, who is identified as the son of Geryon, the tyrant-monster that Hercules conquered: "His sonne was this, *Geryoneo* hight, / Who after that his monstrous father fell / Under *Alcides* club, streight tooke his flight / From that sad land, where he his

monster Zeus defeated, or a Satan-figure that opposes the Son, but is something more contemporaneous. For Protestants of Milton's time allusion to the "old Dragon" and to Typhon could signify nothing else but Rome and its tyrant allies. As Milton identifies Christ's routing of Apollo with the triumph of Christ the king over contemporary monarchs, so also he identifies the Herculean Christ's contest with and defeat of Typhon with the triumph of Protestant nations over Catholicism. In the double-time scheme of the ode, Christ's defeat of monsters in his cradle can prefigure both the defeat of Satan with the Resurrection and also the defeat of Satanism in modern Europe by a Herculean England. Milton in *The Tenure of Kings and Magistrates* connects a king-killing parliament with a tyrant-killing Hercules.[63] In the Nativity ode he is addressing a Protestant nation—now reborn with the birth of its Savior—and advising it to keep the Heraclean sinews of its Christianity taut—to rout the pagan influences in its culture. Just as Christ from Bethlehem had routed the pagan gods, the Protestant nation from London must control the "damned crew" and keep the snaky twin of Typhon—Rome's dragon—from enveloping a free England. The young Milton in the Nativity ode was skillful in conflating his classicism and his Christianity to urge the ascension of Protestant England over Typhoean tyrants at home and abroad.

The final image of the Nativity ode gives us a sun, purged of its Apollonian association, that is about to rise—about to declare its new day as the shadows flock to an infernal jail. Milton's treatment of Apollo in the Nativity ode gives evidence of his early political convictions and the strength of his militant Protestantism; it also demonstrates his versatility in handling mythic symbols in his poetry. The very Apollo whom he can adopt as a sexual and poetic alter ego in "Elegia 5," he can sacrifice on a political altar when that Apollo takes on the robes of monarchy. Yet when that Apollo puts down his bow and takes up his lyre once more or puts on his singing robes, Milton can wholeheartedly readmit him as the symbol for poetry. A poetic "Apollo" will applaud the goddesses of "L'Allegro" and "Il Penseroso"; a nurturing "Apollo" will assist and aid in *A Mask;* and Apollo will reappear in person in "Lycidas" and be triumphant in the mature Latin poems that crown Milton's achievement in the 1645 volume.

---

syre did quell, / And came to this, where *Belge* then did dwell (*The Faerie Queene* 5.10.11, 1–5).

63. Hughes, ed., *Complete Poetry and Major Prose,* 760.

4

"L'ALLEGRO" AND
"IL PENSEROSO"

Invoking the Goddess

In the Nativity ode Milton demonstrated his ability to adapt the genre
of the classical hymn-ode to honor the birth of Christ and to address
personal and political issues that faced him as a young Protestant poet.
Attempting to repeat the performance the next spring in "The Passion,"
an ode for Eastertide, he fails, finding the subject "above his years" and
abandons it unfinished, "nothing satisfied with what was begun." Yet the
ode genre continues to fascinate him, and he later has better success with
the three short occasional odes: "On Time," "On the Circumcision," and
"At a Solemn Music."[1] In "L'Allegro" and "Il Penseroso" he turns to classical
hymn-ode as a poetic model, not, however, for a serious Christian ode on
a religious occasion, but for twin sportive odes addressed to the mythic
goddesses Mirth and Melancholy. Although "L'Allegro" and "Il Penseroso"
in the course of their critical history have been assigned to a variety of
traditions or modes—from the academic prolusion to the rural excursion
to the argumentative verse essay—their basic connection with classical ode
or hymn has not gone unnoticed.[2] As long ago as 1900, Charles Grosvenor

1. These three short odes are undated, their composition usually assigned to 1632
or 1633, and so may have been composed either before or after the composition of
"L'Allegro" and "Il Penseroso," usually assigned to the years 1632 through 1635. See
Variorum (The Minor English Poems), 2.1. 163, 224–27.

2. E. M. W. Tillyard argues that the poem belongs to the tradition of the academic
prolusion. See "Milton: 'L'Allegro' and 'Il Penseroso,'" *Miltonic Setting*, 1–28, esp. 14–
21. Sara R. Watson investigates their indebtedness to pastoral and georgic tradition:
"Milton's Ideal Day: Its Development as a Pastoral Theme," in *PMLA* 57. Maren-Sofie
Røstvig explores the link between these poems and classical philosophic traditions
in *The Happy Man: Studies in the Metamorphosis of a Classical Ideal, 1600–1700*. A.
S. P Woodhouse and Douglas Bush suggest the poems' connection with Renaissance
encomia (See *Variorum: The Minor English Poems*, 2.1. 227–69).

Osgood, in his study *The Classical Mythology of Milton's English Poems,* pointed out their association with several of the Homeric hymns and with Pindar's ode *Olympian 14.*[3] Yet because Homeric hymn and Pindaric ode are essentially religious genres, however light their tone sometimes may become, and because classical deities, even in the Renaissance world, retained serious symbolic significance, the link between Milton's sportive exercises and formal classical hymn and ode has generally been neglected. Nevertheless, Mirth and Melancholy are not merely imaginative figures, but actual classical goddesses with specific attributes, daughters of important deities in the Olympic pantheon. The odes addressed to them are no less formal odes on the classical model than is the Nativity ode, which, as we have seen, is linked to the classical and Renaissance hymns and odes to Apollo.

Yet it is a giant step from framing a "birth ode" to Christ on a classical prototype to framing on the model of serious classical hymn such sportive little trifles as "L'Allegro" and "Il Penseroso" at first appear to be. Indeed, such a step would not even have been possible were it not for the Renaissance imitators of classical hymn-ode—from the fifteenth-century humanist poet Giovanni Pontano to the Scottish neo-Latinist John Leech, Milton's contemporary. These odes extend the range of the formal classical ode and often conflate it with Horatian ode and anacreontics, making possible the kind of light, but serious mythic exercises that we find in "L'Allegro" and "Il Penseroso." For though Milton addresses Mirth in a sportive way and offers sprightly rejoinders to Melancholy as well, he asks from both special powers of poetic inspiration and performance, appropriate to request from such deities. These "gifts" of imagination are no less than those he had requested from Apollo in "Elegia 5"—to be admitted to the company of inspired poets and to receive from the god the authority for his own song. Hence "L'Allegro" and "Il Penseroso" should be looked on as serious poems in which the poet explores his relationship to patron deities of inspiration. In some way these odes are "transitional" exercises that bridge the early appeal to the "heavenly Muse" in the Nativity ode and the various invocations to female goddesses of inspiration in the shorter English and Latin odes; they lead us inexorably, however, to Milton's espousal as his goddess and patron the Muse Urania in *Paradise Lost.* The twin goddesses of inspiration of "L'Allegro" and "Il Penseroso" also temporarily take the place of Apollo, the classical male god of poetry, whom Milton in the Nativity ode has displaced from authority.

---

3. Charles Grosvenor Osgood, *The Classical Mythology of Milton's English Poems,* liv, 39.

ACADEMIC EXERCISES

As his academic prolusions demonstrate to us, Milton learned his classical myths not only from the leading writers of Greece and Rome whose authority he often cites, but also from Renaissance sources closer at hand, the so-called myth books of the fifteenth, sixteenth, and seventeenth centuries that catalogue the mythic lore of these authors and provided Renaissance poets with a wealth of information about classical deities. From Boccaccio's *Genealogie deorum gentilium* and Gyraldus's *De deis gentium* to Conti's popular *Mythologiae* and Cartari's illustrated *Le imagine de i dei de gli antichi,* they were widely known and used throughout the Renaissance.[4] The myth books drew their treatment of gods and goddesses from classical poets and philosophers as well as from the mythological treatises of ancient writers such as Cornutus, Fulgentius, and Hyginus (reprinted and available in the sixteenth century). They retold the stories of gods and goddesses and described genealogical relationships and also interpreted mythic figures and accounts allegorically for humanists of their own eras. As a university man, the young Milton knew and freely used these valuable, ready-at-hand sources of information while at Cambridge, as the careful and frequent citation of classical myth in his prolusions and Latin verse elegies and his reference to different ancient and Renaissance authorities testify.[5] Moreover, the mythical allusions in these elegies and academic prolusions show us that Milton could approach his sources seriously or sportively.

E. M. W. Tillyard demonstrated long ago that an academic debate such as Prolusion 1, "Whether the Day is more excellent than the Night," is intimately related to an implied debate between a daytime, light-loving goddess Mirth and the nighttime, shade-loving goddess Melancholy. Milton employs in "L'Allegro" and "Il Penseroso" the mythic atmosphere of "either-or" that pervades the prolusion, offering us alternate and sometimes contradictory genealogical possibilities for its deities. In Prolusion 1 he entertains us by whimsically exploding Hesiod's preposterous myth that Night is the mother of Day. His wit extends so far as summoning Martial's epigram on a well-matched quarrelsome husband and wife to justify Night's preference of her "dark" brother Erebus as a mate over the "fair" and well-favored

4. For a fuller account of the Renaissance myth books and dictionaries see De Witt T. Starnes and Ernest William Talbert, *Classical Myth and Legend in Renaissance Dictionaries,* 3–28.

5. For information concerning Milton's knowledge and use of myth books see Starnes and Talbert, *Classical Myth,* 226–339. Joseph Mead purchased copies of Comes's *Mythologiae* and Calepinus's *Lexicon* for the Christ College Library; see Harris Francis Fletcher, *The Intellectual Development of John Milton,* 2:575, 583).

Phanes (Light); like prefers like. The good humor of the prolusion extends into Milton's odes. But whereas Milton in the prolusion comes down solidly on the side of Day, he balances the mythic "debate" between Mirth and Melancholy.

The Latin poem "De Idea Platonica" of the 1645 *Poemata* is also related to "L'Allegro" and "Il Penseroso," for it not only employs the disputatious and mythic methods of the Latin prolusions, but also makes use of the formal structure of the classical hymn-ode. Paired in *Sylvarum Liber* with the discursive "Naturam Non Pati Senium," it has affinities with its odic opposites in the English volume.[6] Like "L'Allegro" and "Il Penseroso," Milton begins "De Idea Platonica" with invocation, calling formally upon a triple set of goddesses—the Muses, Memory, and Eternity, addressing them—as Greek and Latin hymn and ode would—with their proper mythic epithets, and making a request of them. Moreover, he invokes them solemnly, the Muses as the goddesses who preside over the sacred grove; Memory as mother of those ninefold deities; and Eternity as the everlasting, incorruptible, and unique goddess who guards Jove's laws and records. Then he immediately undercuts these solemnities by making a request that can hardly be taken seriously. Tongue-in-cheek, Milton, posing as a literal-minded follower of Aristotle, frames an all-too-literal-minded question: where, he asks, is the "idea" man that Plato described to be found. As Carey notes, Milton in this Aristotelian burlesque is pretending to take seriously the literal existence of those abstract ideas that Plato posits in his philosophy; as a would-be Aristotelian he challenges the goddesses to locate the ideal abstraction of man for him—the idea man. Milton's joke extends beyond the folly of the literal-minded request to the pomposity of framing the request in a formal classical hymn. Poetically, the hymn-ode develops, as though in reply to the request, offering a range of negative and positive possibilities. The idea man clearly is *not* the unborn twin of Athene, still lurking in Jove's mind. Then, maybe he *is* to be found somewhere, unnoticed—wandering in the spheres of heaven, sitting on Lethe's bank, or walking about like a giant in some remote land. Milton uses the digressive style of ode to develop the central section of the poem in the either/or style. Negatively he tells us who has *not* seen the idea man—Teiresias, Mercury, the Assyrian priests and other assorted seers. Positively, he demands that Plato either admit the hoax or produce him. The whimsy of the ode is evident both in its far-

---

6. John Carey has argued persuasively that "De Idea Platonica," rather than "Naturam Non Pati Senium," was the Latin poem that Milton sent to Alexander Gil in the letter of July 2, 1628, noting he was enclosing some light trifles ("leviculas nugas"), written for the use of a fellow of Christ College in a philosophical disputation at the Cambridge commencement (see headnote to "De Idea Platonica," in Milton, *Complete Shorter Poems*).

fetched examples and in the grandiose presentation of them in hymn-ode form. Moreover, Milton submits his poem to the same academic audience that had heard his prolusions. Yet "De Idea Platonica" is more than an academic performance in verse; it is Milton's first exercise in the "light" ode. With its many rhetorical turns and tricks it taught him how to undertake and in some sense replicate in English the sportive ode to the deity.

HYMNS TO THE GODS

The classical hymn or ode to the pagan deity became popular at the end of the fifteenth century, first in Italy, and then was translated to France by the mid-sixteenth century, finally to make its way to England, the most famous examples being Spenser's *Fowre Hymnes* to Love, Beauty, Heavenly Love, and Heavenly Beauty—serious exercises that address two abstract classical and two abstract Christian deities.[7] Milton was undoubtedly affected both by the Renaissance imitations in Latin and in the vernaculars and the classical originals—the so-called Homeric hymns, the Orphic hymns, and the hymns and odes of Pindar and Callimachus, for which he expresses admiration in *The Reason of Church Government*.[8] Although many of the classical hymns and odes are addressed to major deities, such as Zeus, Apollo, Aphrodite, and Athene, others honor minor deities of the Olympic pantheon, such as the Graces, the Muses, Hestia or Vesta (Melancholy's mother), and Dawn and Zephyr (Mirth's mother and father according to the second genealogy in "L'Allegro").[9] The classical hymn usually opens

7. The classical hymn and ode were popularized in France by Ronsard in the 1550s, were imitated by Ronsard's followers, and were brought to England by Spenser and the little-known Elizabethan poet John Soowthern. Most of these Renaissance imitations are modeled on the Homeric hymns, the Orphic hymns, and the odes and hymns of Pindar, Callimachus, and Theocritus. The original hymns and odes would have been available to Milton in separate editions and in Henri Estienne's folio edition of the principal Greek poets and his octavo edition of the minor Greek poets, as both were in the library at Christ College, Cambridge (see Fletcher, *Intellectual Development*). Experiments in English in Pindaric ode before Milton include Spenser in "Aprill" of *Shepheardes Calender,* Soowthern in *Pandora,* Drayton in *Odes,* and Jonson in the Cary-Morison ode. See Robert Shafer, *The English Ode to 1660;* George N. Shuster, *The English Ode from Milton to Keats;* and Carol Maddison, *Apollo and the Nine: A History of the Ode.*

8. See *The Reason of Church Government* in Milton, *Complete Poems and Major Prose* (ed. Hughes), 669.

9. There are Homeric hymns to Heracles, Asclepius, the Dioscuri, and Pan, as well as to Hestia, the Muses, and Apollo. See *Hesiod, the Homeric Hymns, and Homerica.* Callimachus has hymns to Apollo, Zeus, and other deities; see *Hymns and Epigrams.* Pindar includes among his odes invocations to major and minor deities as well as to the Muses and Graces. There are Orphic hymns also to the Muses and Graces, Mnemosyne, Dawn, Zephyrus, and Hestia; see Orpheus, *Orphei Hymni,* 43, 52–56.

with invocation and description—sometimes followed by brief or extended digression or myth—and closes with supplication and praise. This basic pattern was established by the Homeric hymns, the earliest poems in this genre, but is also characteristic of the Orphic hymns, certain odes of Pindar, and hymns by Callimachus and Theocritus. The invocation often includes the genealogy of the god or goddess, the citation of his or her birthplace or special dwelling places, and an allusion to the deity's attributes or epithets. For example, the Homeric hymn to Pythian Apollo addresses Apollo directly, names the places he rules over, and, after identifying him as Leto's all-glorious son, describes him at rocky Pytho, playing on his lyre and clad in ambrosial garments. As we have noted in the previous chapter, Homeric hymns sometimes included birth accounts and therefore provided Christian hymnists with models for Nativity hymns to Christ.

There is no doubt that Milton is following the classical hymnic formulas in his invocations to Mirth and Melancholy. First, he addresses the goddess directly; next, he names her parents and alludes to the circumstances of her birth or conception; finally he asks her to come. Milton's "birth accounts" are brief, but important. In "L'Allegro" Venus bears Mirth to Bacchus; Aurora, her alternate mother, conceives her "on Beds of Violets blue, / And fresh-blown Roses washt in dew" ("L'Allegro," 21–22). In "Il Penseroso" Vesta bears Melancholy to Saturn, who courts her "in glimmering Bowres, and glades . . . in secret shades / Of woody *Ida's* inmost grove" ("Il Penseroso," 27–29). Each goddess is described with attributive adjectives or epithets: Mirth is "fair and free," "buxom, blithe, and debonair"; Melancholy is "pensive," "devout and pure." Each is invoked to come well-disposed to the initiate, who seeks her favors and promises (if she grants them) to choose her as his special goddess. She is asked to come, moreover, not alone but in company with her associates, Mirth with the nymph Liberty and Melancholy with the cherub Contemplation, as well as with a host of other allegorical persons, Jest and Jollity with Mirth, Peace and Fast with Melancholy. Here too Milton follows Greek hymn and ode, for the classical hymns describe the allegorical companions who particularly consort with the god or goddess.

"L'Allegro" and "Il Penseroso" are particularly modeled on odes to protective female divinities connected with poetry. As we saw in the last chapter, Milton disempowered the Delphian Apollo, even as he framed his birthday ode for Christ who assumed the powers of Apollo the sun god, the healer, and the god of prophecy. After this important ode, Apollo does not reassume his place as inspirer of poetry until the Latin poetry of the late 1630s. Who takes over in his stead? Curiously enough, it is not the heavenly Muse of the Nativity ode but other Muse-like goddesses, especially here the twin goddesses of "L'Allegro" and "Il Penseroso"—one sportive and mirthful, one serious and melancholy, whom the poet invokes to inspire, nurture, and sustain him. These goddesses turn out to be the feminine alternatives to Apollo. Mirth is after all the third of the Graces, deities that Renaissance poets and classical hymnists associate with Apollo and with poetry. Melancholy, as we shall see, shares many of the qualities of Urania, the eighth of the Muses—and no goddesses are closer to Apollo than the Muses. The Homeric hymn to Pythian Apollo alludes to the Muses as the companions who make music with Apollo and to the Graces and Hours as the goddesses who, together with Harmonia, Hebe, and Aphrodite, dance before him. Pindar describes Apollo's relationship with the Muses in *Pythian 1* (lines 1–2) and with the Graces in *Olympian 14* (lines 10–11). Renaissance poets—as we shall see—were fond of addressing hymn-odes to *both* the Graces and the Muses as inspirers of poetic performance.

Although there are many hymns and odes in antiquity in which poets ask for gifts and favor from inspiring goddesses, one universally admired and often imitated in the Renaissance was Pindar's *Olympian 14*. What more likely model was there for his invocation to the heaven-born Mirth, the Grace Euphrosyne, than an ancient ode which addressed the Graces and asked them to appear? Although composed to celebrate an athletic victory, *Olympian 14* has always appeared to commentators more an ode celebrating the Graces or Charites than an ode for an athletic victor.[10] Shorter than the usual Pindaric ode and composed of two strophes only, it intimately describes the poet's relationship with these goddesses. Its invocations not only provided Renaissance poets with a model on how to address the Graces, but also gave Renaissance mythographers a major source of information about how the Graces function to favor human beings and confer special grace on the poet.

Olympian 14 follows closely the formulas of Homeric hymns, describing the Graces as the protectors of the ancient Minyae and enumerating the special qualities and the particular gifts they grant to human beings. Pindar calls them "queens of song" and implies that it is their song particularly that brings delight and sweetness to human beings. The Graces also grant particular favor to individual men, especially to the poet. If a man is wise (σοφός) or handsome (καλός) or renowned (ἀγλαός), he owes these gifts to the Graces. He especially singles out the attribute *sophos,* which for

---

10. Both Renaissance and modern editors of Pindar suggest that *Olympian 14* was originally composed to be sung in the temple of the Graces at Orchomenus, where there was a cult of these goddesses. See Basil L. Gildersleeve's comments in Pindar, *The Olympian and Pythian Odes,* 237.

Pindar describes not just wisdom, but skill in composing poetry. The Graces are therefore not merely benefactors of humanity but also patrons of poetry. Throughout his odes Pindar often invokes the Graces to inspire his verse.[11] As queens of song, they order all festivals of song and dance in heaven and on earth and without them neither banquet nor choral performance exists. Further, as they minister and arrange celebrations for gods and men alike, they sit on thrones in heaven beside golden-bowed Apollo, the god of song, and with him evermore honor *in song* Zeus, the Olympian father.[12]

Olympian 14 is not merely a collective hymn to the Graces. In the second strophe of the ode, Pindar individualizes each Grace by name and attaches her epithet: Aglaia is queenly and Euphrosyne and Thalia are lovers of song. Invoking them as the children of the greatest god, he bids them listen to and attend on him (lines 13–18).

> ὦ πότνι' Ἀγλαΐα
> φιλησίμολπέ τ' Εὐφροσύνα, θεῶν κρατίστου
> παῖδες, ἐπακοοῖτε νῦν, θαλία τε
> ἐρασίμολπε, ἰδοῖσα τόνδε κῶμον ἐπ' εὐμενεῖ τύχᾳ
> κοῦφα βιβῶντα . λυδῷ γὰρ Ἀσώπιχον τρόπῳ
> ἐν μελέταις τ' ἀείδων ἔμολον.

> O honored Aglaia,
> And Euphrosyne, lover of song, children of the
> Greatest of gods, hear now, and Thalia,
> Desirous of song, look down with favoring aspect
> On this lightly stepping procession. For I have come
>   for Asopichos,
> Singing with care in the Lydian manner. (my translation)[13]

Olympian 14 is unusual in invoking the Graces in the second rather than the first strophe of the ode. In "L'Allegro" Milton also delays the formal

11. Invocations to the Graces to assist in the composition of poetry include the following passages in Pindar's odes: *Pythian* 9.1–8; *Nemean* 10.1–4; *Nemean* 4.6–8; *Nemean* 6.35–39; *Pythian* 5.43–45. See Pindar, *Carmina* (1935).

12. This picture of the Graces celebrating the festival in Olympus has obvious affinities with the portrayal of the Muses, who, seated by Apollo, sing antiphonically with him and render praise to Zeus. See, e.g., the conclusion of Homer's *Iliad* 1.603–4.

13. Gilbert West's translation of this stanza of *Olympian 14* demonstrates that he understood the relationship of Pindar's ode to Milton's "L'Allegro," for he imitates the latter: "*Aglaia*, graceful Virgin, hear! / And thou, *Euphrosyna*, whose Ear / Delighted listens to the warbled Strain! / Bright Daughters of *Olympian Jove*, / The Best, the Greatest Pow'r above; / With your illustrious Presence deign / To grace our Choral Song! / Whose Notes to Victory's glad Sound / In wanton Measures lightly bound. / *Thalia*, come along! / Come, tuneful Maid! for lo! my String / With meditated Skill prepares / In softly soothing *Lydian* Airs / *Asopichus* to sing" (Pindar, *Odes of Pindar with Several Other Pieces in Prose and Verse* [1749]).

invocation, banishing Mirth's opposite before he calls upon Euphrosyne by name and urges her to appear, applying to her the first and most classical of her epithets, "heart-easing": "But come thou Goddess· fair and free, / In Heav'n yclep'd *Euphrosyne,* / And by men, heart-easing Mirth" (11–13). He immediately adds her genealogy, making an interesting choice when he bypasses the Graces' usual parentage and associates Euphrosyne not with the highest of gods, Zeus or Jove (as Pindar does) but with Bacchus and Venus: "Whom lovely *Venus* at a birth / With two sister Graces more / To Ivy-crowned *Bacchus* bore" (14–16). Milton's Grace, like Pindar's, brings sweetness and delight to human beings—those special qualities that a young poet in his lyric poetry tries especially to capture and convey. But the Grace can also give beauty and renown (that is, fame) and finally poetic skill, the sophia, that Milton like Pindar would especially desire from an inspiring goddess. Pindar's ode concludes by asking implicitly that the Graces admit him and the young victor to their company and give them the gifts that are theirs to give. As such it is a perfect model for Milton's ode of invocation and supplication.

Milton probably chose Euphrosyne as the special patron of his ode because as a Grace, she possessed those gifts a young poet might most covet. In "L'Allegro" the young poet asks both to be admitted into Mirth's company and to share in her pleasures or gifts. Many of the pleasures enumerated, particularly those that conclude the catalogue and come at the very end of the poem, are the pleasures of music, dance, and poetry, the ones most closely connected with the Graces. The final request of the young initiate is to be lapped "in soft *Lydian* Airs" and "Married to immortal verse" (136–37). Lydian airs, says Pindar, are most appropriate to commemorate the victory of the young hero from Orchomenus; similarly, Lydian airs are the strains that the poet in "L'Allegro" requests to raise the soul of Orpheus.

In *Olympian 14* Pindar tells his Graces to enter dancing. Dance and song and poetry are inevitably intertwined in a Pindaric ode where the chorus sings and dances to the verses the poet has composed. But dance and song are especially prominent in *Olympian 14,* where the Graces—the queens of song—lead the procession for the young victor. In "L'Allegro" Milton tells Mirth to enter dancing; further he tells her not to come alone, but with her associates in procession. For Pindar, the coming of the Graces clearly coincides with the inspiration to sing the victory song for Asopichus and the house of the Minyae. For Milton the invocation of the Grace Euphrosyne inspires the very poem we see unfold before us.

Milton did not draw direct inspiration for "Il Penseroso" from Pindar's odes, although there are many invocations to the Muse in the Pindaric corpus and odes to other goddesses, who resemble in one way or another Milton's Melancholy. *Nemean 11,* for example, opens with a striking invocation to Hestia (Vesta), the goddess of the hearth. Vesta is, of course, Melancholy's mother in "Il Penseroso" and is a far more somber goddess than the lighthearted Graces of *Olympian 14*. *Nemean 11* celebrates a *prytanis,* a festival of thanksgiving that marked the beginning of the year in office for a magistrate. Like the ode to the Graces, it was probably performed in the temple of Hestia before the altar and was certainly meant to be accompanied by song and dance. Pindar alludes to the procession and dedicates his song and lyre music to the goddess. In the opening invocation of *Nemean 11,* Hestia is named daughter to Rhea and sister to Zeus and Hera; she is particularly characterized as a goddess who maintains purity and justice and so guards magistrates in preserving order and good government. This solemn invocation resembles that in "Il Penseroso," and though Pindar's Hestia is certainly not Milton's Melancholy, both have a somber appearance. The prominence of this ode among Pindar's poems may even have suggested to Milton that Hestia (Vesta) was an appropriate mother for his sage and serious goddess.

"COME, AND TRIP IT"

Milton was not the first poet to look on Pindaric ode as a proper model for neoclassical poetry. In his twin poems he is responding to ancient song and dance in a reorchestrated Renaissance choreography. "L'Allegro" and "Il Penseroso" are the direct beneficiaries of Renaissance experimentation in the light classical ode. Among Pindar's odes *Olympian 14* had become a favorite model for fifteenth- and sixteenth-century Italian and French neo-Latin and vernacular poets. Responding to Pindar's invocation to the Graces, Renaissance poets transformed *Olympian 14* from an address to the Graces that celebrates the victory of a young athlete to an ode that celebrates both the Graces themselves and those who worship them. The Graces appear and reappear in Renaissance poetry, sometimes dancing to the rhythm of Pindar's joyful procession, sometimes adopting a lighter step and appearing in the company of Venus and Cupid and Bacchus.[14]

The Neapolitan poet and founder of the academy at Naples Giovanni Pontano (1436–1503) was acquainted both with Pindar's Charites, the givers of wisdom, beauty, and renown, and also with Horace's Gratiae, the associates of Venus and her son Cupid. Although Horace's ode (*Carmina* 1.3) is not an ode to the Graces, but an ode to Venus, its popularity established in the Renaissance mind the Graces' close connection with Venus. Thus,

14. In some of Pindar's odes Aphrodite is directly connected with the Graces; in Horatian and in later Renaissance ode, she becomes their inevitable companion.

when Horace invokes Venus, the Graces come along—quite gratuitously—
in response to his appeal to the goddess of Love to leave the delights of
Cyprus and to come to the shrine of Glycera.

> solutis
> Gratiae zonis properentque nymphae
> Et parum comis sine te Iuventas
>   Mercuriusque (1.30.5–8)[15]

[let] the Graces with loosened waistbands
and let the nymphs hasten together with Youth
And Mercury, no fitting companion without you.

When Pontano proposes in one of his hendecasyllabics to send his
mistress Neaera off on an expedition to the baths at Baiae, he is probably
thinking more of Horatian than Pindaric delights, for he sends as Neaera's
companions Venus, Cupid, Jest, the Loves, and—of course—the Graces!
For Neaera, the Graces sing, make light of cares, and lead the dances, with
Cupid and Venus looking on with favor. Moreover, Pontano makes sure to
tell us that the proper attendants for the Graces are Jest and Smiles and
Pleasure. The Graces, he says, banish care and mix jest and tears. Now this
is exactly what Milton asks his Grace Euphrosyne to do, summoning her
to appear in the company of

> Jest and Youthful Jollity,
> Quips and Cranks and wanton Wiles,
> Nods, and Becks, and Wreathed Smiles,
> . . . .
> Sport that wrinkled Care derides,
> And Laughter holding both his sides. (26–28, 31–32)

Undoubtedly, Milton, like Pontano, had been reading his Horace together
with his Pindar. He may also have been reading Pontano, for the dancing
feet of Milton's octosyllabics have the same wonderful light-hearted effect as Pontano's hendecasyllabics. To Pindar's invocation of the heavenly
Charites, Pontano adds a salute to more earthy goddesses, ones who can
grant not only the gifts of skill and renown and beauty, but also smiles and
pleasure and love.

Pontano invokes the Graces not once but many times. In another hendecasyllabic, he introduces us to his poet-friend Chariteus (Benedetto
Gareth), who takes his name from the Graces or Charites, and whom these

15. Horace, *Odes and Epodes* (1984), 39.

ministering goddesses serve, granting him the gifts of poetic inspiration, as well as the gifts of pleasure and love. Remembering the Graces' association with gardens, Pontano evokes for him moonlit glades, soft Zephyrs, myrtle bowers. In still another hendecasyllabic, Pontano extends the favors of the Graces to a group of boys and girls, who, sitting under myrtle shades, are invited to hear the Graces singing. For them the Graces lead the dance, and Pontano, urging them to dance and enjoy their youth, summons joy and bids farewell to sorrow. Another of Pontano's lyrics to the Graces is a Sapphic ode to Fannia in which Pontano invites the Graces once more to appear. Here the principal focus is on the goddesses themselves, whom Pontano bids to sing, pleading, like Pindar in *Olympian 14,* the special relationship of the poet to these goddesses of song.

> Hoc, deae, hoc, hoc, O Charites, ministrae,
> Cyprides blandae, hoc agite et remissae
> Fila pulsantes citharae canorum
>   Fundite carmen.[16]

> Here, goddesses, here, here, Charites, ministresses
> Of charming Cypris, come here and plucking
> The strings of the gentle lyre,
> Pour out your tuneful song.

For Pontano, poetics and pleasure are inextricably intertwined, the Graces and Venus and Love inevitable companions. The young Milton is not so frankly sensual a poet as the elder Neapolitan poet, Pontano, but he does follow Horace's and Pontano's lead in closely connecting his Grace with Venus. Like Pontano's Graces, Milton's Euphrosyne is also particularly at home in rural settings ("Meadows trim with Daisies pied, / Shallow Brooks, and Rivers wide") (75–76). Although she does not wait on his mistress, he may lead him—who knows—where "some beauty lies / The Cynosure of neighboring eyes" (79–80). Pontano's dancing youths and maidens have their counterparts in the young men and women that Milton's Allegro views in the country dances: "many a youth and many a maid / Dancing in the Chequer'd shade" (95–96). The rural gaiety that is so much a part of Pontano's lyrics to the Graces is also amply present in Milton's joyful ode.

What Pontano begins, poets of the next generation continue. Andrea Navagero follows Pontano in associating the Graces with Venus and Pleasure and in joining Lucretian and Horatian to Pindaric sensibilities. His Graces, like Pontano's, wait on Venus, who herself is attended by choruses

16. Ioannes Iovianus Pontanus, *Carmina* (1948), 366.

of youths and girls, dancing and singing to the goddesses. Echoing both Lucretius's hymn to Venus and Pindar's *Olympian 14* (Pindar was for him the first of poets), Navagero tells us that nothing is joyful, loving, and pleasing without Venus and the Graces.[17]

> Qua nihil laetum sine, amabile est nil:
> Nilque iucundum: sine qua nec ipsae
> Gratae erunt cuiquam Charites, nec ipsa
> blanda uoluptas: (24r and v)[18]

> Without whom, nothing is happy, nothing lovable,
> And nothing joyful: without whom the Graces
> themselves will not be graceful to anyone, nor
> Pleasure itself pleasing.

In "L'Allegro" too the Lucretian principle joins with the Pindaric, for Milton's Grace Euphrosyne is a generative goddess like her mother Venus and inspires love and joy—all pleasures. Like Navagero, Milton summons Pleasure as the Grace's inseparable companion, promising, "To live with her, and live with thee, / In unreproved pleasures free" (39–40).

Where does Bacchus and his mirth fit into this scenario of dancing Graces, Venus, and Pleasure? The Graces are closely connected with the pleasure-giving goddess Venus as well as with Bacchus, and it is not only the mythographers, but also the poets who exploit this association. At the very outset of his "Monodia de Saltatione Bacchica" Pietro Crinito, Pontano's contemporary, contributes the Bacchic connection, banishing heaviness and welcoming the lightness and good cheer associated with Bacchus. He first bids farewell to father Mars and greeting the nymphs and the Satyrs, also salutes freedom from care.

> Iam curae valeant graues.
> Non hic fluctisonans tridens
> Non toruae resonent tubae:
> Sed gratus lepor: & charis . . . (G4r)[19]

---

17. Without Venus, Lucretius said, pleasure was impossible: "nec sine te quicquam dias in luminis oras / exoritur neque fit laetum neque amabile quicquam" (Without you nothing rises into the bright realms of light nor is anything made joyous or lovely). See *De Rerum Natura*, 1.22–23.

18. Andreas Naugerius, "Precatio ad Venerem, ut pertinacem Lalagen molliat," in *Carmina Quinque Illustrium Poetarum* (1558), 24r and v.

19. Petrus Crinitus, *Poematum Libri Duo* (1508), 2, G4r.

> Farewell now to heavy cares;
>> let neither the surging-sounded trident
>> nor the grim trumpet play here,
>> but pleasing Charm and Grace . . .

His "Monodia de choro sybaritico" also banishes sorrow and exhorts the Grace to bring along with her Venus and Joy, inviting them to the dance:

> Sed laeti atque hilares ioci:
>> Et molles veneres simul
>> Inter delicias fluant,
>> Grato non sine luxu.
> Sic poscit Veneris calor
>> Dum noster Genius viget
>> Et blandas Charites refert:
>> Dulces iungite amores
> Carpamus celerem diem . . . (F4v)

> But [come] joyful and happy jest,
>> And let sweet loves flow at the same time,
>> amid delight, not without pleasing charm.
> Thus the warmth of Venus demands,
>> While our Genius thrives and
>> brings back the charming Graces,
>> you, sweet Loves, join in,
> let us seize the passing day . . .

Like Pontano, Crinito chooses lightly dancing measures—glyconics—to suggest the movement of the Graces.

All Graces dance, but some dance in courtly measures while some come, like Crinito's Graces, tripping along. Milton bids his Grace to come trippingly: "Come, and trip it as ye go / On the light fantastic toe" (33–34). Like Crinito, he prepares her way by banishing her opposites—melancholy and care: "Hence loathed Melancholy / Of *Cerberus,* and blackest midnight born, / In Stygian Cave forlorn / 'Mongst horrid shapes, and shrieks, and sights unholy" (1–4). He also connects her with Bacchus; in fact, he makes her his daughter. Bacchus is the god whose gift of wine dispels sorrow and heaviness, bringing ease from care, and Mirth is a heart-easing Grace. She inherits an exuberant nature from her father, her ode sharing in many ways the quality of the dithyramb, which is, of course, the proper salute to Bacchus.[20]

20. There was a revival of the dithyrambic ode in the late fifteenth century; Pontano, Sannazaro, Crinito, Flaminio, and others composed hymn-odes to Bacchus.

It is Renaissance poets who combine the hymn to the Graces with the dithyramb to Bacchus, a combination that continues right up to Milton's own time in the Latin anacreontica of the Scottish poet, John Leech. Leech pronounces Catullus, Anacreon, and Pindar among his poetic fathers and calls upon the Graces to appear with Venus, Bacchus, and Love.

> Ita me iuuent Iacchi
> Comites, Venusque Amorque;
> Ita me Iuuenta praeceps:
> Risusque candidique
> Cum Gratiis Lepores . . . [21]

> So may the companions of Iacchus [Bacchus]
> Cheer me, Venus and Love;
> So may princely Youth cheer me
> And Smiles and lovely
> Pleasures with the Graces.

Leech makes Pleasure and Smiles inseparable from the Graces, adding also a veritable Miltonic procession of Games and Jokes and a thousand Charms and all kinds of Laughter.[22]

"L'Allegro" could have been a dithyramb to Bacchus; it could have been a hymn to Venus. It has the right meter; it glances in the direction of these exuberant gods and then glances away, putting its pleasures into the custody of a Grace who dances, rather than consigning them to Bacchus and his orgiastic troop or Venus and her seductive company. There is moderation in Milton's mirthful measures. In choosing these two gods as Mirth's parents, Milton is highly selective, as we shall see, about what aspects of Venus or of Bacchus he will admit to the person and company of his Mirth. He maintains a delicate balance. Although both of these gods are implicitly present in Mirth's enthusiastic dance, Milton sublimates the Bacchanalian elements by calling upon Bacchus's chaste and sober daughter and not on the tipsy god himself. With her he enjoys the day; he does not seize it.

21. John Leech (Joannes Leochaeus), "Sodales ad bibendum inuitat," in "Anacreontica," *Musae Priores, sive Poematum* (1620), 1.49.

22. See Leech (Leochaeus), "Leges bibendi" in "Anacreontica," 2.63: "Adsint dii benigni: / Liber pater. Cythere. / Cupido. Gratiaeque / Cum Lusibus. Iocique / Leporibusque mille. / Atque omnibus Cachinnis." Also see Leech's "Ad Bacchum," also in "Anacreontica" (2.66). Leech follows the example of his more famous Scottish countryman George Buchanan. See "Calendae Maiae" where Buchanan welcomes a chorus of the Graces with joy and wine and games and jesting. See Philip J. Ford, *George Buchanan, Prince of Poets, Miscellaneorum Liber,* 152–53.

MILTON AND THE MYTHOGRAPHERS

What Renaissance poets suggest through their poetry about the Graces' association with Venus and Bacchus the mythographers Giraldi and Conti and Cartari and many others confirm in more orderly fashion.[23] In "L'Allegro" and "Il Penseroso" Milton often follows the mythographers' as well as the poets' authority. Renaissance myth books are a compendium of information and offer a wide range of possibilities, informing their reader not only what the ancient writer said about the gods and goddesses, but also how these views were modified by later writers. Milton knew perfectly well that the Greek poets Hesiod and Pindar, as well as Milton's own poetical father, Spenser, had named Zeus and Eurynome the parents of the Graces and made Venus or Aphrodite merely the Graces' companion.[24] The Renaissance myth books present this as the first genealogy. But it was the myth books' practice also to list second and third and often even more alternative genealogies. Milton could ignore the authority of ancient poets and follow a myth book's secondary listing. Hence he makes Venus the mother, rather than the associate, of the Graces and Bacchus

23. Milton's sources are difficult to pinpoint exactly. He can refer directly to a classical poet; he can also refer indirectly to a classical source that cites a classical poet, or to a Renaissance poet using a classical reference, or to a myth book's citing a classical authority. Further, we cannot restrict Milton to those myth books of the Renaissance that authorities such as Starnes and Talbert or Fletcher believe he had access to. The sources cited in the notes merely identify material available to Milton as he selected the variant mythic details he uses in "L'Allegro" and "Il Penseroso."

24. In *Theogony,* Hesiod describes the Graces as the daughters of Zeus and Eurynome (907–9); he alludes also to their ability to stir love and desire (910–11) and their association with Himeros, or Desire (64–65). Sappho connects the Graces with Aphrodite; the Homeric hymn to Pythian Apollo shows the Graces dancing with Aphrodite (194–96). Spenser names them "Venus' Damzels" but retains Hesiod's account of their parentage (*Faerie Queene* 6.10.21–22). Many mythographers, while retaining the Hesiodic account of the Graces' parentage, allude to an alternative genealogy—Bacchus and Venus— and to several others still. Charles Estienne (Carolus Stephanus) lists Venus and Jove, Venus and Liber (Bacchus), Jove and Autonoe, and Jove and Eurynome (*Dictionarium historicum, geographicum, poeticum* [1596], 146v). More conservatively, Conti (bk. 4, chap. 15) lists Jove and Eurynome first but also names other possible parentages (Comes, *Mythologiae sive Explicationum Fabularum* [1581], 273). Although Conti says in chapter 15 that the Graces are the associates of Venus, in bk. 4, chap. 13 he calls Venus the mother of the Graces (260). According to Vincenzo Cartari, some call Venus the mother of the Graces and Bacchus their father (*Le imagine de i dei de gli antichi* [1571], 556–57). Lilius Gregorius Gyraldus (Giglio Gregorio Giraldi) lists Venus and Bacchus as parents in an alternative genealogy (*De deis gentium varia et multiplex historia* [1560], 402). Beginning with his early prolusions and elegies, Milton is flexible in his myth-making. In "Elegia 5," for example, he can adhere closely to myth in describing Cephalus as the lover of Aurora or depart freely in describing the love affair of Phoebus Apollo and Tellus.

her father. He even adds, following the myth books' habit of freely listing alternatives, a totally gratuitous parentage, Aurora and Zephyrus, which no other authority records. Such fanciful mythologizing owes much to the myth books' descriptive rather than proscriptive listings of "possible" parents and to their tendency to interpret the qualities of the mythic child according to his or her assigned parentage.

We learn a good deal about Milton's myth-making by observing how he adds the authority of the studious mythographers to his knowledge of the practice of ancient and Renaissance poets. The mythographers told him that Venus was an appropriate parent for the Graces, for they, like her, are beautiful, young, and lighthearted. In "L'Allegro" he seems to follow this kind of logic in making the laughter-loving Venus—to allude to her Homeric epithet—the mother of Mirth. In choosing Bacchus as father, he also follows the myth books, remembering perhaps that the god of wine was young and handsome and that his gift of wine brought joy and banished sorrow. Poetry like Crinito's or Leech's that described Bacchus's connection with the Graces merely made that selection easier. Certainly, Bacchus, paired with Venus, possesses none of the baleful aspects of the Bacchus of Milton's *Mask,* who mates with the spellbinder Circe to produce Comus. He is a sociable god; from him, as from Venus, the Grace inherits her "youthful Jollity." The god of comedy and dithyrambic verse nurtures a daughter who loves "Jest . . . / Quips and Cranks, and wanton Wiles, / Nods and Becks, and Wreathed Smiles" (26–28). Pageant and festival originate with him; his daughter presides therefore over "pomp, and feast, and revelry, / With mask and antique Pageantry" (127–28). Pindar calls the Graces the organizers of festivals and leaders of choruses in heaven and on earth. By choosing Bacchus as father of his Grace, Milton reinforces this role.

For the ancients poetry was essential to the well-ordered society, and the Graces as patrons of poetry also function to preserve social order. In fact, their ordering of festival or dance symbolizes the infusing of grace and well-being to promote good government on earth. Their very name in Greek, (χάριτες), signifies the favor or grace, (χάρις), that they grant to mortals. The Renaissance mythographers take this ancient description and apply it to a Christian context, identifying the grace of the Charites with the ultimate grace or mercy of God toward human beings.[25] They also interpret the dance of the Graces as an emblem for Christian charity. The Graces dance in a circle with linked hands, the one Grace turned

---

25. Comes, *Mythologiae* (1581), 274–75. Carolus Stephanus says that the Graces, as daughters of Liber and Venus, are moved by reason to grant the gift of grace to humanity (*Dictionarium historicum, geographicum, poeticum* [1596], 146).

away, the other two facing, their dance signifying the giving, receiving, and returning of benefits. Through this visual symbol, they say, God teaches us that as he gives good gifts to us through his heavenly grace, we should return the favor to our fellow human beings and live with them in peace, felicity, and communality. They also reconcile the nakedness of the Graces' dance with the purity of their virginity, commenting that to dance unveiled before all encourages guilelessness, purity, and openness in social behavior. The flowers that the Graces bear in their hands—rose, lily, and myrtle—are also symbolic of the social good they promote on earth, for they are emblems of prosperity and flourishing life. Although their names—Aglaia, Thalia, and Euphrosyne—were variously interpreted in the Renaissance as splendor or beauty, prosperity or growth, and joy or happiness, the mythographers emphasize once more that these flourishing graces are qualities most desirable in social life.[26] From the mythographers Milton inherits a Grace that is both Christianized and socialized.

Whereas all three Graces were depicted as smiling and happy, it is the third, Euphrosyne, Milton's Grace, who symbolizes joy or happiness itself, a quality Milton in "L'Allegro" understands in its full range from mirth or jollity to spiritual bliss. Euphrosyne was sometimes thought of in the Renaissance as the highest and most spiritual of the Graces, her joy the elevated joy of heavenly things and her special gift wisdom.[27] Milton inevitably connected the gift of wisdom (sophia) with poetical insight, and in this he is one with the Greek poets, particularly Pindar, who thought of "wisdom" as a god-given—or should we say "goddess"-given—attribute of the poet's craft. Throughout his poetry, Pindar uses the word σοφός to describe the poet and his art. This sophia is always an inborn gift (see *Olympian 2*.85–88) and is here connected, I believe, with the gift of insight that the poet owes to his patrons, the Graces or, as some might argue, to the highest of the heavenly Graces Euphrosyne.[28] Further, because the highest gift of the Graces is "wisdom," which the poet possesses in abundance, the Renaissance, following the ancients, designated Hermes, or Mercury, as leader of the Graces, for he symbolizes divine reason and order, the means

26. See Gyraldus, *De deis gentium varia et multiplex historia* (1560), 404–5; Natalis Comes (Natale Conti), *Mythologiae, sive explicationum fabularum. Libri decem* (1581), 274–75; Cartari (1571), 559–62. Also see Wind, *Pagan Mysteries,* for interpretation of the names of the Graces (50–80).

27. Wind, *Pagan Mysteries,* 55. Although Milton's Mirth is clearly a joyful goddess, Milton does not use the word *joy* to describe Euphrosyne in the first ode: *joys* first appears in "Il Penseroso" when the "vain deluding joys" of Folly—quite different from Mirth's joy—are dismissed by Penseroso. *Joy* itself is a word that Milton can elsewhere apply to heavenly bliss (See "On Time," 13).

28. See Pindar, *The Odes of Pindar* (ed. Conway). Euphrosyne is associated with "wisdom or talent, particularly poetic talent" (77).

by which the gifts of the Graces are directed to and dispensed among human beings.[29]

To the list of poets who connect the Graces with poetical inspiration, we must add Spenser, whose description of the Graces on Mount Acidale dancing to the pipe of the shepherd-poet Colin Clout is an important forerunner to the portrait of Milton's own patron Grace (*Faerie Queene* 6.10.8–28)[30] Spenser draws a general description of the Graces from Conti's *Mythologiae* and describes them as givers of all gracious gifts and symbols of the virtue, courtesy, that he has been exemplifying throughout book 6 of *The Faerie Queene*. In canto 10, however, he links them specifically with the gift of poetical inspiration. The Graces appear to Colin Clout alone and, freeing him from trouble, inspire his music and direct the composition of his song. When the unwitting Calidore breaks in on the moment of poetical composition, the Graces disappear, and the poet cannot recall them no matter how he tries. In explaining to Calidore who the Graces are, Colin Clout makes clear that they are not only the inspirers of his music and the organizers of the dance but also, by implication, the composers of the world of beauty, harmony, and peace that flourishes about the poet. In naming the Graces, Spenser places Euphrosyne first, perhaps inspiring Milton's choice of this Grace.

Like Spenser's Graces and the goddesses described by the Renaissance mythographers, Milton's Euphrosyne presides over both the making of poetry and the ordering of society. At her side is the mountain nymph Liberty, who urges her to rule with openness and freedom and who links freedom and pleasure (40).[31] The landscape over which the Grace leads Allegro is peaceful, and each of its occupants—plowman, milkmaid, mower, shepherd, and country swain—is engaged in productive work or harmonious pastime. Similarly, in the "Towred Cities" with their "busy hum of men" (117–18), we find concord and cooperation; knights and barons bold are holding "high triumphs" in the "weeds of Peace" (119–20), so illustrating in their activities the social contracts and peaceable assemblies that the Grace promotes. In the midst of this pomp, "Ladies, whose bright eyes / Rain influence . . . judge the prize / Of Wit, or Arms" (122–23); they are earthly counterparts to the heavenly Graces. Such is the society over which Euphrosyne reigns; in city or in country, in elaborate pageant or in simple

29. See Gyraldus, *De Deis Gentium* (1560), 404; Joannes Baudoin, *Mythologie ou Explication des Fables* (1627), 392–93. In the final plate of the *Imagine* (1571), 564, Cartari illustrates Mercury leading the Graces.

30. Edmund Spenser, *Poetical Works,* 380–82.

31. In making Liberty the associate of Mirth—and a feminine divinity—Milton is perhaps feminizing a quality of Bacchus—his epithet Liber and his well-known attribute of freeing, loosening, liberating the individual, especially from care.

natural setting she creates the harmonious order that none but a Grace can sustain.

Since Milton specifically identifies Mirth as the third of the Graces, it has been easy to trace her poetic and her mythic credentials in antiquity and in the Renaissance. But what about Melancholy, the patroness of "Il Penseroso" and the goddess to whom the poet-speaker of the second ode appeals as Allegro had to Euphrosyne in the first? The patron goddess of "Il Penseroso" is also a member of the classical pantheon, a goddess herself invoked in many hymns and odes and a closer relation to Mirth than we might at first expect. But, whereas Milton openly identifies Mirth as Euphrosyne and clearly sets down the primary set of parents, he is nowhere so explicit for Melancholy. He calls Melancholy the daughter of Saturn and Vesta and, like most mythographers, identifies Vesta as Saturn's own child. But neither classical poets nor Renaissance mythographers list a child of Vesta and Saturn, for most mythographers and poets make Vesta a virgin. An alternate genealogy does identify Vesta as Saturn's mother, and the very existence of this alternate may explain Milton's willingness to make Vesta a mother to a heavenly daughter.[32]

Certainly, mythographers linked Vesta, as Conti notes, with the heavens, especially the fiery ether. Saturn, Melancholy's other parent, as the god of science was also connected with the heavens and with contemplation.[33] Their daughter would inherit from both parents a heavenly disposition. Milton describes Melancholy's "Saintly visage" as "too bright / To hit the Sense of human sight" (13–14); her identity, likewise, is elusive, deliberately so. But if we collect all the clues that Milton has given us, we may hit on a goddess whom, under another name, we and Milton know well. She must be a thoughtful virgin—most divine, "sage and holy," "devout and pure," whose looks commerce with the skies and whose soul is held there in "holy passion" (39–41). The goddess who most closely fits this description is the eighth of the Muses, Urania, the goddess who will become the patron spirit for *Paradise Lost*. May "Il Penseroso" not present us with an early study of this heavenly Muse?

The myth books can assist us in establishing Melancholy's identity as the Muse. Homer, Hesiod, Pindar, and most classical poets are unanimous

32. This alternate genealogy lists Vesta as wife to Uranus (Coelus), hence Saturn's mother. See Carolus Stephanus, *Dictionarium historicum, geographicum, poeticum* (1596), 443v; Gyraldus (1560), 149.

33. Comes, *Mythologiae* (1581), bk. 8, ch. 19; bk. 2, ch. 2.

in naming Zeus (Jupiter) and Mnemosyne (Memory) as the parents of the Muses; most Renaissance poets follow their authority. But older authority, as the myth books tell us, assigns the Muses to the line of Saturn.[34] Begotten by Saturn's father, Uranos (Coelus), they are closely linked to the heavens and to science and contemplation, over which Saturn presides. All the Muses share this genealogy, but it has particular significance for Urania, who rules over the eighth heaven and is called the heavenly Muse.[35] Therefore, the Muses in the Renaissance are patronesses of poetry as well as of science and philosophy.[36] So closely connected are they with science and inquiry that the name Muse is construed by some mythographers to mean "mind" or "inquiry" or "memory," the attribute usually assigned to the Muses' mother, Mnemosyne.[37] Some mythographers extend this connection to make the

34. Comes says that the Muses were born like Saturn from Coelus or Uranus (the Heavens), belonging therefore to the same line (*Mythologiae* [1581], 506). Giraldi names two generations of the Muses, the older from Coelus and Terra, the later from Jove and Mnemosyne or some other mother (*De deis* [1560], 253); Geofredius Linocerius, (Geoffroi Linocier), *Mythologiae Musarum libellus* (1583), names Coelus and Terra as the Muses' parents asserting that the Muses were from the beginning and before Jove (1074–75). On the Muses see also Ernst Robert Curtius, *European Literature and the Latin Middle Ages,* 228–46.

35. The line of Urania, says Linocerius, is from Uranos as father, whom others call Coelus or Sky, to whom Saturn was son; collected in this one Muse are all things celestial (*Mythologiae Musarum libellus* [1583], 1102). Conti (*Mythologiae* [1581], 506) and following him Baudoin (*Mythologie ou Explication des Fables* [1627], 788) also cite Urania's descent from Uranos or Coelus, the father of Saturn. It is possible that there is some conflation of the two gods, such as occurs in *Ovide Moralisé* (see bk. 1, chaps. 14 and 15 in *Ovide Moralisé en Prose,* 47–48). On Urania, see John M. Steadman, *Milton's Biblical and Classical Imagery,* esp. 88–101. The alternate genealogy of the Muses also has some implications for Vesta as a putative wife/mother. A Vesta, who is wife to Uranus and mother of Saturn, might also be mother to a daughter—Urania—named for her heavenly father.

36. Conti says that the Muses inspire those arts that bring wisdom (Comes, *Mythologiae* [1581], 511). In some mythographies the Muses number seven because they are the patronesses of the seven liberal arts or nine because they were the inventors of the nine disciplines, as, e.g., Clio of history, Polyhymnia of agriculture, Urania of astrology or astronomy, Calliope of poetry. (See Gyraldus, *De deis* [1560], 254–56; Linocerius, *Mythologiae Musarum libellus* [1583], 1080–81). C. Stephanus says all learning and discipline are joined in the Muses (*Dictionarium historicum, geographicum, poeticum* [1596], 309r).

37. Several mythographers remark on the ancient theory, usually attributed to Aratus or Cicero, that the Muses as qualities of mind were at first three: *mneme* (mind or memory), *melete* (exercise or meditation), and *aoede* (song); or four: *mneme, melete, aoede,* and *thelxiope* (charm). Both Giraldi and Linocier attribute the Muses' descent from Jove as a descent of mental activity. (Linocerius, *Mythologiae Musarum libellus* [1583]). Giraldi notes they derive from Jove who is the property of understanding *(to noktikon),* and from Mnemosyne who is the property of memory *(to mnemonikon)* (Gyraldus, *De deis* [1560], 254). Linocier says that since Jupiter is the parent of all things, he, as cognition, generated the Muses from memory their name signifying conception of mind *(conceptus mentis).* They are the contemplators of eternal things, such as can

Muses daughters of Prince Memnon, merely because the name *Memnon* means "mind" (Comes, 511). It is a genealogy not without application to "Il Penseroso," since Milton compares Melancholy in her dark robes to Prince Memnon's sister, a comparison that, as we shall see, will connect Melancholy to Mirth in an interesting way.

The association of the Muses with mind and memory extends to their very function as inspirers of poetry, for, as the mythographer Linocier argues, there is a connection between the Greek words (εἰδειν), "to know," and (ἀείδειν), "to sing" (1076). Through their song, he says, the Muses dispense their wisdom and so lift learned and studious men to heaven (1102). In turn, through their devotion to the Muses, men elevate their souls and minds to celestial contemplation (1076).[38] The mythographers frequently cite Platonic and Pythagorean theory on the Muses. Plato in the *Symposium,* says Linocier, made Venus Urania identical to the Muse Urania (1102), for he understood that the Muses were the intelligences that govern the spheres, hence the very souls or movers of the heavenly bodies they animate.[39] Urania, most often assigned to the eighth sphere or starry heavens, is apart from Calliope, the intelligence of the sphere closest to God. Linocier interprets Plato's discussion of the Muses in this way: Jupiter is the mind of God, who first illuminates Apollo, the head and leader of the Muses; Apollo in turn inspires the Muses, and they finally arouse the spirit of the poet (1105). The ancient commentator Fulgentius argues that the Muses with Apollo, who perfects their number at ten, represent the steps in the intellective process by which human beings come to knowledge, hence to God (154).[40] Giraldi, following Fulgentius, constructs an allegory whereby the order of the Muses (eight orders of heavenly spheres plus the earth itself) composes celestial harmony. In this order Giraldi makes Urania the sublimity of human intelligence (*De deis* 358). Pythagoras influences the mythographers, in that the Pythagorean number eight is associated with the eighth sphere that Urania governs and the Pythagorean theory of the

---

be conceived by the intellect. Linocier, citing Plato, says the name *Muse* is derived from *inquiry* (μάθαι), for the Muses are the searchers into things who through the use of the senses and external things come to know things celestial and above (1080). Also see C. Stephanus, *Dictionarium historicum, geographicum, poeticum* (1596), 309r. As companions of philosophers, Muses encourage work that is solitary, nocturnal, and meditative (Lucius Annaeus Cornutus, *Natura deorum gentilium commentarius* [1505], 63–64). For further etymological interpretations, see Steadman, *Milton's Biblical and Classical Imagery,* 96–101.

38. Linocerius, *Musarum libellus* (1583).

39. The idea that the Muses are the intelligences of the spheres probably goes back to Macrobius. See Macrobius, *Commentary on the Dream of Scipio,* 194. See Steadman, *Milton's Biblical and Classical Imagery,* 94.

40. Fabius Planciades Fulgentius, *Mythologiarum libri tres* (1556), 154.

music of the spheres is closely connected with the notion that music tunes the Muses' spheres and enables the Muses to establish order throughout the universe.[41] Milton knew all this, as his discursive Prolusion 2 on the music of the spheres amply illustrates.

Although all the Muses are connected with heavenly harmony and learned thought, Urania is supreme in both. Always associated with the heavens and the sciences, astronomy or astrology, she takes her very name from the sky, and she is the Muse most closely connected with Uranos and Saturn, who preside over heavenly contemplation. Often depicted in engravings or described in epigrams as the Muse who fixes her eyes on the stars, she is portrayed as rapt in silence and serious thought. Plato and Plutarch remark on her seriousness, and Ovid tells us in the *Fasti* that Urania is so potent in her silence that no voice can be heard but hers.[42]

Milton's Melancholy, who brings with her the cherub Contemplation and mute Silence, seems more than an image of Urania; she must be the Muse herself. Although, unlike the Grace Euphrosyne, she is left without her proper classical name, she matches in many attributes that heavenly Muse whom Milton first calls on, also without naming her, in "On the Morning of Christ's Nativity." As Mirth can lead Allegro into fellowship with her sisters ("two sister Graces more," 15), so Melancholy can lead Penseroso to hear her sisters—"the Muses in a ring / Aye round about *Jove's* Altar sing" (47–48). She is both guide and instructress to her willing devotee, and this insistence on learning and serious study is exactly the quality in the Muses that the mythographers most stressed. She can direct Penseroso's glance to the heavens, "to behold the wandring Moon" (67) and to "outwatch the *Bear*" (87); she can lead him also to study heavenly things—to unsphere "the spirit of *Plato* to unfold / What Worlds, or what vast Regions hold / The immortal mind" (89–91). She has the power to call up the souls of dead poets, two of whom, Orpheus and Musaeus, had Muses for mothers. She presides over the music that breathes about Penseroso in his waking,

41. Linocerius 1073, 1075, 1077; Gyraldus *De deis* (1560), 358. Milton in Prolusion 2 connects the dance of the Muses with the Pythagorean theory of the music of the spheres (*Complete Poems* [ed. Hughes], 603–4). As we shall see in the next chapter, he can conflate the Muses with the Sirens whom Plato made the intellective spirits as well as the singers of each of the spheres.

42. Urania, says Linocier, is the patron of learned and studious men whom she draws to the sky (Linocerius, *Mythologiae Musarum libellus* [1583], 1102). Being particularly of the heavens, remarks the classical mythographer Cornutus, Urania imparts all knowledge to human beings (*Natura deorum gentilium commentarius* [1505], 63–64). In the mnemonic epigram "De Musarum inventis," usually attributed, though erroneously, to Vergil and often reprinted in the myth books, Urania is described with her gaze fixed on the heavens: "Vranie coeli motu scuratur & astra" (Comes, *Mythologiae* [1581], 512). Linocier (1583) cites Plutarch as assigning to Urania all things celestial and Ovid as remarking on her powers of silence and meditation (1101–2).

music being the special province of the Muses and the means by which they tune the heavenly spheres. Finally, Penseroso calls on Melancholy to "dissolve [him] into ecstasies, / And bring all Heav'n before [his] eyes" (165–66). Who but a heavenly Muse could accomplish such a feat, and who more than Urania could inspire the young, contemplative poet-prophet of "Il Penseroso"? Although Milton does not name Melancholy as the Muse, he expects us, while we read and experience the poem, to discover her identity with a kind of dawning awareness. Penseroso's thoughtful contemplation can only lead to the heavens and the heavenly Muse.[43] It may be that Milton in "Il Penseroso" avoids the title Muse because he is investigating at this point his own connection with the ancient goddesses of inspiration, so often called upon by poets. It may be that he refrains from naming the Muse because he is already inquiring, as in *Paradise Lost* 7, into the meaning that lies beyond the name.

MUSES AND GRACES

"L'Allegro" and "Il Penseroso" are twin poems; nowhere is this more evident than in the relationship of the "sister" goddesses who are their patron spirits. Throughout classical literature poets treat the Muses and the Graces as the closest of kin. They appear together in Sappho (127), in Hesiod's *Theogony* (lines 63–64), and in Pindar's *Isthmian 6* (63–64; 74–75); Alcman calls the Graces the sisters of the Muses (25).[44] Theocritus includes the Muses in his idyll to the Graces, remarking that the Muses grant great renown and the Graces such gifts that nothing in life is desirable without them (206–7). In the usual genealogical scheme, they share a father, Zeus (Jupiter); they also share many attributes, associations, and epithets.[45] Pindar calls both sets of goddesses "fair-haired" and "deep-girdled."[46] Renaissance mythog-

---

43. Throughout his early poetry, Milton seems to be reevaluating the conventional role of the Muses as inspirers of poetry. He refers in the Nativity ode to "Heav'nly Muse" (15), without ever naming her and refers to his Muse in "The Passion" (4) and the sonnet on the nightingale without further exploring her relationship to him or his to her. "Il Penseroso" takes us a step further.

44. Sappho, *Poetarum Lesbiorum fragmenta*. Hesiod describes the Muses and Graces as having homes and dancing places contiguous to one another (*Theogony*, 63–64). Also see Pindar, *Carmina;* and Alcman, *Greek Lyric Poetry*.

45. See Theocritus's *Idyll 16* in "The Poems of Theocritus." The Orphic hymns to the Graces and to the Muses invoke these goddesses directly, list their genealogies, and call them each by name. Epithets or descriptive phrases describe and honor the goddesses; both the Graces and the Muses are called "bright in honor" and "holy" and are invoked to come "well-disposed" and eager to "grant bliss and prosperity" to their initiates.

46. Pindar uses the epithet *fair-haired* for the Graces in *Pythian* 5.45 and for the Muses in *Olympian* 6.92.

raphers comment on the close relationship of the Muses and Graces, and Renaissance poets present them in each other's company.

Neither Milton nor the Renaissance poets that precede him forget that the Graces who grant the poet inspiration for his verse are, as in antiquity, the sister goddesses of the Muses. Many Renaissance poets, like the poets of antiquity before them, summon the Muses and the Graces jointly. In the ode, "Ad Musas," Michele Marullo asks the Muses to come in the company of the Graces, Venus, Jest, and Love, and to inspire his poetry. Marc-Antonio Flaminio composes odes both to the Muses and the Graces, asking Graces to add sweetness to his numbers. Celio Calcagnini invokes the Muses and the Graces together: "Adeste w charites, adeste musae."[47] This association continues in vernacular poets such as Ronsard in French and Spenser in English. In his ode to the Muses, Pierre de Ronsard calls upon the Graces to join them in a nocturnal dance. To serve as proper attendants for his Elisa, Queen Elizabeth in shepherdess dress, Spenser escorts Ronsard's Muses and Graces across the English Channel. The Muses arrive bearing bay branches and play their violins, while the Graces dance deftly and sing sweetly. In his ode "The Sacrifice to Apollo" Drayton explains that the Graces and the Muses rise "from one Stem, / They grace the Muses, and the Muses them" (23–24). In Prolusion 6 Milton twice names the Graces and the Muses together as goddesses of delight.[48] In "L'Allegro" and "Il Penseroso" he follows this Renaissance tradition, summoning the Grace Euphrosyne to inspire him in the first ode and in the second asking the Muse-like Melancholy to lead him to hear the Muses sing.

Both the Graces and the Muses have special relationships with Apollo, who holds the dancing Graces in his right hand and who leads the Muses. Apollo is sometimes even named (as by Conti and by Spenser) father of the Muses.[49] Muses and Graces alike are associated with music, dance,

47. Michaelis Marullus, *Poetae Tres Elegantissimi* (1582), 24r; Marcus Antonius Flaminius in *Carmina Quinque Illustrium Poetarum* (1558), 64v, 127r and v; Caelius Calcagninus, "De Pistophilo," *Carminum, Lib. 3* in *Io. Baptistae Pignae Carminum* (1553), 181.

48. Spenser, "Aprill," *The Shepheardes Calender,* in *Works,* 100–112. Michael Drayton, *The Works of Michael Drayton.* Henry Peacham remarks that "the *Muse, Mirth, Graces,* and perfect *Health* haue euer an affinitie each with either" (Henry Peacham, "Of Poetrie" [1622], 1:118). Milton, *Works* (ed. Patterson), 12:212, 214.

49. On the placement of the Graces at the right hand of Apollo see Gyraldus, *De deis* (1560), 403; Cartari (1571), 563. Some illustrated editions of Conti's *Mythologiae* include illustrations of the Graces dancing in the right hand of Apollo; see e.g., Comes, *Mythologiae* (1637), 131. Also see Cartari (1571), 60. For Apollo as the leader of the Muses (the one who perfects their number at ten) see "Apollo" in Joannes Boccacius (Boccaccio), *Genealogie deorum gentilium* (1492); Fulgentius, *Mythologiarum libri tres* (1556), 154; Gyraldus, *De deis* (1560), 254; Cartari (1571), 61; and Linocerius, *Mythologiae Musarum libellus* (1583), 1081. In his chapter on the Muses (bk. 7, chap. 15) Conti

and poetry. Although, in the myth books, the Muses seem more closely connected with instrumental music and the Graces with dance, both are pictured singing and dancing, and both inspire these arts in human beings. Accordingly, Muses and Graces have a close connection with choral celebrations and festivals. Linocier tells us that the Muse Thalia is the goddess of banquets, which she orders and arranges for human beings. (Nothing in life, he adds, is more delightful to the soul than a well-instituted banquet.) All the Graces, particularly the Grace Thalia, who shares both the name and the function of the Muse Thalia, favor banquets. Linocier also tells us that twelve is the ideal number for a festive company, for it comprises the number of the Muses, nine, and the number of the Graces, three (1089–90). So entirely complementary are these goddesses that it seems inconceivable that a poem celebrating a Grace should not be complemented by a poem celebrating a Muse, particularly when the two poems appear in tandem.

While the Graces and the Muses are complementary, they are by no means identical. Both favor the arts and encourage music and poetry in the lives of human beings, but the Graces incline more to the active and social aspects, the Muses to the reflective and intellectual. The myth books, moreover, support this diversification. Further, in choosing one Grace and one Muse as patron goddesses, Milton has extended this differentiation by selecting as patroness for "L'Allegro" the most active and social of the Graces, Euphrosyne, and as patroness for "Il Penseroso" the most remote and contemplative of the Muses, Urania.[50]

While both Mirth and Melancholy inspire poetry, each encourages a different kind. In the alternative genealogies of Milton's twin poems, the two goddesses are both called children of Aurora, or Dawn. Mirth springs from Aurora and her own son Zephyr, a mother-son incest no doubt quite as innocent as the father-daughter incest of Saturn and Vesta that Milton quietly excuses in "Il Penseroso."[51] Melancholy—named Prince Memnon's sister in a Miltonic comparison, where more is "meant than meets the

---

calls Apollo their leader but in the chapter on Apollo (bk. 4, chap. 10) notes that some authorities think Apollo is also their father (Comes [1581], 231). Spenser makes Apollo father to the Muses in "Aprill," "Teares of the Muses," and *Faerie Queene* 1 and 3, but not elsewhere in the *Faerie Queene* or in other of his works. Edgar Wind reproduces Gafurius's illustration of the music of the spheres, which shows Apollo on his throne, lyre in hand, with the Graces to his right and the Muses below him, also to the right; facing the Muses on the left are the nine spheres that they animate (43, facing).

50. Wind has pointed out that Euphrosyne, the third of the Graces, is often identified with the active as opposed to the contemplative life (*Pagan Mysteries in the Ranaissance*, 79). He also notes that she is sometimes represented—in Pico, for example—as the highest vision of pleasure or good in that she is the focus and end of her two sisters, Beauty and Love (see 55–74).

51. Although the myth books condemn incest in human beings, they interpret it allegorically among the gods, where father-daughter, mother-son, and brother-sister

ear"—must also be born of Aurora, who was Memnon's mother.[52] She is therefore sister to Memnon's brother, Zephyr, as well as to Mirth herself. In this playful mythologizing, we find that Mirth, "So buxom, blithe, and debonair" (24), takes on the rosy qualities of her mother Aurora and the frolic lightness of her father-brother, the "Wind that breathes the Spring" (18). Melancholy, in contrast, takes on the somber darkness of a dawn half begun, where the stars of night still linger and her brightness, like her brother Memnon's, is "Ore laid with black staid Wisdom's hue" (16). This differentiation extends also to the poetry that each goddess inspires. The lighthearted Grace is patroness to the festive poet: both Jonson with his "learned Sock" and Shakespeare with his "Wood-notes wild" are of her company (132–134). The somber-suited Muse, however, who inspires "Gorgeous Tragedy / In Scepter'd Pall" (97–98), is patron to such tragic poets as Aeschylus, Sophocles, and Euripides, who told the tale of Thebes, of Argos, and of Troy. In music Mirth calls forth "soft *Lydian* Airs" that ease care, and for this reason Milton names her "heart-easing Mirth," mindful that the ancient poets and Spenser as well, when he showed the vision of the Graces dancing on Mount Acidale, designate as one of the most important functions of poetry the easing of care.[53]

Melancholy's music is yet more sublime; the "pealing Organ" sounding to the "full voic'd Quire" (161–62) infuses the sweetness that brings heavenly vision. It is significant that both Allegro and Penseroso call on Orpheus, as though to tell us that the archetypal poet and father of song is supreme master of the kinds of poetry both goddesses, Mirth and Melancholy, inspire. At the very end of "L'Allegro" such music sounds as would have caused Orpheus to lift his head from Elysian slumber, and in "Il Penseroso" Orpheus is summoned to sing such notes as those that "drew Iron tears down *Pluto's* cheek, / And made Hell grant what Love did seek" (107–8). Perhaps Milton is suggesting that though some poets favor the inspiration of Mirth and others that of Melancholy, the supreme poet, like Orpheus, masters both genres.[54] By the time Milton came to write "L'Allegro" and "Il Penseroso," he had experimented in both the genres of Mirth and Melancholy, but apart from the serious ode "On the Morning of Christ's

---

relationships predominate. In glancing at the lovemaking of Aurora and Zephyr, Milton ignores the question of incest and treats Mirth's generation as a springtime allegory.

52. See the discussion of Memnon in Baudoin, *Mythologie ou Explication des Fables* (1627), 549–53.

53. Hesiod, *Theogony*, 97–103; Pindar, *Nemean* 4.1–8 (both Graces and Muses grant favor here to soothe and heal humanity); Spenser *Faerie Queene* 6.10.8. The easing of care is also an attribute of Mirth's father Liber Bacchus and his gift of wine.

54. Both "L'Allegro" and "Il Penseroso" focus on the Orpheus-Eurydice episode in the Orpheus myth—both associating Orpheus's power to conquer hell with the impulse of his love for his wife.

Nativity," he had had greater success with less serious modes—with elegy, pastoral, and lyric. Tragedy and epic lay ahead; Melancholy had yet to assert her full influence.

THE CHOICE OF HERCULES

In "L'Allegro" and "Il Penseroso" Milton is not merely composing twin odes to sister goddesses of poetic inspiration, he is working out a theory of poetry, based on his past experiences with different genres of poetry and projecting his future course as an English epic poet. In Chapter 1 we noted the young Milton's attachment to ancient and Renaissance elegy and his flirtation with a career as a neo-Latin elegiac love poet. With the composition of the Nativity ode Milton's directions were changing. He was not only turning away from Latin elegy, having composed his final Latin "love" elegy only months before, he was turning seriously to English religious verse. To mark that turn Milton writes "Elegia 6" to Charles Diodati, in which he outlines a newly declared dedication to Plato and to religious poetry that has resulted in his first English religious ode. In "Elegia 6" Milton also sportively delineates the difference between those poets devoted to lyric and elegiac poetry and those devoted to epic and more serious genres.

This differentiation between less serious and more serious genres of poetry is not unique to Milton's "Elegia 6." It underlies "L'Allegro" and "Il Penseroso" and like many other themes Miltonic, may find its precedent in classical literature and in one of the favorite authors of Milton's youth: Ovid. In his proem to the third book of the *Amores,* Ovid discusses the attractions of two different kinds of poetry, elegy and tragedy, which he personifies as two ladies who come to visit him in a woodland glade. Each urges him to compose poetry in her genre, offering a defense of her kind of verse and promising him success. Ovid confesses himself attracted to both but yields to the blandishments of Lady Elegy, putting off the claims of Tragedy to a later age (3.1).[55] The setting of this rural visitation and the appearance and manner of the two women themselves—one buxom and lighthearted, the other dark-robed and imperious—have more than incidental likenesses to the settings and characterizations of the goddesses of "L'Allegro" and "Il Penseroso." They also resemble two ladies, Voluptus and Virtus, who were involved in another "choice" scenario—the ladies who met Hercules at the crossroads, each of whom appealed to him to choose her way. This myth

55. Ovid, *Heroides* and *Amores* (1977), 444–49.

underlies both Ovid's poem and also, I believe, Milton's two odes, for the story of Hercules' choice was as well-known in the Renaissance, as it was in antiquity, inspiring poetic and pictorial representations.[56]

In Ovid's elegy, the serious "Muse"—Melancholy's Latin counterpart—the dark-robed imperious Tragoedia speaks first, accusing Ovid of yielding to nequitia—of endlessly making love and writing of it. Will he never tire of such pastimes? She demands that he respond to the pulse of another and greater thyrsus. Sing of heroes, she exhorts, begin the greater work ("maius opus"), write the Roman tragedy that awaits composition. In making Tragoedia describe this new poetry controlled by the greater but still "Bacchic" thyrsus, however, and in making her phrase her demands, as Lady Elegia remarks, in elegy's own uneven limping couplets rather than in her own hexameters, he neatly undercuts the proposal. Even so, the demand cannot be passed off lightly with excuses that until now he has only "played" at poetry. *Lusit* is the word, a word Milton uses in "Ad Joannem Rousium" to describe his mood when he composed the poems of the 1645 volume. John Milton also knew something about "playing" at poetry.

The very fact that Ovid permits Elegia to speak second assures her victory. She doesn't even try to weigh her lightness *(levitas)* against Tragoedia's heaviness *(gravitas)*. She merely states the incontrovertible fact—she it was who first inspired him as a poet, who made the seeds of his mind move, who brought his poetry to first fruition. Ovid himself rejects neither Tragoedia nor Elegia. But addressing himself to Tragoedia, he pleads the other's case. Admitting Tragoedia's power and the pressing demands of the eternal work before him, he asks only for a brief respite to finish the poetry that glorifies his love. Concede a little time to your vates. That he uses the

56. Ovid's account of the visitation of Elegia and Tragoedia is based on the Greek myth, included in Xenophon's works, but widely retold, of Hercules' choice. Two ladies, one carefree and light, the other somber and serious, accost Hercules at a crossroads and ask him to choose one of the two roads ahead: one easy, the other rugged. During the late sixteenth century, Annibale Carracci (1560–1609) painted a version of it in Rome (now in the Museo Nationale, Naples), whose striking depiction of the two ladies might also serve to illustrate Ovid's elegy or Milton's "L'Allegro" and "Il Penseroso." It shows Hercules with a lightly veiled nude, much resembling a Grace, at his left hand; she gestures toward a woodland glade, and at her feet, in the corner of the picture, are a musical instrument and the masks of drama. At Hercules' right hand is another lady, crowned with laurel and wearing dark blue robes and a red mantle; she holds a tablet in one hand and gestures with the other upward to a mountain path. In her corner of the picture is a bearded god, holding a book. Although Milton could not have seen the picture before he composed his poems, he could have seen it in Rome during his visit there, for it was part of the Farnese collection. Its ladies are almost perfect realizations of Mirth and Melancholy.

Annibale Carracci, *Hercules at the Crossroads*. Museo Nazionale, Capodimonte, Naples, reprinted by permission of the Ministero per i Beni Culturali.

term *vates* for himself is hardly to be ignored. He is promising eventually to turn to serious poetry.

The poetic debate that Ovid set forth in the *Amores* has relevance both for "L'Allegro" and "Il Penseroso" and for "Elegia 6." "Elegia 6" is often taken as his renunciation of the light genres of poetry for the heavier genres and ultimately for epic. But to do so is a mistake. Like the young Ovid, Milton recognizes the claims of both kinds of poetry. The merry dialogue that he stages with the absent Diodati, to whom "Elegia 6" is addressed, is provoked by Diodati's excuse that he has been feasting in the country and therefore could not produce an appropriate poetic epistle for his friend. Milton not only sportively chides his friend for enjoying the banquets too much and neglecting appropriate poetic composition, but also explodes Diodati's excuse. Wine and feasting do not preclude poetry—rather they inspire it. He goes on to set down the distinctions between the poets of mirth and of contemplation, assigning Diodati to the first, himself to the second sort. Depicting the composers of lyric, elegy, and the lighter genres of poetry as wine drinkers and lovers of festival and the composers of epic, tragedy, and serious ode as water drinkers and devotees of solitude and spare diet, Milton implies a direct connection between poetry and the forces that inspire it. He tells Diodati that wine and feasting inspire the poets of light, happy song, for song loves Bacchus and Bacchus loves song: "Carmen amat Bacchum, Carmina Bacchus amat" (14). Phoebus himself wore the ivy garland, and the Muses were often the companions of the Bacchic throng. Poets of this sort, such as Ovid, find no inspiration when banished from the world of merriment, for all this company—Anacreon, Pindar, and Horace, for example—sing of wine and roses, of festival, and of love. The gods most propitious to these poets are Bacchus and Venus and Ceres, and their favorite Muses, Thalia and Erato. But, continues Milton, different deities nourish the serious poet who would sing of wars, of divine heroes and gods in council, and of heaven and hell. Such a poet—and Homer serves as prime example—must have the character of a priest, abstain from banqueting, and live sparely. Philosophers such as Pythagoras and the prophets Tiresias and Calchas are also of this company, and the poet of poets, Orpheus, having sung in his youth in tapestried halls, became in old age the poet of quiet and contemplation.[57]

Milton's discussion of wine-drinkers and water-drinkers, of festive and contemplative poets has a long history—both in antiquity and the Renais-

---

57. William Riley Parker views "Elegia 6" as having, like Prolusion 1, elements of the rhetorical debate. ("Review of *The Miltonic Setting, Past and Present*," in *MLN*, 216–17).

sance.[58] Some sportive poets like Milton's contemporary John Leech take the wine-drinking side and praise Bacchus in lines very like Milton's own praise of the god.[59] Others condemn wine and insist on water-drinking, taking a religious as well as an aesthetic view of the matter. Although "Elegia 6" is not a Puritanical tract condemning the cavalier love of wine and revelry and "Bacchic" poets, it does have affinities with serious poetic satires such as Baptista Mantuan's "Contra impudice scribentes." Mantuan denounces venereal wine-drinking poets and the scandalous works they produce and defends serious divine poets—David and Orpheus are both cited—who devote themselves to holy writings.[60] Keep Bacchus's ivy away from Apollo's laurel, warns Mantuan. Let the vates drink only from Helicon, the pure streams of the Muses, and not from Venus's streams. Let him be chaste. Although he could very well have drawn his description of the water-drinking holy vates from Mantuan's poem, Milton does not dissociate Bacchic ivy from Apollonian laurel. Unlike Mantuan, he neither excoriates Venus nor banishes the festive poet. He merely marks the vates's choice of chaste life and spare diet as the one which must be made in order to write epic, in order to sing of the starry heavens.[61] He allows Horace and Anacreon and Ovid their place, and he even allows his own friend Diodati to enjoy Christmas feasting with the cavaliers. "Elegia 6" is descriptive, not proscriptive. Although Milton in "Elegia 6" suggests that it is Diodati—not he—who is the festive elegiac poet, Diodati merely serves here as Milton's alter ego. What is "Elegia 6" but a festive Christmastide elegy that could be set beside "Elegia 5," the spring elegy and contrasted to the recently composed Nativity ode, which Milton tells Diodati he is dispatching with the elegy. Yet Milton also alludes to another set of poems that he is sending, written in Diodati's own native tongue. Surely these are (as Carey argues) the Italian sonnets and hardly the work of a water-drinking vates. The composer of love sonnets is obviously still the poet of Mirth, even if the composer of the Nativity ode has inclined to Melancholy.

As critics have often noted, Milton's elegiac study of fostering deities and favoring lifestyles has implications for "L'Allegro" and "Il Penseroso." The progenitors of Mirth are those very gods, Bacchus and Venus, who in

---

58. See *Variorum, (The Latin and Greek Poems)*, 1:115–26. Horace, Ovid, and Vergil (see esp. note 14) are among those who say wine drinking promotes poetic composition. On water drinking, see esp. note 71.

59. Leech (Leochaeus) dedicated his *Musae Priores* (1620) to Prince Charles. See "Elegia 2": "Bacchus amat vates, Bacchum veneramur amantes" (Bacchus loves poets; lovers revere Bacchus) in "Elegiae," 1.88.

60. Baptista Mantuanus, *Aureum contra impudice scribentes opusculum* (1508).

61. In a letter sent to Richard Jones in 1657, the mature Milton advises Jones to dilute the "must of Liber with more than a fifth part of the more liberal drink of the Muses" (*Complete Prose Works of John Milton* [ed. Ayers], 7:503).

"Elegia 6" are patrons of the festive poet, and Mirth herself is closely kin to the Muses of banquet and love elegy—Thalia and Erato—also named there. The philosophers, prophets, and poets whom Penseroso invokes to preside over the world of the serious poet are those Milton names in "Elegia 6." Further, the strict regimen of spare diet that he prescribes for the epic poet in the elegy resembles the program of abstinence and solitude that Melancholy dictates for the contemplative man. So entirely indeed do the festive poet's habits and preferences in the elegy agree with Allegro's in the ode, and the epic poet's with Penseroso's, that we may suspect that Milton's true agenda in the twin odes "L'Allegro" and "Il Penseroso" has more to do with poetics than with a simple differentiation of lifestyles.

"SUCH SIGHTS AS YOUTHFUL POETS DREAM"

Yet, while critics acknowledge the presence and even the importance of references to poetry throughout "L'Allegro" and "Il Penseroso," they do not usually regard as the main subject of these twin odes the difference between poetic inspiration in the elegiac as opposed to the epic poet. More often they read these poems as catalogues of general pleasures that Mirth or Melancholy might grant. Such readings, however, tend to ignore the structure of the poems as petitional odes and the key roles that the Grace Mirth and the Muse-like Melancholy play as deities who specifically inspire poetic vision. But both the nature of the goddesses and the genre of the classical ode strictly control the odes as Milton develops them. For after the invocation to each goddess, which identifies her through a résumé of her person, parentage, and powers, the speaker asks for such gifts of poetic inspiration as a poet might most properly request from the inspiring Grace or Muse. Allegro and Penseroso ask not for random pleasure but only for such pleasure and vision as might inspire and facilitate the composition of poetry. They do not ask their goddesses to lead them into the valley of pleasure but into the vale of poetry making.[62] Milton is not writing odes to mistresses but to deities, and in so doing he redefines for the poet the "come live with me" formula of Marlowe and his followers.

Both "L'Allegro" and "Il Penseroso" unfold as though Mirth or Melancholy were infusing her power and the poet composing to her dictation. From the very moment that the goddess descends to her poet until the conclusion of each poem, she directs the poet's composition as she moves

---

62. Samuel Johnson in *Lives of the Poets* complained about the solitary nature of both Allegro and Penseroso; but if both Penseroso and Allegro are portraits of the poet—not just the sociable versus the pensive man, as Johnson takes them to be, this solitariness is not only appropriate, but also indispensable for the composition of poetry.

him over the landscape, diverting his attention from one to the next object of inspiration and exercising him in those genres of poetry that are in her special province. The movement of each ode mimics in a sense the process of its composition. After the invocation proper, the poet in each ode summons the poetical bird—lark or nightingale—that is the emblem both of his goddess and of the poem that follows. The notes of the lark in "L'Allegro," which "startle the dull night" (42), announce the opening of an aubade as surely as the song of Philomel in "Il Penseroso," "in her sweetest, saddest plight" (57), suggests a serenade. Allegro describes the dawn rising before him and paints the spring scene outside his window with its sweetbrier and eglantine; Penseroso sets the contrasting tones for his evensong with the moon rising over the oak tree and the "Chantress of the woods" adding her music. Both Mirth and Melancholy inspire their poets with the pastoral mode, but the light pastoral of Mirth—with its strutting cocks and cheerful hounds, its whistling plowman and singing milkmaid, and its concluding holiday dances and goblin tales—is necessarily different from the sober pastoral of Melancholy. The poetry that Allegro pours forth at the Grace's inspiration marks him as a poet in the style of the lyric Horace, the elegiac Tibullus, and the bucolic Vergil and Theocritus. And it is not surprising to find, as the editors of Milton tell us, that Milton echoes these poets and chooses the names Corydon, Thyrsis, Phyllis, and Thestylis from Vergil's and Theocritus's eclogues.[63] In this pastoral section of "L'Allegro" the poet carefully composes a country landscape, choosing such details as "Russet Lawns," "Fallows Gray," "Meadows trim," and "Shallow Brooks" as will seem to epitomize scenes from the pastoral genre. For what Milton wishes us as readers to experience is the process of poetical composition, directed by the inspiring goddess and ordered by the aspiring poet. Accordingly, what we are presented with is a highly compact, illustrative idyll.

The corresponding section of "Il Penseroso" follows a similar formula, but it is the intellectual and contemplative idyll, rather than the re-creative, that Melancholy inspires. Milton found precedent for these different kinds of idylls in Vergil and Theocritus and also, of course, in Spenser's *Shepheardes Calender*.[64] In Penseroso's idyll, there are no nibbling flocks, no sound of merry bells or jocund rebecs; instead, the tone of the far-off mournful curfew sets the mood. Melancholy lights the midnight lamp and directs her devotee's eyes to Plato and "thrice great Hermes." And the poetic section

63. See Hughes, ed., *Complete Poems*, 70 n. 83.
64. It is worth noting that E. K. divided Spenser's eclogues into three types: the plaintive, the re-creative, and the moral. See "The Generall Argument of the Whole Booke," *Shepheardes Calender*, in *Poetical Works*, 419.

that ensues turns our attention from earthly landscapes to the stars, much as Beatrice leads Dante from the earthly paradise through the spheres of the heavens, or as Socrates, though sitting under a plane tree, discourses with Phaedrus on higher things. Penseroso's is the pastoral of the mind.

In the next two sections of "L'Allegro" and "Il Penseroso" Milton moves on to the poet's inspiration for comedy and romance on the one hand and tragedy and epic on the other. Once more each genre is presented to us in epitome. Allegro strings together several incidents from comic or goblin tales: "How *Faery Mab* the junkets eat" (102) or "how the drudging *Goblin* sweat / To earn his Cream-bowl duly set" (105–16); turning to loftier themes of romance next, he summons up scenes of tournament with knights, barons, and ladies as arbiters of the contests. He makes the whole world of romance appear in a single figure, Hymen, whom he describes in his "Saffron robe, with Taper clear" (126). Penseroso, in contrast, makes the world of tragedy appear, symbolized by the "Gorgeous" figure in "Scepter'd Pall"—a reminiscence of Ovid's Tragoedia—who sweeps by, as Penseroso alludes to the great tragic cycles of antiquity. Before moving on to epic, he presents in miniature his own re-creation of tragedy, the unhappy tale of Orpheus's tragic quest for Eurydice in hell. For epic he proposes that Melancholy call up the ghost of Chaucer to inspire him as she had inspired Spenser to complete the Squire's Tale of "*Cambuscan* bold, / Of *Camball*, and of *Algarsife*" (110–11).

Neither in the sections on comedy and romance in "L'Allegro" nor in those on tragedy and epic in "Il Penseroso" do we have in full what the comic poet might compose at Mirth's urging or the epic poet at Melancholy's. We have instead two poets recounting the effects of such inspiration or alluding briefly to previous poets who might move them to compose poetry in each genre. The outcome is a poetic apology, not unlike that the young Ovid offers as he explores the opposing poles of his genius and expresses his attraction to both elegy and tragedy. For in describing elegy and tragedy, Ovid had given a brief epitome of each. Similarly, Milton has first Allegro, then Penseroso project his feelings about such different arts as comedy and tragedy, romance and epic, presenting, as he describes each, its characteristic style and manner. Thus, in summoning the goddess that presides over these different schools of poetry, the devotee is proposing the poetic program he might undertake at her command.

"L'Allegro" and "Il Penseroso" conclude with poetic apotheoses. In both, the poet, having enumerated the poetic genres that his goddess inspires and in which she exercises him, attains the acme of poetic vision or dream. Allegro, his inspiration almost complete, tells us that the "sights" that have appeared to his inner eye are the very stuff of poetic dream: "Such sights as youthful Poets dream / On Summer eves by haunted stream" (129–30).

Asking to be "married to immortal verse" (137) and for music to sound, "such as the meeting soul may pierce / In notes . . . of linked sweetness long drawn out" (138–40), the aspiring poet of "L'Allegro" will meet the supreme poet, Orpheus, who wakes in hell to the same music. The dream of poetic composition is about to become reality; Milton's youthful poet, like Shakespeare's in another "dream," has "as imagination" bodied forth "the form of things unknown" and given "to aery nothing / A local habitation and a name" (*Midsummer Night's Dream* 5.1.14–17).[65] Allegro renews his pledge of loyalty to his inspiring Grace, and poem and poet conclude at once: "These delights, if thou canst give, / Mirth, with thee, I mean to live" (151–52). Can we doubt that the delights requested are the delights of the imagination and their product poetry?

For Penseroso the final apotheosis is no less the fulfillment of a dream. As civil-suited Morn, Melancholy's "second" mother, arises "kerchieft in a comely Cloud," Penseroso retreats to the sacred precinct of wood nymphs and spirits. To the sound of humming bees and waters murmuring, the dream that is the melancholic counterpart of Allegro's appears. "Strange" and "mysterious," it waves "in Airy stream, / Of lively portraiture display'd" (147–49), and, as in "L'Allegro," sweet music sounds. With the assistance of music, the Muses' special medium, Penseroso aspires to that vision of the heavens that Urania promises him from the beginning. Turning his eyes to the stars, the poet pledges himself to fulfill the goal of poetry as prophecy, choosing to live with the Muse if she can give him these ultimate pleasures.

Some may be tempted to connect Milton's ascent to heaven at the end of "Il Penseroso" with his declared preference at the end of "Elegia 6" of epic over elegy. Some may wish to elect the year of the twin odes' composition as the time that Milton added the retraction to "Elegia 7," affirming his choice of Platonic contemplation and repudiating the nequitia of his early elegies. But to introduce such choices would seriously upset the balance of the twin odes and the progress of Milton's future poetry. Must the Graces of "L'Allegro" be banished? Must we forbid their reappearance in Eden with the procession of eternal spring?

"L'Allegro" and "Il Penseroso" have presented two differing but complementary accounts of the genesis and progress of poetical inspiration. Milton does not demand that we choose between the two, any more than he requires us to favor the Muses above the Graces or vice versa. Both Muses and Graces assert their presence in the Eden of *Paradise Lost.* These youthful poems are framed as neoclassical odes that request powers and pleasures—gifts from the goddesses. But nothing yet has been granted or received. Both the reader and the poet-speaker or speakers have yet to

65. William Shakespeare, *The Riverside Shakespeare,* 242.

choose.[66] The goddesses have yet to assent or deny. It is a paradise where all things are yet possible. These goddesses dance—as in antiquity—in each other's company; Penseroso can enjoy the companionship of Allegro and the reader can enjoy them both. It may be that the festive Orpheus of the first ode will become (with age) the pensive poet of the second's "peaceful hermitage." To muse upon the Graces in youth can lead one to be graced by the Muses in later years. Or perhaps in addressing the first ode to Mirth and the second to Melancholy Milton was merely following the protocol of ancient banquets, where the first toast was always offered to the Graces—but the last to the Muses.[67]

66. A recent article comments on Milton's use of the conditional, commenting that "the structure of the poems constitutes the grammatical enactment of asking and waiting for grace." See Marc Berley, "Milton's Earthly Grossness: Music and the Condition of the Poet in *L'Allegro* and *Il Penseroso*," in *MS* 30.
67. Lilius Gregorius Gyraldus, "De Musis libellus," in Hyginus (1577), 317.

SABRINA AND THE CLASSICAL
NYMPHS OF WATER

A Mask Presented at Ludlow-Castle

In Milton's *Mask Presented at Ludlow-Castle,* two semidivinities control the outcome of the drama: the Attendant Spirit, who comes from the heavens to succor the Lady, and Sabrina, who rises from the water of the river Severn to release her finally from Comus's spell. Male and female, the Attendant Spirit and Sabrina are divinities of sky and water, who play their roles as the local gods of the English borders and protectors of the children of an earl of "mickle trust, and power." Milton has clad both these divinities in pastoral dress and has given them the appropriate local manners and accents. But at the same time he has also classicized them, connecting them with the ancient divinities that populate his early poems and most especially with the twin progeny of Jove—Apollo, the god of poetry and music, and Artemis-Diana, his sister, the virgin goddess, the huntress, and the protectress of young women. As with his other pastoral divinities, Mirth and Melancholy, their classical identities will be crucial to our understanding of these two spirits.

In his first speech, the Attendant Spirit tells us that he is a dweller of the upper air, a messenger whose mansion is "before the starry threshold of *Jove's* Court" (1). At the end of the mask he ascends to the Hesperides, the paradisiacal garden in the broad fields of sky beyond Ocean. As a semideity or "genius," he is allied both to the supreme god Jove who sent him and to the gods of water—Ocean, Neptune, and his "blue-hair'd deities." When he dons the rustic garments of a shepherd and assumes the pastoral name Thyrsis, he takes on the third realm of the woods and becomes by implication a favoring pastoral deity, a devotee to Apollo, Pan, or Mercury. Milton has made the Attendant Spirit a figure with specific mythological connections—not just a Christianized guardian angel. He expects us to interpret his role classically as well as allegorically. When he joins with the Lady's two brothers and attempts to save the Lady from Comus—three males in heroic assault to break Comus's power—he represents the masculine world of classical power. He acts as the representative of the all-powerful Jove, the potent Neptune, and the pastoral Apollo. But though the Attendant Spirit and the two brothers succeed in routing Comus, they do not free the Lady. It is not until the feminine deity rises from the nurturing water that the Lady is truly released. With Sabrina and her attendant nymphs the power of the feminine enters the mask.

Sabrina, the other "saving" deity, appears to be the only specifically British deity in the *Mask*, a transformed human-being-turned-divinity that critics have been content by and large to conflate with the goddess of the Severn River, a figure that Milton could have drawn from several sources as diverse as Geoffrey of Monmouth's *History,* Spenser's *Faerie Queene,* or Drayton's *Poly-Olbion*.[1] Yet if we accept Sabrina merely as a local British river nymph, who supplies a little local color and serves as the virgin savior of the Virgin Lady, we miss some important classical associations that clarify her person and role in the mask. Although locally connected with the river Severn, Sabrina belongs to a larger family of water deities—well-known classical gods, with whom the Attendant Spirit takes care to associate her—Ocean, Neptune, Tethys, and Nereus, deities who purify and by whom the magic of Comus and his potent parents Circe and Bacchus may be countered. The Attendant Spirit associates himself and the Egerton family with these gods of water at the beginning of the mask and when the Attendant Spirit calls upon Sabrina to appear, he invokes her as a representative of this classical family of water deities.[2]

Sabrina appears in a mask within the *Mask*. The Attendant Spirit invokes her in a song; she rises, attended by water nymphs, and replies in a song of her own. The Attendant Spirit explains the Lady's distress and Sabrina expresses her willingness to help, performs the rites necessary to undo Comus's charm, and descends, while the Attendant Spirit praises her and invokes a charm of his own to protect her. From the first invocation of Sabrina until her descent, the Attendant Spirit treats her in three ways: first, as the nymph of the river Severn, thus a local British place deity; second, as the virgin daughter of Locrine, a maiden connected by way of her father to the native British dynasty that descends back by way of Brutus to Anchises, the father of Aeneas, to the line of Troy; and finally, a transformed human-being-turned-water-nymph who is allied to classical gods of water and to other classical nymphs who have undergone a "sea-change."

---

1. For commentary on Milton's sources for Sabrina see *Variorum (The Minor English Poems),* 2.3, esp. 956–73; also see William S. Miller, *The Mythology of Milton's Comus.*

2. Maryann Cale McGuire in *Milton's Puritan Masque* notes that the maritime motif reappears with the appearance of Sabrina (93).

In the narrative that precedes his formal invocation of Sabrina, the Attendant Spirit describes her history, explaining how she has become a part of the family of classical water deities. It was the god Nereus, the father of classical water nymphs such as Thetis, who saved Sabrina from drowning in the Severn, transforming the human daughter of Locrine into his own adopted daughter, making her, as it were, another Nereid. Thus she joins the family of water gods, invoked by the Attendant Spirit.

> Listen and appear to us
> In the name of great *Oceanus,*
> By the earth-shaking *Neptune's* mace
> And *Tethys'* grave majestic pace,
> By hoary *Nereus'* wrinkled look . . . (867–71)

Milton could have drawn this roll call of deities from Spenser's catalogue in book 4 of *The Faerie Queene* that describes the procession of water dignitaries attendant at the wedding of the Thames and the Medway. But his roll call has more than just a decorative processional function in the *Mask.*[3] As the Trinity manuscript attests, he carefully revised the catalogue. Following Oceanus, he adds Neptune and several other male deities, much strengthening Sabrina's connection with the classical water deities he had specifically referred to at the beginning of the mask as the rulers of this western isle.[4] In so doing he also establishes Sabrina's proper classical credentials. When she departs, moreover, Milton reminds us for a second time that she belongs to a classical court: "I must haste ere morning hour / To wait in *Amphitrite's* bow'r" (920–21). Amphitrite is, of course, the reigning female water deity, consort to Neptune. The daughter of Locrine has left one "royal" family to join another, transferring her fealty to a new set of paternal monarchs—Ocean, Neptune, and Nereus.[5]

3. Neptune, Ocean, Tethys, and Nereus appear together (*Faerie Queene* 4.11); Severn, the river, not the nymph, is also attendant at the wedding (4.11.30, 6). Spenser also alludes to the history of Sabrina, saying that Sabrina gave her name to the river (2.10.19.1–9).

4. See Cedric Brown's commentary on these revisions in *John Milton's Aristocratic Entertainments,* 116–17. Milton, "The Trinity Manuscript," 426–27. Also see Milton, *A Maske. The Earlier Versions;* Milton, *A Maske at Ludlow. Essays on Milton's Comus. With the Bridgewater Version of Comus.* The original invocation of Sabrina was divided between the Attendant Spirit (designated in the Bridgewater manuscript as Daemon) and the two brothers. In the Trinity manuscript, the lines after "songs of Sirens sweet" that name Parthenope and Ligea are canceled. See Louis L. Martz, *Poet of Exile,* 22.

5. Milton may, in fact, be following Drayton, whose Sabrina refers to Neptune as her father.

If the beginning of the Attendant Spirit's catalogue is male and hierarchical, its conclusion is female and nurturing. The Attendant Spirit goes on to invoke a different set of water deities—all female, sister nymphs, all of whom are, like Sabrina, water spirits and are closely identified with her in person, in history, and in function.

> By *Leucothea's* lovely hands,
> And her son that rules the strands,
> By *Thetis'* tinsel-slipper'd feet,
> And the Songs of *Sirens* sweet,
> By dead *Parthenope's* dear tomb,
> And fair *Ligea's* golden comb,
> . . . .
> By all the *Nymphs* that nightly dance
> Upon the streams with wily glance,
> Rise, rise . . . (875–80, 883–85)

These nymphs are not just a random list of female water deities; all are closely connected to mortals, often responding to those in peril. The sea nymph Leucothea, the water deity who helps Odysseus, is, like Sabrina, a transformed human being. The Nereid Thetis is sister goddess to Vergil's Cyrene and Ligea, the latter sometimes referred to as a Nereid (as in *Georgics* 4.336), sometimes a Siren. Parthenope, like Sabrina, is a place deity—a Siren (sometimes sister to the Siren Ligea) whom Vergil also names in book 4, the Cyrene book of the *Georgics*.[6] All of these attendant nymphs have undergone trials of their own, and all have something to tell us about Sabrina and her function in the mask.

"LISTEN AND SAVE"

Sabrina is modeled not only on those goddesses of water specifically named in the catalogue, but also on Cyrene, a goddess of place and a water deity, not directly named in the mask, but closely linked to those goddesses who are named—to the Nereids Thetis and Ligea and to the place goddess Parthenope. Cyrene appears prominently both in Vergil's *Georgics* and in Pindar's *Pythian 9,* where her transformation is recounted. John Arthos has argued for the importance of Vergil's Cyrene as a model for Milton's Sabrina.[7] In the *Georgics* Cyrene answers the prayer of a mortal, her son, and then performs with her sisters a purification rite that cleanses him and

6. Parthenope is the classical name for Naples just as Sabrina is for the Severn.
7. John Arthos, "Milton's Sabrina, Virgil and Porphyry," *Anglia* 79.

undoes the ban laid upon him.[8] As a mother goddess who responds to the pleas of her son, Vergil's Cyrene is closely related to Homer's Nereid Thetis. When Vergil describes the Nereid Cyrene sitting with her sisters beneath the waves, he models this scene on Homer's description of Thetis, also sitting with her Nereid sisters, when the news comes to her of her own son's peril. Milton places Sabrina in a similar position, sitting beneath the waves with her attendant water nymphs, when she hears the pleas of the Attendant Spirit on the Lady's behalf. Like Cyrene and Thetis before her, she too comes to assist a mortal, performing a purification rite for the Lady. There is nothing quite like this in the British accounts of Sabrina, either in Geoffrey of Monmouth or in Spenser or in Drayton. Although Drayton's Sabrina is sympathetic and listens compassionately when the nymphs of her train appeal to her for protection from the Satyrs in the wood of Dean who are raping them, she does not assist them herself, but only protests in their behalf to Father Neptune. Milton's Sabrina is powerful in her own right. She takes on the role of the mother goddesses—Cyrene and Thetis— when she comes to the aid of the Lady, herself undoing the charm, and assuming the role of nurturing "mother" for an imperiled "daughter."

In Pindar's *Pythian 9,* Cyrene appears as a nymph pursued by a god and also as a city-protector transformed by this god from a mortal to a goddess. She thus resembles both Milton's Lady wooed by a persistent demideity and Milton's Sabrina, translated mortal and goddess of place, conflating in one figure the imperiled virgin and the place nymph, and providing hence a useful link between the two principal females of the mask. Cyrene is also, like Sabrina, a protectress of young women, feeling a natural bond of sympathy for them, since she too was once a maiden in distress.

We first encounter Pindar's Cyrene right at the moment when she is about to face great peril. A committed virgin—a huntress-devotee to Artemis, who does not stay at home with girls her own age doing household tasks—she is ranging through the forest pursuing beasts of prey. In the glens of Mount Pelion she is wrestling with a lion, and the lion is getting the worse part of the encounter.[9] Milton's Lady is also a committed virgin, and Milton takes care to link her to the cults of Diana-Artemis and Minerva, two aggressive and independent virgin goddesses who prize their freedom.[10] Although lost

8. Milton's allusion to Cyrene's sister, Ligea of the golden comb, shows that he was at least thinking of the *Georgics* as he wrote this passage in the mask.

9. Cyrene is frequently pictured in this posture, often in African statuary. A statue and a relief, both of which were taken from the African site of the city Cyrene and are now in the British Museum, show the nymph wrestling with a lion. Sometimes this wrestling match is connected with the founding of the city itself.

10. John Rumrich investigates the question of Milton's use of Artemis and Minerva as classical goddesses. See *Milton Unbound,* 76–78.

The Nymph Cyrene Overcoming a Lion, copyright British Museum. A.D. 120–150. Found in the Temple of Apollo at Cyrene. Copy of a larger sculpture now lost. BM cat. sculpture 1384.

in the woods and alone, the Lady is independent and unafraid. The Elder Brother assures us that she is capable of taking care of herself, comparing her to a "quiver'd Nymph with Arrows keen," who "May trace huge Forests, and unharbor'd Heaths / Infamous Hills, and sandy perilous wilds" (422–24). Because of her chastity "she may pass on with unblench't majesty" (430). In defending the Lady's absolute power as a virgin, the Elder Brother specifically connects her with Diana-Artemis, who tames wild beasts.

> shall I call
> Antiquity from the old Schools of *Greece*
> To testify the arms of Chastity?
> Hence had the huntress *Dian* her dread bow,
> Fair silver-shafted Queen for ever chaste,
> Wherewith she tam'd the brinded lioness
> And spotted mountain pard, but set at nought
> The frivolous bolt of *Cupid;* gods and men
> Fear'd her stern frown, and she was queen o' th' Woods. (438–46)

In connecting the Lady with Artemis, Milton is linking her not only to the cult of the virgin goddess, but also to the beast-taming feats such as the subduing of lionesses, a skill needed by the Lady when she encounters Comus and his bestial crew and wrestles verbally with him to win supremacy. The Elder Brother places his sister in the line of Artemis and her beast-taming nymphs, thus making strong virgin goddesses and nymphs such as Cyrene appropriate models for this young aristocratic woman.

Strong though Cyrene and the Lady are, they are in real danger when we first encounter them. The Lady has attracted Comus's attention, Cyrene Apollo's. Apollo is notorious for his courtship of unwilling maidens, the most famous of which is, of course, Daphne—a nymph whose plight Comus himself alludes to when he describes the Lady—"root-bound" as Daphne that fled Apollo (661–62). Daphne is a nymph closely related to Cyrene— in Pindar they are cousins, both descended from the god Oceanus.[11] Their myths obviously are doublets with different conclusions. One story results in honor, favor, and royal eminence for the pursued maiden; the other in transformation and the dubious honor of becoming a laurel tree, thereafter Apollo's favored emblem.[12] *Pythian 9* tells the story of Apollo's lawful

---

11. In Vergil's *Georgics* and in some Renaissance myth books both Daphne and Cyrene are designated as daughters of Peneus, hence sisters rather than cousins. See, for example, Boccaccio, *Genealogiae deorum Gentilium* (1511), 7, 28, 29. For the accounts of Apollo's wooing of Cyrene and Daphne, see Comes, *Mythologiae* (1581), 358–60; 233.

12. Pindar never mentions the story of Daphne, but it is the alternate tragic-story that underlies the happy account of Apollo's wooing of Cyrene. See Charles Segal's

wooing of Cyrene. Catching sight of Cyrene, Apollo proposes to pursue her (as he had Daphne). But he first calls upon the Centaur, Chiron, to advise him how he may win her "lawfully," plucking, as he puts it, the honey-sweet flower of love. The Centaur advises him to try persuasion, not violence. Following his advice, Apollo woos the girl and takes her away to Libya, installing her in the garden of Zeus at Cyrene and making her the queen and patron of the newly founded city. Transformed from nymph to goddess, she becomes the deity of the freshwater spring in the city, her cult and worship closely connected with that of Artemis and Apollo, both of whom also had temples there. Like Daphne, she loses her former nature, but her transformation to goddess, rather than laurel tree, is a happy one. Now consort to Apollo and the mother of his son Aristaeus (whose story Vergil tells), she remains a devotee to Artemis, whose cult she continues to serve.

Cyrene's connection with Artemis-Diana is more complex than it might at first appear. Artemis is not just a goddess of virginity, but a deity who guides young women through all the stages of their life from maidenhood to marriage to motherhood. She permits her devotees to move from committed virginity on to other roles appropriate to women. Hence Pindar's Cyrene, who at the beginning of the ode is a virgin committed to Artemis, continues to be a devotee of the goddess, after she becomes consort to Apollo and a city protectress. A similar progress is possible for Milton's virgin Lady.

The Lady is threatened in a real sense with a "Daphne" scenario. A powerful demigod courts her, apparently seeking her as a consort-queen, but actually imprisoning and enchanting her. As a demideity, Comus partakes of the ruthless aspect of the Olympians—of his drunken father Bacchus, who coldly revenged himself on the Tuscan sailors by transforming them into dolphins (a story Milton alludes to), of Apollo, so intent on enjoying Daphne that he forces her transformation into a tree. Hence Pindar's account of an averted rape has an interesting application to Milton's story. Pindar's Cyrene is Daphne with a difference, the pursued virgin who becomes consort, city goddess, mother to Apollo's favored son (the bee-keeper Aristaeus), as well as mother to the Cyrenian people. Cyrene's story turns out happily, her myth providing an alternative conclusion to the Daphne story. The Lady also escapes Daphne's fate, defeating the would-be rapist

---

discussion of *Pythian 9* in *Pindar's Mythmaking: The Fourth Pythian Ode,* 165–71. Segal comments on the difference between the Daphne and the Cyrene stories and the averting of rape in the latter by the wise counsel of the Centaur Chiron. He notes that Cyrene is no passive victim of the god, but a nymph descended from the powerful gods Gaia and Oceanus, and the granddaughter of Peneus who in the Daphne myth intervened against Apollo.

Comus and returning to her parents, restored to her city, Ludlow, and to its citizens.

That Sabrina, the deity who releases the Lady, is an alter ego of Artemis-Diana, and the Attendant Spirit, the deity who escorts her back to Ludlow, is the alter ego of Apollo, only adds to the complexity and subtlety of Milton's mythmaking. As we have noted in previous chapters, Milton accommodates myth to the demands of his context, freely adapting one or another aspect of a classical story as he needs it. The Attendant Spirit, the genius of music, represents the nurturing aspect of the Apollo figure; Comus, the god of discord represents the violent Bacchic aspect of the Olympian gods. He is not just a "bad" Bacchus, but also a bad Apollo. Unlike the god of the Cyrene story, this demideity cannot become a consort to the Lady.

What Pindar has given us in *Pythian 9* is, of course, the prototypical dynastic myth. He recounts the history of Apollo and Cyrene in order to honor the city Cyrene, its king, and in this specific case its winning athlete.[13] Milton adapts a dynastic myth when he honors the Egertons, taking Pindar as an example on how to use myth to compliment a family. The Cyrene myth is relevant in one way to the Lady's story, in another to Sabrina's. Cyrene and Sabrina are place nymphs, protectresses respectively of Cyrene, the African city, and Ludlow, the town adjacent to the lands that Sabrina's river, the Severn, flows through.[14] When Milton has the Attendant Spirit invoke the nymph of Severn-Ludlow, rather than just any nymph, he is establishing Sabrina's authority over that place. He even goes so far as to have the Attendant Spirit narrate her history, a history that we must recognize is like Cyrene's: a prototypical founding myth. An endangered royal daughter faces death, but is rescued and made immortal, becoming the protective deity of place. In the legendary account that Spenser (for one) gives, Sabrina gives her name to the river just as Cyrene had to the city. Pindar's Cyrene starts out as a model for Milton's Lady; she becomes ultimately a model also for Milton's Sabrina, and so reinforces the link between Lady and Sabrina. The potentially "tragic" story of a destroyed Daphne—Cyrene's double—turns into the "happy story" of a transformed nymph, a city goddess, and a rescued lady. The ode reverses the mythic pattern of the male offering violence to the female, giving the female the victory over the male. In a similar way in the mask the Lady, in resisting a

13. Pindar often uses local dynastic myths when he wishes to honor athletes, aristocrats, and rulers connected with a favored city. Other odes also refer to gods wooing nymphs and so establishing cities. Pindar tells how Zeus wooed both the sister nymphs—Thebe and Aegina—who became the city protectors for the respective cities that took their names.

14. The Severn does not actually flow through Ludlow itself, as does one of its tributaries, the Teme.

powerful god figure, also reverses this mythic pattern, acting the part of a female Odysseus outwitting a male Circe.[15]

But there is more to Cyrene's role as city goddess. As a goddess, whose rites are closely connected to those of Artemis, her cult in Cyrene involved, as did Artemis's, women at puberty, at marriage, at motherhood—during periods of transit from one aspect of womanhood to another, when they need the protection of Artemis and an associate cult nymph. The myth of *Pythian 9* specifically relates to one of these rites of passage—when Cyrene moves from virgin to consort. Pindar was writing the ode to honor the victory in the footrace of the young athlete, Telesicrates of Cyrene. In the ode *marriage*—illustrated specifically with the account of Cyrene's marriage to Apollo—is a symbolic touchstone, a metaphor that designates the individual's arriving at a crucial point in life. Cyrene's marriage and the athlete's victory both celebrate a transitional point. Milton's Lady also, like Cyrene or the athlete, has arrived at a transitional moment in her life, leaving girlhood and approaching young womanhood. She is at the point when she will soon move from her role as daughter and sister to a role as wife and ultimately mother. Like girls in antiquity, her devotion to Artemis and to virginity is perfectly appropriate to her stage of life. The *same goddess*—Artemis-Diana—would continue, however, to be an object of devotion as she becomes wife and mother. The critics who makes Milton's Diana only the goddess of virginity ignore the fact that in antiquity Diana was a cult figure. Artemis-Diana was venerated not only by virgins, but also by women at childbirth. Moreover, at other stages in life, girls and women underwent rites at the temples of Artemis or Cyrene, receiving ritual purification from the goddess or from her nymph Cyrene. What the Lady is experiencing in the mask is a similar rite of purification and passage. Sabrina, who performs a rite of purification and who assists the Lady to complete successfully her transitional passage is, like the place nymph Cyrene, intimately related to the goddess Artemis-Diana.

Some critics have connected the rite Sabrina performs with Christian baptism whereby the "grace" of Christ releases the sinner from original sin.[16] But the Lady in this case is not bound by sin: she has been im-mobilized by Comus's wand, by the evil Bacchic thyrsus, and bound to a "marble venom'd seat / Smeared with gums of glutenous heat" (916–17). Like Daphne, imprisoned within the tree, she is unable to move or free herself. Comus's comparison is apt. Releasing the lady involves restoring

---

15. Charles Segal recognizes, interestingly enough, in the account of Cyrene's and Daphne's resistance to Apollo a variant of the Circe myth where Odysseus overcomes Circe through the use of moly (169).

16. See A. S. P. Woodhouse, "*Comus* Once More," in *UTQ* 19.

her mobility as well as dissolving the gums that hold her to the chair. It is a two-part rite that Sabrina must perform.

What Milton describes is the equivalent of the ancient rite of purification that a female goddess would perform for a female devotee.[17] Sabrina directly addresses the Lady: "Brightest Lady look on me." Although bound and immobile and silent, the Lady can and must respond to Sabrina through her eyes. Like a devotee she must give her consent, must participate in the lustral rite Sabrina performs by sprinkling water from her "fountain pure": first on the Lady's breast, then "Thrice upon thy finger's tip, / Thrice upon thy rubied lip" (914–15). Sabrina repeats the classically correct *thrice* ("ter") that Vergil's Cyrene used in the *Georgics* (4.384–85) when she and her sisters released Aristaeus from the spell cast on him. It is not insignificant that Milton twice in the *Mask* describes a similar rite of purification. The rite Cyrene's nymphs perform resembles both the lustral rite that Nereus's daughters perform for Sabrina—bathing her in "nectar'd lavers strew'd with Asphodel" (838)—and the rite Sabrina herself performs for the Lady.[18] Not Nereus, but his daughters, goddesses of the water—female deities—revive the afflicted female. Not the Attendant Spirit, but Sabrina releases the Lady from Comus's numbing spell.

Sabrina is a divinity who heals. The Attendant Spirit tells us she can "unlock / The clasping charm, and thaw the numbing spell" (852–53); she helps "all urchin blasts . . ." and with her "precious vial'd liquors heals" (845–47). Heal is a crucial word. The Apollonian Attendant Spirit had employed the healing herb haemony to rout Comus, but a more efficacious healer must release the Lady from the chair. This requires the second part of the rite. After sprinkling the water, Sabrina must touch the seat with her moist and cold palms in order to dissolve the "gums of glutenous heat" (917) that bind the Lady to the chair. It is not the lustral water with which she has purified the Lady, but the actual touch of her chaste divinity that breaks the spell—breaks the hold of the "venom'd seat."

17. See for example, Gyraldus, *De deis gentium* (1560), 365; and Comes, *Mythologiae*, 176; for description of Diana as the "releasing" goddess—the one who loosens (λυοῦσα) the ties. In the temple of Cyrene in the ancient city, the priestess of the nymph or of the goddess Artemis would have performed rites of passage and purification for the young women who came to the temple. Such rites were described in the myth books. When a woman becomes pregnant, the priestess of Diana loosens or releases her waistband or zone; when a woman delivers a child, Diana delivers her in her aspect as Lucina or Eilytheria. Diana is also the nurse for children and young people. (See Comes [1581], 176–77; Gyraldus [1560], 352). Thus it is perfectly appropriate for Sabrina (like the priestess or nymph) to come to the aid of the brothers and to help release the sister.

18. There are multiple influences involved here. Vergil's purification rites resemble those that Thetis's nymphs in the *Iliad* performed for the dead Patroclus or Aphrodite for Hector. In turn, Spenser in *The Faerie Queene* used the Cyrene passages for his account of Nereus's saving of Florimell and his nymph mother's reviving of Marinell.

No crux in the mask has provoked wider comment than the "gums of glutenous heat." Some critics suggest these gums are a sticky by-product of Comus's lust (semen); others that they are the secret sign of the Lady's own response to that lust; for still others they are merely birdlime.[19] The word *glutin* occurs in a contemporary Latin poem by the seventeenth-century Scottish poet John Leech. Describing an erotic fancy or dream, he uses the word *glutin* to refer to a kind of venereal glue (the "glutin of Dione") that holds fixed those warming to desire: "Tunc glutino Diones / Simul haesimus calentes."[20] Leech is probably speaking metaphorically when he refers to the glue of Dione, Venus's mother, but his description and his use of the words "glutin" and "calentes" has some implication for Milton's "glutenous heat." Erotic desire binds the lustful in Leech's poem; the gums produced by Comus's lustful desire for the Lady (metaphorically and actually) bind her, even though she has not responded to his erotic importuning. Milton has added one more word to this description that is crucial to our interpretation: the gums smeared on the seat are not only hot and sticky but also "venom'd." Comus has poisoned the marble chair. "Venomed," "envenomed," "venom" are words that Milton consistently connects with drugs or poisons such as a serpent or toad produces. In *Paradise Lost* he describes Hercules' robe as "envenom'd" by the Centaur's poisonous blood; he refers also to the venom that Satan the toad inspires and, in *Arcades*, to the venom of the serpent's bite.[21] In an early citation in the O.E.D., venom is connected with Circe's drugs, with poisonous herbs. Comus has not been able to make the Lady taste the Circean cup, to consent to his lust, but he has envenomed her chair with glutenous gums of Circean poison that fix her like the venom of the serpent. These toxic gums continue to immobilize the victim even after the serpent has fled. What Sabrina must do then is

19. See J. W. Flosdorf, " 'Gums of Glutinous Heat': A Query"; John Shawcross, "Two Comments"; Stanley Archer, " 'Glutinous Heat': A Note on *Comus*. 1.917"; also William Kerrigan, *The Sacred Complex*, 47–48; Margaret Hoffman Kale, "Milton's 'Gums of Glutinous Heat': A Renaissance Theory of Movement." In an unpublished paper Debora Shuger has suggested that the glutin is connected with the word for semen emitted in a wet dream and therefore implies the involuntary concupiscence that Augustine describes. I retain Milton's spelling: glutenous.

20. Leochaeus (Leech), "Somnium, ad G. Drummondum, ab Hathorneden," "Anacreontica," in *Musae Priores, sive Poematum* (1620), 2.73. The passage in question begins with a prayer to the goddess of the fountain to be gracious to the suppliant in the name of Venus. It continues with the description of the goddess embracing the suppliant, causing him to warm with desire and to be stuck or fixed by the glutin of Dione, and to respond with a kiss. The line is clearly erotic: "Tunc glutino Diones / Simul haesimus calentes" (Then at the same time warming, we stick with the glue of Dione).

21. See "As when *Alcides* from *Oechalia* Crown'd / With conquest, felt th' envenom'd robe" (*Paradise Lost* 2.542–43). Also see "Or if, inspiring venom, he might taint / Th' animal spirits that from pure blood arise" (*Paradise Lost* 4.804–5): "hurtful Worm with canker'd venom bites" (*Arcades* 53).

not only to purify, but also to detoxify. As a divinity who heals, Sabrina must touch that seat with her moist cooling hands to neutralize the Circean poison and to decontaminate the chair in order that the Lady may rise.

However important Sabrina's role, she is only one of the two "deities" who effect the Lady's salvation. If Sabrina functions in the *Mask* as a deity closely allied to Artemis, the Attendant Spirit is a deity closely linked to her brother, Phoebus Apollo. He descends from the "starry threshold of *Jove's* Court"; he brings with him the Apollonian presence of music.[22] He is the main singer throughout the mask, fittingly so since his part was performed by the Egerton children's own music master, Harry Lawes, whom Milton himself (in a commendatory sonnet) dubbed the "priest of Phoebus' Choir." The Attendant Spirit functions in no lesser a role than as stand-in for his patron god. Like Phoebus he even takes on the weeds and pipes of a shepherd, disguising himself, even as Apollo had when he served Admetus. As a shepherd he contrasts with the other disguised shepherd, Comus, who plays the part of a baleful Bacchus, associating with shades and dark and fleeing from the "tell-tale Sun" (141), Apollo's symbol. As Apollo the healer, the Attendant Spirit uses his saving herb haemony; as sun god, he defends the Lady and her sun-clad power of chastity and restores her with the renewed day to her parents. Working in tandem with Sabrina, he is like a brother who summons his sister goddess. The twin children of Latona— Apollo and Artemis—are present symbolically in this mask in the persons of the two saving "deities"—the Attendant Spirit and Sabrina—male and female working together.

"SONGS OF SIRENS SWEET"

Two of the immortals that the Attendant Spirit alludes to in his invocation of Sabrina are Sirens, one of them Ligea, the other Parthenope, the protectress of the city Naples, hence a place deity like Sabrina and Cyrene. Allusion to the Sirens once more supports the role of music in the mask, for the Sirens are singers. But when Milton connects his Sabrina with the Sirens and their sweet songs, he is alluding not just to Parthenope and Ligea and the nymphs of water, but also to another kind of Siren, whose music is perhaps more attuned to the sphere-born melodies of the Attendant Spirit. For Milton there are two kinds of Sirens—the water nymphs who enchant with their song and the heavenly Sirens who create the music of the spheres.[23] The first

---

22. See Louis Martz's comments on the importance of music in the mask: *Poet of Exile*, 21–24.

23. Giraldi alludes to several kinds of Sirens. He first cites Plato's Sirens of the spheres, noting that they are also described by Macrobius and Proclus. He later describes the Siren

were the daughters of the Greek river god Acheloos and usually three in number, often identified as the goddesses who enticed Odysseus and other voyagers.[24] The second are the celestial beings (described by Plato) who govern the spheres of heaven and were often in the Renaissance regarded as synonymous with the Muses.

Some critics have been puzzled by the Attendant Spirit's praise of the Sirens' songs in his invocation, for in the Renaissance the Sirens were usually thought of not merely as water nymphs but as singers who lure mariners to their doom.[25] Why should the Attendant Spirit invoke Sabrina in the name of such seductive goddesses?[26] It is clear, moreover, that when Comus alludes to the Sirens earlier in the *Mask*, he is describing dangerous alluring singers.

---

daughters of the river god Acheloos, citing several possible Muse mothers (Terpsichore, Melpomene, or Calliope). He does not connect the two types. (See Gyraldus [1560], 169, 174). Others, following Plato, cite the heavenly Sirens in connection with Necessity (see Cartari [1587], 301).

24. See, for example, Vincenzo Cartari's description of the water Sirens: *Le Imagine de i Dei de gli Antichi* (1587), 196–99. Cartari numbers the Sirens at three, daughters of Acheloos and Calliope, and names them Ligea, Leucosia, and Parthenope. He connects them with the Sirens who lured Odysseus and cites their appearances in Homer, Vergil, Xenophon, Pliny, and Aristotle. Also see bk. 7, chap. 13 of Comes, *Mythologiae* (1581), 495–501; Baudoin, *Mythologie* (1627), 768–78.

25. See Janet E. Halley, "Female Autonomy in Milton's Sexual Poetics," in *Milton and the Idea of Woman*, 236–40. Halley finds both the watery Sirens and the Platonic Sirens dangerous seductive figures. Another critic who raises questions about the Sirens of the Attendant Spirit's invocation is Thomas O. Calhoun, who views Parthenope and Ligea negatively, describing Parthenope as the erotically frustrated Siren and Ligea as introverted and narcissistic (177). See "On John Milton's Mask at Ludlow," in *MS* 6.

26. Although the Sirens, as Homer describes them in the *Odyssey*, try to allure Odysseus and his sailors and shipwreck them, their seduction was not specifically sexual. They promise Odysseus knowledge. The Renaissance, however, understood them as sexually alluring singers. See, for example, the English version of Cartari, *The Fountaine of Ancient Fiction,* translated by Richard Linche: "But howsoeuer the Poets varie in their opinions, they generally vnderstand by those Syrens the delicate purenesse of beautie, wantonnesse, pleasure, & enticing allurements to the daliancie of amorous embracements. And it is read, that they sing so melodiously, and with such a sence-besotting sweetnesse, that the suspectlesly inchaunted sea-trauellers are infinitely beguiled and lulled asleepe with the harmony and pleasing blandishment thereof." Cartari (in Linche's version) reports that the Sirens dance in a green meadow strewn with the bones and carcasses of dead men, "vnclouding thereby the assurednesse of ruine, decay, and perishment to those that so voluptuously addict themselues to the vnbridled affection of such lasciuious and soule-hazarding concupiscence" (101). Giraldi suggests that the Sirens are "meretrices" (prostitutes) who metaphorically lead men to shipwreck (*De Deis Gentium* [1560], 174). In a letter to Richard Jones (dated 1657), commending him for having avoided the temptations of Paris, Milton takes a similar view of the Sirens: "as long as you stay there you will be in safe harbor; elsewhere you would have to beware the Syrtes and Scopulos, and the songs of the Sirens" (*Complete Prose Works of John Milton*, 7:503). On the Sirens as sexually seductive, also see Starnes and Talbert, *Classical Myth*, 109–10.

> I have oft heard
> My Mother *Circe* with the Sirens three,
> Amid'st the flowry-kirtl'd *Naiades,*
> Culling their Potent herbs, and baleful drugs,
> Who as they sung, would take the prison'd soul,
> And lap it in *Elysium* . . . (252–57)

Comus associates these wily enchantresses with his mother Circe and describes how their songs (though sweet) lull the sense in slumber and "in sweet madness" rob it of itself (260–61). Although Comus does not specifically say so, the temptation of the Sirens (as the Renaissance understood it) is sexual. Their introduction at this point in the *Mask* reminds us of the dangerous and deceptive sexuality that Milton connects with Circe, Bacchus, and Comus himself. We remember that it was from this kind of allurement that the young Milton at the end of "Elegia 1" was trying to escape, when, having first heard the "siren" voice of sexual love, he flew from London and from the deceptive halls of Circe. We also remember that in sonnet 4 the young sonneteer says that he has been enthralled by the Siren-like song and the blazing eyes of an Italian beauty.[27] But surely the Attendant Spirit would not invoke Sabrina to free the Lady from Comus's sexual enthrallment by naming Sirens who sexually allure. Whether it is the songs of Sirens that are "sweet" or the singers themselves, nothing in the invocation specifically threatens or misleads.[28] The "fair" Ligea of the golden comb sits on diamond rocks, "sleeking her soft alluring locks," offering beauty and sexual charm, but beckoning no mariners to their doom. And the dead Parthenope, invoked by her "dear" tomb, is a protective, not a destructive deity. Could it be that Milton here makes these watery sisters share the function of the other Sirens—the heavenly sisters that he refers to so often in the course of his poetry and prose?[29]

27. The young Milton was susceptible to seductions of the eye and ear. Having been allured in "Elegia 1" by the sight of a lovely chorus of young maidens when he was wandering in the fields outside of London, he longs to leave London and return to the safe confines of Cambridge, while Cupid still grants him leave. In the Italian poems he fears the Circean bondage of ear as well as the seduction of the eye.

28. Cartari notes that Xenophon differs from other writers in describing the Sirens as pleasing and virtuous, insisting that they sing only true praises and exalt virtue (Cartari [1571], 247).

29. There is actually a third kind of Siren—a winged one. Cartari and Baudoin refer to this type, basing their citations on Ovid, *Metamorphoses* 5.552–63. Like the water Sirens, they are also the daughters of Acheloos. Erstwhile companions of Proserpina, they prayed to become part bird so that they could join Ceres in her search for her lost daughter. And like the water Sirens, the bird Sirens, too, are represented in Renaissance art. Cartari actually pictures the bird Sirens and the water Sirens together in a single illustration. Three bird Sirens are on land, surrounded by the bones of their victims; the

From his earliest works Milton was fascinated with the transforming, the protective, and the compelling powers of music. When he describes the music of the spheres in Prolusion 2, he remarks how the honey-sweet songs of the heavenly Sirens hold men and gods in admiration ("quae mellitissimo cantu Deos hominesque mirabundos capiant").[30] The songs of the heavenly Sirens, like those of the watery sisters, are honey-sweet and compelling, holding the senses rapt, yet not in a dangerous way, for the heavenly Sirens lead human beings to the stars and not to shipwreck on the rocks. In this prolusion (and elsewhere) Milton closely connects the heavenly Sirens with the Muses, who, as they dance night and day about the altar of Jove, fill the heavens with song. In a tradition that extends back to Macrobius, the Muses and the celestial Sirens were thought of as the same divinities.[31]

The ode, "At a Solemn Music," appears to conflate the heavenly Sirens with the Muses. Milton invokes Voice and Verse, as a "Blest pair of *Sirens* . . . Sphere-born harmonious Sisters" (1–2), whose song recreates on earth the divine sound that Plato's celestial Sirens originally made, the so-called music of the spheres that sin-born creatures may no longer hear. These two Siren sisters function to link heaven and earth in a melodic continuum and also to prompt earth to answer heaven once more (as it had before) with "melodious noise." Their role goes significantly beyond that which Plato originally assigned to the celestial Sirens, who are essentially cosmological beings, whose music is a product of their governance of the orbits of heaven. Joining their voices in harmony with the Fates, they control the fixed laws of eternity. Although their music is sometimes heard on earth,

---

water Sirens swim in the water, two of them playing on musical instruments, the third singing. (Cartari [1571], 245). Also see the illustration of bird Sirens playing instruments in Comes, *Mythologiae* (1616), 395. Although Milton undoubtedly knew Ovid's account, he does not allude to the bird Sirens or depict his Sirens with wings. It is possible that these bird Sirens had protective functions in antiquity; they are depicted with Orpheus as protectresses of tombs. A sculpture group, now at the J. Paul Getty museum, shows the bird Sirens with Orpheus. Baudoin associates them not only with Ceres but also with Orpheus, who conquered them with his lute (*Mythologie* [1627], 770–71). Cartari cites Servius as well as Ovid on the bird Sirens.

30. In Prolusion 2 Milton, alluding to his source in Plato, notes that this music (now unheard by mortals) was heard by Pythagoras, who first described it. See the myth (the dream of Er) that concludes the *Republic* (10.617 B and C). Plato describes the vision of the heavens Er sees. Necessity holds a spindle from which eight concentric circles emerge, turning; on the rim of each circle there is a Siren who is borne around as the sphere turns, and who emits a single sound, one tone. The eight tones combined make one harmony, which Pythagorean philosophy terms the music of the spheres. The Fates also sing, adding their voices to the harmony of the Sirens (ὑμεῖν πρὸς τὴν τῶν Σειρήνων ἁρμονίαν, 617 c. 3–4).

31. Gafori conflates the Platonic Sirens with the Muses, as his illustration of the heavenly spheres illustrates. Franchinus Gafurius, *Theorica Musice*, G1.

they neither sing to or for human beings.[32] In contrast, Milton's blest pair of Sirens exist specifically to bring these songs down to earth and inspire human beings to lift their own voices, to make their own music rise again to heaven. Hence, they are more like Muses, indeed Christianized Muses, who are "pledges of Heav'n's joy," that is, who inspire human beings to heal the breach that sin made, to heal it with vocal music that ascends where the soul would follow.

In *Arcades* the Genius of the Wood—a daemon very like the Attendant Thyrsis of the Ludlow *Mask*—listens to the celestial Sirens and puts their heavenly music also to earthly use. In this mask Milton describes the Sirens sitting upon the nine enfolded spheres, having raised Plato's eight spheres to nine and his Sirens to a Muse-like nine. Once more the music they make ravishes the senses, for it is heard "in deep of night when drowsiness / Hath lockt up mortal sense" (61–62). John Carey has noted that Milton diverges from his Platonic source in making the Sirens sing to, rather than with the Fates, lulling them and thereby binding and unbinding the forces of necessity.[33] "Such sweet compulsion doth in music lie" (68), remarks the Genius of the Wood. This compulsion keeps unsteady nature steady; hence rapture is innocent, even beneficent. The Sirens' effect on human beings also causes rapture, but no human being can hear their music, can experience the rapture, "with gross unpurged ear" (72–73). One must metaphorically remove the human wax to listen to these Sirens. Such heavenly music also keeps earthly nature in balance, assisting the Genius of the Wood to perform offices of nurture in Jove's wood. Such music would be worthiest, he also implies, to praise the Countess of Derby. However transcendent in the heavenly spheres, heard music on earth can be put to earthly uses.

Both celestial and water Sirens have their roles in the *Mask*. The first singer to be connected to both is not Sabrina, however, but the Lady. When Comus first hears the Lady's song to Echo, it wakes in him the

32. The Platonic Sirens are essentially cosmological beings whose music is instinctive with the movement and the working of the heavens. The Muses, however, are singers, who have two principal functions: first to make song and dance for the festivals of the gods in cooperation with their brother Apollo and second to be the patrons of poetry and music, hence inspire poets and musicians to compose for earthly occasions. Thus while human beings may hear the music the celestial Sirens make, these Sirens in no sense perform for an audience either earthly or heavenly. The third kind of Siren—the watery singer—makes music that is also sweet and compelling, but may be dangerous to hear.

33. John Carey noted that Milton makes the Sirens lull the daughters of Necessity—the Fates. By lulling them, the Sirens' music "releases the actual from transcendental imperatives; by keeping Nature to her law, it asserts transcendental imperatives again." Thus, comments Carey, "music both unbinds, and binds" (See "Milton's Harmonious Sisters," in *The Well Enchanting Skill,* 257).

memory of the Sirens who sang with Circe. Yet even as he recalls their sweet seductive music and its power to lull the sense, he realizes that this song is different: it breathes "Divine enchanting ravishment" (245) and wakes the soul to bliss. This son of Circe is hearing something very like the music of the spheres, sung by an earthly Siren—the Lady—who, like the sphere-born twins of "At a Solemn Music," knows how to move the vocal air with rapture. Although she and her song are innocent (she is only calling for aid), the effect is not. The rapture she causes may be heavenly, but it is not without sexual implications, for Comus is aroused and enticed by the Lady's singing. She inadvertently enthralls Comus the enchanter. Milton has subtly complicated the matter by making the Lady resemble both the celestial and the water Sirens. Like the Italian beauty he praises in sonnet 4, the Lady has the power to draw down the laboring moon with her singing. Like her, too, she captures her admirer with such blazing beauty that it is vain to seal up the ears with wax. Milton makes plain here how powerful is the sexual allure of women's singing, even when they sound like the celestial Sirens.[34]

But it is not just the Lady who is Siren-like in her singing, but also Echo, the nymph she invokes with her song. At the beginning of the song, the Lady describes Echo as a nymph of stream and wood—the "sweetest Nymph that liv'st unseen / Within thy airy shell / By slow *Meander's* margent green" (230–32). Echo seems here a pastoral sister to Sabrina, whom Milton will later describe as the gentle nymph who "with moist curb sways the smooth Severn stream" (824–25). The connection of the two is more than incidental. By the end of the Lady's song the pastoral Echo has ascended from earth to the spheres and become a "Sweet Queen of Parley, Daughter of the Sphere" (241). Drawing perhaps on a hint from the mythographers, Milton transforms the pastoral nymph who loved Narcissus into a kind of heavenly Siren.[35]

In translating Echo to the spheres, Milton seems to be exploiting a Platonizing agenda. Although critics have often been content to restrict Milton's Platonism to the elder brother and his strictures to his younger sibling, the Lady too is an excellent Platonist. She understands the relationship between earthly forms and heavenly ideas both in her song of Echo and later in her

34. Perhaps Milton was recalling Ovid's advice to ladies to learn to sing and to imitate the Sirens in order to enthrall their lovers (*Ars Amatoria [The Art of Love]*, 3.311–20).

35. See Starnes and Talbert, *Classical Myth*. They believe that Milton takes his characterization of Echo as the "queen of the sphere" from Carolus Stephanus's dictionary where she is described in such a fashion (249). Cartari (1571) also notes that Macrobius connects Echo with the harmony of the spheres (136).

rejection of Comus's coarse earthly materialism.[36] Further, by transforming the pastoral Echo into a sphere-born Siren, the Lady's song prepares us for Sabrina's transformation from nymph to water deity to savior. "Sweet" is the key word that links the charming song of the water Sirens who "in sweet madness" rob the sense with the song of "Sweet Echo, sweetest Nymph," that comes "sweetly" to ravish Comus. Even as the Lady's song invokes Echo's aid, so the Attendant Spirit's song invokes another gentle nymph, invoking her aid by "Songs of Sirens sweet," the counterparts to the sweet song that Comus heard the Lady singing. Echo does not reply, but Sabrina responds to the Attendant Spirit's song with her own song announcing her presence: "By the rushy-fringed bank . . . Gentle swain at thy request / I am here" (890, 900–901). She comes as an enchantress whose song neither deceives nor destroys, but, like her touch, has the power to create and to break spells. Nymph, Naiad, Siren, all in one, Sabrina is the ultimate metamorphosis of the water Siren, the ultimate manifestation of the heavenly Siren—a spirit who saves.

Persistently throughout the mask Milton moves (Platonically) from heaven to earth and back again to heaven.[37] As Voice and Verse, the sphere-born goddesses, link heaven and earth in "At a Solemn Music," so Echo, the pastoral "siren," links the Lady to the spheres above. Finally, Sabrina, a nymph, like Echo, who has both a pastoral "earthly" (or, if you will, "watery") aspect and a heavenly one, will finally rescue the Lady, turning her eyes and thoughts once more to the spheres.

"How charming is divine Philosophy!" (476), exclaims the Second Brother, after his elder sibling has explained how the soul, released from earthly pollution, may converse with heavenly habitants and become immortal. Not only is philosophy "charming" but also musical, he continues, as is Apollo's lute—"a perpetual feast of nectar'd sweets" (479). With the songs of the seductive Sirens, the soul could be imprisoned as though with those "Potent herbs and baleful drugs" that Circe and the water Sirens gathered as they sang. But with the song of Sabrina, the "charmed band" can be undone and the true virgin soul released from the "unblest enchanter vile" (904, 907). Like divine Philosophy, music can charm and release from charms. Milton answers the charms of the first kind of Sirens with the more potent charms of an earthly-heavenly Siren-singer.

---

36. When the Lady rejects Comus and his coarse sensual love, she does so not only by appealing to a Platonic doctrine of "Sun-clad" chastity, but also to power that the rapt spirit has to move dumb things to sympathize by the flame of sacred vehemence, that is to translate them to the skies.

37. For commentary on the Platonism of *A Mask,* see Sears Jayne, "The Subject of Milton's Ludlow *Mask,*" in *PMLA* 74. Jayne insists that the Platonism of the *Mask* is the Christian Neoplatonism of Ficino.

PARTHENOPE: NAIAD OF THE SHORE

Milton rehabilitates the water Sirens, in a sense, when he links them with his good goddess Sabrina and makes them participate with her in the breaking of Comus's charms. But long before Milton invoked Parthenope and Ligea as part of Sabrina's company, Neapolitan writers had rehabilitated the reputation of the Siren Parthenope and her Siren sisters. From antiquity Parthenope had been the patron goddess of Naples. Her dead body, reputedly, was found on the shore when the Greek founders established the city, naming it for the nymph, building a tomb for her and instituting games in her honor. Parthenope became the symbol as well as the name for Naples.[38]

Milton was well aware of the status of Parthenope as Naples's own goddess when he wrote a set of epigrams in 1638 or 1639 to the Neapolitan singer Leonora Baroni whom he heard sing in Rome. He not only compared her to the Siren Parthenope, but also to the Muses and to other heavenly singers, demonstrating once more that he had no difficulty conflating the different types of Siren-singers.[39] In one epigram he calls the Neapolitan singer a revived Parthenope, who did not die but yet lives, holding men and gods spellbound by her songs—just as the heavenly Sirens are reputed to do ("Ad Eandem").[40] In another, the "watery siren" Leonora becomes a heavenly angel whose songs speak of God ("Ad Leonoram Romae Canentem"); and in a third, she is a Muse who possesses a Pierian voice ("Ad Eandem"). If Milton can make the "angelic" Muse-like Leonora a good Siren, a living Parthenope, who holds men enchanted with her song, he can also make Parthenope and Ligea into fitting attendants for his good goddess Sabrina. When Sabrina rises with her nymphs from the Severn and sings, she too, like the Neapolitan Siren Leonora Baroni, holds her audience spellbound.

Sabrina's connection with Parthenope extends further, however, than her identity as a Siren and her prowess as a singer. Parthenope—like

38. See Comes (1581), who cites Strabo's account of Parthenope (496).

39. Milton may have been influenced in these epigrams by a celebrated neo-Latin poem of Balthazar Castiglione to Elisabella Gonzaga: "De Elisabella Gonzaga Canente" (*Carmina Quinque Illustrium Poetarum,* 33v-34v). Castiglione compares Elisabella's song to that of the Sirens and other deities of the Ocean. The fish-tailed Siren, like the bird Siren, is a popular figure in Renaissance art, and like her often appears to have protective qualities. See, for example, the fish-tailed goddess in the mosaic floor of the cathedral at Otranto.

40. See Milton, *Complete Poems and Major Prose* (ed. Hughes), 130–31. Also see Diane Kelsey McColley, "Tongues of Men and Angels: *Ad Leonoram Romae Canentem*," in *Urbane Milton.* McColley asserts that Leonora is a "Platonic Siren, not a Homeric one luring men to wreck" (143).

Sabrina and Cyrene—is both a protectress of young women and a goddess of place, a dynastic nymph, whose myth is closely connected with the city's founding. To employ a local nymph as a city emblem is an ancient classicizing device that Neapolitan poets readily adapt when they celebrate the city and its people. Renaissance Naples was attempting to recover its Greek and Latin past. By invoking Parthenope, by employing her as a character in eclogue, in mask, in wedding song, Neapolitan poets were offering a compliment to Naples's dynastic past and were following the tactics of classical poets such as Statius, Vergil, and Pindar. They were also furnishing Milton with an example of how a local dynastic nymph could be employed to compliment a noble family.

Just as Pindar had given the nymph Cyrene a prominent place in an epinician ode in order to compliment Arcesilas of Cyrene, so the ancient Neapolitan poet Statius had employed Parthenope in an occasional poem of a different sort. In a celebratory song for the wedding of the Roman nobleman, Lucius Arruntius Stella, and the Neapolitan Lady Violentilla, he alludes to the bride's Neapolitan heritage, making Parthenope her foster mother.

> at te nascentem gremio mea prima recepit
> Parthenope, dulcisque solo tu gloria nostro
> reptasti.[41]

> But at your birth my Parthenope first
> received you in her bosom, and you in our land
> alone were its sweet glory.

In this way Parthenope becomes not just a protectress of the city, but a nurturer of the city's marriageable young women. Further, Statius heightens the wedding motif by alluding to the mythic marriage of Parthenope, the local place nymph, to Sebethos, the local river god. The river Sebethos swells with pride in honor both of Parthenope and the bride. Statius's Parthenope and Sebethos stand behind the Elizabethan nymphs and river gods in the topological weddings of Spenser and Drayton, the very poets who gave Milton his nymph Sabrina.

Later Neapolitan poets carried on the tradition. Parthenope appears in Sannazaro's Latin and his Italian poetry, functioning sometimes as a city deity, sometimes as a nature deity, and still other times as a protectress of young women.[42] In the piscatorial eclogue that he composed for Ferdinand

---

41. Statius, "Silvae," 1.1.2.260.

42. Wilfred P. Mustard, *The Piscatory Eclogues of Jacopo Sannazaro;* also see Jacopo Sannazaro, *Arcadia & Piscatorial Eclogues.* For commentary on Sannazaro's pastorals, see William J. Kennedy, *Sannazaro and the Use of Pastoral.*

of Aragon, the exiled son of King Frederick, Sannazaro advances the golden-haired Siren in her ancient tomb as a nationalistic symbol for the city. Expressing, as Milton would in "Mansus" and "Epitaphium Damonis," his ambitions as a poet, he promises to sing (under Parthenope's auspices) both of Naples's past and future—of the scepters restored to her city and kings broken under Frederick's lance. This appeal to Parthenope is in fact a call for political action; Sannazaro is urging Ferdinand to free himself from captivity in Spain, to return to Naples, and to reclaim his right.[43] Parthenope represents here not only the city's past but a hope for its future. Like Parthenope, the nymph Sabrina can also be a political symbol, standing, as we shall see, for the ancient British past, for the region about Ludlow, and for the hopes and aspirations of the ruling family, the Egertons.

Sannazaro is not content to make Parthenope merely a convenient dynastic symbol for Naples's kings. She is related to the common people as well and is a nature deity revered by the community of fishermen, who in the fourth eclogue invoke her with the Nereids and the other Sirens as a protective deity of water. Milton could have limited Sabrina's role in the *Mask* to her rescue of the noble daughter of the Egertons. But he too tells us that this place nymph is a deity loved by the shepherds around Ludlow: she often visits their herds and they carol her goodness "loud in rustic lays, / And throw sweet garland wreaths into her stream" (849–50). But most important, Sannazaro's Parthenope plays a personal role in eclogue 1 as the drowned maiden, the dead Siren who not only became an emblem for Naples, but also became a protectress of her young women.

Sannazaro's eclogue 1, the dirge for Phyllis, is one of the pastoral poems that critics cite as a model for Milton's "Lycidas." In it Lycidas and Mycon lament the death of Lycidas's beloved Phyllis; Lycidas sings a funeral song, in which he complains, as does Milton's shepherd-swain, of the harsh fate that took away the loved one. He invokes the presence of the Nereids, the sea deities, and Parthenope to lament for her, and at the conclusion of his song, he consigns Phyllis to the protection of Parthenope, residing in a double tomb with the Siren, both of them honored by Parthenope's beloved, the river Sebethos. The inscription that Sannazaro composes for Phyllis echoes Statius's for Violentilla. Just as Statius placed Violentilla at her birth in the bosom of the Siren, Sannazaro places Phyllis at her death in Parthenope's bosom: "In Gremio Phyllis Recubat Sirenis Amata / Consurgis Gemino Felix Sebethe Sepulcro" (104–5) (Beloved Phyllis lies in the bosom of the Siren / You surge happily about the twin sepulcher, Sebethos). Hence, the dead Phyllis becomes, as it were, another place deity, to be enrolled

---

43. See Kennedy, *Sannazaro,* 170–71.

with Parthenope and with Milton's Sabrina, as an unfortunate maiden, transformed to the protector of her native place.

Giovanni Pontano, Sannazaro's contemporary and friend, links Parthenope with marriage rather than dirge, giving her a prominent place in his pastoral mask *Lepidina* and in the wedding songs that he composed for his daughters.[44] The pastoral mask, like Milton's own mask, is celebratory, composed to honor Naples's nobility and her citizens on the occasion of the expansion of Neapolitan water works in the 1480s.[45] Like most masks, its plot is minimal. It recounts from the vantage of two young peasants—Macron and his wife Lepidina, pregnant with their first child—the festal processions through the streets of Naples celebrating the metaphorical wedding of the Siren Parthenope and the river god Sebethos.[46] Lepidina, the young bride who watches the "wedding" pageant, is in fact a double for Parthenope, identifying with her as bride and seeing in the city's future her own future prosperity. The two leading females of Pontano's mask are as closely linked to one other as Milton's virgin nymph is to his virgin Lady. The destiny of Naples joins them, just as the future of Ludlow joins Sabrina and the Lady.

Pontano's *Lepidina* makes the mythic wedding of the local nymph and her river into a personal as well as a civic occasion. Key to the celebration is not just Parthenope the bride (whom Triton introduces in the third pompa) but also Antiniana, the daughter of Nesis and Jove, patron nymph of Pontano's own villa, who sings the wedding song in the seventh and final pompa. She is the very nymph that Pontano chose to sing the wedding carmina for the marriages of his daughters Aurelia and Eugenia (*De Amore Coniugale* 3.3,4).[47] The concluding song of a conventional wedding mask blesses the bride and groom and promises a fruitful union. Adapting this

---

44. *Lepidina cuius Pompae Septem,* in Ioannes Iovianius Pontanus, *Carmina* (1948), 3–33. Pontano's book of lyrics is called *Parthenopeus,* a title he assumes for himself as the spokesman for Parthenope or Naples. Among the carmina is a celebration of Sebethos's conversion into a river and his wedding to Parthenope (119–21).

45. See Carol Kidwell, *Pontano,* 256–68.

46. The pompae of Pontano's *Lepidina* will inevitably remind English readers of the wedding of the Thames and the Medway in *The Faerie Queene* 4, created by Spenser to celebrate Florimell's and Marinell's spousals, or of the topological pastoral of Drayton's *Poly-Olbion,* especially the passage that celebrates the marriage of the Isis and the Cherwell. Yet, of course, Pontano's topological wedding mask antedates both of these and must surely have been one of the models for both Spenser and Drayton and later for Milton, since its topological strategies are so like those the English poets employ.

47. Pontano, *De Amore Coniugale* 3 in *Carmina* (1948), 176–80, 180–85. At both these weddings Antiniana, Parthenope's representative, presides. Among his poetry in honor of the nymph Antiniana are two odes in her honor (*Lyra,* 3, 4), which describe her as a water nymph sprung from Jove and Nesis. In 6 Pontano invokes her specifically to sing the praises of the city Naples. She also appears as the singer of a city-ode in celebration of Naples.

convention, Pontano confers a blessing on the city, predicting that heroes will spring from this union who will tame bulls, plant and harvest crops, raise vines, hunt and fish, and lay down laws. Like Pindar in *Pythian 9*, Pontano narrates the wedding of a nymph to a god to promise prosperity to a city.

The use of Parthenope in Pontano's mask can tell us a little about Milton's purposes in introducing Sabrina at the critical juncture of his own mask. For the Lady, Sabrina is an Artemis-like savior, but for Ludlow, Ludlow's people, and its ruling aristocratic family, she is a place nymph who promises prosperity. Although the *Mask at Ludlow-Castle* does not celebrate a wedding—either metaphorical or actual—it does conclude with a celebration that guarantees future prosperity to city and people. With the foiled seduction, the rescue of the Lady, and her restoration with her brothers to their parents, the future of the Egertons and of Ludlow and its citizenry is secure. Moreover, as both Milton and his audience understood, the future for all the Egerton heirs—including the Lady—involved marriage.

With the Lady's rescue, the theatrical mask becomes a processional mask. The Lady rises to greet her brothers, the Attendant Spirit leads the Lady and her brothers back to Ludlow, the three children follow as though in procession, and the Attendant Spirit presents the children to their parents and departs. Much has been made of the fact that the rescued Lady does not speak. But in a processional mask the central person does not speak; the attendant person or persons speaks for her. In Pontano's "wedding" mask Parthenope appears, but other characters speak for her, describe her, and praise her virtues. With the children's rescue and return to Ludlow, the Attendant Spirit speaks for them, praising their triumph over vice and intemperance—their winning of crowns of praise. The arrival at Ludlow Castle is celebrated with mask-like pageant—pastoral and formal dance—communal celebrations like those that Pontano created for his Neapolitan mask, *Lepidina*. The Lady and her brothers are restored to the community at Ludlow, and the ensuing festivities celebrate the future of that community.

"DAUGHTER OF LOCRINE"

Family and nation work in tandem in Milton's mask. Classical myth acts, moreover, in behalf of both as an allegorizing and a historicizing medium to place the events in Ludlow in a national and an international perspective. Once more Pindar's example is important, for in his odes family and national identity are interconnected. When he chose the Cyrene myth, Pindar was not only praising Arcesilas the ruler, but also the young athlete Telesicrates as a citizen of Cyrene and a promising member of an aristocratic family. In a similar manner Milton employs the Sabrina myth to praise Lady Alice as a daughter to the Egertons and as a member of British aristocracy. But the Sabrina myth actually functions to provide a wider historical perspective. Sabrina is a historical character, an erstwhile mortal, the daughter of the British king Locrine, and so the ancestral link between the aristocrats of the past and the present.[48]

As a royal daughter, however, Sabrina had a history that can hardly be called fortunate. Milton only tells us that she threw herself into the waves, fleeing from the wrath of her "step-dame" Guendolen; he suppresses two facts: that she died with her mother, Locrine's mistress, and that she was not a legitimate offspring of Locrine.[49] Her misfortunes as a royal daughter, however, connect her with another nymph named in the Attendant Spirit's invocation: Leucothea—the Theban Ino, daughter to Cadmus. Ino-Leucothea was fleeing from the anger of her maddened husband, just as Sabrina was fleeing Guendolen, when she cast herself into the waves. Like Sabrina, she was revived and became a protective water deity, winning happiness for herself and giving aid to human beings in distress. (In the *Odyssey,* Ino-Leucothea saves Odysseus from drowning.) The likeness, however, does not end there, and here, once more, another Pindaric analogy is helpful. Pindar composed *Olympian 2* for Theron of Acragas, a Sicilian ruler who traced his forebears to Thebes. He narrates Ino-Leucothea's myth to show how unhappy circumstances may be reversed, how her Theban descendants under Theron of Acragas may enjoy the happiness that she as royal daughter did not enjoy. They, as Pindar tells us in his ode, experience good fortune and win divine favor.

Like Ino, Sabrina is closely related to a noble dynasty; like Thebes's unfortunate royal daughter, her fortunes were reversed and she now enjoys happiness as Severn's nymph, protecting the future for others. Milton twice reminds us that Sabrina is the "daughter of Locrine." Further, he connects her with British royalty that goes back to Troy by way of Brutus, Aeneas, and Anchises, reiterating twice that connection too: "*Locrine,* / That had the Scepter from his father *Brute*" (827–28); "*Locrine* / Sprung of old *Anchises* line" (922–23). Milton is eager to establish both Sabrina's link with the paternal ancestry of old Britain and her connection to the Lady, another aristocratic daughter, whose fortunes are also happily reversed.

---

48. See Dean A. Reilein, "Milton's *Comus* and Sabrina's Compliment," in *MQ* 5. Reilein sees Milton's suppression of Sabrina's past—her illegitimacy—as Milton's indirect reference to the more unpleasant aspects of the family's past. He suggests that Sabrina rises above her background, as did the Egertons.

49. For an account of Sabrina's past see Leah S. Marcus, "Justice for Margery Evans: A 'Local' Reading of *Comus,*" in *Milton and the Idea of Woman,* 80. Also see Christopher Kendrick, "Milton and Sexuality: A Symptomatic Reading of *Comus,*" 69.

Milton's *Mask* was being performed in the great hall of Ludlow Castle in honor of a dynastic occasion—the installation of the Earl of Bridgewater as President of Wales.[50] Ludlow had been the site of a royal castle and one of the major residences of the British royalty until London took over in importance in the sixteenth century. Bridgewater held Ludlow Castle by virtue of royal appointment, having been granted his charter as President of Wales by Charles I. But despite the prestige of this royal appointment and Bridgewater's close connections with Charles I, Milton never mentions Charles directly or indirectly in the *Mask at Ludlow*. In contrast, in *Coelum Britannicum,* performed, also in 1634, for Charles at Windsor, Carew includes more than a few compliments for Charles.[51] Mercury advises the high senate of the gods to reform itself on the model of Charles's court. Some critics wish to see Milton's reference to "the Imperial rule" of the "Sea-girt Isles" as a compliment to Charles. John Creaser, however, believes exactly the opposite. Far from alluding to Charles, Milton evades Charles's authority, stating that the Earl holds his charge directly from Jove himself and Jove's brother Neptune:[52]

> *Neptune,* besides the sway
> Of every salt Flood, and each ebbing Stream,
> Took in by lot 'twixt high and nether *Jove*
> Imperial rule of all the Sea-girt Isles
> . . . .
> Which he to grace his tributary gods
> By course commits to several government,
> And gives them leave to wear their Sapphire crowns,
> And wield their little tridents; but this Isle,
> The greatest, and the best of all the main
> He quarters to his blue-hair'd deities;
> And all this tract that fronts the falling Sun
> A noble Peer of mickle trust, and power,
> Has in his charge, with temper'd awe to guide
> An old and haughty Nation proud in Arms" (18–33).

50. See William B. Hunter Jr., *Milton's Comus: A Family Piece.*

51. For a discussion of *Coelum Britannicum* (and other masks) in connection with Milton's *Mask,* see John G. Demaray, *Milton and the Masque Tradition.*

52. John Creaser has argued that the presentation of *A Mask at Ludlow* in 1634 was an important state occasion comparable in its way to the presentation at Windsor Castle of Carew's *Coelum Britannicum* in the same year. See "'The Present Aid of This Occasion': The Setting of *Comus*" in *The Court Masque.* Warburton suggested that the king is honored under the name of Neptune, a suggestion that the editors of the *Variorum* approve. See *Comus, Variorum, (The Minor English Poems),* 2.3.861. Creaser argues (and I agree) that the connection of Charles with Neptune is mistaken (129).

Milton has a subtle political point to make here. He bypasses the present English monarch by invoking the gods of sea and sky, who grant their "charter" to the Earl as a representative of the ancient British nation. Milton is silent about the Egertons' connections with the Stuart court, all the more remarkable since the Egerton brothers had danced at Windsor in *Coelum Britannicum.*[53] He emphasizes instead their descent from Locrine, Brute, Aeneas, and Anchises. As Spenser had created for Elizabeth in *The Faerie Queene* a specifically British dynastic past, Milton in *A Mask* stresses that the Earl of Bridgewater, like the virgin queen Elizabeth, was the descendant of a "haughty Nation proud in Arms" (33). It is with the British line from the "Faerie Queen" rather than with the line of James and Charles that he chooses to identify the Egertons. It is certainly true that in this decade of his life Milton had begun to think of himself, like Spenser, as the future bard for the British, as the later Latin poems "Mansus" and "Epitaphium Damonis" both testify—the celebrator of Brutus, of Arthur, and Britain's dynastic past.[54] Nevertheless, the emphasis on the dynastic British past rather than the Stuart present cannot be accounted for merely by Milton's ambitions to write an Arthurian epic.

Moreover, the presence in the *Mask* of two "virgin" ladies who are aristocratic daughters cannot fail to recall the virgin queen of Spenser's epic and of the previous royal reign in England. Moreover, these virgin ladies contrast implicitly with another royal female—Henrietta Maria—who was often appearing in masks during this decade.[55] Not long before, when he composed *Arcades,* Milton placed a female at the center of a mask, Lady Alice's grandmother, the Dowager Countess of Derby. There too he avoided connecting the female with the dynastic present, but exalted her by linking her to mythic figures from classical antiquity—the mother goddesses Cybele and Latona—founders of mythic families and mothers to illustrious children such as Apollo and Diana, the leading prototypes for the Attendant Spirit and Sabrina.

53. Creaser, "'The Present Aid,'" in *The Court Masque,* 124.

54. Even though this aim never materialized into the projected epic, it did result in the prose *History of Britain,* where Milton would once more have the opportunity to tell the story of the daughter of Locrine. See Nicholas von Maltzahn, *Milton's History of Britain: Republican Historiography in the English Revolution,* who argues for a continuity between the classical and the British myth, noting that "at the triumphant moment of the Lady's release, the Attendant Spirit recalls Sabrina's Trojan heritage" (101).

55. See John Peacock's discussion of Henrietta Maria's influence on court mask: "The French Element in Inigo Jones's Masque Design," in *The Court Masque.* Also see Kendrick, "Milton and Sexuality," who argues that the Lady is contrasted with Henrietta Maria "in order to differentiate true chastity from this exotic idol" (47).

This, this is she alone,
> Sitting like a Goddess bright,
> In the center of her light.

Might she the wise *Latona* be,
Or the tow'red *Cybele*,
Mother of a hundred gods;
Juno dares not give her odds;
> Who had thought this clime had held
> A deity so unparalleled? (17–25)

The countess, mother to a dynasty of future aristocrats, is also the metaphorical mother to the mythic land of Arcady, honored by its rivers, the divine Alpheus and the sandy Ladon, by its shepherds, and by the Genius of the Wood, its native pastoral daemon. When he composes the *Mask at Ludlow-Castle,* Milton honors Lady Alice by the attendance of the pastoral deities Thyrsis and Sabrina and also makes the pastoral river nymph double as a dynastic ancestor. Milton's classicizing myths have political relevance.

The return of Lady Alice and her brothers to Ludlow-town reminds us once more that we are in a court setting. The Attendant Spirit bids the shepherds give way "Till next Sun-shine holiday" (959) and the assembled company rise in a courtly dance to welcome these "fair offspring nurs't in Princely lore" (34). The purpose of the children's journey to Ludlow has been, as the Attendant Spirit tells us at the beginning of the mask, "to attend their Father's state, / And new entrusted Scepter" (35–36). It has also, as the Spirit now tells us, "timely tri'd their youth, / Their faith, their patience, and their truth" (970–71). If Comus and his unruly rout represent certain decadent members of the British aristocracy—Buckingham, Castelhaven, and their ilk—the Earl, his wife, the Lady, and her brothers represent their idealized counterparts.[56] The Lady and her brothers triumph over these unworthy aristocrats, even as they triumphed over "sensual Folly and Intemperance" (975).[57]

---

56. That implicit doubling of Apollo in the Cyrene story is also useful. It permits Milton to dismiss the rapist-god of the Daphne myth—his stand-in for the dissolute courtier of Charles's or James's courts or for "Comus" of the Castelhaven or the Buckingham scandals—and at the same time to accept the dynasty-founding Apollo of the Cyrene myth. He even uses Sabrina-Cyrene's triumph specifically to cancel this "false" Apollo's power. For the contemporary implications of the *Mask,* see Barbara Breasted, "*Comus* and the Castelhaven Scandal," in *MS* 3. Also see David Norbrook, "The Reformation of the Masque," in *The Court Masque.*

57. Even though the mask focuses upon the Lady's virtuous refusal of Comus, it also celebrates her brothers' heroic efforts to rescue their sister and so they are rightly praised with their sister in her triumph.

Like many court entertainments, the mask portrays mythically the strug-gle between the virtue and vice—the virtuous courtly children overcoming the corrupt court of a son of Bacchus. But it neither alludes mythically nor allegorically to representatives from Charles's court at Windsor or Whitehall where the Caroline court mask flourished to praise so-called aristocratic virtues. At the moment in a royal mask when a prince or princess might have appeared, moreover, Sabrina rises. That she, a representative of a far distant and distinctively British past, is the saving "royal" presence, not a Stuart prince or princess, king or queen (or their representative), is surely significant.[58] Here Milton may be commenting tacitly on the difference between his mask and the typical court mask that existed to afford en-tertainment to or compliment those aristocrats or royal children who took part in it.[59] It is an interesting paradox that as Prince of Wales the future Charles I had first appeared in the Jonsonian mask, *Pleasure Reconciled to Virtue,* the mask that most resembles Milton's *Mask* and from whom Milton may have drawn the character Comus.[60] In 1634 Milton distances himself and the Egertons from Whitehall and its masking.

In 1634 and again in 1637 (after he revised the mask) and still more forcefully in 1645 when he printed the mask with his other poetry, Milton enthusiastically approved of the virtue of the Egertons, Britain's free-born nobles. His inclusion of prefatory material that identified the patrons and the occasion of the mask certainly implied his willingness to be associated with the Earl of Bridgewater and his family. After 1645 he did not retain, of course, the same view of the Egertons nor they of him. It is a rueful reflec-tion on his view of British aristocracy that he removed the complimentary letters and even the names of Lady Alice and her brothers from the 1673 text of the Ludlow *Mask*.[61]

---

58. Sabrina contrasts with the kind of allegorical stand-ins for Stuart royalty that had appeared in royal masks for Charles I or Henrietta Maria. Creaser remarks that "In other courtly masques and entertainments, the mere presence of royalty or nobility undoes the enchantments of evil" ("'The Present Aid,'" in *The Court Masque,* 127).

59. The Egerton children had taken part in *Tempe Restored* (1632) as well as *Coelum Britannicum.* See Creaser, "'The Present Aid,'" in *The Court Masque,* 117

60. See Norbrook, "The Reformation of the Masque," in *The Court Masque,* 104–5. *Pleasure Reconciled to Virtue* was not printed until 1640, but many critics urge that Milton could have obtained a copy.

61. In the 1673 *Poems* nothing connects the Egertons to the *Mask*—Milton deletes the separate title page, giving information about its presentation before the Egertons, the two letters (Lawes's and Wotton's), and even the dramatis personae that identified Lady Alice and her brothers as performers. As John Creaser and Peter Lindenbaum have suggested, he no longer wishes to identify the *Mask* as a patronage piece nor to associate himself with the Egertons. See Creaser, "'The Present Aid,'" 117; Peter Lindenbaum, "John Milton and the Republican Mode of Literary Production," in *YES,* 131.

PSYCHE

The Attendant Spirit has the first and last words in Milton's mask. In one way it is the triumph of the Apollonian spirit of music over Dionysiac discord and noise. Comus, the Bacchus of the dismal shades—of Cotyttean dark and of Circean charm—is banished. Yet in the Attendant Spirit's final song or epilogue (composed by Milton for the revised version of his mask) Bacchus, father of Mirth, is implicitly present in the garden of the Hesperides, and Venus, Mirth's mother, reasserts her power as she heals Adonis and consents to the wedding of her son Cupid and Psyche. From Cupid and Psyche will be born Youth and Joy. Joy, of course, recalls Euphrosyne or Mirth, the Bacchic offspring in Milton's ode "L'Allegro." Milton concludes this revised version of the Ludlow *Mask* with the celebration of a divine wedding that can be an allegory of virtue triumphant or the prediction of future nuptials at Ludlow.

As the Trinity manuscript shows us, the extended description of the garden of the Hesperides in the Attendant Spirit's parting song is a late addition to the mask. Milton originally included in the Attendant Spirit's opening song references to the Hesperidean gardens and to the dragon guarding the tree. But when his revisions relocate the Hesperides to the parting song, he omits allusion to the dragon, and expands the description and the flower catalogue. The final revisions add, moreover, the descriptions of the two couples that inhabit the garden: Venus and Adonis, and the Celestial Cupid and Psyche. As critics have pointed out, Milton's Hesperidean gardens are a conflation of the gardens of Hesperus's daughters (which contained the dragon-guarded tree with its golden apples) with Elysium or the Isles of the Blessed, those kingdoms located by the ancients not in the mountains of Atlas and his brother Hesperus, but beyond Ocean.[62] Milton, however, locates his Hesperides not merely beyond Ocean, but specifically in the fields of sky:[63]

> And those happy climes that lie
> Where day never shuts his eye,

62. See *Comus* in *Variorum, (The Minor English Poems)*, 2.3.975–80. The principal classical sources are Ovid and Hesiod, but Milton also makes use of descriptions of paradisiacal gardens in Callimachus, Pindar, and the Homeric hymn to Pythian Apollo. Renaissance sources include Spenser's gardens, principally his Garden of Adonis in *Faerie Queene* 3.6. Also see *In Mythologiam Natalis Comitis, Obseruationum libellus,* in Comes, *Mythologiae* (1616), 588, which associates the garden of the Hesperides with the garden of Adonis.

63. Conti and Baudoin explain that the Hesperides can take their name from the star Hesper or Hesperus and so be stars as a heavenly paradise. See bk. 7, chap. 7 in Comes, *Mythologiae* (1581), 482; Baudoin, *Mythologie,* 311–12; 732.

> Up in the broad fields of the sky:
> There I suck the liquid air
> All amidst the Gardens fair
> Of *Hesperus,* and his daughters three
> That sing about the golden tree (976–83)

Milton refrains from making the garden of the Hesperides a compliment to Stuart England—another famed western isle—as masks of the period were fond of doing.[64] Removing the threatening presence of the dragon, he populates the garden with beautiful female singers and dancers from classical myth: Hesperus's three daughters, the Graces, and the "rosy bosom'd Hours." These tuneful goddesses are still another version of the heavenly Sirens, now inhabiting a pastoral sky-garden. Once more Milton has raised his pastoral singers from earth to heaven. The mask's Hesperidean garden is a conflation of earthly and heavenly paradises; it recollects those elysiums referred to in the early elegies and anticipates the pastoral heaven of "Lycidas" and "Epitaphium Damonis." It looks forward also to the pastoral Eden of *Paradise Lost* 4, called by Milton a *"Hesperian* Fable true," with golden trees, attendant Graces and Hours, together with the West Winds that assure eternal spring or summer. No less in *Paradise Lost* than in the *Mask* Milton's classicizing and Christianizing go hand in hand.

In the *Mask* Milton even goes one step further to include in his garden two amorous couples, Venus and Adonis and Cupid and Psyche, risking the charge that he has admitted to the *Mask* the sexual dalliance he earlier appeared to disapprove. While there is no classical authority for associating the Garden of the Hesperides with the Garden of Adonis, Renaissance poets often conflate the two.[65] Giovanni Pontano, for example, not only reports in "De Hortis Hesperidum" that Venus took Adonis there, but healing his wound transformed her erstwhile lover into a wondrous citrus tree with golden fruit—the very tree of the Hesperides. Milton has no such transformations in mind, but he does make his garden a place of healing—hence carrying over the theme of cure and restoration that he introduced when he had the Attendant Spirit and Sabrina save and also heal the Lady of Comus's baleful charms. Adonis—"waxing well of his deep wound"—reposes on beds of *"Hyacinth,* and roses," drenched with Elysian dew. The flowers described, like floral "herbs," heal him, and the dew is a counterpart to Sabrina's reviving water. Venus, the Assyrian Queen, sits sadly on the ground next to the sleeping Adonis, appearing not so much as the lover but as a deity—not unlike Sabrina—who is effecting his cure.

---

64. See Ann Coiro's discussion of Stuart mask in "Herrick's Hesperides: The Name and the Frame," in *ELH* 52.

65. See *Comus* in *Variorum (The Minor English Poems),* 2.3.975–80.

In the Eden of *Paradise Lost* Milton does not draw back from engaging his resident lovers in lovemaking. But the *Mask* was composed under the shadow of the Platonism that he tells us in the retraction to "Elegia 7" ruled his heart. Triumphant sexual love must be allegorized. Celestial Cupid is heavenly Love who, in holding "his dear Psyche sweet entranc't" (1005), is contemplating the Soul as well as embracing his bride.

Psyche is the last mythological female figure named in Milton's mask, another endangered virgin, who, like the Lady, is destined for marriage, not, like Sabrina, for resurrected virginity. Milton's ultimate source of the Psyche story is Apuleius's *Metamorphoses,* but Psyche's story is told and retold in many versions, one of the most notable being the allegorical account in Boccaccio's *Genealogiae Deorum Gentilium*. Apuleius's narrative is divided in two parts, the first part recounting how Cupid became Psyche's secret lover, visiting her at night and keeping his identity secret until Psyche, egged on by her jealous sisters, lights a lamp and discovers her god-lover, causing him to flee, burned by the lamp's oil.[66] The second part of the story involves the trials of Psyche inflicted on her by Cupid's jealous mother Venus, who, unwilling to admit a beauty rival to hers, attempts to destroy her. Psyche is forced to accomplish three difficult labors, the last two life-threatening. As she is faced with these trials, she almost despairs and throws herself into the water to drown. But she is helped and eventually completes all her tasks. Finally Jupiter consents to Cupid's pleas and, persuading Venus and the other gods, makes Psyche immortal and celebrates her wedding to Cupid. Psyche—long pregnant with Cupid's child—brings forth their offspring: Pleasure.

It is on the laboring, wandering Psyche that Milton places his emphasis and on her reunion with Cupid. Psyche is a mortal, who must undergo a series of trials in order to prove that she is worthy of becoming a god's consort. She is courted by a god, the patient and gentle Cupid, whose wooing contrasts with the demigod Comus's coercive wooing of the Lady. Here is an example—like Apollo's wooing of Cyrene—of a god successfully winning a consort and forming a union that attains fruition. Milton places in the future Psyche's wedding to Cupid—as well as the birth of her offspring, not the single child Pleasure, but the twins Youth and Joy. The change is significant. The example of Psyche's "wand'ring labors long" (1006) provides us with yet another instance of suffering that is rewarded. In using the key word "wand'ring" and in referring to a "labor," Milton connects Psyche to the Lady on both a figurative and a literal level. Milton's Lady must wander, lost in the woods; must face trial, must repulse Comus's

---

66. See Apuleius, *The Golden Ass, Being the Metamorphoses of Lucius Apuleius,* 4.28–6.24.

indecent offer before her virtue, like Psyche's, is confirmed and she is freed. When we encounter Psyche in the epilogue, she too has just succeeded in her trials and now awaits a future that will include a happy marriage.[67]

As the Attendant Spirit has told us right at the outset of the mask, the Lady's trial is also that of the virtuous soul, a trial that is symbolically figured in the Apuleian story of Psyche, the Soul, overcoming the obstacles to attain Heavenly Love. Milton's reference to Psyche in *Areopagitica* demonstrates, moreover, that it was Apuleius's account of Psyche's trials that particularly interested him. He compares Psyche's first assigned task—"the incessant labor to cull out and sort asunder" the confused and intermixed seeds of grain—with the Christian's task of sorting out good from evil. Good and evil he describes as twins cleaving together, that grow up together in the field of this world "almost inseparably," so alike in "many cunning resemblances" that they are "hardly to be disarm'd." Yet it is the task of the Christian to distinguish them. The person who "can apprehend and consider vice with all her baits and seeming pleasures, and yet abstain, and yet distinguish, and yet prefer that which is truly better," Milton calls "the true wayfaring Christian" (Hughes, 728). Such a description fits exactly the trial of the Lady at Comus's table; she considers vice's baits and seeming pleasures, she abstains, she distinguishes, and she prefers "that which is truly better." With the allusion in the epilogue to Psyche's reward after "wand'ring labors long," Milton brings us full circle round. In his first song the Attendant Spirit, descending from the sphery clime, had referred to the heavenly rewards that Virtue promises to her "true Servants / Amongst the enthron'd gods" (10–11). In his parting song, he urges those mortals who would follow him to love Virtue, who "alone is free" and can teach us how to climb "Higher than the Sphery chime" (1019–21). The Attendant Spirit's re-ascent promises mortals—the Lady, her brothers, and indeed the whole company—a similar re-ascent to heavenly joy. The Lady's reward, like Psyche's, will be to give birth to the Christian offspring—eternal Youth and heavenly Joy— not to "Voluptas" or Pleasure, the offspring of a Comus-like allegory. That the allusion to future marriage can function both on the dynastic level, in predicting the Lady's future dynastic marriage and continuance of old Anchises's line, and on the Christian level, in fulfilling her trial as the virtuous soul, is only testament to the complexity of Milton's mask.

The Lady enters the mask as its sole female character; but in the unfolding of the action a sequence of mythic females is summoned—metaphorically and actually—to assist her and help her to triumph, the most important of whom is, of course, Sabrina. In classicizing the native British river goddess

---

67. See Cedric C. Brown, *John Milton's Aristocratic Entertainments,* 150–51. Brown emphasizes the Christian rather than the Platonic allegory inherent in Psyche's story.

Sabrina, in linking her and the Lady persistently with Greek and Roman deities, ranging from water nymphs to Artemis-Diana to Parthenope and finally to Psyche, Milton is not supplying decorative classical borders to a central panel that honors certain members of the British aristocracy. Milton's classicizing works to reveal the mask's true significance and can finally even affirm his Christianity, as one virgin Lady, who has won her laurels, releases another. In fact, Milton's classicizing permits him to have it both ways—to celebrate the triumph of the Earl of Bridgewater's daughter at the same time he celebrates the triumph of Virtue.

SPORTING WITH AMARYLLIS

"Lycidas"—Classical Ode and Renaissance Pastoral

ycidas" and the Ludlow *Mask* are the concluding items of the *English Poems*—pastoral and mythological works that interweave ancient classical originals and Renaissance imitations. Yet, as I have argued in the previous chapter, the contribution of the classical tradition to *A Mask* is often overlooked. The opposite, however, is true for "Lycidas," which is often treated as having sprung full grown from so-called pastoral elegy—the ancient idylls or eclogues of Theocritus, Bion, Moschus, and Vergil. Other traditions are often ignored.[1] Further, although critics have glanced at the contribution of Pindaric ode to the genre of monody or have mentioned in passing the influence of neo-Latin pastoral, no one has investigated fully how Pindaric ode shapes the structure and meaning of "Lycidas" or how knowledge of Renaissance as well as classical pastoral might deepen our understanding of Milton's use of the pastoral motifs.

1. It is only within the last few years that scholars have begun to pay closer attention to the rich legacy of Hebraic prophecy that informs the monody or to look more closely at the context of contemporary politics. Both Edward Tayler and Michael Lieb comment on the echoes from the Old Testament, particularly in the opening words, "Yet once more." See Edward W. Tayler, "*Lycidas* in Christian Time" in *Milton's Poetry;* and Michael Lieb, *The Sinews of Ulysses: Form and Convention in Milton's Works.* Two unpublished papers by Carter Revard (presented in Binghamton in 1987 and in Florence at the Third International Milton Symposium in 1988) comment on the relevance of 2 Samuel (with the account of David's census) to the punishment of Bastwick, Burton, and Prynne, and to the interpretation of the two-handed engine. Some of these Hebraic texts support the political contexts of both 1637 and 1645. In 1645 when he added to the headnote of the monody that besides bewailing the death of a learned friend, it foretold "the ruin of the corrupted Clergy then [in 1637] in their height," Milton placed "Lycidas" in a clear political context. Also see Leonard, "'Trembling Ears': The Historical Moment of 'Lycidas,'" in *JMRS* 21.

The ode tradition that included the Pindaric corpus was in antiquity the older ancestor of Theocritean idyll and Vergilian eclogue and itself shaped these later forms. Renaissance commentators, such as J. C. Scaliger, Antonio Minturno, and Benedictus Aretius, understood the relationship between Pindar's odes or ἔδεα and the little odes or εἰδύλλια of Theocritus and the eclogues of Vergil.[2] Milton in turn would have been familiar with these Renaissance critics and would have known their definitions of these terms as well as their definition of monody. As we have noted in Chapters 2, 3, and 4, Milton had been experimenting with different techniques of Pindaric ode since his earliest English funereal ode, "On the Death of a Fair Infant," and by the time he composed "Lycidas" he had written a number of odes—long and short—that employ Pindaric methods. In planning "Lycidas," he would have turned directly both to Pindar's odes as odic models and to many neo-Latin or vernacular Pindarics that had been produced on the Continent during the sixteenth century.[3] He might also have known Ben Jonson's Cary-Morison ode, the most ambitious Pindaric ode that had yet appeared in English, although he does not follow it directly as a model. We know from his remarks in *The Reason of Church Government* (1642) that he approved of Pindar and Callimachus as fitting models for odes and hymns.[4] We know further that after composing "Lycidas," he would continue to think about the potentials of ode, especially Pindaric ode, for at least ten years more, culminating in his composition of the Latin Pindaric "Ad Joannem Rousium." We can no longer disregard Pindaric ode as a shaping influence on Milton's odes and his pastoral monody "Lycidas."[5]

It is also imperative to look more closely at Renaissance pastorals and their influence on "Lycidas," since Renaissance poets had modernized the ancient genre and had given it contemporary significance. Yet apart from the pastorals of Spenser's *Shepheardes Calender,* Renaissance eclogues are hardly mentioned or, if so, only in isolation as individual rather than

2. See, for example, Scaliger, Minturno, or Aretius for explanation of these genres: Julius Caesar Scaliger, *Poetices Libri Septem,* 48–50; Antonio Minturno (Sebastiani), *L'Arte Poetica* (1563), 171–86; Benedictus Aretius, *Commentarii Absolutissimi in Pindari Olympia, Pythia, Nemea, Isthmia* (1587), 16, 19, 21.

3. Beyond Jonson's experiments in Pindaric ode (the Desmond and the Cary-Morison odes), Drayton's forays into Pindar and Anacreon, and Soowtherne's clumsy imitations of Ronsard's Pindarics in *Pandora,* imitation of Pindar was hardly existent in English.

4. See Milton, *Complete Poems and Major Prose* (ed. Hughes), 669.

5. I am not the first to suggest Pindaric influence in Milton's monody. Both F. T. Prince and Clay Hunt thought that the verse techniques of "Lycidas" had affinities with the Pindaric ode and came to Milton indirectly through the medium of the Italian canzone. They prefer, however, to see "Lycidas" as an Italian canzone in the style of Tasso and others, rather than as a Pindaric ode. In this John Carey follows them. See Clay Hunt, *Lycidas and the Italian Critics;* F. T. Prince, "*Lycidas* and the Tradition of the Italian Eclogue," in *English Miscellany* 2; and also Prince's *The Italian Element in Milton's Verse.*

collective models. Bush and Woodhouse in the *Variorum* and Louis Martz in *Poet of Exile* glance at Sannazaro's contribution to "Lycidas," and William Harrison made a similar claim for Castiglione's "Alcon."[6] But recognition of importance of Sannazaro or other individual neo-Latin poets has not led to an investigation of the genre of neo-Latin pastoral.[7] Even Watson Kirkconnell's catalogue of Renaissance pastoral and W. Leonard Grant's review of neo-Latin pastoral literature have not led to study of this genre in connection with the genesis of Milton's pastoral monody.[8] Yet Milton would have been familiar with many other neo-Latin poets who had worked to expand the scope of ancient pastoral literature. Closer in their concerns to Milton than ancient writers such as Vergil and Theocritus, they wrote, as he did, as Christian humanists, devoted to modernizing the best of ancient literature and to making it relevant to their times. Hence their poetry contributes significantly to our understanding of "Lycidas" as a contemporary Christian pastoral poem.

"Lycidas" was written at a crucial moment in Milton's career as a poet and in his development as a man—at a time of personal and political crisis. His mother had died in the spring of 1637, and Milton was planning his first trip abroad. He was leaving behind a political and religious situation in England that would only worsen over the next three years, and he was also turning to contextualize himself in the larger political, social, and poetical world of the Continent. "Lycidas" was probably the last poem that he wrote before he left. It was also the English poem that he would place in his 1645 volume opposite the Latin epitaph, "Epitaphium Damonis," composed on his return to England to mourn his closest friend, Charles Diodati. Before he left England Milton had begun to reevaluate his aims as a poet; when he returned he would voice more fully those goals as a poet that he had defined during his journey.

When he fulfilled the request in 1637 to contribute a poem for the Cambridge volume memorializing Edward King, Milton defined himself vis-à-vis that university and the English world to which he once belonged even as he prepared for the "fresh Woods, and Pastures new" that lay ahead in Italy. Although several of his Latin poemata and the epitaph on Jane Paulet might have been intended for Cambridge publications, "Lycidas" was the only poetic contribution Milton ever actually made to a collection by his university. Other Cambridge poets, including Cowley, Crashaw, Marvell,

---

6. William P. Harrison Jr., "The Latin Pastorals of Milton and Castiglione."

7. Even Paul Alpers's comprehensive treatment of "Lycidas" in the context of pastoral, while alluding to Marot, Sannazaro, Castiglione, and Ronsard, relies largely on Vergilian and Theocritean prototypes. See Paul Alpers, *What is Pastoral?*, 93–112.

8. W. Leonard Grant, *Neo-Latin Literature and the Pastoral;* Watson Kirkconnell, ed., *Awake the Courteous Echo.*

and Edward King himself, had regularly contributed to Cambridge com-memorative and occasional volumes.[9] In submitting "Lycidas" for the King volume, Milton openly acknowledged his role as a Cambridge alumnus in a way that he had not done since he wrote the group of Latin funera ten years previous. But "Lycidas" is not a narrow provincial commemorative poem. Even as it situates itself in the rural English landscape, its pastoral by its very genre extends it to the humanistic world of the Continent where John Milton the man was planning to go.

ELEGY OR ODE?

"Lycidas" is often called a pastoral elegy. But it was not so called by the man who wrote it. Milton was careful to designate its genre as ode—an ode for a single voice or, as he called it, a monody.[10] In the early seventeenth century the ode was not a dominant or even a popular form. Monody was a term almost unknown in English. Yet so important to Milton was ode as a poetic form (both odes for "choral performance" and for a single voice) that they are the dominant poetic form of the English volume, holding the place of preferred genre that elegy holds in the *Poemata*.

Experimentation with Pindaric form and meters and poetical devices had been widespread on the Continent since the end of the fifteenth century,

9. For a discussion of Cambridge University publications and Milton's possible connection with them, see Alberta T. Turner, "Milton and the Conventions of the Academic Miscellanies," in *YES*. Also see Norman Postlethwaite and Gordon Campbell, eds., "Edward King, Milton's 'Lycidas': Poems and Documents," in *MQ* 28. Most of the surviving poems of Edward King are occasional pieces on the birth of the royal children. There is also a poem on the safe return of King Charles from Scotland. Milton may have had strong political reasons for refraining from commemorating such royal occasions. For further commentary on the historical Edward King as Lycidas, see Lawrence Lipking, "The Genius of the Shore: Lycidas, Adamastor, and the Politics of Nationalism," in *PMLA* 111.

10. Although Milton termed his pastoral lament "Lycidas" a monody, critics since James Holly Hanford in 1910 usually call it a pastoral elegy; scholars, investigating the relevant traditions, compare the poem to everything from eclogue to idyll to ode. A monody, I hasten to say, as the Renaissance critics J. C. Scaliger and George Puttenham agree, is simply an ode for a single rather than choral voice. See James Holly Hanford, "The Pastoral Elegy and Milton's *Lycidas*," in *PMLA* 25. Both Scaliger and Puttenham define monody as a funeral song. Scaliger puts it simply: "Etiam monodia dictus cantus lugubris" (*Poetices Libri Septem* [1581], 129). Puttenham goes further to call it a funeral song for a single voice: "Such funerall songs were called *Epicedia* if they were song by many, and *Monodia* if they were vttered by one alone" (*The Arte of English Poesie* [1589], 63). B. Rajan in *"Lycidas"* in the *Milton Encyclopedia* and Scott Elledge in *Milton's "Lycidas"* (107–14), cite Scaliger's and Puttenham's definitions of monody. Also see J. W. Binns's definitions of the different genres of lament in *Intellectual Culture in Elizabethan and Jacobean England*, 60.

particularly in Italy. And Italians had almost invented the form of monody. With experiments in monody, moreover, neo-Latin poets such as Poliziano and Joannes Secundus were seeking to adapt Pindar's voice to Renaissance Latin poetry. One of the earliest monodies is Poliziano's lament for Lorenzo de' Medici. At only thirty lines it is much shorter than "Lycidas," but it too adapts Pindaric devices for lament. Further, there are some interesting thematic parallels with "Lycidas." Both poems describe the shattered laurel; both invoke choruses of Muses and nymphs that mourn, and both express their grief figuratively in fountains of watery or "melodious tear[s]." Who makes my eyes a fountain of tears, asks Poliziano: "Quis oculis meis / Fontem lachryarum dabit?"[11] We cannot know, of course, to what extent actual Continental monodies such as Poliziano's affected Milton's choice of the genre for his pastoral lament. Besides, as a poetic form, Renaissance monody was not restricted to laments for the dead.[12] But when they were so directed, as we shall see later in Joannes Secundus's monody on the death of Thomas More, they could be expansive odes that employed figures and digressions in a manner very like Pindaric ode.

Like Pindar's odes, "Lycidas" fills the category of "occasional poetry." In composing the monody as a part of the official collection of commemorative poems for the dead Edward King, Milton is engaging in a public performance that is comparable in its way to the public occasions that called forth Pindar's choral odes. Pindar composed his odes, of course, to commemorate athletic victory, but many times as he celebrated the winners of athletic contests and their patrons, he also remembered important men— living and dead—connected with them and the commemorative occasion. By employing commemorative ode as a poetic form, Milton could include in "Lycidas" a range of utterances and themes and could move digressively over topics that at first appear to have little to do with the lament or song for the dead. A contemporary of Milton's, in fact, remarked that Milton was an excellent Pindarist.[13] Without the model of Pindaric ode, Milton

---

11. Angelus Politianus, *Omnia Opera* (1498), n.p.

12. Pietro Crinito, Poliziano's contemporary, uses monody for exuberant lyric celebrations as well as complaints. Right on the heels of Poliziano's monody to the dead Lorenzo is Crinito's monody to the living Poliziano, a sportive little narrative that recounts how a southern Siren, flying back to Daulia, hears Angelo singing a new kind of melody beside the slowly flowing Arno. The most serious of Crinito's monodies is one on "Fortune and Her Men" that reflects philosophically on Fortune's power to raise men to the clouds and throw them down. Monody, however, is not a form that Crinito uses for lament for the dead. See *Poematum Libri Duo* (1508).

13. See Nicholas von Maltzahn, "Laureate, Republican, Calvinist: An Early Response to Milton and *Paradise Lost* (1667)," in *MS* 29:181–98. Von Maltzahn notes that a contemporary John Beale (1608–1683) refers to Milton as an "excellent Pindariste," remarking that "Lycidas" best illustrates the "Pindarique way" (184).

could hardly have made "Lycidas" the poem that it is structurally and thematically.[14]

Whereas critics have proposed that Pindaric ode has an influence on "Lycidas," few have gone so far as it show how and where this influence is manifested. To discern characteristic Pindaric devices and a basic Pindaric structure in the monody, however, is not difficult. First of all, the overall pattern of "Lycidas" resembles the basic five-part "rhetorical" structure that editors and commentators had identified in most of Pindar's odes: exordium, proposition, confirmation, digression, and epilogue.[15] Further, Milton is also using within this structure certain distinctive Pindaric devices: the striking opening figure or apostrophe, the use of the odic "I," the abrupt interruption of poetic sequence, interlinking mythic figures and digressions, moral *sententiae,* to mention a few. Second, Milton imitates Pindar's subtle indirectiveness as a poet. Pindar always—whatever the occasion—has his own agenda and is often writing a poem whose ostensible subject is different from its real one. On one level Pindar may be celebrating in *Olympian 1* Hieron's victory in a horse race, but on another he is considering the delicate issue of what piety or impiety to the gods means. Milton may be lamenting the dead shepherd Edward King, but he too has a separate agenda. The themes he explores transcend the ostensible occasion of commemorating King. Milton does not directly refer to this separate agenda, however, until he reissues "Lycidas" in the 1645 *Poems,* whereupon he adds to the headnote the comment that it by occasion foretells "the ruin of the corrupted Clergy then [in 1637] in their height." In this indirection Milton resembles Pindar, who never commemorates an occasion alone without probing the meaning of the event and often raising those very basic questions about human existence. Issues of life and death, success and failure, joy and grief, good and evil are basic to his odes.[16]

14. We do not know which edition of Pindar Milton used. As Samuel Adkins and Maurice Kelley have demonstrated, the copy of Pindar's odes (ed. Joannes Benedictus, Saumur, 1620) owned by Harvard University with annotations attributed in the Columbia edition to Milton cannot be directly connected to the poet. The Benedictus edition and the edition by Erasmus Schmidt (Wittenberg, 1616) were the most impressive scholarly editions available to Milton; Cowley used Benedictus when translating Pindar for his 1656 *Pindarique Odes.* There was also available, however, the popular edition of Pindar's odes (with facing Latin translation but without textual or explanatory notes), first printed by Henricus Stephanus in 1560 and frequently reprinted up through the first part of the seventeenth century.

15. See for example the diagrams of odes in Schmidt's edition.

16. Pindaric ode is always offered to commemorate a specific and usually official occasion and is always addressed to a specific person on that occasion, usually an athlete who has been victorious in one of the games. Occasionally, however, it celebrates other persons and other events, as, for example the founding of the city Aetna in *Pythian 1* or the celebration of a prytanis in *Nemean 11;* it can even, as we shall see, remember the

It is hardly coincidental that Milton raises these very issues in the course of "Lycidas."

The complexity of "Lycidas" is probably due in part to the fact that it is not Milton's first excursion into Pindaric ode. He had experimented before, as we have noted, with Pindaric figure when he composed the figurative opening of "Fair Infant"—the image of the "blasted blossom." The opening figure in "Lycidas"—the shattered garland—also replicates Pindar's bold figures not only in its striking poetic vividness, but also in its allusive design. To take a direct example, the first words of Pindar's *Pythian 1* apostrophize the "golden lyre" (χρυσέα φόρμιγξ), the musical instrument, which he describes as the joint possession of the Muses and Apollo, and which he invokes almost as though it were an entity in itself—a symbol for music. By placing the lyre first in the poem, Pindar puts it visually and vividly before our eyes at the same time as he makes it the ruling symbol for his ode. It signifies the order and harmony in the cosmos (the lyre moves the universe as it creates the music of the spheres); it is also the symbol for order and good government on earth (the choruses on earth move to the sound of the lyre). *Pythian 1,* addressed to Hieron and his son, the ruler of the new city Aetna, is an ode about governing. By beginning his ode with a figural representation of the good governance—the golden lyre— Pindar makes clear to his audience at the outset that as heaven and earth are united by the rule of music, so rulers on earth ought to be united by the rule of the gods.[17] The opening figure is not only impressive in itself, but also directly relates to the themes that Pindar will develop in the ode.[18] Is it accidental that Milton begins his monody not with statement but with figure—the figure of the shattered garland?

By shattering the would-be laurel crown that he would bestow or gather to himself—both actions are implicit in the statement—Milton opens his poem with a metaphor that will guide him throughout. The laurel crown was the victory reward both for the poet and for the athlete in the Pythian games in Apollo's honor. Death has shattered Lycidas's garland; untimely

---

dead. Typically, an ode deals with some problem crucial to human life and considers through a series of passages, some juxtaposed abruptly against one other, a universal question about human beings and their relationship with divine beings. The probing usually takes the form of a series of so-called digressions, often centered on or about a myth or myths. Pindar never proceeds directly; it is the very essence of his ode that as he celebrates the ostensible occasion he has come to commemorate, he raises other basic questions.

17. As the ode develops and Pindar considers Hieron and his son as rulers, we come to understand how the figure of the "golden lyre" or music underlies what Pindar has to say about government on earth. See my article, "Building the Foundations of the Good Commonwealth: Pindar, Marvell, and the Power of Music," in *The Muses Common-weale.*

18. Figures in other odes work similarly, such as the figure of the brimming cup in *Isthmian 6* or of the golden pillars in *Olympian 6.*

plucking shatters the garland the poet-swain would pluck as would-be poet. The paradox in the action is implicitly Pindaric. Metaphorically, the laurel is the poet's praise, and in an epinician ode or in a monody it is the poet's responsibility to bestow the crown of praise. Yet tragic circumstance can make him hesitate and reflect on the appropriateness of bestowing that laurel. Consider Pindar's reticence and anguish of heart (ἀχνύμενος θυμόν, 5–6) at the beginning of *Isthmian 8* when he must sing at a time of national mourning, just at the end of the wars with Persia; he must invoke the Muses, but he hesitates to do so.[19] He knows, however, if human beings are to go on, the poetic garland must be bestowed—indeed it is part of the process that gives comfort and ultimately relief.[20] In the opening section of "Lycidas" Milton works his way from the figure of anguish—the shattered garland—to the assertion of the appropriateness, indeed the necessity, to lay poetic praise: Lycidas "must not float upon his wat'ry bier / Unwept" (12–13). "Praise"—the praise both by and of the poet—continues to be an issue throughout the poem.

The Pindaric ode at its best is a very delicate poise of seemingly discordant parts. It proclaims an occasion in a straightforward way and then digresses from it erratically, introducing mythic characters, themes, and events that may at first seem to have little to do with the commemoration of a victorious athlete. Take, for example, *Pythian 12,* an ode, composed of four strophes or stanzas, commemorating the victory of Midas, a Sicilian flute player in a Pythian contest. Pindar opens the ode with praises of Midas's native city together with an invocation of its ruling goddess.

> ὦ ἄνα,
> ἵλαος ἀθανάτων ἀνδρῶν τε σὺν εὐμενίᾳ
> δέξαι στεφάνωμα τόδ' ἐκ Πυθῶνος εὐδόξῳ Μίδᾳ
> αὐτόν τέ νιν' Ελλάδα νικά
> σαντα τέχνᾳ τὰν ποτε
> Παλλὰς ἐφεῦρε θρασειᾶν Γοργόνων
> οὔλιον θρῆνον διαπλέξαισ' Ἀθάνα (*Pythian 12.3–8*)

> O Mistress,
> Be gracious with the favor of men and gods,
> Receive this crown from Pytho in behalf of glorious Midas,
> the one who has conquered in Hellas in the art that once
> Pallas Athene invented, weaving it from the dreadful
> dirge of the bold Gorgons.

19. Citations of Pindar's verse are from Pindar, *Carmina* (1935), ed. C. M. Bowra. Also see Pindar, *The Olympian and Pythian Odes* (1908), ed. Basil L. Gildersleeve.

20. We must not fall "orphaned" of garlands, Pindar asserts. *Isthmian 8* is unique in being a "victory" ode that commemorates the dead even as it celebrates the living who have survived.

In alluding to Pallas Athene and her invention of flute music, Pindar appears to be doing no more than offering a perfunctory compliment to the winner of a flute contest. (Pallas Athene invented the flute, Pindar tells us, after she heard the wailing of the gorgon-sisters of Medusa, whom Perseus slew). But very soon Pindar's digressive allusion becomes an extended digression when, with the naming of Perseus as the slayer of Medusa, Pindar goes on gratuitously (it appears) to recount the story of Perseus's birth, his killing of the gorgon, and his vengeance for his mother. What is Pindar's purpose in introducing Perseus into the ode and in recounting his adventures in such detail? If he had merely been celebrating flute playing, there would appear to be none. But Pindar is playing a more elaborate tune on his own odic flute. Even as he considers the miraculous genesis of lovely music from hideous wailing, he reflects how often beauty comes out of ugliness, victory out of defeat, and miracle from the commonplace. These miracles can only occur, however, when the gods aid human beings to transcend the limits of their mortal nature. Side by side in the ode are Athene, the all-powerful, all-wise virgin goddess; the gorgons, once beautiful women, transformed to snaky-haired monsters; the great hero Perseus; and the flute player Midas, for whom the ode was composed. What do they have in common; how has Pindar made their stories interlock in an ode that ostensibly is no more than a celebration of a flute victory? The clue lies in the figure of Athene and her relationship to the persons in the ode—to the gorgons, to Perseus, and even to Midas the flute player. As a goddess, she has the power to transform both human beings and things—and transformation is one of the crucial issues in the poem. First of all, Athene transformed the gorgons from lovely maidens like herself to snaky-haired horrors, who turn all to stone. She petrified their beauty, and they in turn petrify all who look on them. But, curiously enough, this transformation works two ways. Not only can Athene transform lovely maidens to gorgons, but she can also transform the wailing lament that they raise for their sister into lovely polyphonic music. The sound of the gorgons' wailing is after all the inspiration for the flute music that Athene creates. Perseus hears that wailing, Pindar points out, both after he kills Medusa and when he employs her gorgon-head to turn the king of Seriphos and his subjects to stone:

> τὸν παρθενίοις ὑπό τ' ἀπλάτοις ὀφίων κεφαλαῖς
> ἄϊε λειβόμενον δυσπενθέϊ σὺν καμάτῳ,
> Περσεὺς ὁπότε τρίτον ἄνυσσεν κασιγνητᾶν μέρος,
> εἰνναλίᾳ Σερίφῳ λαοῖσι τε μοῖραν ἄγων. (9–12)

> the (sound) which Perseus heard coming from the horrible
> maidenly heads of serpents with anguished suffering,

when he conquered the third of the sisters
and brought death to sea-girt Seriphos and its people.

Perseus also is touched by the divine, for Athene uses her power to guide him, leading him to the gorgons, assisting him in killing Medusa, and inspiring him to effect his mother's liberation. She transforms him into a hero even as he transforms others with the gorgon's head. Pindar introduces Perseus's mother Danae into the ode to remark how her son freed her from servitude, and also to remark how she too was transformed by divine power. The gorgons, once lovely maidens, are imprisoned in ugliness; Danae was also a victim of her beauty, first confined by her father to the brazen tower and then by the king of Seriphos to her island prison. She is liberated from both by divine intervention and her sorrow is ultimately transformed to joy. Zeus came to her in the brazen tower and impregnated her with the hero Perseus who ultimately freed her from a second captivity. Zeus came to Danae, as Pindar reminds us, in a stream of gold. Here Pindar works his most daring metaphoric transformation. As he describes Perseus's conception from the spontaneously flowing stream of gold, he links it with the flute music, itself golden and flowing, that also was conceived when through divine intervention its sorrowful wailing became beautiful music.

In the final strophe of the ode, Pindar binds up his moral, connecting now the figure of the flute player Midas with the hero Perseus, as he had earlier connected the antithetical figures of the gorgons, Danae, and Athene. Joy does not come to light, comments Pindar, without laboring or pain. The flute music was born of the pain of the gorgons, Perseus from the laboring pain of his mother, and Danae's liberation from captivity through the pain of the islanders and king turned to stone. Even the flute player Midas, if the legend that the scholiasts hand down is true, won victory from apparent pain and defeat. As he was playing, his mouthpiece broke and he was forced to play upon the reeds, but nonetheless was victorious. Pindar's ode reaches beyond the celebration of a flute player or even the celebration of the origin of flute music to comment upon a universal truth—how the divine has the power to transform human experience, bringing joy or sorrow, success or failure.

Much has been written about the disconnections of Milton's "Lycidas," about the abruptness of its transitions, the intricacies of its digressive design, the subtleties of its mythic connections. When we place it beside even a brief ode such as *Pythian 12*, we can locate many of its so-called complexities and disjunctions in the typical pattern of a Pindaric ode. Consider what we have observed about Pindar's interweaving of mythic characters. Something similar happens in "Lycidas." Milton begins with the dead poet-pastor Lycidas, whom he links throughout the ode to Orpheus, to Apollo, to Neptune and Triton, to St. Peter, to Alpheus, and finally to the archangel Michael and Christ. In *Pythian 12,* the reader must work out the pattern of interconnection in order to understand the relationship of the mythic characters to the theme Pindar is investigating. Something comparable must be done in working out Milton's themes. For his ode involves more than the praise of a poet-pastor or lament for his untimely demise.

If the underlying image in *Pythian 12* is the flowing stream: of melody, of lament, of generative power—now golden, now brazen and dissonant—the underlying image of "Lycidas" is water: the water that drowned Lycidas; the watery tears—melodious and lamenting; the water that causes the sisters of the sacred well to revive their song; the freshwater stream that bears the head of Orpheus in contrast to the Alpheus's amorous stream that pursues the fountain nymph Arethusa and mingles its waters with hers; the water of triumph on which Christ walked; and the water of other streams in the kingdom of the blest. The water imagery in "Lycidas" has been studied by Brooks and Hardy and other critics; no one has commented, however, on how Milton's use of water as a linking image may be related to Pindar's imagery.[21] Water flows as persistently in Milton's ode as the stream of gold in Pindar's and its meaning changes as it is linked now with one, now with another figure. It destroys Lycidas and Orpheus; it is the medium of Alpheus's and Arethusa's transformation; it triumphs as Christ rises from the ocean like a resurrected sun; and it is the final benison for the saved Lycidas whose oozy locks are laved with nectar pure—heaven's transformed water.

Milton is not the only poet in the commemorative collection to use water imagery to comment on King's death. Many of the poets who eulogize King (both in the Latin and the English section of the book) refer to melodic tears, the water of baptism, and the water of King's drowning. Isaac Olivier, a fellow of King's College, even alludes to Pindar's *Olympian 1* with its celebrated opening figure: water is best ("ἄριστον μὲν ὕδωρ"). Olivier quips:

> Had the Thebane Swan
> Who lov'd his Dirce (while it proudly ran
> Swell'd by his lyre) now liv'd, he would repent
> The solemn praises he on water spent.[22]

21. *Poems of Mr. John Milton* (New York, 1951), 169–86; reprinted in *Milton's Lycidas: The Tradition and the Poem,* ed. C. A. Patrides, 140–56. Also see Wayne Shumaker, "Flowerets and Sounding Seas: A Study in the Affective Structure of *Lycidas,*" in *PMLA* 66.

22. Isaac Olivier, "What water shall vertue have again," in *Obsequies to the memorie of Mr. Edward King* (Cambridge 1638) in *Justa Edovardo King. Reproduced from the*

This awkward witticism attempts to connect Pindar's famous aphorism on water with King's unfortunate demise from the same element. Although his allusion is clumsy, Olivier does demonstrate a contemporary awareness of Pindar's use of figure and does attempt to replicate his methods. Yet, even though Olivier directly alludes to Pindar and Milton does not, Milton is more successful than Olivier in exploiting Pindar's imagistic techniques, succeeding where Olivier fails. Milton's is the sole truly Pindaric voice in the 1638 volume.

Milton's use of brief allusion and extended mythic digression owes as much to Pindar as his treatment of the transformed image. Milton introduces the first person from a classical myth just at the point when he poses the question, why did the nymphs not save Lycidas? As though to reply, he poses two other interlinked questions—"Had ye been there—for what could that have done?" and next "What could the Muse herself," (57–58), leaving the rest of the question incomplete. At this point, he alludes to Orpheus as the first of a series of mythic persons to whom he will contrast Lycidas. He chooses, just as Pindar had for Perseus, only very select details of his story—his birth from a Muse mother, her absence at his death, his enchantment of Nature and Nature's lament for him, his dismemberment by the "rout that make the hideous roar" (61), and the voyage of his "hoary visage," decapitated by the Bacchantes, down the Hebrus to the Lesbian shore. It is clear that he has suppressed details from the Orpheus story that might bring comfort at this juncture—that Calliope beheld from afar her son's death, that Orpheus's head still spoke Eurydice's name as it journeyed down the Hebrus, and that this head conferred the gift of song on Lesbian poets.[23] Further, he seems only to connect Orpheus with Lycidas in a deceptively simple and direct way—both were young poets who suffered untimely deaths. But the resemblance masks two decided differences. Lycidas at his birth was neither so divinely favored as Orpheus, nor was he at his death so tragically nor violently destroyed. And perhaps, though Milton is not ready to assert it, Lycidas was not abandoned by heaven after all.

The example of Orpheus provokes a second poetic sigh and still more impassioned questioning. Why should anyone serve a Muse, who begrudges thanks and abandons her children to a blind and fury-ridden fate? The question brings upon the scene the next important mythic figure in the ode, Orpheus's father, Phoebus Apollo, the god of poetry and the patron of

---

Original Edition, 1638, 15. Olivier also alludes to the Arethusa myth and to St. Peter walking the waves.

23. When Pindar recounts the story of Pelops in *Olympian 1*, he carefully eliminates details that might detract from Pelops's heroism—such as Pelops's bribe of Oenomaus's charioteer to assure his victory. Pindar is a model for selective myth-telling.

poets, who, as Pindar tells us in *Pythian 1,* holds the lyre in common right with the Muses. As with the appearance of Athene in *Pythian 12,* Apollo's appearance here raises the level from the human to the divine. Further, it bridges the gap between Orpheus and Lycidas. Phoebus as the divine father of Orpheus and the patron god of poets is metaphorically a father to Lycidas and to the shepherd-swain as well. As such, he affirms that heaven does not abandon the poet nor deny him appropriate fame. He insists that we consider Jove's ultimate purpose in all things.

Phoebus's speech—dramatic or epic in its style—is another instance of Milton's adopting a Pindaric device. Pindar does not use the device of dramatic speech except in very special instances when he wishes to give vivid realization to a moment in a narrative sequence. In *Olympian 1,* for example, when he is recounting how Tantalus's son Pelops plans to undertake a very dangerous chariot competition with Hippodamia's father in order to win her in marriage, Pindar breaks into his narration at the climactic moment with speech. Pelops has come to the seashore alone to seek the aid of the god Poseidon, and Pindar allows us to hear Pelops's prayer to the god. The speech makes vivid for us the sincerity, the courage, and above all the piety of this young man, a young man whose father Tantalus, after all, had been guilty of the greatest impiety. It is a turning point in both the narrative and the ode. Thereafter, Pelops is rewarded with victory and Pindar uses the mythic example to point out to his patron Hieron (who has also been victorious in a contest) the virtue of following the pious son who attributes his success to the god's help and not to his arrogant father who sinned against the gods.

Pindar uses dramatic speech in other odes to bring the word of the god to human beings. In *Olympian 13* we hear the voice of the goddess Athene urge Bellerophon on to heroic daring—as she tells him to bridle the winged horse Pegasus. In *Pythian 3* we hear Apollo determining to save his son Asclepius from death, even as he has decided to punish Asclepius's mother. In *Nemean 10* Zeus speaks in reply to Polydeuces and grants his request that he honor Castor and permit him to share his immortality. Moments of crisis provoke Pindar not just to describe the action but to present it with dramatic voice. Further, dramatic speech in Pindar's odes often marks a point of encounter of the mortal with the god, a point when the god must decide on a matter crucial for that mortal. The voice of the god changes the fate of the human being and at the same time changes the direction of the ode—lifting it from the human to the divine.

Dramatic speech punctuates the narrative not once but several times in this "digressive" section of "Lycidas." Apollo replies to the shepherd-swain; a series of mourners comment on Lycidas's untimely death; St. Peter regrets the good shepherd's loss and pronounces on the fate of the unworthy shepherds. When Phoebus Apollo interrupts the swain's angry indictment of divine justice, he reassures him that Jove's judgment is just, as Pindar's Apollo in *Pythian 3* or Pindar's Zeus in *Nemean 10* had offered reassurance of the faith and justice of the divine. In "Lycidas" the swain asserts that "*Fame* is the spur that the clear spirit doth raise," a fame prematurely dashed to disappointment (70); Phoebus replies, "*Fame* is no plant that grows on mortal soil" (78), correcting the swain's vision as he repeats the key word.

Phoebus's speech has the ring not only of Pindar's dramatic utterances, but also of Pindar's *sententiae*—the often-praised aphorisms that Pindar so frequently employs to assert the moral and the divine purpose of his odes. Both Warton and Jerram point to Pindar in their comments on Phoebus's remarks on fame, Jerram citing specifically *Nemean 7*. 31–34 (45): "τιμὰ δὲ γίνεται / ὧν θεός ἁβρὸν αὔξει λόγον τεθνακότων. / βοαθόων" (But honor comes to those whose report the god increases, assisting them, even though they are dead).[24] The context for this remark in *Nemean 7* is striking, for Pindar is reminding a young athlete at the very moment he has achieved fame how uncertain life is. Death comes to all, both those who foresee it and those who do not. True honor exists only in the divine—not in the human frame.[25] As Milton comments on the rewards of poetic fame, he has made Phoebus's words sound very like Pindaric sententia. That it is Pindar's own Phoebus Apollo who insists on the eternal perspective of "fame" (itself a classical concept) is important here. With Phoebus's reassurances, the poet-swain need not quite abandon the goal of earthly fame, the hope that his name will be set beside those classical poets—Homer, Vergil, Pindar—even as he wins his meed in heaven.

At this transitional point in the ode, the swain invokes two deities of water connected with Theocritean and Vergilian pastoral: the Sicilian fountain Arethusa and the Italian river Mincius, who return the ode to its pastoral note: "But now my Oat proceeds." A diverse procession of mythic figures now appear—Triton and Hippotades, next Camus and St. Peter—to disclaim responsibility for or to express sorrow at Lycidas's death. They present alternate perspectives on the question of human mortality and are both thematically and dramatically differentiated. Triton and Hippotades, representing nature as sea and wind, and Camus, the river god who represents the shepherd community at Cambridge, speak only from the perspective of

24. See Elledge, *Milton's "Lycidas,"* 275.
25. Pindar is probably referring here to Achilles, the father of Neoptolemus (the principal character in the myth of *Nemean 7*); Achilles died young because he valued his honor above his life (Plato cites him as an example in *The Apology*). His son Neoptolemus, though aspiring to the same honor, did not fare so well. It is the god, comments Pindar, who is the ultimate judge of a man's lasting fame.

earth, and so are unable to account for Lycidas and his fate. Peter, however, representing both human and divine realms, can speak authoritatively. As with the earlier figures, Orpheus and Apollo, Milton chooses selectively the biblical aspects of Peter's character he wishes to present. He names him the pilot of the Galilean lake, the holder of the keys of heaven, and the shepherd of the church, for in these roles he is related both to the pastor Lycidas and other shepherds, able to offer earthly guidance and heavenly sanction. Peter is a Christian father to the pastor Lycidas, for he is the head of the Church, just as Apollo is poetic father both to Orpheus and Lycidas as the head of the poetic congregation. Like Phoebus, he raises the dialogue from the earthly to the divine, vindicating heaven of the charge that it does not value the faithful herdsman and promising the punishment of the reprobates. Once more Milton uses the device of dramatic speech to make his point vivid. Just as Athene in Pindar's ode had brought Danae and Perseus from their unfortunate beginnings to triumph and liberation, punishing those who had done them evil, Peter assures us that the greedy shepherds will be ultimately struck down with swift heavenly vengeance: "But that two-handed engine at the door / Stands ready to smite once, and smite no more" (130–31).

But in many ways it is the treatment of Arethusa and Alpheus that demonstrates Milton's most subtle use of Pindar's mythic techniques. Why are they invoked—Arethusa, immediately after the Phoebus passage, and Alpheus after the Peter passage? Milton invokes Arethusa right at the point where he begins to consider the fate of the tragically drowned Lycidas; he invokes Alpheus immediately after Peter's denunciation of the bad shepherds. In the myth, well known to Milton in versions by Pindar, Theocritus, Vergil, and other writers, Arethusa had fled from Alpheus, who pursued her undersea and joined his waters with hers as she was transformed in Sicily into a fountain. In one aspect she is yet another example of a tragically pursued nymph like Daphne, who loses her life and her form in attempting to escape an unwanted lover. In another, she is the miraculously transformed being, who attains her true purpose in joining as fountain to river with that lover she first fled from—a Cyrene or even a Sabrina. Both Arethusa and Alpheus experience a sea-change; both undergo a kind of death in order to attain, as transformed gods, immortality in another realm. Pindar alludes to their story at the beginning of *Nemean 1* when he names Sicily the "Ἄμπνευμα σεμνὸν Ἀλφεοῦ," (1) the holy breathing place of Alpheus, the site where the river god attained his second breath as the immortal husband of Arethusa, the place where the colonizing Dorians may also attain new life.[26] From the human perspective, Alpheus,

26. Alpheus and Arethusa appear also in Theocritus, in Moschus (where the story of the river god and the nymph are told), in *Aeneid* 3. 694–96. See J. Martin Evans,

in vain pursuit of a fleeing nymph, heard a dread voice that shrunk his streams; from the divine perspective, that voice gave him renewed life in Sicily. So the poet proclaims reassuringly, "Return, *Alpheus,*" joining his invocation of Alpheus with a second command, "Return *Sicilian* Muse" (132–33).

Who is the Sicilian Muse? At first we might simply take this as another name for Arethusa, here made the Muse of pastoral poetry. But why *Muse*— a name used both harshly and reverently in this ode? Milton begins with an invocation of the Muses that sweeps aside their "denial vain, and coy excuse" (18); he appeals to a fellow poet as "some gentle muse" who may favor him with a future monody. The Muse is both the mother of Orpheus who could not save her son and the thankless Muse that offers scant rewards. But here, as he calls for return, the Muse is the spirit of comfort—the gentle mother who calls "the Vales, and bid them hither cast / Their Bells and Flowerets of a thousand hues" (134–35), the returning maiden who brings with her the spring. Milton seems to have conflated Arethusa with Proserpina—and Sicily is, after all, home to them both. In *Nemean 1* Pindar associates Sicily not only with Alpheus and Arethusa, but also with Proserpina, to whom Zeus gave the island of Sicily. Milton's flower catalogue—so like Perdita's in Shakespeare's *A Winter's Tale,* recalls the spring flowers that Proserpina let fall, those very flowers that will return when she returns to the earth. Without ever naming Proserpina, Milton has introduced her into the ode; without ever directly connecting Alpheus with Lycidas, he has made him the figure of the restored "god." Like Pindar, Milton lets his mythic figures subtly unlock his ode's meaning.

The return of the feminine comfort at this juncture in the poem is important, for "Lycidas" has been up to now a poem of masculine loss and abandonment, where the strong feminine presences of "L'Allegro" and "Il Penseroso"—the nurturing Muses—are helpless and where the saving female—the Sabrina figure of *A Mask*—is absent. The shepherd-swain wanders alone in a desolate landscape where the masculine figures who come—even the "fathers" Phoebus, Camus, and Peter—offer excuse, or moral sentence, or express regret or anger but do not comfort. Up to now the feminine too is impotent. The nymphs have not heard Lycidas's dying cries; the unnamed Muse Calliope does not appear; the pastoral mistresses—Neaera and Amaryllis—have been cast aside, unable to provide facile comfort or negligent pleasure. The shadow of the mother's death is omnipresent—the surviving son looks everywhere, but cannot find her, the sense of the feminine having been extinguished in his life. Bereavement breathes throughout the ode with its accompanying fear of death and

---

The Road from Horton: Looking Backwards in Lycidas. Also see Tayler, *"Lycidas* in Christian Time," in *Milton's Poetry.*

dissolution. Then the words sound, "Return, *Alpheus*" and with Alpheus, the restored lover, comes once more the feminine Muse, "Return, *Sicilian Muse*"—the mother, who has not abandoned him after all. For Milton, as for Pindar, who calls upon the Muse as mother at the beginning of *Nemean 3,* the Muse *is* the nurturing female presence who brought him both life and inspiration.

With the linking of Proserpina to the Sicilian Arethusa, there is also an implicit linking of Lycidas to Alpheus. Early in the ode Lycidas was associated with the tragic Orpheus whose "divine head" was destroyed and brought down the Hebrus river to the sea. Now, he is linked with another classical demigod, the river Alpheus, who in pursuing Arethusa undersea enacts the pagan version of the Christian resurrection, anticipating in fact Lycidas's second breath and redemption in heaven.[27] Milton indirectly alludes to Alpheus's undersea voyage as he describes how the dead Lycidas visits "the bottom of the monstrous world." Then, closing the circle, he alludes to still another classical figure—the poet Arion, who was not drowned, but also came safely through the seas to shore, saved by the dolphins. Milton never names Arion; he doesn't have to. Merely by referring to the dolphins, as J. Martin Evans has observed, he recalls the Arion story and also other mythic accounts of salvation by dolphins.[28] Ultimately, however, it is not the dolphins that save Lycidas. The myths of resurrected Alpheus and the rescued Arion are stories of salvation that parallel, but do not replicate, the Christian story. Missing from their accounts of rescue is the one who alone can effect Lycidas's resurrection. The angel of the guarded mount calls Lycidas homeward, but it is only through Christ that he is saved: "Through the dear might of him that walk'd the waves" (173). Because of Christ, Lycidas can rise from the waters, and like the day-star (Christ's own planetary aspect) mount high.

The vision of Lycidas, redeemed in heaven, hearing the songs of the

27. Milton is not the only poet in the Cambridge volume to link King with Alpheus. Isaac Olivier, who, as we noted, conspicuously employed water imagery, also makes the comparison, wishing that King, like Alpheus (whom he erroneously calls Achelous), might have run under the sea and come safely to land like a bridegroom: "As Achelous with his silver fleet / Runnes through salt Doris purely, so to meet / His Arethusa; the Sicanian maid / Admires his sweetness by no wave decai'd; / So should he, so have cut the Irish strand, / And like a lustie bridegroom leapt to land" (*Obsequies,* in *Justa Edovardo King,* 16). Milton deals with the bridegroom motif with greater subtlety.

For commentary on the English poems of the King collection and mythic, thematic, and imagistic connections to Milton's "Lycidas," see Michael Lloyd, " 'Justa Edouardo King,' " in *N & Q.* Lloyd does not discuss the Latin poems of *Justa.*

28. See J. Martin Evans, "Lycidas and the Dolphins," *N&Q* 25 (15–17). Several of the poems in *Justa* and *Obsequies* also refer to dolphins; see, for example, Isaac Olivier: "Why did not some officious dolphine hie / To be his ship and pilot through the frie / Of wandring Nymphs" (*Obsequies,* 15). Olivier also alludes to St. Peter as the one who "trode the waves" (16).

solemn troops and sweet societies, not sunk beneath the waves, is the last of the mythic transformations that Milton enacts in his monody. This final transformation is dependent, however, upon those he has effected earlier: Lycidas, Orpheus, Apollo, Peter, Alpheus, even Arion are all mythic characters that lead us ultimately to Christ, who mythically interconnects with them all. Like most of the figures in this ode, Christ is not directly named, but is identified through a "myth" connected with him, the story of his walking the waves (see Matthew 14.33). Milton actually alludes to the story twice, the first time indirectly when he names Peter, "the Pilot of the *Galilean* lake" (109). In Matthew, Peter, sailing the ship on the sea of Galilee with the other disciples and seeing Jesus walking on the water, first expresses his faith by asking Jesus to bid him come to him, but then falters in his faith and begins to sink in the water. Only when Jesus reassures him and takes him by the hand does Peter recover his faith, declaring that Jesus is the Son of God. At the final juncture in the ode, the shepherd-swain, who has also, like Peter, doubted, regains his faith and is able to declare to the other shepherds: "Weep no more . . . / For *Lycidas* your sorrow is not dead" (165–66).

The affirmation that Lycidas is not dead does not come through the process of intellective reasoning and debate, but through the series of mythic transformations whereby we are led from the dead Orpheus to the living Lycidas, saved, as Peter was and as the poet-swain hopes to be, by the redeemer who walked the waves. From an abandoned classical poet Lycidas has become the saved Christian, entertained in heaven by "all the Saints above." Yet he still retains on earth a classical persona as the "Genius of the shore," himself the safeguard "To all that wander in that perilous flood" (183, 185). By employing Pindar's techniques of mythic transformation Milton can convey by implication, by allusion, by digression an intricate design that is both classical and Christian.

There is perhaps at the very end of "Lycidas" an acknowledgment of the part Pindar has played in monody. In calling the song a Doric lay, Milton connects it both to the idylls of Sicily and to the odes of Greece. Pindar sang in the Doric dialect—and he too was the poet of Alpheus and Arethusa. In "warbling his *Doric* lay," Milton tells us that the swain "touch'd the tender stops of various Quills." (188). These various quills can apply to the different modes adopted in the monody—ode and pastoral eclogue and lament and invective—and its exploitation of a range of styles and voices, not the least of which are the magnific odes of Pindar, the ancient singer of Dorian Thebes.

WHO IS LYCIDAS?

In the course of its critical history the impact of ancient pastoral on Milton's "Lycidas" has been well documented. Although Theocritus's and Vergil's and even (as I have been arguing) Pindar's influence is evident in Milton's poem, Milton was intent on making his monody a poem of its own time, not an ancient ode or idyll. "Lycidas" identifies itself as a Renaissance poem in several ways, one being its attitudes toward its subject—the dead Lycidas—as a poet and pastor; the other being the voice of the unnamed shepherd-swain, who sings the lament. In the interaction between these two Milton develops a poem that is uniquely contemporary, however much the techniques and the poetic voices from the Roman and Greek past echo and re-echo throughout.[29]

The title "Lycidas" immediately identifies the poem as pastoral and Milton consistently maintains this convention throughout. Its use of the pastoral convention distinguishes it, as critics have often remarked, from the other poems—both Latin and English—in the Cambridge collection. Other poets of *Justa* and *Obsequies* assume the poetic "I" and address King directly or refer to him as Edvardus or as King, but Milton distances himself from his subject by giving King the role of Lycidas and by assuming for himself the persona of a shepherd-swain who represents a pastoral community. We can understand better Milton's stance in "Lycidas" by placing it in its Renaissance pastoral context and by contrasting this context with that of the other elegies in the collection.

The conventions of Renaissance pastoral are particularly helpful in elucidating Milton's distinctive treatment of the speaker and the subject—Lycidas. Besides "old Damoetas" (35), the pastor-teacher of the Cambridge community, Lycidas is the only shepherd named in the poem. In a gesture uncharacteristic of pastoral, ancient or modern, where pastoral names are abundant, Milton refuses to assign a name to his "uncouth swain." Neither does he allude to or create a dialogue with other shepherds nor set the scene at the beginning with a pastoral frame. The swain's song opens the poem, and only at the end when the song has ended does Milton close the missing opening frame and describe the singer. We must supply the context at the beginning and must learn from what he tells us who the singer is and why he has come to sing.

It is useful then to ask right at the outset, "Who is Lycidas?" Critics have usually answered the question by turning to those characters in ancient pastoral that bear the name or to characters closely associated with them. A goatherd named Lycidas appears in Theocritus's sixth idyll and Vergil's ninth eclogue. A dead shepherd—Daphnis—is mourned in Theocritus's first idyll

---

29. Many critics have noted how the refrains and echoes from Bion, Moschus, Theocritus, and Vergil are present throughout "Lycidas," continually reminding the reader of the tradition of pastoral from antiquity. But Louis Martz has reminded us that it is the *entire* tradition of pastoral that Milton evokes, both ancient and modern. See Martz, *Poet of Exile,* 60.

and in Vergil's fifth eclogue. The shepherd—Lycidas—of Milton's monody is usually considered a composite of the two. Daphnis as the twice-mourned shepherd, prominent in both Theocritus and Vergil—would seem to claim precedence over Lycidas the goatherd as a poet-figure. Why Milton passes the name Daphnis by and fixes on Lycidas is somewhat of a puzzle—one to which we will return. Theocritus's goatherd Lycidas is a modest fellow, whom Simichidas meets along the way and engages in a good-natured singing match—Lycidas gives Simichidas the prize. Vergil's Lycidas is also a goatherd, whom Moerus encounters en route to town; Lycidas agreeably consoles him in his troubles—he declines to sing, however, praising Moerus as a singer. If Milton models his Lycidas on either of these goatherds—good fellows though they are—I should be much surprised. Both Louis Martz and J. Martin Evans attempt to justify Milton's choice of the Theocritean-Vergilian Lycidas.[30] Martz correctly observes that Lycidas continues to be a name popular in later pastoral, citing specifically Sannazaro's use of it in his first piscatorial eclogue. But there are many more Renaissance Lycidae.

Lycidas as a character occurs in many Renaissance eclogues—well over thirty neo-Latin poems, according to W. Leonard Grant's count.[31] In some he is a much lamented shepherd who has, like Milton's own Lycidas, recently died; in others he is the principal speaker; and in still others he is one of several pastoral interlocutors engaged in dialogue.[32] Sometimes he is a shepherd who, together with other shepherds, mourns a companion. Lycidas joins Thyrsis in Basilio Zanchi's eclogue to lament the passing of Damon who represents dead poet Castiglione and in another pastoral he mourns Meliboeus, the great pastor of pastors, Pietro Bembo.[33] In these poems Lycidas is doing for another poet what the swain of Milton's poem

---

30. See J. Martin Evans's discussion of Milton's use of these eclogues: *The Road from Horton*, 14–15. Also see Louis L. Martz, *Poet of Exile*, 60–75.

31. For an account of the Renaissance Lycidae, see Grant, *Neo-Latin Literature and the Pastoral*, esp. 116–204; and Kirkconnell, *Awake the Courteous Echo*, esp. 141–243. Kirkconnell includes both ancient and Renaissance analogues to "Lycidas" in this collection. Also see Thomas Perrin Harrison Jr. and Harry Joshua Leon, *The Pastoral Eclogue, An Anthology*.

32. See Martz, *Poet of Exile*, 63.

33. See Lawrence V. Ryan, "Milton's *Epitaphium Damonis* and B. Zanchi's Elegy on Baldassare Castiglione," in *Humanisticia Lovaniensia* 30. Ryan points out that Zanchi first wrote the elegy to mourn the death of Celso Mellini in 1519, but later rewrote it, adapting the details for the Mantua-born Castiglione, who died in 1529, and publishing it in this version in 1553, this final version being the one that prevailed. Zanchi also wrote pastoral elegies for Pontano ("Meliseus"), for Lorenzo Gambara ("Alcon"), and for Navagero ("Myrtilis"). "Meliboeus" is one of three anonymous laments for Pietro Bembo. Amyntas asks Lycidas why he is mourning and Lycidas replies that all nature is grieving for Meliboeus. Amyntas comforts him, telling him that Meliboeus is adding new glory to the gods, and advises him to cease grieving. Together they depart for new pastures as the night comes on. (in Gherus, ed., *Delitiae CC Italorum Poetarum*, 1.379–81).

does for him. At other times Lycidas is not a mourner for another shepherd, but a forlorn lover sighing for an unresponsive Neaera or Amaryllis, sometimes, as in Sannazaro's piscatorial eclogue, a lover who grieves for his dead mistress. It is useful to examine these Renaissance Lycidae according to the role or roles they play: as lover, as interlocutor, as mourner, as dead shepherd. First, let us look at several prominent sixteenth-century Latin eclogues in which Lycidas pleads his case as a disappointed lover. Although neither Milton's Lycidas nor his shepherd-swain is primarily a lover, both may have listened to the voices of passionate shepherdesses and even considered the claims of pastoral love.

"NEAERA AND AMARYLLIS"

At the beginning of "Lycidas" the shepherd-swain plucks the myrtle leaves —the emblem of Venus and love—as well as the Apollonian laurel and the Bacchic ivy—and shatters all three. Lycidas died young, before he could marry and enjoy the fruits of Venus; the anxious swain who mourns Lycidas seems to have forsworn both Neaera and Amaryllis and the amorous delights of shepherd life.[34] Love and its promised joys are themes often unnoticed in Milton's monody, undercurrents in the plaintive lament for lost pastoral life. As Michael Lieb has rightly observed, "despite the great amount of attention devoted to *Lycidas* in recent years, the amatory dimension of the poem remains largely unexplored."[35] Lieb has explored this amatory note in ancient pastoral, pointing, for example, to the cruel Amaryllis of Theocritus's idyll 3, to Daphnis's betrayal by a mistress in idyll 1, to Vergil's Gallus and his affair with the heartless Lycoris in eclogue 10. But apart from Sannazaro's eclogue 1, which both he and Louis Martz cite, he leaves Renaissance pastoral unexplored. Renaissance pastoral, however, is rich in disappointed lovers, many of whom resemble Milton's Lycidas or his shepherd-swain.

In Sannazaro's piscatorial eclogue, the fisherman Lycidas is one of the speakers who mourns for the dead Phyllis, his beloved and bride-to-be. Establishing his credentials as a singer and lover in the ancient Theocritean

---

34. For the Renaissance Neaerae, see R. J. Schoeck in *N & Q*. Also see John Carey's note on Neaera's hair (John Milton, "Lycidas," *Complete Shorter Poems* [1971], 245) that locates Neaera in Vergil, Tibullus, and Horace as well as in Secundus, Buchanan, and others. In Lygdamus Neaera's hair is described as "longos incompta capillos" (3.2.11–12), in Secundus as "tortiles capillos" (*Basia* 8.20). Renaissance poets who write to Neaera include not only Secundus and Buchanan, but also Marullo, Crinito, Amalteo, Leech, and many, many more. It is probably the most popular name for a mistress in all the neo-Latin corpus.

35. Lieb, *The Sinews of Ulysses,* 67.

and Vergilian line, he pours out his heart to his friend Mycon in a song lamenting Phyllis. The death of the bride has a mythic resonance. Although it is never mentioned directly, the subtext here—as also in Sannazaro's *Arcadia*—is the story of Orpheus's loss of Eurydice.[36] A sense of desolation pervades the eclogue, for in losing Phyllis, Sannazaro's Lycidas, just like Orpheus, has lost not only his beloved, but also his connection with society, his vocation as a poet, and even his desire to live. The sea and the shore ("deserta litora") now seem desolate; he thinks of the ungrateful sepulcher that holds Phyllis. Just like Milton's shepherd, he feels the "heavy change" in nature, now joyless and dead, as though nature were responding to the death of the beloved. Both Sannazaro and Milton effectively exploit the pathetic fallacy. In both poems there is a bitter sense of youth blighted, hopes disappointed, and emptiness and grief left in the place of solace, love, and wished-for reward. Milton's shepherd reproaches the Muse who did not save Lycidas and who offers scant reward for service. Sannazaro's Lycidas reproaches Venus who has taken the joys and expectation from his youth. With a brief glance, Milton's swain also regrets that he has not enjoyed the sports of love that now seem past. But we will return later to Milton's Neaera and Amaryllis—the absent shepherdesses.

Images of water are integral to both Sannazaro's and Milton's poems. Sannazaro looks at the barren seascape; Milton thinks of the waves that still hold the body of Lycidas, of the "sounding Seas" that hurl his bones, of the "whelming tide" that covers him. Sannazaro's Lycidas, saying farewell to the shore, imagines himself wandering on the empty desolate ways, far from the community of fishermen and memory of his dead Phyllis. But at this point he remembers the protective sea deities—Nisaea, Cymodoce, Lycothea and Palaemon, Panope, Galatea, Proteus—some also named in "Lycidas," others in the Attendant Spirit's catalogue of Sabrina's attendants. From the sea—first viewed as comfortless and desolate—comes comfort in the form of these sea deities who dance, sing, and finally frame a dirge for Phyllis. Now Sannazaro's Lycidas is able to see Phyllis herself translated into a protective deity, a goddess of the waters, plucking immortal amaranth and mixing it with seaweed. She now looks down on them, like the other protective goddess Parthenope, with whom she now dwells. Like Milton's Lycidas, she becomes a protective genius.

In *A Mask at Ludlow-Castle* Milton used Sabrina and her accompanying train to bring purification and release to the Lady and to return her to

---

36. See David Quint, "Sannazaro: From Orpheus to Proteus," in *Origin and Originality*. In *Arcadia*, as Quint points out, Meliseo mourns the death of Fillide three times repeating her name, just as the decapitated Orpheus three times cries out the name of Eurydice, as his head is carried down the Hebrus (66).

her family. Neptune and the sea-deities act as neutral forces, however, in "Lycidas." Triton, their representative, declares them blameless: although they did not save Lycidas, neither did they destroy him. Milton's sea-deities come to sympathize, but do not tender the kind of assurance offered in Sannazaro's poem. Neither do companionable shepherds like Sannazaro's Mycon offer comfort to the swain of Milton's monody. The swain of "Lycidas" must find comfort and answers for himself. He merely witnesses and does not hold colloquy with the procession of nature deities. Milton avoids the pagan apotheosis and pagan comfort. Unlike Sannazaro, who entrusts Phyllis to a tomb protected by the Siren Parthenope, Milton leaves Lycidas's body to the resurrection that all Christians may expect.

But Sannazaro's poem is not the only Renaissance eclogue where we find an unhappy lover named Lycidas. In Francesco Berni's "Amyntas," in Basilio Zanchi's "Phyllis," and in Joannes Secundus's Orpheus eclogue a lover named Lycidas suffers the pangs of rejected love. Zanchi's Lycidas at first denies Mycon's request to tell of his unhappy love: "Ne miserum me coge Mycon memorasse superbos / Fastus, & tristes saeuae mihi Phyllidis iras; / Dum refero, crescit dolor: & nova cura recursat." (Do not urge me, who am miserable, Mycon, to remember the haughty pride and woeful anger of savage Phyllis toward me. When I relate, sorrow increases and new cares return.) But he at last consents to tell of his unhappy love, and at the conclusion of his tale, he lays down in the grass to await Phyllis, hopeful that when she passes by she will reward him with a kiss. Although scorned by his mistress, this lover neither dies for love, nor altogether abandons hope. Such is not the case with the Lycidas of Francesco Berni (1497–1535).[37] Berni models his shepherd on the tragic dying lovers of Theocritus's first and Vergil's tenth eclogue.[38] Like them, Berni's Lycidas is a supreme singer, whose song has resounded to the hills and caves and groves, and who has through his singing caused other shepherds to identify with him as he determines to die, forsaken by the fair Amyntas. The pastor Meliboeus, who tells of Lycidas's plight, shares in his distress, grieving that neither Cupid nor Apollo can save him. The Naiads weep about his virgin

37. Basilius Zanchius, "Phyllis," in *Delitiae CC. Italorum Poetarum* (1608); Francesco Berni, *Tutte le Opere* (1538).

38. See J. Martin Evans, "Lycidas, Daphnis, and Gallus," in *ERS*. Evans argues convincingly that Theocritus's Daphnis and Vergil's Gallus—while both languishing for love—are actually opposites. Daphnis is a Hippolytus figure, who having forsworn love, is the victim of an avenging Aphrodite; Gallus, however, is a victim of his own sexual passion. Milton's Lycidas and his swain, he asserts, more resemble the Theocritean figure. Evans comments how Renaissance commentary on Theocritus and Vergil would have made this contrast clear. Evans does not deal, however, with other Renaissance attempts (such as Berni's) to make a composite of Vergil's and Theocritus's shepherds.

tomb and bring violets and cups of milk to mourn him, blaming love as the cause of Lycidas's death. Lycidas bids farewell to his flocks and to love.

Love also plays a part in Milton's monody. The shepherd-swain mourns the untimeliness of Lycidas's death, regretting the loss to "Shepherd's ear" and regretting also (although he never fully voices it) the fact that he died unmarried. The bridegroom Alpheus unites with Arethusa, fulfilling the love Lycidas has lost. The flower passage at the close of the ode indirectly mourns his unfruitful demise, for the flowers of the spring that strew Lycidas's laureate hearse are those associated with forsaken love—"the rathe Primrose that forsaken dies, / The tufted Crow-toe and pale Jessamine, / The white Pink, and the Pansy freakt with jet, / The glowing Violet . . . And every flower that sad embroidery wears" (142–45, 148). In the Christian apotheosis that follows, the swain promises a kind of fulfillment to forsaken love. Milton does not follow Vergil's, Theocritus's, or Berni's example and leave his Lycidas desolate of love. The amatory note of Milton's poem achieves a different resolution. Lycidas will hear "the unexpressive nuptial Song / In the blest Kingdoms meek of joy and love" (176–77). Like the unmarried Damon of "Epitaphium Damonis," he will share in the marriage of the Lamb. It is a specifically "Christian" wedding song that Lycidas will hear. David Quint has noted that Milton does not lose hope that the consummation of his own Lycidas may yet have its place in a transcendent pastoral world of heaven.[39] Further, although sexual disappointment is part of the tragedy of Lycidas, it is not Milton's last word on pastoral love. When he creates the pastoral scenes of Eden in *Paradise Lost,* he will rewrite the sexual idyll and grant fulfilled love to the shepherd Adam and his faithful shepherdess Eve.

The Lycidas of Joannes Secundus (1510–1536) not only laments an unhappy love but also connects his fate to that of Orpheus, the unfortunate poet-lover whose loss of Eurydice Milton alludes to in "L'Allegro" and "Il Penseroso" and whose own death he mourns in "Lycidas."[40] Like Zanchi's and Berni's Lycidas, Secundus's Lycidas is the victim of a hard-hearted mistress—the cruel Neaera. By making Lycidas the narrator of Orpheus's tragedy, by allowing him to feel a kinship with the ancient poet, Lycidas's loss of Neaera becomes inextricably involved with Orpheus's loss of Eurydice. Secundus creates a pastoral frame for his "Orpheus" eclogue;

---

39. David Quint, "Sannazaro: From Orpheus to Proteus," in *Origin and Originality.*

40. Joannes Secundus, "Orpheus, ecloga," in "Sylvarum Liber," *Opera* (1541), 5–53r. See also John R. C. Martyn, "Joannes Secundus: Orpheus and Eurydice," in *Humanistica Lovaniensia* 35. Martyn points out the link between Orpheus and Neaera in Milton and Secundus. I wish to thank John Dillon for providing me a photocopy of the 1541 Secundus and for calling my attention to Martyn's transcription, translation, and commentary on the Orpheus eclogue.

he introduces the shepherd Lycidas and lets him narrate his own story before he sings Orpheus's song of unhappy love. The introductory frame is important, and obviously has biographical and poetical overtones, since Neaera, as we noted in Chapter 1, is cruel mistress of Secundus's own *Elegies* and of the *Basia*.

The song that Secundus's Lycidas sings resembles the song of Sannazaro's Lycidas, a lament of a lover for a dead loved one. But the song is not his own. Secundus makes his Lycidas take on Orpheus's voice, as though the dead poet himself were singing for the lost Eurydice, the living poet being totally absorbed in his character and voice. Lycidas not only sings of Orpheus, he sings *for* Orpheus. It is as though Orpheus were living still and grieving still for his beloved wife. Ironically enough, Secundus's Lycidas has lost no beloved to death. He himself is the forsaken one, enthralled by the gray eyes and golden hair of "urbana Neaera" and cast aside and abandoned. He mourns by the deserted mountains and icy crags, so completely absorbed in the Orphic personality that he forgets his flocks and pastoral duties. Yet, as different as his case is from Orpheus's, it is through singing in Orpheus's voice that he finds relief for his grief. The Muse Calliope hears him and, thinking that her son still lives, kisses Lycidas and grants him inspiration.

In the song proper, Lycidas as Orpheus addresses himself to Eurydice, singing as though he has just lost her the second time and repeating the refrain: "Euridice, misera Euridice, misera uxor amantis." Appealing to his Father Apollo to assist him in song, he rehearses the whole story: how he first sought Eurydice in Hades, how the Furies and Cerberus grew kind at his song, but how his success in singing did not save him from losing his wife a second time. Now—desolate and abandoned—he swears that he will die remembering his first love. At this point Calliope interrupts Lycidas's song, refusing to let him proceed since she knows the inevitable sequel—the dismemberment of Orpheus.

In his Orpheus eclogue Secundus has created a speaker so totally absorbed in his woe that Orpheus's grief becomes indistinguishable from his own. In his monody Milton achieves a similar kind of poetic involvement, making his shepherd speaker feel not only Lycidas's misfortune as his own, but also that of the archetypal poet Orpheus, who represents, as we have noted, them both. The three "fatal" figures intersect—two of them having been cut off by a savage fate—and the third, even as he sings, dreading the fatal shears. Milton deals with the same paradox that Secundus so poignantly permits his Lycidas to express in his song—the poet who enchanted universal nature, who made the shades of Hades mild, could neither save himself nor his beloved nor be saved by Calliope. Milton alludes to the Muse mother, and Secundus brings her upon the very scene to lament once more her failure to save her son. But while Secundus shrinks from telling the horrific end to Orpheus's story, Milton does not, making us look on Orpheus's gory visage, sent down the stream to the Lesbian shore.

In Secundus's poem, lost love is a dominant theme. Orpheus's Eurydice and Lycidas's Neaera ironically become one, Neaera becoming a symbol of loss, delusion, and death. Both Secundus's shepherd and his Orpheus are helpless to win their loved ones—and this helplessness inevitably dooms them. Milton associates Orpheus's death both with lost vocation and lost love, for immediately after his shepherd has told how "the rout that made the hideous roar" tore Orpheus, he breathes a poetic sigh—alas—echoing Secundus's pastoral "heu."

> Alas! What boots with uncessant care
> To tend the homely slighted Shepherd's trade,
> And strictly meditate the thankless Muse?
> Were it not better done as others use,
> To sport with *Amaryllis* in the shade,
> Or with the tangles of *Neaera's* hair? (64–69)

Is it only coincidental that Milton's shepherd-swain cries out against the fate of Orpheus immediately before he complains of the pitiful rewards for poetry and the vain temptations of love? Is it only coincidence that he regrets Neaera and Amaryllis? Lurking in the shade are the pastoral mistresses whom others have courted. Were it not better for him also to yield to their blandishments: "to sport with Amaryllis in the shade / Hid in the tangles of Neaera's hair"? The lines, here quoted from the 1638 text, possess an even greater sensuous immediacy than their 1645 counterparts.[41] The lover is hidden in the tangles of his mistress's hair, completely absorbed by her person, yielding as Secundus did to Neaera. Is it a wonder he revised this line in 1645? Significantly, neither in 1638 nor in 1645 does the poet-swain answer the question he poses. Like Secundus, he may not have altogether forsworn Neaera and her tangled hair. The juxtaposition of Orpheus as fatal lover and fatal poet in both Milton's and Secundus's poem casts Milton's shepherd at a crucial moment in a double role. If Milton knew Secundus's "Orpheus" eclogue, he also knew that Secundus—like his own Lycidas—did not live to enjoy his Neaera. Like Edward King or Milton's Lycidas, the poet of the celebrated *Basia* died young, having prophesied unwittingly in the Orpheus eclogue his own fate.

The "Lycidas" of Giambattista Amalteo (1525–1573) is also a poem of exclusion and lost love, but exile, rather than death or infidelity, separates

---

41. See Milton, "Lycidas," *Obsequies to the memorie of Mr. Edward King,* in *Justa* (1939), 22.

this Lycidas from his Amaryllis and from the pastoral shades of Florence, where he has enjoyed his youth, his loves, and his poetry-making. Amalteo, like Secundus, uses a frame for his eclogue, introducing the single singer, sitting by the side of the Arno lamenting, and explaining the reasons for his grief, even as he offers at the outset a few words of dedication to Cosmo de' Medici. Assuming the character of Lycidas himself, Amalteo regrets that he must depart for Spain, forced to leave the lovely banks of the Arno, as well as his lovely Amaryllis, whom he has courted under evergreen laurels.[42] Amalteo develops, as had Secundus and Berni, not only a strong identification of the poet with his speaker, but also an identification with place—a pastoral Florence, where he feels that nature, companions, loves are perfectly in harmony with poetry. Leaving Florence and journeying across the vast Pyrenees, he leaves behind the happy fields and woods, where his flock grazes, where he first felt the fires of love for Amaryllis, and goes to an unsympathetic world desolate of all comfort. The eclogue builds through repeated reference to this native landscape, to the evergreen gardens that Lycidas will see no more, that evoke both a sense of nostalgia and are the symbol for youth and love and companionship lost forever on his departure. His two last farewells are to Amaryllis and to the laurels of Florence. If only she might remember their loves, if only she might weep still and sigh for him, if only these plaints could call him back.

> Huc gemitum, & nostras referetis saepe querelas,
> Quas fors accipiet madidis Amaryllis ocellis.
> O mihi, si veteres recolens Amaryllis amores,
> Et nostri desiderio crudelius ardens
> Illacrymet, si sollicito suspira corde
> Ducat, et insanis reuocet me tristis ab undis!

> Here you will often reply to our sigh and plaints,
> Which perhaps Amaryllis will receive with wet eyes.
> Ah me, if only Amaryllis, thinking of our former loves,
> And burning more cruelly, might weep for our desire,
> If only she might draw sighs from a solicitous heart, and
> Sad, call me back from the raging waters!

The lovely Amaryllis of this poem is a contrast to the heartless Neaera of Secundus's eclogue. If we accept Amaryllis as a type for the loyal but lost love, we might even read the "Amaryllis" passage of "Lycidas" with

---

42. Giambattista Amalteo's "Ad Ludovicum Dulcium" is a pastoral that alludes to wooing Neaera in a *locus amoenus*. See Sukanta Chaudhuri, *Renaissance Pastoral and its English Development*, 94.

less cynicism. The poet-swain appears to conflate the thankless mistress and thankless Muse and look on sport with Amaryllis or Neaera as vain as his devotion to the Muse. But his attitude toward the mistress may be colored by his own despair. Milton's sportive Amaryllis may be as innocent of reproveable pleasures as was the sportive Mirth of "L'Allegro." To sport with Amaryllis in the shade may be only to enjoy those pleasures of youth that hard fate now denies to the prototypical shepherd—whether by death or exile. Amalteo's "Lycidas" allows us to entertain an alternative reading, and pass a less harsh judgment on mistress and muse.

Much as he regrets the loss of his mistress, Amalteo reserves the final farewell for the Florentine laurels themselves, under whose shadows their hearts grew warm with love while Pan meditated his song.

> At vos o lauri, quarum fragrante sub umbra
> Et nostra insolitis caluerunt pectora flammis
> Nostraque Maenalios meditata est fistula cantus,
> Sic ver assiduum foveat, nev frigora laedant,
> Neve unquam laeto rami spolientur honore.

> But you, o laurels, under whose fragrant shade
> Our hearts grew warm with unaccustomed flames,
> And our pipe meditated Pan's songs,
> Thus may eternal spring ever warm, and frost never harm
> Nor ever may your branches be spoiled of rich honor . . . [43]

In these laurels survive his poetry and the remembrance of his love. The complaint is bittersweet, very like that of Milton's swain who comes to shatter the laurel before its due season and to express regret for the joyful days when he and the other Lycidas joined in their pastoral songs and dances. Perhaps an Amaryllis looked on those pastoral dances, too.

Secundus's and Amalteo's poems share with Milton's "Lycidas" a strong sense of personal involvement. Both Secundus and Amalteo make their poet-speaker their spokesman—the means through which they can speak their deepest feelings. Through him they voice their sense of loss, of regret, of disappointments in love and in life. Love has passed these shepherds by. Neaera or Amaryllis is lost, as they turn regretfully away from the amorous shades. But what awaits them? Both Secundus and Amalteo refrain from being too specific. They leave us with a sense of loss, perhaps even of impending doom. Their poems are deliberately valedictory. The conclusion of "Lycidas" is valedictory too, but with a difference. We do not know, of

---

43. Joannes Baptista Amaltheus, *Carmina* (1550), 71r–72v. See J. E. Sandys, *TRSL* 32, for a discussion of Amalteo.

course, exactly what awaits Milton's shepherd-swain either. But as he ends his song and comes to the end of the pastoral day, he twitches his mantle blue, rises, and goes on, departing with a sense of renewal. There is hope—and perhaps love, too.

DAPHNIS OR LYCIDAS?

In 1587 Oxford University printed a twin volume to commemorate the untimely death the previous year of one of its most illustrious alumni, Sir Philip Sidney. It included many different poems—most of them in Latin—that commemorate Sidney, some of them, inevitably, pastoral eclogues or laments. The Continental tradition that we have been following had crossed the channel and expressed itself in these Latin eclogues.[44] Sidney is mourned in the university volume both under the names Lycidas and Daphnis.[45] It is tempting to focus only on the anonymous eclogue "Lycidas"—a poem, like Milton's own monody, that was written for a university collection and that names a dead poet the very name that Milton chose many years later for Edward King. It is tempting also to speculate that Milton, in choosing the name Lycidas for his dead poet-friend, was thinking also of Sir Philip Sidney, a much more renowned poet, who had been honored with the same name.[46] It is even more tempting to make some political as well as poetical speculations about the use of the name. Sidney was more than a poet; he was a young Protestant leader, who died in the Netherlands fighting for a Protestant nation that was trying to maintain its religious freedom against the much more powerful Catholic Spain. His death left both the world of poetry and politics bereft. Mars would grieve for him as well as Mercury and Apollo. And the Protestant world—not

44. Warren B. Austin has pointed out that some of the earliest pastoral laments written by English poets are those Giles Fletcher the Elder wrote for the collection lamenting the death of the poet Walter Haddon and his son Clare Haddon, a scholar at Cambridge drowned in the Cam, also in 1572: "De obitu Clarissimi viri D. Gualteri Haddoni, Elegia." He proposes these as possible analogues to "Lycidas." See "Milton's Lycidas and Two Latin Elegies by Giles Fletcher the Elder," in *SP* 44.

45. Jan Dousa the Younger also wrote an eclogue for the death of Sidney in which Lycidas on the banks of the Thames mourns for the passing of Daphnis. See Jan Dousa Filius, *Poemata* (1704), 102–5.

46. The volume is organized into two parts, the first *Exequiae Illustrissimi Equitis, D. Philippi Sidnaei Gratissimae Memoriae ac Nomine Inpensae*, the second *Peplus Illustrissimi Viri D. Philippi Sidnaei Supremis Honoribus Dicatus*, both published in Oxford by Joseph Barnes in 1587. The eclogue "Daphnis" by William Gager occurs in the first part, the eclogue "Lycidas" in the second. I wish to thank James Riddell for calling my attention to the volumes. He and Stanley Stewart remark how the commemorative elegies from the obsequies to Sidney to *Lycidas* "served as a vehicle for the expression of native poetic ambition." See *Jonson's Spenser: Evidence and Historical Criticism*, 135.

just England—would especially feel his loss.[47] Milton might indeed have looked upon the Sidney of this commemorative volume as a figure for "good shepherd" who was tending his sheep, tending them in a different way from the Anglican priest Edward King, about to set off for a pastorate in Ireland when he was untimely struck down. Sidney played skillfully upon his pastoral pipes and served well the "faithful Herdsman's art." The England of Elizabeth unanimously mourned for a Protestant political leader as a good pastor. Milton's own England was, in contrast, producing shepherds who were both bad poets and bad pastors—venial men who fed themselves and served neither people nor country and let "their lean and flashy songs / Grate on their scrannel Pipes of wretched straw" (123–24). The difference in status between the Elizabethan Protestant poet-pastor Sidney and the Caroline poet-pastors could not have failed to strike Milton.

Both the anonymous Sidney "Lycidas" and Milton's "Lycidas" speak for university communities that their poets choose to picture in idealized pastoral colors. The Sidney "Lycidas" is a dialogue between two shepherds—Damoetas and Amyntas; Milton's "Lycidas" a monologue that implicitly addresses the "pastoral" community. The Sidney "Lycidas" opens as Amyntas asks Damoetas why he comes, neglected in appearance and obviously suffering some inner grief. Damoetas replies that Lycidas is dead—a shepherd who used to please the other shepherds with his songs, and it is fitting, therefore, to spend the day in song mourning his passing. These conventional words, entirely appropriate to the pastoral, anticipate the sentiments of Milton's swain. Yet though conventional, these words have force within their respective poems, because they express the conviction that the untimely loss of a poet-pastor is a tragic loss that must be appropriately recognized and mourned by his fellows. Both poems almost announce a national imperative. "Lycidas is dead," says Milton's swain, as he begins to frame the ode in his honor, quickly adding, "he must not float upon his wat'ry bier / Unwept" (12–13).

The 1587 "Lycidas" makes the death of the shepherd an occasion of national mourning: Damoetas insists that the whole realm is plunged into grief for Lycidas. Not only do the nymphs of wood, tree, and dell and the Graces lament, but Mars sets his shield aside and Apollo and the Muses weep. Sidney was, after all, both a soldier and a poet. The poet's reward, the laurel, is dry—shattered, as in "Lycidas," by the premature death, and the waters of Hippocrene are stagnant. Nor is there any hope that another such

---

47. There were elegies written in the Netherlands for the death of Sidney. Milton may have known the poem by the Dutch poet Janus Dousa the Younger. Recently, Raphael Falco has dealt with the presence of Sidney in Milton's "Lycidas": *Conceived Presences: Literary Genealogy in Renaissance England.*

as Lycidas will come; for, as Milton was to phrase it for the other Lycidas, he "hath not left his peer" (9). Amyntas responds, approving Damoetas's sentiments, but reassuring him that Lycidas has entered heaven—now the woods resound with joy, not sorrow. Reconciled, Damoetas bids Lycidas hail and farewell, promising that so long as dawn rises in the east and Phoebus dips in the waves at sunset, so long will the pipes of Arcady resound with song for Lycidas. In Milton's "Lycidas" a single shepherd offers both complaint and consolation, weeping first for Lycidas and finally bidding the shepherds to "weep no more" (165), assuring them that Lycidas has entered the "blest Kingdoms meek of joy and love" (177). He also pledges to remember the dead Lycidas (183). Milton's monody, like the Oxford "Lycidas" and many pastorals before it, concludes with the setting of the sun and the anticipation of a new day: "And now the Sun had stretch'd out all the hills, / And now was dropt into the Western bay" (190–91). There may be a political as well as a personal renewal anticipated with the ending. The Sidney "Lycidas" is interesting not just because it uses pastoral conventions that anticipate Milton's later pastoral. It begins to be something else—a poem of national mourning that touches on, though it does not extensively develop, the issue of how the loss of the "good shepherd" who had labored in the cause of Protestantism affects the survivors who labor on. We might dub it a *Lycidas manqué*—a poem that leaves off just at the point that Milton's monody takes up—the point of protest for that loss and for the shattered hopes of Protestantism.

In this same 1587 collection that memorializes Sidney as the shepherd Lycidas, he is memorialized twice by William Gager as Daphnis, first in the pastoral poem, "Bellesita," then in an eclogue, "Daphnis." Lycidas may seem only a random name chosen for Sidney. None of the Continental Lycidae that we have looked at joined the roles of pastor or political leader and poet in the same way that the Cambridge "Lycidas" does. Such is not the case with the name Daphnis which had political as well as poetical resonance. While in Theocritus's idyll 1 Daphnis is the name of the dying poet-shepherd, in Vergil's eclogue 5 he is the newly dead political leader, Julius Caesar. Both the Theocritean and Vergilian precedents are especially appropriate for the poet-soldier Sidney.[48] Gager's poems, moreover, pay attention to both poetry and politics, looking back on both the Theocritean and Vergilian roles that Sidney-Daphnis played. In "Bellesita" the alma

48. See J. W. Binns, "William Gager on the Death of Sir Philip Sidney," in *Humanistica Lovaniensia* 21. Although "Bellesita" and "Daphnis" are the only two poems in which Gager addresses Sidney as Daphnis, he wrote other laments for Sidney, one of them, as Binns points out, that exists only in manuscript. Watson Kirkconnell includes a translation of Gager's "Daphnis" in *Awake the Courteous Echo*, 220–25. Like Milton and King, Gager and Sidney were fellow students at the university.

mater Oxford (here called Bellesita) mourns Sidney the man, recounting his death in battle, linking him with classical heroes, and alluding to his brothers and sisters and wife who mourn him. Gager's Oxford-Bellesita knows that in mourning Daphnis, she is mourning an alumnus that held a special place in the university and the court. In "Lycidas," Camus fulfills a similar role as representative of Cambridge, coming upon the scene as the first of the mourners and making the point that in losing Lycidas the university has lost an alumnus important not only to the university community, but to the world of pastors that was about to receive him. Although "Bellesita" does not fully develop the pastoral topos, its evocation of Oxford's nymphs and rivers (Cherwell and Isis) suggests the pastoral and anticipate Gager's second poem, "Daphnis" a full-fledged pastoral realization. There Gager attempts to join more fully Sidney's two roles as poet and political leader, lamenting the fact that Sidney honorably espoused the same military destiny that killed him. Gager fully exploits the pastoral conventions of the classical tradition, describing Sidney as Daphnis the *vates*, the poet who, like Orpheus, Calliope lamented and Apollo loved, whom the pastoral nymphs and Satyrs mourned. While we could pass this poem off as simply another pastoral precursor to "Lycidas," Gager's "Daphnis" as well as the anonymous "Lycidas" have more to tell us about Milton's pastoral monody than is first apparent. They point the way to the political-religious protest of "Lycidas."

Milton's monody is far more bold than the Oxford poems in its political and religious statements. Milton is not merely mourning the loss of a Protestant pastor, but is also indicting the world of church and state that has let the "bad" pastors thrive and has said little or nothing about the ravagings of the "grim Wolf with privy paw" who "Daily devours apace" (128–29). Gager and the anonymous "Lycidas" poet engage pastoral figures in conventional dialogue, as they protest Sidney's death, as they mourn and offer comfort. But beyond regretting that grim war has gathered the young shepherd before his time, they enter into no dialogue about the political-religious cause that prompted Sidney's involvement. No Christian "pastor"—such as St. Peter—strides across their pages to engage more serious issues. These pastorals do not resound with the righteous anger that Milton puts into the mouth of St. Peter against the contemporary Church. Milton writes as no other poet in this or any other university volume wrote, taking on the zeal of the pamphleteer and anticipating what he himself would write of the Church in the antiprelatical tracts of the early 1640s. Milton upsets the tone of "pastoral" mourning, of "University" grief—as St. Peter brushes aside Camus and his pastoral sigh for his "dearest pledge"—a sentiment worthy of the Oxford pastorals—and with only the briefest mention of the "young swain" he might have "spar'd" launches into an attack of those who "creep and intrude, and climb into the fold" (113, 115).

Before we dismiss these Oxford pastorals as interesting, though bland, precursors to the type of pastoral Milton would write, however, there is one more nagging question to consider. If Milton knew the Oxford volume, if he chose the name Lycidas, thinking of Sidney, why did he select it and not Gager's Daphnis as the more appropriate name for his poet-pastor? The answer involves the after-history of the name Daphnis. Although Sidney was honored in 1587 with this name, by Milton's time, Daphnis had become a name closely associated with another important political figure—namely, James I. In the commemorative collection gathered to mark the death of Queen Elizabeth in 1603 and the accession of James I, one shepherd, Thyrsis, mourns the passing of Elysa, while another, still one more of our Renaissance Lycidae, welcomes the arrival of Daphnis (James) from the north.[49] *Daphn-Amaryllis,* another collection published in 1605 by the Scottish poet David Hume (c. 1558–1630), also follows the same practice. Queen Elizabeth is the dead Amaryllis, mourned in the first two eclogues, but Daphnis is James come to take her place. In eclogue 3 two shepherds, Moeris and Lycidas, announce that Amaryllis, dying, praised Daphnis and told those who loved her to love him as well.[50]

Since Vergil in his fifth eclogue had used the Theocritean name Daphnis for Julius Caesar, it is logical for Renaissance poets to apply it to Julius-like Vergilian rulers rather than to the Theocritean poets. In the sixteenth century, Continental eclogues had previously used the name Daphnis for princes, with Henri III of France being honored with the name. Vergil, as David Quint points out, had already softened the Theocritean context, changing the character of Daphnis the shepherd god, and all but eliminating disappointed love as a motif in his eclogue. He made mourning for Daphnis-Julius a national occasion and he provided an apotheosis for Daphnis, who becomes a pastoral god.[51] Although Milton retains for his Lycidas an apotheosis, he makes it into a Christian Redemption, not a pagan deification such as Vergil awarded to the future god Julius. Further, he carefully avoids the royal subtext that a name like Daphnis would convey.

From the time James assumed the throne, the name Daphnis was consistently and repeatedly applied to him, particularly by Scottish poets.[52] James's return to Scotland in 1617 was popularly celebrated by many

---

49. See *Threno-thriambeuticon* (1603). Also see J. W. Binns on this and other university volumes, in *Intellectual Culture in Elizabethan and Jacobean England,* 34–45.

50. David Hume, *Daphn-Amaryllis* (1605). The sequence of eclogues to James is reprinted in *Iacobaea* in Hume's posthumous works, *Poemata* (1639), together with Hume's epigram to James and other members of the royal family.

51. Quint, "Sannazaro: From Orpheus to Proteus," 53.

52. See Grant, *Neo-Latin Literature and the Pastoral,* 347ff.

Scots poets. James is Daphnis in John Leech's second eclogue, "Daphnis Redux," where three shepherds—Lycidas, Moeris, and Alexis (pseudonyms probably for Leech and his fellow Scots poets, William Drummond and William Alexander)—welcome Daphnis back to Scotland. Alexis announces Daphnis's return, describing Daphnis as the wonder of poets and the glory of shepherds, and asks Moeris and Lycidas to sing a song in his honor. They oblige.[53] Henry Anderson in eclogues 1 and 2 celebrates the same visit, with Amaryllis now representing the city of Perth who welcomes the king as Daphnis into Scotland.[54] The Daphnis figure is obviously a princely one, but Lycidas could also be princely. In an anonymous pastoral dialogue printed in the Cambridge collection that commemorated the death of James I in 1625, two shepherds remark on "Lycidas'" grief for his father Scotus, thereby designating Charles by the name Milton ironically was to adopt for King twelve years later.[55] The royalist King, however, would not have been displeased by the coincidence.

Although we do not know exactly why Milton chose the name Lycidas, we can suspect the reason he avoided the name Daphnis. In 1637, as he protested the corruption of the Stuart clergy and by implication the Stuart kingship, he must have felt reluctant because of its well-known royal and Stuart associations to use the name Daphnis for his dead shepherd, however honorable its classical pedigree and its application to Sidney some fifty years earlier. When he named his pastor, he wanted to dismiss as far as he could James and his son and their pastor, William Laud. Hence the Renaissance Lycidas becomes Milton's much lamented poet-pastor.

Lycidas had become one of the most popular of pastoral names, one assigned to happy and tragic pastors and to poets and to lovers and

53. John Leech, "Ecloga Secunda," in "Idyllia, siue Eclogae," *Musae Priores* (1620), 6–11. Several of the other eclogues have political overtones. Leech dedicates his volume to Prince Charles and includes epigrams addressed to him as well as to other figures in the court: to James I, Buckingham, royal secretaries, and other officials. (See "Epigrammata" Libri 4 in *Musae Priores*.)

54. See Henry Anderson, "Musarum Querimonia," in *Delitiae Poetarum Scotorum* (1637), 1.33–36. John Barclay (1582–1621), another poet of Scots heritage, in his 1615 eclogues adopts the pastoral pseudonym Corydon for himself and describes James I as the god of the shepherds, Phoebus, as the one who brings life and song to his subjects. Apollo or Phoebus, as we have already noted in Chapter 3, was a favorite designation for James, especially by English poets, who celebrate his return to England as the return of Apollo-Sun. In a collection that contains poems to Carolus (Prince Charles) as well as to Prince Henry, the name Daphnis is used only once—in an eclogue that mourns the death of a prince, perhaps Prince Henry, but more likely Henri IV of France who was assassinated in 1610 (John Barclay, *Poematum Libri Duo* [1615]). In a collection on Prince Henry's death, *Eidyllia. In obitum Fulgentissimi Henrici Walliae Principis Duodecimi* (1612), however, Daphnis is obviously Prince Henry (C2r–C3r).

55. *Cantabrigiensium Dolor & Solamen: seu Successio Beatissimi Regis Jacobi Pacifici: et Successio Augustissimi Regis Caroli* (1625).

even to most idealized Protestant poet-pastor-political leader, Sir Philip Sidney. The Renaissance Lycidas could play many roles, and he had in a sense taken over the role of the prototypic poet-shepherd of classical tradition, making us all but forget that he began in Theocritus and in Vergil as a goatherd. The classical goatherd Lycidas is not altogether forgotten, however. Just three years after the composition of "Lycidas," in the midst of his deep grief for his friend Charles Diodati Milton alludes in "Epitaphium Damonis" to this carefree and good-natured character. There Lycidas is restored to a Theocritean-Vergilian context; he is Tuscan countryman—very much alive—overheard in a poplar grove beside the Arno competing in a song contest with Menalcas. The classical tradition is still contemporary for Milton as he turns this Lycidas into a genial Italian, very like those poets whom he met in the academies in Florence in 1638. In so doing he gives us still another version of the Renaissance Lycidas.

RENAISSANCE MONODY: MILTON AND SECUNDUS

If the neo-Latin tradition affected Milton's choice of the name, *Lycidas,* it also affected his choice of genre—monody—and the development of that genre in Continental poetry of the sixteenth century. One of the most interesting of the Renaissance monodies that precedes Milton's "Lycidas" is the one Joannes Secundus composed on the death of Thomas More, a poem that not only mourns the passing of the poet-saint, but also decries the injustice of his execution at the hands of Henry VIII.[56] Like Milton's "Lycidas," it draws on both classical and contemporary traditions, being both a formal lament for the dead and also an intellectual investigation of the underlying causes in the cosmos for that death. Secundus exploits a range of emotions, as in succession he grieves for More who has been snuffed out by cruel murder, is disconsolate over the changes of Fortune, and angry at the savagery of Venus who spurred Henry on and at Henry for his deceit and treachery in executing More. At the same time his monody, like "Lycidas," is a technical experiment. Secundus, who after his death was compared to Pindar, was affected by the attempts of contemporary neo-Latin poets to imitate Pindar's techniques in the serious ode. Hence he appropriates many of Pindar's poetic devices. His apostrophes, his abrupt juxtapositions, his digressions, his use of *sententiae* all speak of Pindaric experiment.

56. Joannes Secundus, "In Mortem Thomae Mori, Monodia," *Poetae Tres Elegantissimi* (1582), 163v–165v. The monody is not contained in the first collection of Secundus's works in 1541, but is included in later editions of Secundus and is generally accepted by scholars as authentic.

There are many similarities between Milton's and Secundus's monodies, for both closely follow the patterns of classical ode, Secundus's, however, without the formal trappings of pastoral. Both poets call upon the Muses—and Calliope in particular—to lament the poet's fall, and both pluck for themselves and for the dead poet the honorific laurel. Secundus places it ceremonially on More's tomb in deference to laurel-bearing poets. Both poets also recognize the fitness of one poet honoring another poet as he would wish also to be honored. As Milton's swain puts it: "So may some gentle Muse / With lucky words favor my destin'd Urn" (19–20). Milton need not have singled out King's poetic profession nor Secundus More's; both men were known for other public roles. But part of each monody is the singular way in which the poet and poetry assumes a central importance.

Even though each follows classical formulas and conventions of eulogy for a departed poet, neither Milton's nor Secundus's monody is just a formal lament for the dead. An integral part of both monodies is the questioning of the justice of that death. In questioning, indeed, in indicting divine justice, both poets raise their poems above their function merely as funeral songs. A worthy man, Milton's shepherd complains, has been arbitrarily cut down by a blind Fury, a poet who should have been protected by Calliope, by Apollo, and by the almighty Jove. But before him Secundus had raised questions very like these, as he investigated the religious, moral, and political implications of More's death. More's fall was not just the death of the poet, but that of an eminent statesman, who was once a councilor, the glory of the realm. And that death was not accidental but deliberate. More was murdered—executed by an all-powerful ruler because he upheld justice and religion. Therefore, with his death justice and religion are threatened. Secundus does not mince words. The king has divorced his legitimate wife, has taken on the title of Pontifex Maximus, and has condemned an innocent man, outraging Virtue, Law, and Religion. What kind of a world is it where a man is killed for professing truth and the man who has killed him thrives, asks Secundus. In a Catholic court that was outraged by Henry VIII's actions, as a Catholic poet who was closely connected to the emperor Charles V, Secundus had no need to censor his remarks. He could be quite forthright in his anger at the political system in England; he could even go so far as to question—for a moment, at least—God's ultimate justice.

The central section of "Lycidas" raises issues very like these. But because it speaks to a Protestant audience divided about religion, it must do so in a more circumspect manner. Not until 1645—after the fall of Laud and the victory of Parliament at Naseby—did Milton dare to add to the headnote of the poem and identify the faithless shepherds as the "corrupted Clergy then in their height." He brings on the scene, however, the first Pontifex

Maximus—with the keys that decide a sinner's fate—"the Golden opes, the Iron shuts amain" (111); and he makes Peter's prophetic allusion to the two-handed engine an assurance that the guilty will be punished. But the guilty shepherds are nameless.

Both in its digressive techniques and in its evaluation of divine reward and punishment, Secundus's monody anticipates Milton's. In the Cambridge collection in which it appeared Milton's monody was unique in denouncing the guilty shepherds, even as it regretted the loss of the good shepherd. Secundus's monody is one of the very few Renaissance odes that maintains the same kind of balance. For Secundus the monody concerns as much the abuses of religion under Henry as it does the loss of the poet-saint More. With angry indignation Secundus raises the question of whether More's brutal death will be unavenged, his murderer getting off scot-free. In fact, Secundus makes parallel those passages in which he considers punishment and reward. First, he depicts More's bloody execution as graphically as Milton describes Orpheus's decapitation by the Bacchantes. As More's head falls, rivers of purple stain his breast. Yet at that very moment God opens heaven for More: Christian angels sing paeans and the swans on the Meander applaud Apollo, Secundus tells us, adapting the classical vision to a Christian context.[57] For Henry, however, not heaven, but the abyss of hell opens. Do you think, Secundus asks, that heaven is pleased with blood? On earth, Henry will suffer the consequences of his act, vainly regretting the loss of the wise councilor More and haunted in his dreams by the ghost of the murdered man. This, says Secundus, is divine judgment for More. With its careful structural balancing of reward and punishment, Secundus's monody provides Milton with a model for his own juxtaposition in "Lycidas" of passages of reward and punishment, of the classical Apollo and the Christian St. Peter, the one promising reward in heaven, the other assuring us of the punishment of the guilty.

The final passage of Secundus's monody offers comfort and farewell to the good vates, who died for religion, laying down his life so that temple and altar would survive. Milton refrains from providing similar moralizing assurances. It is true that Lycidas, like More, is received into heaven, where the saints above entertain him "in solemn troops, and sweet Societies" (179). It is also true that he, like More, becomes a guide to human beings left behind. But Milton, unlike Secundus, does not tell us that Lycidas died for religion, although such a statement would have been easy enough to make

---

57. Secundus may be taking this extravagant description from the Homeric hymn to Apollo. There the swan, alighting on the banks of the eddying Peneus, sings to the god as he beats his wings, and the sweet-voiced bard, holding his lyre, always honors the god first and last in his songs (21.1–4).

about a young pastor about to serve his church. For him the "grim Wolf with privy paw" continued to "devour apace." In 1637 Milton could not assure us that the cause of religion—temple and altar—was secure.

Yet despite the obvious differences in religious orientation, Secundus provided Milton with a powerful poetic example.[58] Secundus's monody had broadened the traditions of ancient ode—had made it both a lament for the dead and a philosophical investigation of the mores of the living. Without approving Secundus's Catholicism, Milton could approve of Secundus's outrage at More's fate and might even have seconded Secundus's anger at a living king licentiously abusing religion. With such a poem as Secundus's as a model, Milton could mourn in a single ode the death of the poet, even as he justified the ways of men to God.

"SO MAY SOME GENTLE MUSE"

Important as is the political agenda of Milton's "Lycidas," we must not make Peter's denunciation of the bad shepherds, signaled out in the sub-note that Milton adds in 1645, the primary aim of the monody and its bewailing of the learned friend the secondary motif. It is often difficult and sometimes undesirable in the works of John Milton to separate politics and poetics. Milton himself indicates, however, after St. Peter's exit, as he turns back to his lament for Lycidas, that "the dread voice is past" (132). The pastoral stream can flow on. "Lycidas" is a living poet's tribute to a another poet who has recently died. Critics have sometimes accused Milton of celebrating himself as a poet and not Edward King, his dead poet-friend. Can "Lycidas" justly be included with those poems, whose primary aim is to look with the eyes of a poet on a fellow who is also a poet? Among such poems are the classical laments, such as Moschus's for Bion and Vergil's for Gallus—actual living poets giving tribute to their friends—that Milton takes pains to echo and imitate in "Lycidas." But among such laments of poet for poet—far closer to Milton's era and to his concerns as a Christian humanist—are numerous Renaissance encomia and naeniae, those poems that Renaissance writers addressed to their friends, and those epitaphs that were the final tribute to friendship on their death. It was commonplace for Renaissance poets during their lifetimes to include poems of poet-friends

---

58. Milton regarded Sir Thomas More with respect and admiration, referring to him in *An Apology for Smectymuus* as a "sublime wit" and in *Pro se Defensio* as a noble man. (See *Works* [ed. Patterson], 3.294; 9.111). His view of Henry VIII is less clear. Although he approved Henry's break with Rome, he notes that the quarrel was more about supremacy than about faultiness in religion (Also see *Of Reformation* in *Works* [ed. Patterson], 3.7).

and associates in a place of honor in their printed *Poemata*. Milton follows that practice in his own *Poemata* when he includes the Latin epigrams of Manso, Salzilli, and Selvaggi and the Italian ode of Francini to preface and introduce his own Latin poems. It was equally commonplace for editors to gather in posthumous volumes epigrams and naeniae that poet-friends had composed on a poet's death. Long before university volumes like *Justa Edvardo King Naufrago* came into existence, naeniae, epitaphs, and odes appeared in posthumous volumes of their works to testify to the regard of contemporary poet-friends. Sometimes entire sections were devoted in posthumous volumes to such poems. Sometimes private volumes were published, such as the one that friends and associates put together after the young Roman poet Celso Mellini drowned in 1519—*Celsi Archelai Melini funere amicorum* (Rome, 1521).

So many of these epigrams, naeniae, and odes exist that it is impossible to survey even a small sample. Toscanus, for example, in his collections of Italian poets, and Gherus in those of Italian, French, Belgium, and German poets often include a number of epigrams on the poet immediately before his selected poetry. The editions of Secundus's works called forth particularly poignant elegies from friends and his poet-brothers since Secundus died young. These are collected with Secundus's own poems and form a substantial section in these posthumous volumes. Yet I will focus not on these nor on the pastoral epitaphs such as Castiglione's *Alcon,* but on two poems that poet-friends wrote some time after 1500 for Michele Marullo, who, like King, was accidentally drowned. The poet-mourners—Giovanni Pontano and Pietro Crinito—knew Marullo well, had exchanged poems with him in his lifetime, and react with grief and shock at his death.[59] But how different are the poems they produce. Yet both poems are from close friends, who have known the poet intimately and who may be said to feel genuine shock at his sudden and untimely death and personal grief at the loss of both poet and friend.

Pontano's tribute to Marullo is in the form of a sepulchral epigram. Even as he laments Marullo's death, Pontano retains the affectionate tones of life. His epigram speaks with loving regret, not despair, as though Marullo, who had so skillfully led the chorus in Greek and Latin song, was only removed to a poetic Elysium, where Corinna joins him in song, where Delia plays the flute, and Cynthia dances. Pontano insists that his friend has been translated to a humanistic heaven. His patron goddesses can warm him in their bosoms; not death, but the Muses, have ravished Marullo:

---

59. Pontano, "Tumulus Marulli poetae," *Opera* (1518), 68r–68v; Crinitus (1508), F4v. In the first book of the "Baiarum," Pontano has a witty poem that he sent to Marullo in response to the present of a cheese included with some verses.

"Nec Parca eripuit, Musae rapuere Marullum" (68r). Pontano is trying to sum up Marullo's life and his art. He is not concerned with speaking the "truth" either about Marullo's life or his untimely death. He wishes only to make us feel, as we are reading his epigram, that the essence of the dead friend is preserved there—or rather of his dead friend as he appeared in his elegant, classically formed Latin verse, that spoke of Muses and of Lucretian equanimity about death. If there is a justification for Pontano's polished lie about a Muse-inhabited Elysium, it is this.

How different is Crinito's poem—no eloquent tribute to the poet of Apollo but a cry of despair that Apollo and the Muses have abandoned the poet. Just like "Lycidas," the naenia opens abruptly: "Ain perisse maximum vatem perisse?" (F3v). ("Is it true? Has the great *vates* died?") Critino continues with repeated questions: "What do I hear? What evil has snatched you from us, Marullo? O the vanity of human expectation! Now we are filled with empty hope, now cast down!" How far are we from the elegant falsehood that the Muses, not death, have ravished Marullo. And how close are we to the anguished questions that the shepherd-swain of "Lycidas" raises in bereavement both at the unexpected death and at the indifference of the world to that death.

It is true that Crinito's poem is only indirectly related to Milton's "Lycidas." We cannot line up close echoes, borrowed lines, nor can we point out how both are indebted to the tradition of the pastoral lament, for Crinito deliberately eschews that tradition. What links Milton and Crinito is the unaffected *cri de coeur* that is at the very center of their responses to the death of a poet-friend and the ultimate tribute of friendship in identifying utterly with that death. Also there is the resolute refusal—time and again— of both poets to indulge in either the humanistic or the easy Christian consolation that the poet is now part of the world of poetry, of nature, or of art to which he by his profession belonged. Indeed both Milton and Crinito vent their outrage and despair in indicting the world of nature and of the gods that permitted the poet to perish. Milton's swain both demands why the nymphs were not there to save Lycidas ("Where were ye Nymphs?" 50) and despairs of their powers to help ("Had ye bin there—for what could that have done?" 57) And in still another insistent query, he questions the efficacy of his vocation, if neither Nature nor the gods of the poets protect him—"Alas! What boots it with uncessant care / To tend the homely slighted Shepherd's trade / And strictly mediate the thankless Muse?" (64–66). Milton is asking the very questions that Crinito also asked—universal questions about the purpose of life and of the poet's place in it.

If Secundus's monody on More was one kind of inquiry into divine justice, Crinito's is another. When Secundus questions divine dispensation, he does so, secure in its ultimate response—that, if the good man suffers on earth, he will be rewarded in heaven. In Crinito's naenia, the Christian consolation is absent, and the poet's complaints against divine justice are far more clamorous. Indicting the gods and divine Necessity that struck Marullo with its thunder from above, Crinito can only raise the faint hope that Marullo may live through the grace of Apollo. He recreates the scene of Marullo's death—describing how the swelling waters of the river doomed him. What god, he asks, was deaf to his prayers and denied Marullo life? What cruel goddess drowned both the poet and his verse, consigning his inspired song to the glittering waves? Can we listen to Crinito's indictment of the gods of nature without thinking of Milton's Orpheus passage, where the clamor of the Bacchic rout drowns both the poet and his song. The mourners stand by helpless, while the scene of drowning occurs all over again. In vain, they ask the gods of sea and wind what hard mischance condemned the swain; in vain they seek comfort in memorial rites. The "whelming tide" covers the body of the poet (157–59), denying it to the "moist vows" of friends. Both poets acknowledge their helplessness as human beings against the incontrovertible fact of their friend's drowning. Both cry against the cruelty of the world of nature and the impotence of human beings to control their destiny. By re-creating for us the scene of the death, both poets make us share in their desperation.

Crinito concludes his poem in the interrogative voice with which he began. The closing lines ask the question that Milton's "Lycidas" also asked. Who is there to fill the poet's place? Now that Marullo is gone, says Crinito, who can fitly join, as he did, the Graces and Venus to the Muses? Who can sing the praises of the god, address the king, or bind his hair with the sacred leaves? His only reply is the affirmation that his tears are vain. "Lycidas" concludes, of course, by wiping away those very tears. Yet Crinito's naenia is a powerful testament to one poet's grief at the death of another—and its very intensity of personal emotion contributes yet another dimension to the poetry of lamentation. It also reminds us that though Milton's swain may be nameless, the J. M. of the Cambridge "Obsequies," the John Milton of the 1645 *Poems* claims our attention as a poet bewailing a learned friend. Not even in "Epitaphium Damonis" did Milton go beyond the total identification of poet with poet that marks "Lycidas," testifying not to a lack of grief, but to a consummate expression of it. What one poet says of another is important in life as in death. Milton included the poetic tributes of his Italian friends at the beginning of his *Poemata* as a mark of the link between poet and poet. And in "Lycidas" he looked forward to those testmonia that might adorn a posthumous tribute—the lucky words that favor a destined urn.

1637

So pervasive is the influence of Continental Renaissance Latin poetry on this "final" ode of the 1645 volume that it is surprising in some ways that "Lycidas" was not written in Latin—the official language of that Renaissance and a language that would connect Milton to the poets of Italy he would visit. The 1638 Cambridge volume that commemorated King is, like Milton's 1645 volume, a double book, composed of twin volumes, each with separate title pages. The first volume, *Justa Edovardo King Naufrago,* is a group of nineteen poems in Latin and three in Greek; the second, *Obsequies to the Memorie of Mr. Edward King,* is a collection of twelve poems in English addressed to Edward King, two to his sister, and also "Lycidas," the last poem both of the English collection and of the double book. How easy would it have been for Milton as an expert Latinist to have joined the university poets of the first volume and composed an epitaph in Latin. When he wrote "Ad Patrem" he took up Latin composition once again—after the lapse of some years—and he would practice his skills as a Latin poet in Italy with commendatory poems and on his return with a Latin eclogue lamenting Diodati. How easy, then, would it have been for "Lycidas" to have marched in Latin hexameters. "Lycidas" resembles the Latin poems in the collection in using classical references—in alluding to Phoebus Apollo, to the Muses, to the nymphs, to Neptune, and to the Nereids that did not save King, in excoriating the "fatall bark," in appealing collectively to the community of fellow Cambridge scholars and poets to mourn the young man. Still, Milton's monody differs from these poems in the intensity with which it delineates the poet-speaker, in its indictment of providence, in its expostulation with God, and in its denunciation of a society that had fallen short of its responsibility both to poetry and to religion.[60]

60. Many themes, allusion, and images connect "Lycidas" to the poem of the Cambridge collection. See, for example, Nicholas Felton's opening Latin poem that refers to Phoebus's grief for Hyacinthus, to the impotence of the Muse, to the necessity to confer due rites on King as an alumnus of Cambridge. John Pullen refers to Deva and to Sabrina. R. Brown refers in his Latin poem to Orpheus's drawing the hills after him and singing songs in Hades. Brown describes in his English poem the sons of Phoebus collectively lamenting the loss. T. Norton alludes to Apollo-Sun "going to bed," sinking in the Irish sea and the ending of the day. Samson Briggs comments that it "ill sutes / With men thus to expostulate with God" (*Obsequies,* 15). William Hall refers to the "fatall bark" (*Obsequies,* 13), and Cleveland, as many critics have noted, exploits the water imagery, referring to Neptune and the Hebrides (*Obsequies,* 10). Cedric Brown has suggested in an unpublished paper that the "Yet once more" that opens Milton's poem may be an allusion to the earlier poems that precede him in the King volumes.

At the very time when he was composing "Lycidas" Milton was already turning his eyes to Italy, but he did so not to confirm his career as a Latin poet, but to finalize that humanistic education that would make him an English vates. While it mines the gold of classical and Renaissance literature, "Lycidas" is an English monody written for an English audience. The old bards, the famous Druids, are summoned to take their places beside Apollo and the Sicilian Muse, the nymphs of the British shore, to join Neptune and Alpheus, just as Cyrene and Parthenope had joined Sabrina. Unlike the commemorative volume for King that places the Latin poetry first, Milton would place his English poems first in his own twin book, reserving the penultimate place in the English volume for "Lycidas." In the Nativity ode he presented himself as a young Protestant poet, eagerly urging his Muse to come before the Magi and present the ode she inspires; in "Lycidas" he simply says, "I come" (3). What he has to say about poets and poetry, what St. Peter says of the pastors who "creep and intrude and climb into the fold" must not be said in clerical or university Latin, but in English, the language of the people, the language he will employ for the political addresses of the 1640s for defending English civil rights and English law. Milton, who dismissed Apollo from the prophetic chair in 1629, is claiming in this ode a "prophetic" voice for the poet; he may also be subtly telling his Cambridge contemporaries why the role of poet-prophet transcends even the honorable role of poet-pastor that the dead Edward King had filled. In 1637 he could hardly foresee what his actual role would be as an English poet-pamphleteer. Yet the choice of English for "Lycidas"— like Milton's other choices—was a deliberate one. When he contributed his English monody to the commemorative volume in 1637, Milton was addressing the Cambridge community; in 1645, he addressed England.

It is also tempting to speculate that Milton may have seen some of these poems before he composed his own lament for King, hence permitting him, as the last poet to speak, to create an intricate kind of intertextuality.

7

APOLLO REDIVIVUS

Milton, Manso, and the Phoenix

One of the problems of the 1645 *Poems* is the arrangement of poetic texts. Critics who look at the English poems alone tend to consider "Lycidas" or *A Mask at Ludlow-Castle* as the climax of the volume, arguing that one or the other, usually "Lycidas," is Milton's crowning achievement and final word as a young poet.[1] This is misleading. An entire volume of Latin poems—the second part of the twin book— follows the English poems and includes works written after the composition of "Lycidas" or *A Mask*. How does Milton signal to his reader that the second volume contains these important works? Reading the volumes consecutively, we come—once we have completed the mask—to the second volume and commence reading the book of Latin elegies. If we do so, our journey is in a sense retrogressive, for reading the elegies after *A Mask* we go back to "prehistory"—to poems that were composed, as we noted in Chapters 1 and 2, before the Nativity ode that opens the English volume. Carefully as Milton has arranged poems within the two volumes, he has provided few clues about how to move from one to the next. Some kind of map of reading is needed, some guide from the pastures of "Lycidas" or the woods of *A Mask* to the elegies and woods of the Latin poems. For we, like the Milton of 1638, are about to take a journey that will climax in the final poems of the Latin book, a journey that will take us to Italy.

Milton does actually give his readers some clues about the interrelationship between the poems of the two volumes—first, in the letters prefixed to *A Mask at Ludlow-Castle,* the last work of the English volume; next, in the title page of the *Poemata,* and finally, in the material prefixed to the Latin volume itself. The two letters prefixed to *A Mask at Ludlow-Castle*—the first

---

1. The placement of *A Mask at Ludlow* as the final work is probably dictated by publication convention as well as by its prominence among the young Milton's works. Masques tended to be printed last when included in a mixed volume of poetry.

Henry Lawes's dedicatory letter to Viscount Brackley, the second Sir Henry Wotton's letter to Milton—commend the mask as Milton's most notable achievement as an English poet.[2] But the second letter, from Wotton, not only commends the mask, but also includes a good deal of specific material about the journey to the continent. Milton had courted Wotton's favor by sending him a copy of *A Mask,* and he had also asked him for recommendations about his coming voyage. Curiously enough, by reprinting the entire letter, Milton has provided his readers useful information about the Latin poems composed in Italy, those that conclude the *Poemata.* He has, so to speak, eased the transit of his readers across the "channel" from one book to the next, just as Wotton's letter has facilitated his own journey from England to Italy.

The prefatory material to the *Poemata* serves an even clearer purpose. Milton's title page prepares us for the first book of elegies and for the opening poems of the book of sylvae by noting that most of the poems following were written by his twentieth year. Milton actually affixes head-notes to many poems noting the age of composition, a not too uncommon practice. (Alexander Gil, for example, dates many of his Latin poems). Next, Milton explains why he has attached the testimonial poems that follow: the three Latin epigrams from Manso, Salzilli, and Selvaggi and the Italian ode from Francini. The testimonia actually serve a double function. They were written to commend the Latin poems that follow—the elegies and sylvae of his Cambridge years—the very compositions that he read before the Italian literati at the academies he visited in Italy.[3] These are the poems that won him the commendations of the international audience, just as *A Mask at Ludlow-Castle* had brought him to the attention of an English audience. In printing them Milton was, as he tells us, both fulfilling an obligation to his Italian friends (thanking them for the compliments they addressed to him) and also observing the common practice, particularly in neo-Latin volumes, of prefixing commendatory poems to a volume. The commendatory poems serve yet another incidental function. The epigrams that Giovanni Battista Manso and Giovanni Salzilli address to Milton introduce these Italian literati, preparing English readers for the commendatory poems to Manso and Salzilli Milton wrote in response. It is in these Latin poems, some written before, others after he embarked for Italy, that Phoebus Apollo, the guardian

2. Not only were the commendatory letters and the names of Lady Alice and her brothers removed in 1673, but "Lycidas" also was privileged above the *Mask* in the "Table of the English Poems," its title appearing in bold face.

3. See particularly John Arthos, *Milton and the Italian Cities,* and also several essays from the collection *Milton in Italy,* ed. Mario Di Cesare, especially Anna K. Nardo, "Milton and the Academic Sonnet," 489–503. Also see Nardo's "Academic Interludes in *Paradise Lost,*" in *MS* 27; and Peter Lindenbaum, "John Milton and the Republican Mode of Literary Production," in *YES* 21

spirit of poetry, returns to play his part in shaping Milton's destiny as an epic poet.

"FOLLOW ME"

The last voice that we as English readers hear at the end of the English volume belongs to the Attendant Spirit in *A Mask*, who, as he departs from the company at Ludlow, offers suitable advice to those who might accompany him on his journey.

> Mortals that would follow me,
> Love vertue, who alone is free,
> She can teach ye how to clime
> Higher then the Spheary chime,
> Or if Vertue feeble were,
> Heav'n it self would stoop to her. (1018–23, 1645 text)

"Follow me," says the Attendant Spirit, now our guide on a further journey. An Apollonian spirit of music and poetry is in some ways the perfect cicerone for our "Latin" adventure. He will take us where the Roman language is spoken: to the academies of Florence, where we may hear Milton's Latin elegies, those poems that so often praise the god Phoebus Apollo—his poetical father.[4] He will also take us finally to Rome and to Naples, where Milton will once more lift his voice in Latin composition to answer his Italian friends and to praise Leonora Baroni, another sublime singer. An Apollonian guide is much to be desired on a journey that will reintroduce us to the god Apollo.

The first poem of Milton's English volume, the Nativity ode, dismissed Apollo, a god who had been a guiding force in the youthful Latin poetry and especially in "Elegia 5."[5] But Phoebus Apollo, the god of poetry, is not so easily banished. He begins to make his presence felt once more in the English poems of the 1630s. He stands behind the Genius of the Wood in *Arcades* and behind the Attendant Spirit in *A Mask at Ludlow-Castle*, but he

---

4. Although Milton uses both the names Phoebus and Apollo, sometimes together, sometimes separately, there are at least twice as many citations of the god as Phoebus—the bright or shining one. See Index to *The Works of John Milton* (ed. Patterson).

5. In the Prolusions Apollo is a frequent and controlling presence. He appears in "Elegia 5" at the poet's calling either as sky god to bring on the spring or as god of poetry to inspire the poetic trance. He is the driver of the sun's chariot in "Naturam non pati senium," where he shines in perpetual youth defying the aging of the earth. He is a lover too: in "Elegia 5" he accedes to the Earth's courtship and in "Elegia 7" he is the failed suitor of Daphne whom Cupid punishes. In "Elegia 6" he is the convivial brother of Bacchus who is not ashamed to wear the corymbus or a crown of Bacchic ivy in his hair.

does not appear in his own person or assert his godhead until "Lycidas." Then he comes forth in response to the shepherd-swain's indictment of the profession of poetry to defend himself and the heavenly rewards of poetry. Phoebus Apollo's speech is one of the explosive moments in "Lycidas." How different from the words of simple reproach that Vergil makes Apollo speak to the dying Gallus in the tenth eclogue! The passage that follows Apollo's speech in "Lycidas" returns us to pastoral song, and the monody itself concludes with a quiet and understated reaffirmation of the vocation of poetry. Phoebus Apollo is, as it were, readmitted as an acceptable poetic mentor, an acceptable "god" for the community of shepherds and poets represented in "Lycidas." Where, however, do we go from here, after the nameless swain has "twitch't his Mantle blue" (192) and departed? How does this renewed commitment work itself out? The ending of "Lycidas" reaffirms but is inconclusive—open. The story of the nameless swain is left half-told.

Since the death of his mother in April 1637, Milton the poet had been proposing foreign travel.[6] The conclusion of "Lycidas" was written with that journey in mind. In Italy, "the seat of civilization and the hospitable domicile of every species of erudition," as Milton himself testifies many years later in *The Second Defense of the People of England* (Hughes, 827–28), he would find both Apollo and his Apollonian commitment. The concluding Latin poems of the *Sylvarum Liber* are products in one way or another of the Italian journey. Moreover, in the last two poems of his Latin book, "Mansus" and "Epitaphium Damonis," he finally affirms his vocation as England's future epic bard. Not "Lycidas," then, but "Epitaphium Damonis" concludes the story for the nameless swain. Assuming his proper Theocritean name, Thyrsis—the pastoral name that the Attendant Spirit had also adopted—Milton explains exactly how he will fulfill his Apollonian calling. The pastoral god of "Lycidas" guides the final poems of Milton's *Poemata* and determines that choice.

APOLLO AND THE MUSES

The poem that most convincingly marks the shift in attitude toward Phoebus Apollo is "Ad Patrem," the Latin hexameter verses that Milton wrote to his father to defend his choice of vocation, a poem that scholars date

6. Both Milton himself in *The Second Defense of the People of England* and Edward Phillips in the *Life* connect the death of his mother with Milton's determination to go abroad. (See *Complete Poems and Major Prose* (ed. Hughes), 828, 1027). Plans for the trip were probably in the making even as he wrote "Lycidas" in November 1637. See David Masson, *The Life of John Milton: Narrated in Connexion with the Political, Ecclesiastical, and Literary History of his Time*, 1.646.

either late in the Cambridge-Hammersmith period or on the eve of Milton's departure for his Italian journey.[7] Apollo and the Muses hold important places in "Ad Patrem"—places they continue to inhabit in "Mansus" and "Epitaphium Damonis," poems that also concern poetic vocation. For this reason John Shawcross has argued for 1638 as its date of composition.[8] It seems clear that Milton placed the three poems close to one another in his *Silvarum Liber*—separated only by the Greek translations and "Ad Salsillum"—because in all three Apollo functions not just as the god of poetry, but as a "father" symbol for the poet or even as his own alter ego.

Despite its title and its affectionate address to the elder Milton, "Ad Patrem" is not a poem that concerns the father, John Milton Sr., per se. To see the difference we need only compare with it another poem of son to father—namely, the verses of Alexander Gil Jr. to Alexander Gil Sr. included in the former's *Parerga*.[9] Gil Jr.'s poem is an occasional one— a genethliacon or birthday poem, commemorating the elder Gil's sixtieth birthday. There are ample references to the relationship of father and son: an affectionate salute to Gil's green old age, some witty asides concerning the old man Aeson, and a final tribute to Gil's stature and achievement in life. The poem exactly fulfills but never transcends its occasion. This is a son writing a graceful tribute to a much-loved father. Although Milton demonstrates in "Ad Patrem" a similar affection and respect for his own father, although he too is not above making witty asides and although he compliments his father on his achievements, his poem completely transcends its occasion. It is far more than a poem of a son rendering thanks to his father.

"Ad Patrem" is as close as Milton came to writing a verse apology for poetry. Following on the heels of Sidney and Puttenham, he defends poetry as a divine art, as the vestige of that Promethean fire that brought art as well as life to human beings, as the power that can defy death and foresee the future. Without a trace of the zealous fervor that asserted in the Nativity ode that the oracles were dumb, Milton, as though echoing another fervent Protestant, Sidney, cites as divine inspiration the poetic prophecies of the "Phoebades" and the Sibyllae—priestesses of Apollo at Delphi and at Cumae.[10] The beginning of "Ad Patrem" might appear at first merely as

---

7. See *Variorum, (The Latin and Greek Poems)*, 1:232–40.

8. E. M. W. Tillyard praised the Latinity of "Ad Patrem" and connected it in theme and style to "Mansus" and "Epitaphium Damonis." See Tillyard, *Milton;* John Shawcross, "Milton's Decision to Become a Poet," in *MLQ* 24; and Shawcross, *John Milton, The Self and the World*, 62, 68–70, 86–7; also see William Kennedy, "The Audiences of *Ad Patrem*," in *Urbane Milton*.

9. Gil, *Parerga*, 14–16.

10. See Sir Philip Sidney in *The Defense of Poesie* (ed. Feuillerat): "the Oracles of *Delphos* and *Sybillos* prophesies, were wholly delivered in verses, for that same exquisite

a replay of "Elegia 5" with its evocation of the Muses, the Castalian spring, and the double peaks of Parnassus as well as its invocation to Apollo to bring on the poetic trance that will convey the poet to the domain of the god himself on Olympus. But there is a difference here. In "Elegia 5" the young poet is hoping for the return of powers of inspiration with the spring; in "Ad Patrem" he is speaking as a member of the circle of Apollonian priests. The laurel crown is in place. In fact, it is all he has, possessing nothing, as he affirms, except that which golden Clio has given him. The vocational uncertainty that marks the sonnet on his twenty-third year has disappeared. The goal of "Elegia 6" now seems within his reach: he can refer to himself confidently as a *vates*. In this context he asks his father not to scorn the divine work, the poet's song: "Nec tu vatis opus divinum despice carmen" (17).

Enrolling himself in the company of priests, he offers with them his own song to Apollo. He can assume for himself the title "Priest of Phoebus' Quire," that he would bestow in 1648 on his friend Harry Lawes, also tuning, as Lawes did, the "happiest lines in Hymns or story" (11). He has advanced beyond the timid stance of "Elegia 5," where he is a lonely initiate responding to the coming of the god. The Apollonian vision of "Ad Patrem" is collective and more controlled than that of "Elegia 5." In the elegy the poet responds ecstatically to the god, leaving his body to rise to the clouds; in "Ad Patrem" he mounts in the company of fellow priests. By using the choral pronoun "nos" (we) to describe that ascent, he connects himself not merely with the priests who are leading the worship of the god, but also with those ancient choral poets who compose and perform songs of worship—Homer and Callimachus and Pindar. Like them, he leads a chorus and ascends to the temples of his "native" Olympus, there performing to the sound of the harp and the beat of the plectrum.

> Nos etiam patrium tunc cum repetemus Olympum,
> AEternaeque morae stabunt immobilis aevi,
> Ibimus auratis per caeli templa coronis,
> Dulcia suaviloquo sociantes carmina plectro,
> Astra quibus, geminique poli convexa sonabunt. (30–34)

> Truly when we seek again our native Olympus,
> and the immovable ages of eternal ways shall stand,
> we shall go with golden crowns to the temples of the sky,

observing of number and measure in the words, and that high flying libertie of conceit propper to the Poet, did seeme to have some divine force in it. And may not I presume a little farther, to shewe the reasonablenesse of this word *Vatis*, and say that the holy *Davids* Psalms are a divine *Poeme*?" (3:6).

and in fellowship sing sweet songs to the sweetly sounding
   plectrum,
to which the stars and the vault will echo to the twin poles.

The Olympus of "Ad Patrem" is a peculiarly Christian-classical place, suggesting both the Christian heaven of saints in solemn jubilee and the
classical heaven of Homer and Pindar, where the Muses or Graces perform
at the side of Apollo and their heavenly father Zeus. Even the suggestion
that the sound of this choral music resounds to the stars and vaults of
heaven has both classical and Christian overtones. Poetically we have here
what Homer describes at the end of *Iliad* 1 or Pindar in *Pythian 1* as the
antiphonal response of the Muses in chorus. The chorus coordinates with
the sound of the heavenly lyre or phorminx—Apollo's constellation—and
resounds on earth with the choral celebration of human beings. Milton is
giving us yet another version of Pythagoras's music of the spheres.

But it is not just music, but vocal music—*carmina*—that holds heaven
and earth in admiration—vocal music that coordinates words, meter, and
melody. Apollo personifies for him, as for the Greeks, the musical composite—voice and verse perfectly fitted together—the singer and the crafter of
words. In "Ad Patrem" he as poet joins with Apollo's priests to make this
music, which, as it sounds to the stars, binds together the heavens and the
entire universe. A fiery spirit ("igneus . . . spiritus") circles the heavens and
sings as he moves; this immortal melody, this ineffable song ("Immortale
melos, & inenarrabile carmen," 37), this too is sphere-music. The spirit's
song has two effects: it holds in check the threatening constellations—the
hissing serpent and the fierce Orion—and thus it lightens the burden of the
starry heavens for Atlas who upholds it all.

Milton does not name the fiery spirit, but he can be no other, as
Shawcross argues, than the cosmic Apollo.[11] Like the Apollo-Sol of Proclus's
and Michele Marullo's hymns to the sun, he is a protogonos, preexistent to
earthly light, a lord of noetic fire, who created and who holds together
the universe.[12] But he does so not so much with light as with music.
Hence he is like the Apollo of Renaissance musical theory—the god of
Gafurius's treatise, *Practica Musicae* (1496), who governs the ninth heaven,
holding sway over the Muses and the planetary spheres that each of them
control.[13] The identity of this singing spirit is not so crucial as his power

11. Shawcross, *John Milton, The Self and the World*, 311 n. 35. Also see *Variorum
(The Latin and Greek Poems)*, 1:245–46.
12. Michele Marullo, "Hymn to the Sun," *Carmina*, ed. Alessandro Perosa (1951);
Proclus, *Inni.*
13. Franchinus Gafurius, *Theorica Musice* (1496), G1. Apollo holds the lute in his left
hand and signals to the Graces with his right. A three-headed serpent, his tail coiled in

to govern the universe with song, even as song thematically governs the poem "Ad Patrem." Like the Apollo of Pindar's *Pythian 1,* the spirit is a deity who controls heaven and earth with music. Pindar describes how Apollo's lyre governs with its sound, moving the circuits of heaven, moving the choruses in heaven and earth who respond to its governance. Pindar was a Pythagorean. For him the harmony of the spheres extended from heaven to earth; it could quell the warlike heart of Ares and with its power hold in check all the enemies of Zeus.[14]

For Milton as for Pindar, song rules earth as well as heaven. At the banquet table the upright ancient king who feasts in moderation seats the vates in honor at his feast; the order of the righteous king's court reflects the musical order that governs the courts of heaven. The vates, it is clear, is the controlling, ordering voice of this earthly society, just as fiery spirit is the ordering voice of the society in heaven. His voice is both Hesiodic and Mosaic; his themes are theogonic. He sings not only of chaos and the foundations of the earth (the Hesiodic and the Mosaic creation), but also of the deeds of heroes, the autocracy of earth. His is the highest musical voice on earth—except for the voice of Orpheus. This semidivine singer transcends all poet-singers in that his song links heaven and earth. Vocal music possesses transcendent power. It was not through his lyre, Milton maintains, that Orpheus performed his supernatural feats—held back rivers, gave ears to oaks, moved dead shades to tears— but through his *singing voice.* Here the human son of Apollo excelled his father. He performed through song alone what not even Apollo's lyre could perform—so powerful is the force of singing word. The Orpheus who in "Lycidas" was torn apart by the bacchantes is here triumphant—neither his lyre nor his voice is drowned.

Milton's poem "Ad Patrem" is not only about the force of song, but also about fathers and sons. It is significant that Milton shifts the attention from Apollo to his poet son, just at the point that he introduces the plea for poetry that is at the heart of his poem. John Milton the son begs John Milton the father not to contemn the sacred Muses: "Nec tu perge precor sacras contemnere Musas" (56). He draws models for this line from a formidable list of classical poets—Lucretius, Ovid, Propertius, and Horace—as well as their neo-Latin followers Vida and Buchanan. All plead with their readers for indulgence—do not despise the Muses, do not contemn the vates.[15]

---

the sky, joins the heavens with earth ("terra"), with the ninth Muse, Thalia, represented on earth. Hence the motto—"Mentis Apollineae vis has movet undique" (The strength of the Apollonian mind moves these things everywhere).

14. Pindar, *Carmina* (1935).

15. See *Variorum, (The Latin and Greek Poems),* 1:242, 248. The list includes not only Horace's but also Vida's *Art of Poetry.*

Milton, however, does not address the plea to the general reader, but to that very father whom he will soon be identifying as a musician with Apollo himself. In fact, he makes John Milton Sr. take on an Apollonian role by wittily suggesting that Phoebus wished to be divided between father and son. The god gave some gifts to the father, some to the son, so that between them they held the entire god. Praising his father's accomplishments as a musician, he subtly makes him a surrogate for Phoebus Apollo, the first possessor of the lyre and so the inspirer of song—the poet's part. Milton slyly implies that his father, as Apollo's surrogate, could not, of course, hate the Muses. Nor, of course, could he send his son into unmusicianly trades—commerce, law, the civil arena—"noisy" professions that would offend the ears and soul of a musician. Instead he left him at his leisure to discover the Muses, recalling as he refers to the Aonian shores the mountain on which Hesiod, the archetypal shepherd-poet of the Greek, met the Muses and where they conferred on him the laurel branch, the emblem of his profession as poet.[16] Thus, Milton implies, his father facilitated the archetypal encounter for his son that made him a poet. He gave him not just the Muses, but, as Milton says, Phoebus Apollo as his companion.

At his father's behest, moreover, Milton continues, he learned languages, adding to Latin and Greek (the first languages of poetry) French, Italian, and Hebrew. Here once more, the father's "gifts" are the gifts of the god— tongues by which human beings may craft music into song and, through song, may convey the mysteries of heaven to earth. Milton uses for his father the title "pater optime" (78), which Vergil used for Jove, indicating to us that his father is a surrogate not just for Apollo, but for Apollo's sire, the father of the gods, who dispenses wisdom to human beings. In alluding to Hebrew, Milton refers specifically to the language by which the Palestinian *vates* uttered the mysteries of heaven. Whether in Greek or Hebrew, song is the means by which the divine communicates with human beings. Milton has included indirect references to the "first" poets both of the Greeks and the Hebrews—Hesiod, the poet who shepherded his sheep on Helicon, and Moses, the shepherd who first taught the chosen seed—both of whom he will allude to in the opening lines of *Paradise Lost*.

In the *Georgics* the poet Vergil prays that he come through his craft to a knowledge both of heaven and earth—that through poetry he discover the face of nature, of wisdom, of science.[17] Milton has a Vergilian motive in alluding in "Ad Patrem" to "scientia" (knowledge). By knowing the science

---

16. See Hesiod, *Theogony*, 22–35, esp. 30–32 where the Muses give Hesiod a rod of laurel and breathe a divine voice into him.

17. See *Georgics* 2.477–86. Milton alludes to these lines again in *Paradise Lost* 3.29. See my discussion in "Vergil's *Georgics* and *Paradise Lost:* Nature and Human Nature in a Landscape," in *Vergil at 2000.*

of words he is able to unlock other kinds of knowing. The poetry of the past (of Rome, Greece, Palestine) and the science of the present (of modern Europe, particularly France and Italy) comes to the English poet through their tongues and also through their poetry. Milton anthropomorphizes Scientia into a beckoning earth goddess who offers her knowledge as kisses. The young poet, like the sun god of "Elegia 5," may incline and accept—or fly from these embraces. She is in a way the ultimate Muse.

Gifts can be dangerous, however, to those who do not know how to use them. Milton introduces at this point one of the most troublesome myths about gift-giving—the story of Apollo's gift of the chariot of fire to his son Phaeton, a fatal bequest that led to the scorching of the earth and the downfall of the unskillful charioteer. Not everything that a Pater Phoebus gives to a Poeta Filius is a safe gift. The Promethean fire Milton alludes to earlier in the poem was both a force of inspiration and a source of a curse. Illumination can be the most dangerous of gifts—if illumination requires that one control the reins of Day and the tiara of the Sun. It is a curiously negative example, particularly when coupled with the commandment to manage well the gift of knowledge. Milton's father, like the almighty Jove, had dispensed both life and knowledge to his offspring. If the management of knowledge is as dangerous for the poet as the governing of the sun's chariot was to the unfortunate Phaeton, then the poet becomes almost as it were the "victim" of a father's generosity. Milton does not say this, of course, but the very inclusion of the myth of Phaeton conveys this implication—an implication that stretches as far as the fatal tree of knowledge in *Paradise Lost.*

Milton's references to poets in this poem have been happy ones—Orpheus charms nature with his song, Arion the dolphin. Yet lurking is the ghost of the hero whose "knowledge" brought him woe—Bellerophon, the rider of the Muses' stallion Pegasus, who tried to come to the heavens and failed, as the proem of book 7, *Paradise Lost,* tells us. The warning that poets from Pindar through Vergil give is that the poet must walk humbly, lest he provoke the envy of the gods or the malice and spite of human beings. It is exactly on this note that he concludes his reflections on his chosen Apollonian vocation. He hopes, he tells his father, to take his place among the poets crowned with ivy and laurel; he hopes to walk free from cares and quarrels and from envy and spite; he hopes for the protection of a paternal Apollo to ward off the viper's tongue. It is almost as though he were invoking Apollo's physicianly, together with his poetic care, calling upon the healer with the serpent's rod. These cautious prayers remind us of the epigraph from Vergil that he later attaches to his 1645 *Poems:* "Baccare frontem / Cingite, ne vati noceat mala lingua futuro" (Eclogues 7.27–28)— "Bind my brow with foxglove, lest an evil tongue harm the future bard."

Like "Mansus," the poem he wrote not long after to the elderly Marchese di Villa, "Ad Patrem" is a poetic gift offered in return for kindness and paternal care, a grace rendered in return for many gifts. Milton is using his poet's talent in a time-honored manner—to memorialize the name and person of the addressee and so to confer a kind of immortality on him. Milton's father, like Manso, was an elderly men who had won—by virtue of his own service to Apollo—a name and reputation in his own right. Thus the poet in offering his verses confers a double-share of immortality, snatching his name from Orcus and granting whatever share of earthly fame a poet's gift can confer. Milton's poem to his father closes with this promise; his poem to Manso opens by promising the fatherly Italian poet a place among the ivy and the laurel. However warm the tribute to his father and to the Marchese, both poems transcend their occasions and are more than epistolary thank-you notes; they proclaim the young Milton's devotion to his ultimate father—the god of poetry.

THE PILGRIM OF THE HYPERBOREANS

References to Phoebus Apollo and the Muses crowd the opening lines of "Mansus," the song ("carmen") that Milton sent before he left Naples to the elderly Neapolitan patron of Tasso and Marino in return for Manso's great kindness and offices of "humanitas." He is thanking Manso not just for his courtesy, but for sharing his humanistic learning. The poem is in the style of the Renaissance panegyric, a genre that dates back, as Ralph W. Condee has demonstrated, to classical panegyric.[18] Renaissance panegyrics—sometimes brief and epigrammatic, sometimes ode-length—were regularly included in editions of a poet's own work. A number precede the text of Manso's *I Paradossi,* printed in 1608, but a whole section of tributes (over 100 in number) appear as the final section of Manso's *Poesie Nomiche,* printed in 1635, just three years before Milton visited the Marchese.[19] Most of the poems are in Italian, rather than Latin, and most are sonnets or brief lyrics, but a few are canzoni about the same length as Milton's hundred-line hexameter poem or song. The number of tributes is unusual and attests to Manso's popularity among his contemporaries, a popularity that Milton alludes to in the headnote to the poem in his 1645 *Poemata,* remarking

18. Ralph W. Condee, "'Mansus' and the Panegyric Tradition," in *Studies in the Renaissance* 15. Also see R. W. Condee, "The Latin Poetry of John Milton," in *The Latin Poetry of English Poets.*
19. See "Poesie di Diversi a Gio: Battista Manso Marchese di Villa." in Giovanni Battista Manso, *Poesie Nomiche* (1635), 225–326.

that Manso held the first rank of renown among Italians both for his literary accomplishments and for his military valor.

It is certainly true that Milton's Latin poem to Manso has the flavor of a humanist compliment, replete with classical references and allusions.[20] Some critics have even argued that Milton adopts for his own address to Manso many of the terms of compliment that Manso's friends used in their commendatory poems.[21] In poem after poem among the encomia of the *Poesie Nomiche* Manso's Italian friends compare the Marchese to Apollo and Mars; it is unlikely that Milton was unaware of these compliments.[22] But Milton does not celebrate Manso, as his Italian friends had, as a Mars in war and an Apollo in peace. Apart from the direct commendation in the headnote of the poem, Milton not only refrains from comparing Manso to these gods, but he also refrains from celebrating Manso's poetic accomplishments. It is as a patron to poets, rather than a poet, that Manso appears in "Mansus," as a Maecenas or a Gallus, rather than as a Horace or a Vergil. This is not to say, however, that Milton avoids the extravagant style or the mythic texture of humanistic encomia. Far from it. With Phoebus's choir, the Pierides prepare songs of praise for Manso; Milton's own Muses—the Camoenae—wreathe for him victor's crowns of laurel and ivy. Although he substitutes Mercury for Mars in his praise of Manso, he remarks how Jupiter, Apollo and Mercury all favored Manso equally at his birth (70–72). He praises his green old age; he remarks that Manso wears the honors of his brow unfallen—alluding, I think, to the many laurels of honor that the old man had had bestowed upon him. He does not, however, call him Phoebus. Although in "Ad Patrem" Milton allowed his father to assume the place of a surrogate Apollo—a Pater Phoebus—Manso, however, remains Father "Mansus"—the patron to poets. The role of Phoebus is reserved

20. See particularly Anthony Low's essay "*Mansus:* In its Context," in *Urbane Milton.* Low comments in detail on Milton's many classical allusions throughout the poem. Also see Condee, "The Latin Poetry of John Milton," in *The Latin Poetry of English Poets.*

21. Estelle Haan, "'Written Encomiums': Milton's Latin Poetry in Its Italian Context," in *Milton in Italy.* Also see Condee, "'Mansus,'" 175.

22. See "Poesie di Diversi à Gio: Battista Manso, Marchese di Villa," in Manso, *Poesie Nomiche* (1635), 257–326. See particularly Margherita Sarrocchi, who says Manso unites Mars and Phoebus (303), Giovanni Battista Comentati, who calls him both a "saggio Apollo" and a "fiero Marte" (304); Scipione Errico, who says he does not know whether to call Manso a "musico Apollo" or a "guerriero Marte" (302); Antonio Gallerati says he employs both Apollo's plectrum and Mars's sword and is honored by both (268); Angelita Scaramuzza calls him the "Pregio di Febò, e Marte" (300). Giovanni Ambrogio Biffi commends his sword in war, his lyre in peace; what Mars and Apollo are in heaven, Manso is alone on earth (267); Antonio Gallerati varies the praise a little by citing Manso, like Apollo, as the conqueror of the Python (267). Encomia prefixed to Manso, *I Paradossi overo dell' Amore Dialogi Di Gio. Battista Manso* (1608), are in a similar vein; some of the encomia printed in *Poesie Nomiche* (such as Biffi's and Gallerati's sonnets) make earlier appearances here. Also see Haan, "Written Encomiums," 536–40.

for the poets Manso assisted—for Tasso, for Marino, and finally for Milton himself. As the biographer and friend to poets, Manso memorializes them; he guards their bones; he ensures that their features will be engraved in marble or in bronze, that their work will be preserved on earth for later ages. But he does not join their ranks as a poet, not even as one who might memorialize them. In fact, the poets themselves, returning favor to Manso, memorialize him in verse—as Tasso and Marino had done, and now as Milton does, the young servant of Phoebus who comes from the north.

It is one of the curious phenomena of Milton's encomiastic verse that he as poet often becomes with those he lauds the subject as well as the speaker of the poem. The speaker's aspirations for fame in "Lycidas" stand side by side his urgent pleas in behalf of the dead Lycidas. In "Mansus" at the central point in the poem, Milton shifts the attention from the elderly Maecenas he has been celebrating to himself, the young visiting poet from the land of the Hyperboreans, come to establish himself in Italy as the third among the sons of light—the third poet, after the great Tasso and Marino, to receive Manso's favor.

The land of the Hyperboreans is not mere metonymy for England; it carries with it an important Apollonian context. In Pindar's *Olympian 3* and *Pythian 10,* the Hyperboreans are the people of Apollo, who live in a distant northern land. Although other poets allude to the land of the Hyperboreans, in Pindar's odes it is particularly designated as a land favored by Apollo.[23] As Apollo's chosen people, the Hyperboreans experience neither sickness nor old age, dwelling free from war and toil, having escaped the judgment of Nemesis.[24] Pindar wrote *Pythian 10* for a boy-victor from Thessaly, one of the more remote areas of northern Greece, far from the thriving centers of Sparta or Athens or even Pindar's own Thebes. To compliment remote Thessaly, he associates it with a never-never land of the Muses and Apollo, where the arts thrive and the Muses are particularly honored. Pindar describes the Hyperboreans sacrificing hecatombs of asses in honor of their patron god, who, Pindar tells us, rejoiced, laughing as the rampant "hybris" of the asses, pleased by the sacrifice, strange and exotic though it might appear to the Greek sensibility. In this land maidens dance to the striking of the lyre and the sounding flute, while the Hyperboreans, their hair wreathed with golden laurel, join in these festivities. Milton goes to great lengths to identify Pindar's Hyperborean land with his native Britain, thus not only making the Britons a people chosen by Apollo, but also making himself an

23. Milton writes the word "Hyperboreans" in Greek in a Latin letter to Diodati (see "Familiar Letters," Epistle 6, *The Works of John Milton* [ed. Patterson], 12), indicating that he thinks of the Hyperboreans in a Greek rather than a Latin context.
24. Pindar, *Pythian 10, 29–44, Carmina.*

Apollonian poet, who, like Pindar, can describe the sacred rites of his own Muse-favored society.

Invoking the Muse Clio and great Phoebus, Milton calls himself a stranger from the Hyperborean sphere. Like Pindar's Hyperborean land, Milton's England is a northern land remote from the thriving "classical" centers—old Greece or the magna Graecia of Renaissance Italy—but England is not now, Milton affirms, nor was it in the past, indifferent to the Muses.[25] The swans of Phoebus are native to England and tune their voices along the Thames while the silver river pours its bright tresses into the ocean. Even in ancient times, Apollo was known and worshipped by the British. Choruses of Druid priests sang hymns to the god and celebrants brought him grain, baskets of apples, and fragrant crocus—pastoral gifts. Milton takes pains to name the native British Druid poet-priests of Apollo, for he thereby establishes that Britain, like the Hyperborean land or far-off Thessaly, was a society devoted to the proper worship of the god Apollo. Druid priests are Phoebades too—full sharers in the rites and sacrifices to Apollo that Milton alludes to in "Ad Patrem." It is hardly an accident that when he describes the poetry of the Druids, Milton even echoes at line 43 of "Mansus" line 46 from the earlier poem.[26] British bards celebrate native British heroes, translating to Britain a tradition of heroic poetry that had begun in Greece—a tradition worthy of emulation that Milton affirms he intends to follow. Classical Greece recognized, moreover, that the Druids were part of a larger cult of Apollo, naming the Druid maidens—Loxo and Upis and golden-haired Hecaërge—when the maiden choruses at Delos, Apollo's birthplace, sang songs of praise to Phoebus. Even as he now proposes that classical Italy recognize him as a fellow poet, Milton insists that as a Briton, descended from the Druid bards, that he already bears the proper poetic credentials as a devotee to Phoebus.

Asserting his vocation as a British poet, Milton announces that he will undertake a British epic on a British theme. But he also boldly claims classical authority for this epic; he deliberately places himself in the line of Homer and Vergil and Pindar as well as their modern Italian counterparts Tasso and Marino. This is part of his program to make himself and his people acceptable in the community of Renaissance humanists in Italy.[27]

25. Milton may even be linking himself to the hero Perseus who came to the land of the Hyperboreans and then went on to accomplish great deeds, such as the slaying of the gorgon.

26. "Heroumque actus imitandaque gesta canebat," "Ad Patrem," 46; "Heroum laudes imitandaque gesta canebant," "Mansus," 43.

27. Even years later in *The Second Defense of the People of England* he remembers with pleasure how he had been accepted as a poet in Florence, in Rome, in Venice, and in Naples. See *The Second Defense of the People of England* in Milton, *Complete Poems and Major Prose* (ed. Hughes), 828–29.

APOLLO AND CHIRON

Milton's next digression reworks the account of Apollo's servitude to Admetus, a myth that moves Milton the poet even closer to his goal. The story is a complex one, involving Apollo's year-long exile at the court of a mortal, a punishment inflicted by Jove because Apollo had attacked the Cyclopes for slaying his son Aesculapius. Some critics believe that Milton's allusion to Apollo's servitude includes reference to this larger framework of the myth— the story of Hercules' rescue of Admetus's wife Alcestis.[28] But Milton does not refer to these events, focusing instead not on Admetus, but the god Apollo and his visit to the cave of Chiron, an event that Milton apparently added to the story.[29] It is to Chiron, moreover, the gentle Centaur, tutor to Achilles and Apollo's son Aesculapius, and advisor to Apollo himself, that Milton compares Manso, punning on Manso's name as he names Chiron ("mansueti Chironis," 60). Clearly, Milton thinks of Apollo's visit to Chiron in the vale of Tempe as parallel to his own visit to evergreen springtime Naples, the garden of Italy, and to Manso's villa. In alluding to the Centaur who was tutor to so many semidivine sons, Milton is probably thinking of Manso's relationship with Tasso, Marino, and now with Milton himself.[30] Further, his emphasis is on the request that Chiron makes of Apollo. At the Centaur's bequest the god of poetry, seated in the idyllic setting by the banks of the Peneus, takes his lyre in hand and pours forth an ecstatic song, soothing, as Milton says, the labors of his exile. What is that song? Milton does not tell us, but he does describe the effects of the singing. The stream overflows its banks; the very rocks become unfixed; the mountain trees, unrooted, hurl themselves downward, and amidst this violent upheaval, the heart of the spotted lynx grows gentle, listening to such strains as were never heard before.

What begins as a compliment to Manso—that the god of poetry visited him, that famous poets dwelled in his halls, as Apollo dwelled with Admetus and Chiron—ends with the praise of Apollo and his song. Critics have pointed out that Milton has transferred to Apollo's song the effects usually associated with Orpheus's singing—rivers halt in their course, rocks and trees are moved, wild animals grow tame.[31] He does so for a purpose. Just as he has associated himself with Apollo and his visit to Manso with Apollo's visit to Chiron, he has made Apollo's song the poet's song—*his own* unstoppable song. Although he has not told us what *Apollo* sang, he

28. See Low, "*Mansus:* In its Context," in *Urbane Milton,* 115–18.
29. MacKellar, *The Latin Poems,* 327.
30. See Low, "*Mansus:* In its Context," in *Urbane Milton,* 114–18. Low also fills in some of the contexts in which Chiron appears in Pindar's odes.
31. *Variorum (The Latin and Greek Poems),* 1.277.

does tell us what *he* himself will sing—he the young foreigner come from a Hyperborean heaven to entertain the ears of a friend to poets who has also encouraged his song. He will sing of the kings of his own country, of Arthur and his wars with the supernatural forces under the earth, of the magnanimous heroes of Arthur's table.[32] Entering into the very subject of his song, Milton tells us, using the first person, "I shall break to pieces Saxon phalanxes under the warfare of the Britons": "Frangam Saxonicas Britonum sub Marte phalanges!" (84).

Milton has done a curious turnabout. We would expect in a commendatory poem such as "Mansus" that the encomiastic poet would take the opportunity here to render a gracious compliment to his host by making "Apollo's song" praise Chiron-Manso, who had called forth that song. After all, Milton has told Manso that wherever the glory of Tasso shall be named, he shall be also. Their fame shall be together on men's lips; together he and Tasso shall enjoy immortal flight. To be celebrated in song is a reward Manso has every right to expect for having befriended poets. But at this juncture Milton deliberately thwarts his expectation. Milton does not make Manso the subject of Apollo's song, nor, as the Italian encomiasts of the *Poesie Nomiche* had, does he compliment the Marchese's own poetry. He categorizes him instead as the friend to poets who has facilitated *their* great work and has revered *their* memory. In helping Tasso and Marino to write, Manso assured their future fame, as he is now assuring fame to another aspiring poet—Milton. Moreover, when Milton speaks of future fame, it is neither Tasso's nor Marino's nor Manso's, that concerns him, but his own. He confides his own plans, predicts his own nationalistic epic and basks in the expectation of fame that will result from that endeavor. The lecture on fame that Phoebus bestows on the shepherd-swain in "Lycidas" would be lost on this aspiring poet.

That the conclusion of "Mansus" focuses on Milton the young poet and not on Manso the older friend of poets merely fulfills what has been the real theme of the poem from the beginning—the development of John Milton as a poet. Even Apollo, a pivotal figure in this poem as in "Lycidas" and "Ad Patrem," exists not for himself, but as the patron god of the sons of Apollo. Fame, a central concern in "Lycidas," reappears to exert its prerogative, as Milton the poet looks forward to the future and imagines his own funeral as a poet. It is a curious vision for a poet barely thirty years old to project. But these imagined funeral exequies, unlike those in "Lycidas," are not motivated by a fear of death. The funeral rites are a measure in some way of his own future status as a poet—of the regard that friends and posterity will have for his poetry. In classical poetry, particularly in the poetry of the

32. See MacKellar, *The Latin Poems,* 330–31.

elegiac poets—Propertius and Tibullus and Ovid—the imagined funeral is
a critical topos for assessing the poet's reputation and place in his society.
By adopting classical motifs for his funeral, Milton looks back on these
Roman elegists, poets he once emulated. He speaks of ashes and urns and
marble busts and Paphian myrtle and Parnassan laurel—all unmistakable
trappings for the classical poet or for poets such as Tasso and Marino
who followed closely in the classical tradition. That Milton imagines for
himself not an English monument, such as he would have at St. Giles
Cripplegate in London, but a Roman urn, a "parva urna," lends the passage
a poetic perspective and specifically links it with passages on funerals and
memorials in the works of his Italian and Roman predecessors.

Milton had already been touched, however, with classical laurel. The
verses "On Shakespeare" that he composed some years previous for the second Folio (1632) had a monumental quality to them that was hardly English.
He had espoused for England's leading dramatist a Horatian reward—no
"Star-ypointing Pyramid" (4), but the "live-long Monument" (8) that his own
living volumes would afford. He lingers in this poem too with words that
suggest the actual monument and the poet's imagined funeral—"Marble"
and "Sepulcher'd" and "Tomb." Already there is a tension here between
the tangible "witness" of an earthly fame and the intangible reward of the
invaluable book. Apollo resides in Shakespeare's book in the "Delphic
lines" and their deep—almost prophetic impression. Writing of another
poet Milton has already told us a good deal about his own hopes and
expectations.

Something similar happens when he writes of Manso and his poetic
friends—Tasso and Marino—and imagines their marble monuments. Among
the encomia prefixed to Manso's *Poesie Nomiche* is a sonnet written by
Giovanni Battista Marino, which is relevant in motif to the "funeral" passage
in Milton's "Mansus."[33] In this sonnet Marino remembers Manso as the
memorializer of Tasso's memory, coming to the Latin hills to see once
more the poet's famous urn and to mourn for the one that all Italy reveres.
Tasso himself is pictured in the Parnassus of heaven, his hair freshly
adorned, while his friend Manso prays that he rest in eternal peace. The
sonnet exploits some of the paradoxes that concern Milton: earthly urns as
opposed to eternal monuments, the poet's Parnassus versus the Christian
heaven, the friend's remembrance in place of posterity's reward. At this
point, Milton moves from describing Manso as a patron to seeing him as
a beloved friend, who (as in Marino's sonnet), executes the last offices
for the poet, who builds a memorial for him, and tends it with care and

---

33. Giovanni Battista Marino, "Tomba del Tasso amico del Marchese," in "Poesie di
Diversi à Gio: Battista Manso, Marchese di Villa," in Manso, *Poesie Nomiche* (1635), 269.

affection. In wishing for such a friend to perform the requisite offices for him, Milton reveals something about his own self-image as a poet. The example of the Italian academies and Renaissance sodalities—as well as exemplary friends such as Tasso and Manso—has made Milton experience in life what he had only found previously in the works of Horace or Vergil, Propertius or Ovid. Milton's literary funeral is just that—the fulfillment of what he had known from literary texts—now made vivid and recreated in his own poem. He envisions a future friend who will tend his urn—a composite of the literary patron and the beloved mistress of the Roman elegiac poet. "He" or "she" composes the limbs, gathers the ashes, and memorializes the poet in marble, remembering him in death by tending his tomb.

This imaginary funeral is an important part of the tradition of elegiac poetry (See Tibullus *Elegies* 1.3; Lygdamus *Elegies* 3.2; Propertius *Elegies* 2.13; Ovid, *Tristia* 3.3). Although Milton had by this time passed beyond his ambitions to be an Ovid or a Propertius, he still cherished, however, the elegiac poet's desire for fame. Intimations of the elegiac poet will still linger—as we shall see—to his last Latin poem "Ad Joannem Rousium." Although he changes the context and many of the details of his imaginary funeral, including the sex of the mourner, we cannot mistake the undoubted debt that Milton has to the Roman elegists. Propertius hopes that his books as well as his mistress Cynthia will accompany him to his grave, that his ashes will be gathered into a "little" jar, and that a laurel will be planted at his grave. The imaginary funeral is a tribute to what he has been as a poet. Ovid's pleas are no less urgent. He asks his wife to gather the ashes in the little urn and to bring at least his bones back from exile to testify that his wit as a poet both made him and unmade him.[34] On earth his books and the tender care that his wife will give for his tomb will testify to his stature as a poet. If the mistresses and the self-pitying expiration are gone from Milton's reenactment of his classical funeral, the desire for an attendant mourner and a belief in the testament of poetry remains. He imagines himself dying full of years ("Annorumque satur"), having fulfilled a long life and his promise as a poet. The anxious prayer for inspiration—"O modo spiritus adsit" (if only the spirit will be present)—has been answered.[35] He does not pray, as Ovid had, that his spirit be consumed with his body. He hopes to enjoy in

---

34. Ovid, *Tristia* 3.3; Milton many times refers to the poetry of Ovid's exile—see for example "Elegia 6," 19–20.

35. In expressing the hope that he will have life and inspiration to write his epic, Milton is probably echoing Vergil's *Georgics* 3.10. He also echoes the *Georgics* in "Epitaphium Damonis": "O, mihi tum si vita supersit" (168).

a classical-Christian heaven the sure rewards of the good—another phrase he borrows from a classical poet, here Vergil.[36]

Nothing is more misunderstood or criticized in this poem than its final lines and particularly the phrase "plaudam mihi."[37]

> (Quantum fata sinunt) & tota mente serenùm
> Ridens purpureo suffundar lumine vultus
> Et simul aethereo plaudam mihi laetus Olympo. (98–100, 1645 *Poems*)

> As much as the Fates permit, and entirely serene at mind,
> Smiling, my face suffused with rosy light, and at the same time,
> Joyful, I shall applaud myself, on airy Olympus.

As the reference to rosy light implies, a phrase taken from Vergil's description of the Elysium fields in *Aeneid* 6 (640–41), Milton's heaven is colored with the light of a classical Olympus, where the poets are gathered as they are in Raphael's celebrated mural of Parnassus in the Stanza della Segnatura. "Mansus" does not concern, as "Lycidas" did, the rewards of the Christian, but focuses on the rewards of the poet, namely the reward of an epic work achieved. Neither Tasso nor Marino, who, as Milton says, sang of the Assyrian loves of the gods, appears in "Mansus" in any other role than that of the poet, the sons of Phoebus, nurtured by the foster father, Pater "Mansus." The phrase itself, "plaudam mihi," Milton had employed in Prolusion 6. The context of its use in this early rhetorical exercise is instructive, for Milton, comparing himself to the poets Orpheus and Amphion, congratulates himself that he has been more successful than they. With their skill on the lyre they have drawn rocks and beasts and trees to themselves; but he with his *words* has drawn the approbation of learned men. He speaks this not boasting, he insists, but merely with satisfaction that he has, he hopes, pleased his auditors.

Although the context for the phrase, "plaudam mihi," seems at first quite different, it is not altogether so. Milton's audience in "Mansus" is the society

---

36. Vergil, *Aeneid*, 1.603–5. Aeneas graciously wishes Dido a proper reward for her kindness. See Low, "*Mansus:* In its Context," in *Urbane Milton,* 122. Milton uses a similar phrase in "Epitaphium Damonis," 36.

37. See Prolusion 6, *The Works of John Milton* (ed. Patterson), 12.210.12–14. Low traces the phrase "mihi plaudam" to Horace's *Satires* 1.1.66–7, arguing that it should be taken satirically, as in Horace. See Low, "*Mansus:* In its Context," in *Urbane Milton,* 123–24. Low also traces the phrase "Quantum fata sinunt" to Vida's "Quantum fata sinunt, et non aversus Apollo" (*De Arte Poetica,* 3.192), where not only fate, but Apollo's favor is invoked. We might remark that even at this point the god of poetry is tacitly present, if not directly invoked.

of learned men, those humanists of Italy who, like Manso, prize poetry—a specifically academic group, learned in the subtleties of Latin, and in that regard not unlike those he addressed at Cambridge and hoped to please. In both "Mansus" and in "Ad Patrem," he aspires to take his place among those who value poetry, among the sons of Phoebus. The hope that he expresses at the end of "Mansus" is for the ultimate self-congratulation of literary, almost "academic" fame, the reward of a life devoted to Apollo that has gleaned not only the laurels of the god, but also the approbation of his peers among the sons of poetry. Perhaps Milton had not despaired of finding on his return to England something comparable to the literary culture of Italy. Perhaps the young pilgrim from a Hyperborean north hoped to build in his native land a society congenial to Apollo and the Muses.

APOLLO THE PHYSICIAN

Although no less affectionate, no less warm a tribute to an Italian poet-friend, "Ad Salsillum" is almost a scherzo in comparison to the elegant andante of the verses to Manso. Yet it too neatly fulfills the expectation of the humanistic circles that Milton had been frequenting in Italy.[38] In it Milton espouses Apollo as a patron god, but in addressing Apollo the physician, he appears at first to concern himself with a different aspect of the god. He chooses the scazontic meter for his address to Salzilli, partly because the little poem is a tour de force, partly because he wishes the meter to convey a cheerful message to a sick friend.[39] In structure the poem recalls the light English odes, "L'Allegro" and "Il Penseroso," for like them it is organized as a hymn-ode to the gods, Apollo and Salus (Health), whom Milton petitions to bring health to Salzilli in return for Salzilli's continued devotion to Apollo and poetry.

The hymn-ode to Hygeia or Salus was a favorite type among vernacular and neo-Latin poets of the previous century, examples of it occurring in Calcagnini, Flaminio, Ronsard, Magny, and others.[40] Ronsard includes his

---

38. See James A. Freeman, "Milton's Roman Connection: Giovanni Salzilli," in *Urbane Milton*, 87–104.

39. This is the only use of scazontes in Milton's Latin verse. In *Parerga* (1632), Milton's friend, Alexander Gil Jr., published in scazontes a mock funeral lament for Tilly, the defeated general of the Catholic League.

40. The hymn to Health (Hygeia) is of ancient authority, occurring among the Orphic hymns. Renaissance poets adapted the type and often made it a familiar address to friends in which they requested the return of health. See Caelius Calcagninus, "Hymnus in Sanitatem," in Gherus, ed., *Delitiae CC. Italorum Poetarum* (1608), 546–47; Marcus Antonius Flamineus, "In bonam valetudinem," *Doctissimorum Nostra Aetate Italorum Epigrammata* (1548), 4r.

petition to Health in an ode to Apollo that he sent to his king, Charles IX, asking Apollo to cure the king.[41] Like Ronsard, Milton combines the format of the familiar ode with the formal hymn-ode, petitioning the god in the proper hymnic fashion by referring to his name—Paean—and his accomplishments, the slaying of the Python.

> O dulce divum munus, O Salus, Hebes
> Germana! Tuque Phoebe, morborum terror,
> Pythone caeso, sive tu magis Paean
> Libenter audis, hic tuus sacerdos est. (23–26)

> O sweet divine gift, O Health, sister
> of Hebe! And you, Phoebus, the terror of diseases,
> since your killing of Python, or Paean, if you prefer
> to hear yourself so named, this is your priest.

Combining formal hymnic structure with informal verse, as he had in his English hymn-odes, he adapts the classical hymn structure to his own purpose. "Ad Salsillum" is an encomium with a difference.

Milton is pursuing an agenda of Apollonian poetics in this poem, too. Although ostensibly he refers to Apollo only as the god of medicine, appealing to him in the name of friendship to restore good health to Salzilli, his poem is very much one of poet to poet. Milton never forgets, moreover, Apollo's other role as god of poets. He has taken care at the outset of the poem to invoke the Muse of scanzontic verse, the "muse" of that other limping meter so like the elegiac couplets he had often employed in his early Latin poetry. His invocation recalls not only Ovid's pleasant jesting references to Lady Elegia—the Limping Lady of *Amores* 3.1—but Ovid's serious considerations in this elegy of his vocation as a poet. Milton places himself conspicuously in his own poem. He alludes, as he had in "Mansus," to his having come from London to the Italian cities (where, he says, the very soil nurtures poets), and he also recalls that Salzilli had compared him in an epigram to the "divine poets"—Homer and Vergil and Tasso. Although Milton demurs that such praise is undeserved, he later includes the epigram in the testimonia of the *Poemata*. Indeed, even in this sportive poem, Milton accepts his vatic role, invoking Apollo to come as a vates would address the god of poetry. When he asks Apollo to show favor to Salzilli because he is a poet-priest ("sacerdos"), he quickly enrolls himself,

41. See Ronsard, *Odes* (5.6) in *Oeuvres Complètes*: "Pasteur parmi les bois." Ronsard asks Apollo to use his physicianly skills to cure his king, Charles IX, saving him as he saved Admetus, bringing Health, for if Health comes, Youth and Pleasure will follow (2:608–11).

as he had in "Ad Patrem" and Mansus," in this select company. Yet he maintains a light touch and good humor throughout, even when he appeals to Apollo and makes extraordinary claims about poetry's sacred powers. It is to Apollo's own advantage, he jestingly reminds the god, to restore Salzilli to health, for then Salzilli will gladden the gardens of Rome once more with his song. Poetry has the power to control nature and govern society, he continues. Were Salzilli to sing again, Rome's ancient king Numa would wonder at his song, and the Tiber itself would submit to his government and, lending fertility and favor to the country, would nevermore overflow its banks. In one sense Milton was returning a fulsome compliment in kind. Yet extravagant though his compliments might be, we should not dismiss them merely as one poet topping another with his wit. This familiar poem continues to express (albeit in its way) Milton's preoccupation with Apollo and with poetry's divine status. It also demonstrates that Milton could still govern mirth as well as melancholy as he courted the deities of poetry.

DAMON, MANSO, AND THE PHOENIX

Apollo does not actually appear in "Epitaphium Damonis," the poem Milton wrote for his friend Charles Diodati on returning to England in 1639/1640. His presence, however, is implicitly felt throughout as Thyrsis, the shepherd-swain of this pastoral eclogue, tries to find his poetic voice to lament his dead friend.[42] In "Lycidas" the god of flocks reproves the shepherd-speaker for complaining about the meager rewards of the homely slighted shepherd's trade. In "Epitaphium Damonis" that same pastoral Apollo remains tacitly present as the patron of the community of poet-shepherds of which Thyrsis is a member. Phoebus Apollo prompts the long epic poem Milton aspires to write, and is the father of the phoenix who unfurls his wings on one of the two poetic cups that Milton tells us Manso presented to him. Even more insistently than in "Lycidas," Milton appeals to the pastoral tradition, choosing as the speaker of "Epitaphium Damonis" the Thyrsis of Theocritus's Idyll 1 and directly alluding at the beginning to Theocritus's Daphnis, not the Daphnis-James of Scottish eclogue. "Epitaphium Damonis" is both a recapitulation, a reconsideration, and a valediction to pastoral, as Milton revolves, but in a different way from "Lycidas," on the poet's place in society, and turns away from eclogue to epic as a medium for poetic expression. Milton may be thinking, as critics have often urged, of Vergil and the dying Gallus's farewell in eclogue 10 to the sylvan

42. See *Variorum (The Latin and Greek Poems)*, 1.282–84 for the dating of the poem.

world of pastoral poetry. Or he may have chosen the classical eclogue as a medium for placing English pastoral landscape, now bereft of the shepherd-physician Damon, side by side the pastoral landscape of ancient and modern Italy from whence finally comes comfort and renewal. Italy— with its Tuscan shepherds and their contests of song, with old shepherd Manso taking old Damoetas's place, with twin pastoral cups reminding us of the cups Theocritus's Thyrsis won with his song—lightens the lament with classical leavening. Apollo may be absent, but the sons of Phoebus inhabit the pastoral world of "Epitaphium Damonis" just as they had in "Mansus" and "Ad Patrem."

Poetry and Italy invade the poem simultaneously at line 13 when Milton explains that the love for the Muse detained him in the Tuscan city, ignorant that Damon has died.[43] Friendship, a basic theme in "Mansus," reappears in a different guise in "Epitaphium Damonis." In "Mansus" Milton had celebrated his own friendship with the elderly Neapolitan nobleman as well as Manso's friendship with the poets Tasso and Marino. In "Epitaphium Damonis," however, the loss of friends poignantly affects him—the death of Diodati, his boyhood confidant, and his removal from and nostalgia for his Florentine friends Dati and Francini, whom he celebrates as the Tuscan shepherds—Menalcas and Lycidas. The Latin word *sodalis* has a special place in "Epitaphium Damonis," signifying not just friend (*amicus,* a word Milton uses for Diodati), but a literary intimate, such as the member of an Italian academy. As he made the pastoral life in "Lycidas" the university life, Milton has deliberately adapted the pastoral he describes in "Epitaphium Damonis" to the life of the literary sodality such as the Italian academies, where familiar and learned friendships flourish.[44] Regret for this association—with shared hopes and aspirations—combines with regret for his lost sodalis Damon-Diodati, who from his earliest youth had provided him with the intellectual stimulation that produced the Latin elegies and familiar letters.[45] As long as fifteen years later, when he was writing *The Second Defense of the People of England,* Milton would recall his Italian friends and the Italian academies where humane studies and

43. Citing his love for the Muse, Milton is probably echoing Vergil, *Georgics* 2.475–76.
44. In Italy Milton confides that he dared to enter into contest with the "Tuscan shepherds," competing in song in their academies. He makes these poetic meetings the equivalent of the song contests described by Theocritus and Vergil in the idylls and eclogues.
45. In a letter to Carlo Dati written April 21, 1647, Milton regrets both friends who have died and friends from whom he was separated by place and distance—connecting (apparently) his loss of Diodati with his separation from his Italian friends: "those whom habits, disposition, studies, had so handsomely made my friends, are now almost all denied me, either by death or by most unjust separation of place" ("Milton to Carlo Dati," "Familiarium Epistolarum" in *The Works of John Milton* [ed. Patterson], 12:47).

friendship went hand in hand.[46] A feeling of lost connections permeates "Epitaphium Damonis." Milton could speak in "Mansus" of the sense of shared community that Italy brought, a community that the England to which he has returned no longer possesses. It is not only Diodati's death that has shattered his dreams, but also the failure of the community of pastor-poets at Cambridge that "Lycidas" so feelingly laments. Hence Milton looks back on Italy with a double regret—the consolation he found there has now vanished.

In "Epitaphium Damonis" as in "Ad Patrem" and "Mansus," Milton tells of both his aspiration to be a poet and his desire to belong to a community devoted to Phoebus Apollo—men of learning who serve the liberal arts.[47] The young physician Damon-Diodati was also a member of that community—a follower of Aesculapius, Phoebus's physician-son and also a son of Phoebus. Damon was the inheritor of another aspect of this many-faceted god, to whom the healing arts, as those of music and poetry, were sacred. Milton connects Diodati with his Italian friends not only because he was of Tuscan blood, but because Diodati too valued that Renaissance ideal of "humanitas." Milton identifies "humanitas" as a collective literary experience when he graciously thanks the old Marchese; it is that literary experience that he longs for here. At this point in "Epitaphium Damonis," he is seeking in the special friend the first audience that is so important to an aspiring poet, an audience he spoke of in "Mansus" when he first outlined his plans for his projected British historical epic. When he speaks of that epic, he employs both in "Mansus" (82) and "Epitaphium Damonis" (103) the same key word—*dicam*, "I shall tell"—almost as though he were speaking the first line of a proemium. In "Mansus" the poet begins his song at the behest of Chiron-Manso; in "Epitaphium Damonis" he holds the song in abeyance to sing to his friend Damon on his return. The projected epic is peculiarly the product both of old Italy and old Britain, inspired by the example of Vergil and Tasso, but made of the materials of British legend. On the one hand, it is conceived, as Milton lies beside the Arno in the company of his Italian friends, but it is withheld from poetic birth until his return to England when he could sing to Damon when they would be

46. Milton, *Complete Poems and Major Prose* (ed. Hughes), 828–29. See particularly Arthos, *Milton and the Italian Cities,* and also several essays from the collection *Milton in Italy:* Nardo, "Milton and the Academic Sonnet"; Diana Treviño Benet, "The Escape from Rome: Milton's *Second Defense* and a Renaissance Genre"; and Dustin Griffin, "Milton in Italy: The Making of a Man of Letters?"

47. See Albert C. Labriola, "Portrait of an Artist: Milton's Changing Self-Image," in *Urbane Milton.* Labriola regards "Epitaphium Damonis" as crucial for Milton's developing view of himself as a poet.

reclining beside an English river, the Colne.[48] But the meeting will never take place—Damon is dead. The poetic pipes have broken their joinings; the weighty song fails. Has his song died with Damon?

The turning point of "Epitaphium Damonis" comes with Milton's reassertion of that song.[49] Not until he accepts Damon's death can he return in a sense to the interrupted strain that he had begun in Italy. Adapting the phrase that Vergil gives to Gallus in Eclogue 10.63 when turning from pastoral song to epic—"vos cedite, silvae" (160)—Milton announces his heroic theme at the same time he renounces Latin pastoral. He has hung up his rustic pipe, the "fistula," and has now determined to sing an English epic for an English audience.

"Epitaphium Damonis," like many Renaissance pastorals, is a framed poem. Its opening section invokes the nymphs of Himera, who remembered Daphnis, Hylas, and Bion, and urges them to repeat their Sicilian song in England. Then it describes how the poet Thyrsis sits alone, grieving for his friend Damon. Just as Milton distances himself from the shepherd-swain at the end of "Lycidas" by providing the concluding frame, Milton separates himself at the beginning of "Epitaphium Damonis" from the persona who sings the lament for Damon.[50] But there are other types of framing devices. The poem is framed also, as it were, by Theocritean and Vergilian pastoral; it begins by alluding to Theocritus's Daphnis and concludes by quoting Vergil's Gallus and his farewell to pastoral poetry.

When Milton begins to sing in "Epitaphium Damonis" the opening lines of his Arthurian epic, the pastoral hexameters take on the weightiness of

48. See *The Works of John Milton* (ed. Patterson), 12:26–27. Milton's familiar letters, like his elegies to his friend, testify how Milton shared his future poetic plans with Diodati. The letter that he wrote before his departure for Italy (September 23, 1637) tells (blushingly) of his hopes to write "immortal" poetry: "Audi, Theodote, verum in aurem ut ne rubeam, & sinito paulisper apud te grandia loquor; quid cogitem quaeris? ita me bonus Deus, immortalitatem. Quid agam vero? πτεροφυῶ, & volare meditor; sed tenellis ad modum ad huc pennis evehit se noster Pegasus, humile sapiamus." (26) (Hear, Theodotus, but let it be in your private ear, lest I blush; and allow me for a little to speak grandly with you. You ask, what am I thinking of. By the good God, immortality. And what am I doing? Growing wings and meditating flight; but as yet our Pegasus raises himself on very tender pinions. Let us be humbly wise.) (Translation adapted from *Works* [ed. Patterson], 27.) The reference to Pegasus provides a specifically classical context for these remarks; the god Milton refers to could very well be an assisting Apollo.

49. We can compare Milton's technique here with Sannazaro's in the eclogue "Phyllis." Lycidas's grief for Phyllis has interrupted his song; but at the end of the eclogue he reasserts his vocation as a poet, insisting on the songs that he shall write ("inscribam"): "Inscribam grandesque notas ferrugine ducam / Praeteriens quas nauta mari percurrat ab alto / Et dicat: 'Lycidas, Lycidas haec carmina fecit'" (123–25). Milton's Thyrsis also is positive, declaring not only that he will sing, but what he will sing.

50. For a comparison of Milton's techniques in "Lycidas" and "Epitaphium Damonis" see Philip Dust, "Milton's *Epitaphium Damonis* and *Lycidas*," in *Humanista Lovaniensia* 32.

epic hexameters. He intones the epic's theme and beginning: "Dardanias Rutupina per aequora puppes / Dicam" (162–63)—"I shall tell of the Dardanian ships embarking on the Rutupian sea." The kings and queens that he alluded to collectively in "Mansus" he now names and begins to fill in their story: Inogen, and Arviragus, and old Belinus. When he arrives at Igraine, he even begins to narrate the circumstances of Arthur's conception. He gathers the momentum of an epic song begun, before he breaks off, but now not in grief, but to tell us the intention of that epic. The native theme told in the native tongue will be his collective legacy for the British people, giving to them the national epic that Tasso gave to the Italians and Vergil to the Romans. It is also in a way a memorial for his English friend of "Latin" ancestry—though he can never hear of it with earthly ears. The reassertion of the work comforts the mourning shepherd Thyrsis, as the condolences of the shepherd-community could not, and allows him to take up the task that death had interrupted.

To confide his future epic plans was, however, only half of the projected conversation that Thyrsis-Milton planned to have with Damon-Diodati. Milton wished also to tell Diodati of Manso and Manso's gifts—the two pastoral cups—one of which pictured the phoenix, the other the heavenly Amor. Most critics agree that these cups were probably books, specifically two of Manso's own books that he had given to his visiting English friend— the first probably the *Poesie Nomiche* that concludes with the poem, "La Fenice," (the phoenix) and the second the *Erocallia* that concerns theories of Love.[51] Milton chooses to allude to these books pictorially, describing their decorative scenes, as Theocritus describes the scenes on the cup in Idyll 1.[52] Central to their tableaux are the twin figures—the phoenix and Amor—used symbolically not just to compliment Manso and allude to his gifts, but also to bring "Epitaphium Damonis" to a climax by applying these figures both to Damon and to the speaker-Thyrsis.

The phoenix appears among the trees in an incense-breathing Arabian forest in the springtime. Milton carefully sets the scene and describes the flash of its cerulean blue plumage and many-colored wings, calling it, as Ovid and others had, a divine bird, unique on earth.[53] It looks out over the sea waiting for Aurora to rise from its glassy waves.

---

51. See Michele De Filippis, "Milton and Manso: Cups or Books," in *PMLA* 51. Also see Ralph W. Condee, "The Structure of Milton's 'Epitaphium Damonis,'" in *SP* 62.

52. See "Idyll 1," in Theocritus, ed and trans. A. S. F. Gow. For commentary on Milton's imitations see Gordon Campbell, "Imitation in *Epitaphium Damonis*," in *Urbane Milton*, 172.

53. Ovid, *Amores*, 2.6.54; *Metamorphoses* 15.393–407. See Lactantius, *De Ave Phoenice*; also see Starnes and Talbert, *Classical Myth*, 272–75; Osgood, *Classical Mythology of Milton's English Poems*, 69–70.

Has inter Phoenix divina avis, unica terris
Caeruleùm fulgens diversicoloribus alis
Auroram vitreis surgentem respicit undis. (187–89)

Among those the Phoenix, the divine bird, unique on earth,
Flashing blue with many-colored wings,
He looks at Aurora rising from the glassy waves.

Milton has condensed a great deal of the phoenix legend in this brief description. Important for him is the phoenix's divinity, its uniqueness, and its quiet expectation of Dawn. According to both Renaissance and classical accounts, the phoenix is the child of Apollo-Sun.[54] When the phoenix comes to the end of its life span, it awaits the rays of the sun that at first striking will consume its body; the new phoenix who emerges from the ashes will bear its "father"—the consumed body of the former phoenix—to the temple of Apollo-Sun in the east where its god-parent will receive it.[55]

The basic story of the phoenix is ancient, dating back in one version to Herodotus. One of its fullest treatments is Claudian's "Phoenix," the poem Manso paraphrased in his "La Fenice."[56] Manso adheres closely to Claudian, not attempting to Christianize the story, as Tasso had; he was undoubtedly aware, as Milton certainly was, of other versions of the phoenix story—in Ovid, in Lactantius, and, of course, in Tasso's *Il Mondo Creato*.[57] Manso's

54. Mary Cletus Carpenter, editor of Lactantius, gives an account of the different classical, Christian, and contemporary accounts of the phoenix. Also see Lilius Gregorius Gyraldus, *De Deis Gentium* (1548), 151b; and M. Antonius Tritonius, in Comes, *Mythologiae* (1616), 54.37.

55. The gender of the phoenix can be (both in Milton and other writers) either masculine or feminine, hence either son or daughter of the sun god. Grammatically, of course, in Latin as in Italian, its gender is feminine. In this passage, Milton does not specify gender—although its designation as "divina avis, unica" might point to feminine. *Avis*, like *phoenix*, is feminine in Latin. In *Paradise Lost*, when Milton compares Raphael to the phoenix, he designates the phoenix as male and echoes the language of "Epitaphium Damonis": "that sole Bird / When to enshrine his reliques in the Sun's / Bright Temple, to *Egyptian Thebes* he flies" (272–74). In *Samson Agonistes*, Milton appears to describe the bird as feminine using the personal pronoun "her" (1704, 1706) in his description: "that self-begott'n bird / In the *Arabian* woods embost, / That no second knows nor third, / And lay erewhile a Holocaust, / From out her ashy womb now teem'd, / Revives, reflourishes, then vigorous most / When most unactive deem'd, / And though her body die, her fame survives, / A secular bird ages of lives" (1699–1708). Although he may be doing no more than marking grammatical gender, this description closely resembles that in "Epitaphium Damonis."

56. See "Phoenix," 27 in "Shorter Poems" *Claudian*, 2.222–23; and Manso, "La Fenice," *Nomiche Poesie* (1635), 242–50. Claudian's poem is 110 hexameter lines. Manso's is in twenty-six 8-line stanzas.

57. Tasso, "Quinto Giorno" (ll. 1278–1626), *Il Mondo Creato*, in *Poemi Minori di Torquato Tasso;* Tasso, *Creation of the World*, 136–43. Tasso connects the relationship

phoenix—his "Augel del Sole" (bird of the sun)—is closely connected to Apollo-Sun, but is also apparently for Manso a poetic symbol. In the dedicatory letter to his friend Giulio Caria, Manso tells Giulio that he is sending him his "phoenix," a poem that has taken new wing from Claudian and is now flying not to the temple of Apollo in Cyrene but to the "Tempio Cario."[58] There Giulio, acting like Apollo, can either destroy or give the phoenix new life. Manso remarks that Giulio, like Apollo, is a son of Jove and a master of song, and is qualified therefore to judge his friend's poem. Manso tells him either to purge his poetic phoenix of its errors or consign it—if it is unworthy—to a fire from which it will never arise again.

Milton calls the "cups" he had planned to show Damon wondrous works of art from a wondrous man. This tardy allusion to Manso's poetry may strike us as odd, particularly since Milton had virtually ignored the Marchese's verse in his commendatory poem, "Mansus." But it is not Manso's poetry, per se, or even Manso's "Fenice," but the poetic work *generically* that Milton describes as the phoenix. Manso's witty dedication had conflated the phoenix and the poetic work, making the latter dependent for its survival on the Apollonian friend, as the former had been on the patron god. Immortality awaits Manso's phoenix only if the friend approves and gives it new life. Milton probably knew Manso's dedicatory letter as well as his poem. When he describes the image of the phoenix on Manso's cup, not only is he identifying the final poem of Manso's gift book, but he is also, like Manso, making the phoenix a symbol for the poetic work—this time his own. Manso had confided to his friend his hopes that his phoenix, like Apollo's fortunate "son," would attain immortality; Milton had hoped to confide to Damon similar hopes for his phoenix—his projected epic. The divine bird as Milton portrays it in "Epitaphium Damonis" is awaiting rebirth, just as his own "would-be" epic awaits the dawning of new inspiration.

While Manso's "Fenice" is a key source for Milton's phoenix, it is not the only one. Milton glances at details in other versions of the phoenix myth in Ovid, Claudian, Lactantius, and Tasso. Ovid takes care, for example, to contrast the phoenix poetically with Phaeton, Apollo's fatal son, whose mismanagement of the Sun's fire scorches the earth and fells him.[59] Gifts of the god can be fortunate and unfortunate, as Milton observed in "Ad Patrem." The very fire that kills Phaeton, however, wakens the phoenix to

---

of the old phoenix and the new—father and son—with that between God the Father and the Son of God.

58. See the letter to Giulio Caria from Il Marchese di Villa, in *Nomiche Poesie* (1635), 251–52.

59. See Rudolf Gottfried, "Milton, Lactantius, Claudian, Tasso," in *SP* 30; and Kathleen Ellen Hartwell, *Lactantius and Milton,* 123–32.

new life. The holocaust is replayed here with a different Apollonian son and a different conclusion.

Milton had spoken in "Ad Patrem" of the Promethean fire of poetic creation, the spark from heaven that a poet awaits to ignite his work. In both "Ad Patrem" and "Elegia 5," he had presented himself as a son of Apollo, awaiting the approving nod from the paternal god. In "Epitaphium Damonis," immediately after he recounts the plans for the future epic, Milton describes the Apollonian bird, the phoenix, quietly looking to the east—waiting for the first ray of the sun that will ignite him too, that will consume the old and give him new life. Poetry is that unique entity on earth, like the unique bird that must continually be reborn. As the phoenix awaits the dawn, the poet, also reaffirming his service to the god Apollo, awaits his own regeneration from the ashes of his old work.

In relating the phoenix to Thyrsis-Milton and in reading it as a symbol for poetic revival, I am not denying the more familiar connection of the phoenix (particularly in the Christian community) with the resurrection from the dead. But to see the phoenix as a symbol for revived Thyrsis-Milton does not preclude applying it also to Damon-Diodati. Damon had been consigned to Orcus at the poem's beginning and now spreads his wings metaphorically to rise to heaven with the phoenix. With the repeated assertion, "tu quoque in his . . . tu quoque in his *certe est*" (198–99) (you also are among them . . . you also certainly are among them), Thyrsis awards Damon a place on Olympus among the gods. It is not, however, through the agency of the phoenix that he wins this place but through that of Amor, the figure on Manso's other cup. Amor is pictured among the clouds in the wide-spreading sky of great Olympus, shooting his arrows upward to set sacred minds afire.[60] Like the heavenly Cupid at the end of *A Mask,* this celestial Amor inspires the flames of heavenly love.[61] If the phoenix looks to the poetic fires of Dawn, Amor rolls his flaming eyes, never looks downward, scattering his fiery darts upward throughout the spheres—inflaming noble hearts. Fire unites the phoenix and Amor. They work in tandem to represent the renewed poet and to lift the resurrected Damon to heaven:

> purum colit aethera Damon,
> Aethera purus habet, pluvium pede reppulit arcum. (203–4)

60. See Condee, "The Structure of Milton's 'Epitaphium Damonis,'" 592–94, for commentary on the role of Amor.

61. Manso's books may again be referred to obliquely, for a good deal of his writing (*I Paradossi overo dell' Amore Dialogi* and the *Erocallia*) concerned Platonic theories of love and dealt thus with the heavenly Cupid. Many sonnets, moreover, from the three books of *Nomiche Poesie* treat of human, sacred, and moral love. See De Filippis, "Milton and Manso," 753.

Damon dwells in the pure aether
Purely he possesses it, he spurns the rainbow with his foot.

Because of the divine Amor, Damon treads the pure ether. At the same time, Thyrsis experiences Amor as the purifying fire, much like Dante who passed through the fire in the final circle of Purgatorio on his ascent to the pure love of paradise. The phoenix and Amor make possible Damon's "flight" to heaven as well as Thyrsis's purified vision.

The Christian and the classical converge at the end of "Epitaphium Damonis, as at the end of "Lycidas," when the shepherd-swain turns from weeping to banishing tears. As critics have often remarked, certain details in each conclusion are complementary: Lycidas listens to the "inexpressive nuptial Song, / In the blest Kingdoms meek of joy and love," (176–77), Damon experiences comparable joys as he too takes part in immortal wedding-song—"immortales hymenaeos" (217). The shepherd-swain of "Lycidas" and Thyrsis also experience revival and renewal. We might even assert that the living pastors experience the greater revival, for they are restored to active life as poets—to the renewed song of Apollo on earth.[62] But despite these similarities, there are some striking differences between the English and the Latin pastoral lament.

Even though Milton alludes in "Epitaphium Damonis" to the rewards of the virgin martyrs, to joyous palms and to the immortal wedding of the Lamb, its concluding celebrations are more classical than Christian.[63] Moreover, unlike "Lycidas," the eclogue ends without a framing denouement. At the end, it is the joyful voice of the poet that we hear—his renewed song—a song mixed with the sound of the lyre and with blissful choruses. Are we not once again in the land of the Hyperboreans, where the rites of Apollo are celebrated—where the Muses are rightly revered? Does Milton not implicitly honor Damon as a Roman hero raised to Olympus, quaffing nectar with reddened lips in the company of gods and heroes, like Augustus Caesar

---

62. See Janet Leslie Knedlik, "High Pastoral Art in *Epitaphium Damonis*," in *Urbane Milton*. Knedlik notes rightly that "Epitaphium Damonis," unlike "Lycidas," does not indict divine justice. Both pastorals, however, show us shepherds who have temporarily left their flocks untended. Also see A. S. P. Woodhouse, "Milton's Pastoral Monodies"; and Fred J. Nichols, " 'Lycidas,' 'Epitaphium Damonis,' the Empty Dream and the Failed Song," in *Acta Conventus* (1973). On the use of Latin in "Epitaphium Damonis" see John K. Hale, "Sion's Bacchanalia: An Inquiry into Milton's Use of Latin in the *Epitaphium Damonis*," in *MS* 16. Hale comments on the strong positive vision in the final lines that the Latin verse particularly supports.

63. Knedlik, in "High Pastoral Art," notes that the closing vision is classical except for the use of Sion in the last line (150). Woodhouse, in "Milton's Pastoral Monodies," takes a different view, citing Revelation 14.1–4 as the source for Milton's view of Damon in heaven (271).

who in Horace's ode sits beside Hercules and Pollux (*Carmina* 3.3.9–12)? As in "Mansus," Milton assumes the rights and privileges of a Roman poet to celebrate friendship in verse. He even fulfills the Roman promise he made to his friend: that (unless a wolf saw him first) Diodati would not in vain possess a poet for a friend.[64]

In "Elegia 6," Milton had celebrated the Dionysiac and the Apollonian aspects of poetry by wittily connecting Dionysian orgy with Diodati's Christmas celebrations:

> Iam quoque lauta tibi generoso mensa paratu
>   Mentis alit vires ingeniumque fovet.
> Massica foecundam despumant pocula venam,
>   Fundis et ex ipso condita metra cado.
> Addimus his artes, fusumque per intima Phoebum
>   Corda; favent uni Bacchus, Apollo, Ceres. (29–34)

> Now also the sumptuous table with its generous store
>   lends you strength of mind and wit;
> The Massic cups foam with creative impulse,
>   and you discant the store of your verses
> From the wine-jug. To this we add the arts
>   and the presence of Phoebus in your innermost
> heart. In you alone Bacchus, Apollo, Ceres are favorable.

For Diodati, Milton continues, the Thracian lyre also sounds, and its music rules the dancing feet of maidens, just as the lyre and Apollo's presence inspired the maiden dances in Pindar's *Pythian 10*. While he surrounds Diodati with a festive company in "Elegia 6," he himself sits apart meditating heavenly song, singing the starry sky, the hosts in the air, and the gods destroyed in their shrines.

The dichotomy Milton created in "Elegia 6" also applies to "Epitaphium Damonis," the last Latin poem of *Sylvarum Liber,* and the last poem that he created for Charles Diodati—his companion, brother-poet, and prime addressee in the *Elegiarum Liber*. Now, while Milton remains on earth, preparing his Apollonian role as England's future epic poet, he addresses Diodati in heaven enjoying, under the auspices of Bacchus, the "orgiastic" rites of Sion, just as he had enjoyed the festive company Milton describes in "Elegia 6." Whatever distinctions Milton makes between Dionysus and Apollo, Milton does not forget that the two brother-gods are alike patrons of poetry. As he told Diodati in "Elegia 6," Apollo does not shrink from

---

64. See *Variorum (The Latin and Greek Poems),* 1.301 for precedents in Vergil and Theocritus and other sources.

wearing the green clusters of Dionysus's ivy in his hair. In "Epitaphium Da-monis" Thyrsis and Damon—Milton and Diodati—still joined in friendship, celebrate poetry under the lyre of Apollo and the Bacchic thyrsus of Sion. No less than "Elegia 6," "Epitaphium Damonis" is a vision of Milton's poetic future that he shares with his best friend.

The last three long Latin poems of the *Silvarum Liber* concern in different ways the question of poetic vocation, and in all three Milton adheres to Phoebus Apollo as his own poetic father. The prophetic pagan god, disenthroned in the Nativity ode, reigns in the late Latin poetry. In "Epi-taphium Damonis" Milton may be announcing his plan to forgo pastoral and to take leave of Latin as a poetic language, but he does not renounce Apollo, who merely leaves off his role as god of flocks to assume once more the robes of Jove's imperial son. We move in these Latin poems not only beyond pastoral, but significantly beyond "Lycidas." Milton refers tentatively at the end of "Lycidas" to fresh woods and new pastures. Having found in Italy a direction for future poetry, he tells us in "Mansus" and "Epitaphium Damonis" where these new woods and pastures are leading him. Significantly, he must put on the pastoral garments one more time in "Epitaphium Damonis" before he can metamorphose the pastoral Apollo into Vergil's imperial patron and take on epic song. At this stage of his life, Milton found an Apollonian patron, however he was clad, indispensable for poetry. But what happens to Apollo and to Milton's future epic plans when Milton in the 1640s forsakes his design to write a nationalistic epic? Must he turn back to the Nativity ode and dismiss Apollo, as he invokes once more a "heavenly Muse" to nurture and govern his song? To answer that question we must look at Milton's final Latin poem—an ode that he composed in 1647 after he had collected and closed his first volume of verse.

"AD JOANNEM ROUSIUM"

Milton's Farewell to His Book

Between the time that Milton composed "Epitaphium Damonis" and the publication of the *Poems, English and Latin* in January 1645/ 1646 Milton wrote no further poetry in Latin and, so far as we know, only a few English sonnets. The composition of "Ad Joannem Rousium" early in 1647 marks the first long poem that he had completed in over six years—a poem that marks the change that had taken place in the young English poet since he set down his plans for the English epic in "Epitaphium Damonis." By 1646/1647 he had changed his stance as man and poet, and "Ad Joannem Rousium" marks to a degree that change. He had probably determined by this time to write *The History of Britain* in prose.[1] No longer was he aspiring to be a Spenserian chronicler of Arthurian glory. As the frontispiece and the title page of the English *Poems* shows, he was raising his Muses higher and was aspiring to the vatic role that his Italian friends had foreseen for him—to be the English Homer or Vergil or Tasso—or perhaps something higher.[2] "Ad Joannem Rousium" is an important poem in that it not only voices those newest aspirations, it also looks back on the poet who had composed "L'Allegro" and "Il Penseroso" and *A Mask* as well as the sportive Latin elegies.

"Ad Joannem Rousium" was written to accompany the replacement volume of the 1645 *Poems* sent to the librarian of the Bodleian at Oxford and was not published by Milton until 1673 when he reissued the poems of

1. According to Milton's remarks in *The Second Defense of the People of England* (*Complete Poems and Major Prose* [ed. Hughes], 832), Milton had completed four books of *The History of Britain* by March 1649. Also see Parker, *Milton: A Biography,* 1:295.

2. The presence of Melpomene and Urania opposite Erato and Clio in the four corners of the portrait suggests devotion to the higher Muses of "Il Penseroso," as well as to golden Clio and to the Muse of love poetry. The quotation from Eclogue 7 of Vergil with its prophecy of the future bard or vates suggests the aspiration to Vergilian rather than Spenserian epic.

the 1645 volume, adding several other poems and the tract *Of Education,* as well as this ode to John Rouse.[3] The ode that originally served as proem to introduce the 1645 *Poems* to Rouse appears as envoy to the 1673 volume, the last poem in the book and the next to the last piece; *Of Education* concludes the volume. The fact that Milton chose to publish the poem in 1673 and to place it after the Latin elegy to Damon (which concluded the 1645 volume) indicates not only that he valued it but also that he regarded it as a kind of valedictory piece, fitting to conclude the section of Latin poems and to sum up the contents of his first and earliest poetic output. Its final placement at the end of the Latin poems is doubly fitting, since it is also one of the last Latin poems that Milton wrote.

Although "Ad Joannem Rousium" has been almost universally praised by the critics who have written of it, the ode has excited interest mostly for its biographical detail or for its poetic form. Both E. M. W. Tillyard and Louis Martz comment on the agreeable portrait of the young poet and the personal tone of his lines. The poem possesses, as Tillyard remarks, a "mixture of stateliness and of half-humorous and urbane elegance," or as Martz says, a combination of learned wit and a carefree air.[4] Other critics, however, are more intrigued by Milton's poetic versatility than by his elegant air or self-portraiture. "Ad Joannem Rousium" represents for them a unique experiment in the formal Pindaric ode and as such looks forward to the experiment with other choral meters in *Samson Agonistes*.[5] It is the only ode Milton wrote after he expressed admiration for Pindar's and Callimachus's lyric compositions in *The Reason of Church Government,* remarking that they were worthy of imitation.[6] Earlier odes from "Fair Infant" to the Nativity ode and "Lycidas," as well as the sportive "L'Allegro" and "Il Penseroso" testify, as we have noted, to Milton's experimentations in the ode form. But "Ad Joannem Rousium" is the closest experiment in actual classical strophes. It is curious therefore that the only poem to use formal Pindaric strophe, antistrophe, and epode is not a hymn or a choral

3. John Hale calls the Rouse ode a "by-blow of the 1645 *Poems* and the Civil War"; "The Pre-Criticism of Milton's Latin Verse, Illustrated from the Ode 'Ad Joannem Rousium,' " in *Of Poetry and Politics,* 20.

4. Tillyard, *Milton,* 71–72; Louis L. Martz, "The Rising Poet, 1645," in *Lyric and Dramatic Milton,* 4–5.

5. Edward K. Rand, Milton in Rustication," in *SP* 19:115; S. E. Sprott, *Milton's Art of Prosody;* F. T. Prince, *The Italian Element in Milton's Verse,* 148 n; Edward Weismiller, "The 'Dry' and 'Rugged' Verse," in *Lyric and Dramatic Milton,* 128; John T. Shawcross, "The Prosody of Milton's Translation of Horace's Fifth Ode," in *TSL* 13:88 (Shawcross analyzes the metrics of the Rouse ode); also see *Variorum (The Latin and Greek Poems),* 1.324–31.

6. Milton, *Complete Poems and Major Prose* (ed. Hughes), 669. Citations of "Ad Joannem Rousium" are from the Columbia Milton by line number.

piece but a personal poem in the mode of the elegiac letters included in the 1645 volume. Tillyard was one of the first to point out that "Ad Joannem Rousium" is more elegiac than Pindaric in tone and to question why Milton had used Pindaric strophes for a poem that resembles the introductory poems that the elegiac or lyric Latin poets attached to their volumes.[7] Hence it would appear that the ode is something of a critical puzzle, admired for its disparate elements, but elusive in its intellectual design, its stately Pindaric manner at odds with its elegiac wit.

We can scarcely doubt that John Milton, who demonstrated his mastery of English and Latin verses in the 1645 volume, knew exactly what he was doing in combining elegiac and Pindaric elements within this ode. He is, in fact, closely following neo-Latin practice in mixing elegiac and odic techniques. From the earliest Pindaric imitations in the fifteenth and sixteenth centuries, neo-Latin poets such as Francesco Filelfo and Benedetto Lampridio, for example, mixed Pindaric and elegiac elements within the same poem.[8] This practice continued with later Pindaric poets. Familiar letter poems in Pindaric measures are hardly an anomaly at the end of the sixteenth century; neo-Latin poets such as Paulus Melissus or Scévole de Saint-Marthe composed epistles in Pindaric strophes. Hence in adapting Greek metrical form for a Latin verse letter to a friend, Milton is demonstrating his knowledge of and penchant for following Continental neo-Latin traditions. But he is also doing what he did in his earliest elegies to Charles Diodati, that is, employing the personal letter form to make some serious statements about himself as a poet and the function of poetry in the world. Although ostensibly the poem does no more than recommend a replacement volume to the care of the librarian at Oxford, it contains some of Milton's more interesting statements concerning the relationship of poetry to society, particularly a society beset with serious civil problems, which felt it had better things to do than cultivate the Muses.

The ode was composed at a crucial period in Milton's life as well as in the life of the nation. Milton's wife had returned to him in the summer of 1645; he moved into a large house in the Barbican, and he, his wife, and their extended family were living there when Milton received the request from John Rouse for a replacement volume of the *Poems* that had been published a year earlier.[9] The ode was addressed to the librarian of the

7. Tillyard, *Milton,* 171–72.
8. See Carol Maddison's discussion of the humanistic ode in *Apollo and the Nine.*
9. Masson dates "Ad Joannem Rousium" on January 23, 1646/1647, remarking that it was written after the death of his father-in-law on January 1 and shortly before the death of his own father in March. I have examined the original manuscript of "Ad Joannem Rousium" (still in the Bodleian Library). Although not written in Milton's own hand, it

now-liberated Oxford, the king and the royalists having vacated the town before Oxford fell to Fairfax, Cromwell, and their armies on June 24, 1646. Since the Parliamentarian victory at Naseby on June 14, 1645, only a year earlier, the climate of the war had changed. In light of the turn in tide of political affairs, Milton may have felt that he could once more turn his mind to private matters. The printer Humphrey Moseley had begun printing poetry, beginning with a volume of Waller's poems at the end of 1644. It is likely that when he approached Milton, the poet felt that he could now put his poetic affairs in order. Moseley registered the book with the Stationer's Register on October 6, 1645. During the summer of 1645, Milton must have been preparing its contents, perhaps reflecting on how the years of the Civil War, during which he put poetry in second place, had changed him as a poet. The Rouse ode reflects that feeling and looks retrogressively at the "displacement" of poetry from Oxford, as from the poet's life. However genial Milton's manners with Rouse, however casual his banter on the subject of the lost book, his remarks about the poet and his role in society must be taken seriously. And the fact that Milton employs now elegiac, now Pindaric tones must be taken as part of that sober purpose.

As the Renaissance often viewed them, Roman elegiac poets—Ovid, Propertius, Tibullus—and their fellow lyric poets—Horace, Catullus—stand in a different relationship to their society and their times than does the committed Pindaric bard. The former (the Renaissance thought) look upon poetry as a pleasant peaceful pastime, to be cherished in quiet, however the din of civil disturbance raged about them. The Pindaric bard—and Pindar stands as the original of the type—though cherishing the Muses no less, takes a more active civic role, speaks directly to his society and seeks to cure, not to retreat from its ills. Milton, of course, is aware of these different types of poets and their different stances toward society. He himself had entertained in his first Latin elegies the prospect of becoming a new neo-Latin Propertius or Ovid. When he assumes first the elegiac, then the Pindaric voice, we can see him now taking on one, now the other role. To trace how Milton progresses from the elegiac to the Pindaric pose in this ode is to watch him recapitulate his career as a poet and to bid farewell to one kind of poetry and commit himself to another. At heart, then, "Ad Joannem Rousium," like the Latin poems that close the *Sylvarum Liber,* is an ode about John Milton and his role as a poet.

---

was attached to the replacement copy of the 1645 *Poems* that Milton sent to Rouse. Rouse had received the eleven prose pamphlets sent him by Milton, but not the book of poetry. Milton sent the replacement volume of *Poems* together with the ode. See Masson, The *Life of John Milton,* 3:644–48. Also see Parker, *Biography,* 1:307.

"CUI DONO LEPIDUM NOVUM LIBELLUM"

Adopting the Roman convention of addressing his own book, Milton begins the ode sounding very much like a Catullus or a Propertius:

> Gemelle cultu simplici gaudens liber,
> Fronde licet geminâ
> Munditiéque nitens non operosâ,
> Quam manus attulit
> Juvenilis olim,
> Sedula tamen haud nimii Poetae. (1–6)

> Book of twin parts, happy in a single cover
> but with a double leaf,
> shining with an unstudied elegance
> once given it
> by a youthful hand—
> a zealous hand but not yet that of an assured poet.[10]

Calling to mind phrases that Catullus, Propertius, and other Latin poets used in their initial poems to refer to their volumes, Milton describes the two-part book of English and Latin poems almost as though it were a Roman scroll whose ends were to be polished with pumice.[11] Like these Roman poets, Milton takes pleasure in the appearance of his nicely bound book and compares by implication the unstudied elegance of the binding with that of the verses themselves.[12] When he addresses it affectionately by name: "parve liber" (13) or "libelle" (37) ("little book"), he expects his reader to recall that Catullus referred fondly to his "lepidum novum libellum" ("pretty new little book"). Like Catullus, he too is about to present it to a friend.[13] Milton may well have thought of Catullus's friendly dedication to his learned friend when he dispatched his book to Rouse, whom he calls a custodian of learning ("AEternorum operum custos fidelis," 54). Catullus

---

10. The prose translation of "Ad Joannem Rousium" is by Douglas Bush, in *The Complete Poetical Works of John Milton,* 179–81.

11. Catullus speaks of his book as being smoothed off with dry pumice stone ("arida modo pumice expolitum," Proem 1, 2) and Propertius begs that his verse run smoothly, polished with fine pumice ("exactus tenui pumice versus eat," Proem 3, 1.8). *The Poems of Catullus,* 1; *Propertius, Elegies I–IV,* 93.

12. As anyone who has looked at a copy of Milton's 1645 *Poems* will remark, this description is accurate. Humphrey Moseley was a printer who took pride not only in the elegant and learned contents of his books, but also in their appearance. See Masson *The Life of John Milton,* 3:445–56 for a description of Moseley and the circumstances of prepublication in autumn 1645.

13. Catullus dedicated his book to Cornelius, whom he commends as the writer of a three-volumed history of the world.

apologizes that his verses are trifles and contrasts them, perhaps ironically, with those of his laboriously learned friend.[14] Here is another convention that Milton imitates. Roman poets express on the one hand negligence and indifference toward their verse, yet on the other hand great pride and boundless ambition. Catullus concludes his proem with a plea to the Muse that his verses, which he has only now called trifles, may last more than an age: "quod, o patrona virgo / Plus uno maneat perenne saeclo" (9–10). Propertius has similar ambitions, attributing to poetry the power to lift him from the earth to the heights: "quo me Fama levat terra sublimis" (Proem 3, 1.9).

Adopting the apologetic voice of the Latin elegist, Milton is both modest and ambitious. The very fact that he is sending his book to Rouse argues ambition, for he urges Rouse to guard it with the great works of Latin and Greek poetry held by the Bodleian (70–72). Yet he is also able to describe himself in an objective manner as young and eager—not yet too much a poet. He refers to his poetry, moreover, as carefree and playful, composed while he wandered now in Italian, now in English fields, alluding both to the places where he wrote many of the poems and the languages in which he wrote.

> Dum vagus Ausonias nunc per umbras
> Nunc Britannica per vireta lusit
> Insons populi, barbaritóque devius
> Indulsit patrio, mox itidem pectine Daunio
> Longinquum intonuit melos
> Vicinis, et humum vix tetigit pede. (7–12)

> . . . while he sported with wandering freedom
> now in Ausonian shades, now in English fields,
> unconcerned with the public world, and following his own
>   devices,
> he indulged his native lute or then with Daunian quill
> sounded a foreign air to his neighbors,
> his feet scarcely touching the ground.

In these lines Milton is carefully drawing for us a picture of the poet he was during the 1620s and 1630s when he composed the elegies, lyrics,

---

14. "Cui dono lepidum novum libellum / arida modo pumice expolitum? / Corneli tibi: namque tu solebas / meas esse aliquid putare nugas / iam tum cum ausus es unus Italorum / omne aevum tribus explicare cartis / doctis Iuppiter et laboriosis!" (Catullus, 1–7) (To whom do I give my pretty new book, freshly smoothed off with dry pumice-stone? To you, Cornelius: for you used to think that my trifles were worth something, once, when you took courage, alone of Italians, to set for the whole history of the world in three volumes, learned ones, by Jupiter, and laboriously done!)

and pastorals of the 1645 volume—a private poet, concerned with his own poetic world of meadows and forest shades, a *persona* close to the those he adopted for "L'Allegro" and "Il Penseroso." As in "L'Allegro" and "Il Penseroso" (as well as in other pastoral odes and eclogues), he distances himself from his poetry by adopting a *persona,* using the third person singular to describe the author of the 1645 *Poems.* He depicts himself as a young elegist, who sported and indulged his native lute or Daunian quill, whose foot scarcely touched the ground. He ignores, interestingly enough, the poetic *personae* of the Nativity ode and the serious pastorals, "Lycidas" and "Epitaphium Damonis." He does so deliberately, I believe, for he wants his reader to look upon him for the moment as a gentleman-poet without serious public, religious, or personal cares, a young Ovid or Propertius or even Vergil. But there is a deliberate design in this self-presentation, just as there is in allowing "L'Allegro" to precede "Il Penseroso."

The Roman gentleman-poet of the first century B.C.—as the Renaissance viewed him—wrote a special kind of occasional poetry for a select circle of friends, young men of his own class and so-called learned ladies or courtesans.[15] He concentrated on lyric, elegy, and pastoral and avoided the more weighty genres, epic or tragedy. When challenged to write a more serious verse, he pleaded his youth, his particular disposition for elegant light private poetry, putting off to mature or old age the commitment to sing of arms and the man. Among the elegiac poets Tibullus, Propertius, and Ovid all offer apologies for preferring elegy to epic, and the lyric poet Horace offers a similar defense of ode. Vergil makes a point of beginning with pastoral, but even while yet a pastoral poet entertaining thoughts of more serious genres.

Two of these apologies for elegy (by Ovid and by Propertius) have particular application to Milton's self-representation in strophe 1. We have already glanced in Chapter 4 at Ovid's apology for elegy, his portrait in *Amores* 3.1 of himself as a young poet courted by the Ladies Elegia and Tragoedia, and his deferral of the latter to more mature years. Both "Elegia 6" and "L'Allegro" and "Il Penseroso" allude obliquely to the Ovidian/Herculean topos of *Amores* 3 with its choice of poetic genres. The Rouse ode also indulges in self-portraiture of the Ovidian sort, as Milton draws a picture of the poet who composed the poems of the 1645 volume, insisting—perhaps too urgently—that "he" was not yet too much of a poet—"nimii Poetae." The modest denial accords well with the self-portraiture of "L'Allegro" and

---

15. Both Ovid and Propertius refer to the audience of young men and women for which they wrote. See, for example, Ovid, *Amores,* 2.1. 5–10, 37–38. Despite their pose as gentlemen-poets affecting aesthetic disinterest, Ovid and Propertius make telling commentaries on the life and the political scene in first-century B.C. Rome.

some of the lighter elegies; it does not at the point, however, take account of the steady march toward epic that had begun as early as the Nativity ode. Milton's Muse already knew how to sing with angels.

Milton's apology in strophe 1 also resembles Propertius's several portraits of himself as an elegiac poet. Unlike Ovid and later Milton, however, Propertius dismisses completely the call of the more serious Muse, justifying aesthetically in each of his three books of elegies his service to elegy (1.7; 2.10; 3.3; 3.5).[16] Propertius speaks of the delights of lyric poetry in terms of landscape and music and with a nostaglia for his youth. Alluding in both 3.3 and 3.5 to the two springs of the Muses, he describes both the higher, Hippocrene (for epic poetry) and the lower, Aganippe (for lyric and elegy), imagining the latter in a lush woodland grotto. His delight, as he tells us, is in the lower springs of Helicon and in the beauty of the Muses before they have ascended to the epic heights: "me iuvat in prima coluisse Helicona iuventa / Musarumque choris implicuisse manus" (3.5, 19–20) (It pleases me to have worshipped Helicon in my early youth, / and to have entwined my hands in the dances of the Muses.)[17] Milton could have spoken these very words, for he too identifies his early poetry with forest shades and grottos and with the music of the Muses.

In the actual poems of the 1645 book, however, Milton, while practicing and even delighting in elegy and light lyric, often tells us how as a poet he is aspiring to the very springs of upper Helicon that Propertius avoids. In "Ad Patrem," for example, he refers to the higher Pierian fountains and calls upon the Muses to spur him to a poetry more sublime than that which he had hitherto written (1–5). By choosing, however, to look on his early works as the poems of youthful indulgence, he deliberately heightens the resemblance between himself and the Roman elegists. Milton tells us in strophe 1 that he was a private person, uncommitted to public responsibility ("insons populi"). He describes how he wandered in pastoral retreats playing and indulging his own art. When he uses the word *lusit* (8), which literally means "he played," he suggests the free sport, amusement, pastime, and even dalliance and banter of elegies 1 and 7 and other lyric pieces. "Indulsit" (10), two lines later, reinforces these meanings; as a poet, he "indulged" his native lyre or lute ("barbaritóque . . . patrio"), yielding to the pleasant sport of poetry, just as Ovid yielded to the graceful Elegia.

---

16. Propertius confesses that he has been entreated by the more martial Muses, but, as he explains in 2.10, he deems that it is fitting for young men to sing of Venus and love, for old men to sing of wars and tumults. Moreover, in 3.3 he states that Phoebus expressly forbade him to aspire to epic poetry, recommending elegy as more suitable to his poetic temperament.

17. See Propertius 3.2, 15–17: "at Musae comites et carmina cara legenti, / nec defessa choris Calliopea meis." Also see Margaret Hubbard, *Propertius,* 72–82.

The light pastoral Muses preside over this idyllic woodland world of youth and spring and poetry, just as they do in Ovid and Propertius. Milton's country retreats in Buckinghamshire or at Oxford are the counterparts of the elegist's Helicon or Parnassus.

In the opening strophes of his ode, it appears as though Milton is sending his little book to a country haven in Oxford very like that described in Propertius's elegiac apology or like that which he celebrates in his own pastoral "L'Allegro" and "Il Penseroso." He deliberately evokes for us the aura of idyllic woodlands and fountains where poets might dwell in peace with their Muses and in company with one another with no further thought than to produce graceful elegant poetry. It is a poetic vision that Renaissance poets often also indulged. The Italian poet Benedetto Lampridio, for example, described the villa of Pietro Mellini in Rome (where the poets gathered) as an idealized pastoral garden, and Pietro Crinito described the Silva Oricellaria near Florence as a *locus amoenus* of private retirement also devoted to the Muses.[18] Milton tempts us to think of the fountains and groves in Oxfordshire—the home of Rouse—as just such places of pleasant retreat. He even recollects for us the conclusion of "Epitaphium Damonis," relocating on earth the thiastic dances of a Bacchic throng in the pleasant meadows near the Father Thames:

> Thamesis ad incunabula
> Caerulei patris
> Fontes ubi limpidi
> Aonidum, thyasusque sacer. (18–20)

> . . . to the cradle
> of blue Father Thames,
> where the clear fountains
> of the Aonides are, and the sacred dance.

It is tempting to connect Oxford's rural retreats with those of the Renaissance sodalities of poets or link the Oxford Muses with those who refreshed Propertius in the woodland grotto. In the biographical remarks in *An Apology for Smectymnuus,* Milton confesses that in this youth he delighted in the "smooth elegiac poets," who, both for "the pleasing sound of their numerous writing, which in imitation I found most easy and most agreeable . . . and for their matter . . . I was so allured to read that no recreation came to me better welcome."[19] But in evoking passages from the Roman elegists

18. See Lampridio, "In Petri Melini Villam, vbi Ille Poetas de More Familiae Coena Exceperat," in *Carmina* (1550); and Crinitus, "Ad Faustum de silua oricellaria," in *Poematum Libri Duo.*

19. Hughes, ed., *Complete Poetry and Major Prose,* 693.

in the Rouse ode or heightening his own resemblance to these elegists, Milton is not merely giving us a piece of autobiography. In describing what he was and no longer is, he is pointing to the difference between a pre- and a post-1640 view of poetry. The Muses of the private contemplation and delight do not flourish in a land beset with civil disturbance. In 1647 Milton must have thought that the time for graceful private elegy was past. As he had reflected in *The Reason of Church Government,* higher poetry— epic or tragedy—"shall be found more doctrinal and exemplary to a nation" (Hughes, 669).[20] To write such poetry a new kind of poet must appear, who, ascending to Hippocrene, shall recall the Muses to their homes. Looking back on the young elegist he once was, he raises the imperative for a different kind of commitment.

Past and present converge also in the description of Oxford, for in referring to the blue father Thames and the limpid fountains of the Muses, Milton is less describing present-day Oxford than calling up the memory of its pre-war counterpart. Oxford was the military headquarters for the king and queen during the Civil War and remained in the hands of royalists late in the struggle. The intellectual activity of the University necessarily had been disrupted, its Muses baffled or silenced by the war.[21] When Milton wrote his ode in January 1647, the city had been recently liberated, having fallen to the Parliamentarian army six months before, after a siege of about a month and a half. Perhaps now its Muses could be safe, its sacred band of poets return.

"PARVUS LIBER"

Although Milton raises the question of the displaced Muses, he does not adopt the voice of the outraged polemicist nor permit references to the king nor to the events of the war to invade the ode. Throughout much of "Ad Joannem Rousium" Milton retains the tone and manner of the genial elegist. This is certainly the case in those sections of the poem (antistrophes 1 and 2) where he enjoys a friendly joke with Rouse concerning the unfortunate book that lost its way after being dispatched to Oxford. We must read between the lines to grasp the serious implication of what he says. When he asks who seduced the book by fraud and how it went astray from its

20. Ibid., 669.
21. In a letter to Carlo Dati, dated April 21, 1647, Milton confides that the Civil War has afforded him little leisure for poetry: "What safe retirement for literary leisure could you suppose given one among so many battles of a civil war, slaughters, fights, seizures of goods?" ("Milton to Carlo Dati," "Familiarium Epistolarum" in *The Works of John Milton* [ed. Patterson], 12:51).

brothers, he appears, as Martz has observed, to be treating the incident as a piece of mock epic.

> Quis te, parve liber, quis te fratribus
> Subduxit reliquis dolo?
> . . . .
> Quin tu, libelle, nuntii licet malâ
> Fide, vel oscitantiâ
> Semel erraveris agmine fratrum.
> Seu quis te teneat specus
> Seu qua te latebra, forsan unde vili
> Callo teréris institoris insulsi,
> Laetare felix. (13–14, 37–43)

> Little book, who thievishly abstracted you
> and left your brothers?
> . . . .
> Yet, little book, although because of a messenger's
> dishonesty or sleepy carelessness
> you once wandered from your brothers' company—
> and may be now in some cave
> or den where you are rubbed by the coarse hard
> hand of a stupid huckster—
> you may rejoice in good fortune.

Affecting a solicitous concern for its welfare, Milton addresses the book directly and treats it like a lost child. He also spins out an entertaining anecdote about the messenger's motives for "losing" the book and the person of the man now holding it. The direct address, the playful concern, and above all the invention of an anecdote link Milton to the Latin elegists who first exploited this kind of situation in verse. He is not so far here from the playful tone he adopted in the epigrams on Hobson.

Once more we must turn to the Roman elegists for elucidation. Ovid and Propertius both have elegies that concern lost or returned tablets, which they address with affected concern or outrage and which they make the subject of imaginative anecdotes. Although neither elegy (Ovid, *Amores* 1.12 and Propertius 3.23) offers an exact parallel to the situation in Milton's ode, both provide interesting perspectives. The Roman elegies concern either the loss of tablets or their return by the lady to the lover, and the situation is, therefore, emotionally charged. Ovid's lady sends the tablets back with a message that displeases him, and he threatens to throw them away and then speculates what might happen to them if he "loses" them. He tells them to lie in the street where they will be crushed by the weight of a passing wheel, exclaiming that it would be better for a judge to read such tablets or that they should lie in a miser's accounts.[22] The tablets sent by Propertius's lady do go astray, and as Milton laments the loss of his book, Propertius laments the lost tablets. He speculates about what was written on them and where they now lie. The tablets and the love messages, perhaps the love verse, are dear to him, and he fears that they have fallen into the hands of an avaricious merchant who will write bills on them.

> me miserum, his aliquis rationem scribit avarus
> et ponit duras inter ephemeridas!
> quas si quis mihi rettulerit, donabitur auro (3.23, 19–20)

> Alas! and now some greedy merchant writes his bills
> upon them and places them among his unfeeling ledgers!
> If any will return them to me he shall have gold for his
>   reward.

In both the elegies and in the Rouse ode a relatively trivial event (the loss of tablets or a book) is treated with mock seriousness; an object is addressed and regarded as a person (in Propertius and Milton, a cherished person), and a likely scenario involving that object is imaginatively created for the reader. In all three poems, the incident imagined is unsavory. Ovid creates a miser, Propertius a greedy merchant, and Milton a stupid huckster who now possesses the cherished tablets or book. All three poets, moreover, expect the reader to share in their mock outrage and, of course, be entertained by their poetic inventiveness. But there is still another "person" who is addressed besides the book or tablets and the reader: the friend for whom the poet writes and from whom the tablets come or to whom the book is sent.

Like the Latin elegies, Milton's ode is a personal poem written to a "learned friend," a *doctus amicus,* as Milton calls Rouse in the first antistrophe (16). The learned friend that Latin elegists such as Ovid and Tibullus and Propertius addressed was not male, however, but female. A *docta puella* inspired the poet, who dedicated his lines to her and described

---

22. See Ovid, *Amores:* "Ite hinc, difficiles, funebria ligna, tabellae, / tuque, negaturis cera referta notis! . . . / proiectae triviis iaceatis, inutile lignum, / vosque rotae frangat praetereuntis onus! / . . . aptius hae capiant vadimonia garrula cerae, / quas aliquis duro cognitor ore legat; / inter ephemeridas melius tabulasque iacerent, / in quibus absumptas fleret avarus opes." (*Amores,* 1.12, 7–8, 13–14, 23–26.) (Go away from here, troublesome tablets, funereal pieces of wood, and you, wax crammed with writing that will tell me no! . . . Lie, there thrown down at the crossing of the ways, useless wood, and may the weight of the passing wheel break you to pieces! . . . It would be fitter for such tablets to receive the imprint of prattling bail-bonds for some attorney to read in harsh tones; It would be better that they should lie among day-books and tables over which a miser weeps for money spent.)

her in his poems, the word, *docta,* applying not only to her learning and wit, but also to her experience as a courtesan. Cynthia, the *docta amica* of Propertius, is perhaps the most famous of these "learned" friends.[23] When Milton gives Rouse the title, "learned friend," which Propertius had so endearingly bestowed on Cynthia, it may be that he is sharing with the Oxonian, well-versed in Latin literature, a subtle joke that is not to a Cynthia but to a "friend" of a different sort that he entrusts with his verses. Or he may be recalling those learned friends that he shared so much with in Italy—friends such as the old Marchese Giovanni Manso, who was close in age to Rouse's own years.

At any rate, he appeals to Rouse for the kind of special care and protection that the Roman elegists often requested for their poetry, hoping for a select audience like theirs—no vulgar or insolent mob, but to a circle of young men and women, learned and sympathetic to the Muses. For these future readers, Milton asks Rouse to shelter his book and to preserve it. Offering thanks for the favor of Rouse ("Roüsio favente"), Milton closes his ode with solicitous urbanity.

"QUIS DEUS, AUT EDITUS DEO"

Despite the familiar accents of the opening and closing strophes and the light banter of antistrophes 1 and 2 recounting the book's possible misadventures, "Ad Joannem Rousium" is no simple Roman elegy in Pindaric dress. Beginning with strophe 2 and more firmly in strophe 3, Milton modulates the personal tone, and the strain we hear is of a higher mood. The elegiac poet and his learned friend retreat to the background and the heroic bard advances. The "elegiac" anecdote of the lost book assumes the proportions of Pindaric "myth." The Muses under the protection of the god Apollo take their places, not now in wood and stream, but in the temple guarded by the priest whose person Rouse now assumes. The little lost book is regretted no longer; its more fortunate brother now dispatched to Rouse will ensure its immortality. Milton turns from deploring its low fate, imprisoned in some cave or den, to imagine its escape from Lethe and flight to heaven.

> profundam
> Fugere Lethen, vehique Superam

---

23. See Propertius 1.7, 9–11: "Hic mihi conteritur vitae modus, haec mea fama est, / hinc cupio nomen carminis ire mei. / me laudent doctae solum placuisse puellae." (So the time of my life is passed. This is my renown, this the fame I wish to claim for my song: let them praise me only that I pleased a learned girl.)

In Jovis aulam remige pennâ; (44–46)

that you may escape the depths of Lethe
and may be carried on oaring wing to the high court of Jove.

With his little book our poet also mounts on high, forsaking the lower springs of Helicon and seeking Hippocrene, which he alludes to as the Pegasean stream ("amne Pegaséo," 36). The Pegasean flight that he envisioned in his 1637 letter to Diodati he is once more vigorously pursuing. Assuming the Pindaric mantle, he makes strophe and subject stride hand-in-hand.

One of the most striking characteristics of the Pindaric style is the abrupt shift in tone, often accompanied by a sudden heightening.[24] In some of his earlier poetry and particularly the monody "Lycidas," Milton had displayed this characteristic. In "Lycidas," for instance, with the entrance of Phoebus Apollo, Milton turns abruptly from the bitter complaints of the swain to the sublime words of the god (76–84). In "Ad Joannem Rousium" the shift is from the elegant banter of the first two strophes to the serious outcry: how may the Muses be saved in a land inhospitable to poetry? This outcry in strophe 2, moreover, is framed as a question and placed directly parallel to the question asked in antistrophe 1. Both questions begin with the interrogative "quis" ("who"), but the first "who" refers to a man, the second to a god or god-sprung man. The first queries in a half-amused way who lead the book astray; the second demands with righteous anguish who will restore a nation lost to learning and strayed from the Muses. The evocation of these Muses follows directly after the idyllic description of the Muses' retreat at Oxford. There Milton creates two effects. The first is playful and elegiac, the second solemn and Pindaric. No sooner have we been shown the pleasant clear fountains of the Muses and the cradle of blue Father Thames than with solemn resonant tones Milton engages a Bacchic throng of poets in a sacred dance with these Muses. The mood is suddenly heightened.

> . . . thyasusque sacer
> Orbi notus per immensos
> Temporum lapsus redeunte coelo,

---

24. Sixteenth- and seventeenth-century editors and commentators frequently mentioned the features of Pindar's style, often citing the views of ancient writers such as Horace, Pliny, and Quintilian. See, for example, the commentary by Erasmus Schmidt in the Wittenberg edition (1616) of Pindar's odes. A useful summary of classical and Renaissance views on Pindar is found in Thomas Pope Blount, *De Re Poetica* (1694), 65–68, 171–74.

Celeberque futurus in aevum. (21–24)

> . . . and the sacred dance
> which has been famous in the world
> while the firmament has turned through vast stretches
> of time and will be famous for ever.

This cosmic dance (like that of Milton's sphere-born sisters or his Attendant Spirit) moves as though in tune with the movement of heaven and eternal time. Those who join in it are not mere pastoral deities and earthly men. The word "sacer" is used to describe the band of poets, a band similar to that Milton had described in "Elegia 5" or "Ad Patrem." The poet himself is no longer a private man amusing himself and indulging in his art, but a man divinely elected. Milton calls him and his power "sanctus" (30)— holy—and refers to the "sacris" (sacred places)—the sanctuaries of poetry's god, Apollo. Milton's poet is now a man with a holy vocation.

As early as "Elegia 5," as we have noted in the previous chapters, Milton had enrolled himself as a sacred bard of Apollo and had directed his path on the "Pindaric" pursuit. Among ancient poets of Greece and Rome Pindar is preeminent as a poet devoted to Apollo and his sacred calling.[25] Unlike the elegiac poets of Rome who described poetry as a private pastime and rarely concerned themselves directly with political issues, Pindar was the poet who used his voice to address kings and nobles. He lived in a society where rulers still listened to the voice of the poet, and where the poet acted as a stabilizing force in society. The claims that Pindar makes for the poet are epic claims, the very ones that Propertius declines and Ovid puts off, the very ones that Milton from the late 1630s has been considering more and more urgently. The Muses are important to Pindar not merely as inspirers of his verse (the elegiac poets, too, called on the Muses for inspiration), but as guardians of religious order and social welfare. Poetry is the organ for future fame, and the poet through the Muses grants glory and preserves the memory of great men, whether statesmen, heroes in battle, or athletes, insuring that their deeds do not go down in darkness.[26] At the same time poetry commemorates the past and passes down history to the future, it binds human beings together. Pindar even goes so far as to measure a good society by its service to the Muses.[27] As we noted in the previous

25. Both Apollo, the god of poetry, and Zeus, the father of the Muses, figure prominently in Pindar's Olympian and Pythian odes as guardians of society and patrons of poetry.

26. For the power of poetry to preserve the memory of great deeds, see the following odes of Pindar: *Pythian* 3.114–15; *Nemean* 1.11–12; *Nemean* 6.30a–30b.

27. For Pindar, how the Muses are served is the touchstone for judging the good of a society. For example, he praises the West Wind Locrians as honorable and straight-

chapter, Milton in "Mansus" defines Britain as a Muse-centered society by associating it with Pindar's land of the Hyperboreans and their cherishing of Apollo and the Muses.

In his odes, Pindar not only defines the poet's social obligations but also his religious ones. As servant of the Muses he is elected by god and not man, and his chief function is to speak the truth. Pindar tells us in *Isthmian 2* that the old poets possessed higher principles than their modern successors, for they sang for the sake of the Muse, not for money (*Isthmian 2.1–10*). Further, he remarks in another ode that when the Muse sings truth, she will grow great in strength: "αὔξεται καὶ Μοῖσα δι' ἀγγελίας ὀρθᾶς" (*Pythian 4.279*) ("And the Muse through a straightforward report will increase in strength"). Poetry flourishes with truth because truth is the defining characteristic of the good poet. In *Nemean 8* Pindar gives us a brief sketch of the ideal poet's selfless commitment to the Muse.

> χρυσὸν εὔχον-
>   ται, πεδίον δ' ἕτεροι
> ἀπέραντον, ἐγὼ δ' ἀστοῖς ἁδὼν καὶ χθονὶ γυῖα καλύψαι,
> αἰνέων αἰνητά, μομφὰν δ' ἐπισπείρων ἀλιτροῖς.
>
> (Nemean 8.37–39)

> Some pray for gold,
> others for land without limit,
> but I pray to hide my limbs in the earth as one who gladdened
>   his fellow-citizens,
> praising that which deserves it and laying blame on workers of
>   evil.

The concept of the poet as the servant of the Muse is common in the ancient world, associated not only with Greek poets such as Pindar, but also the Roman poets such as Horace and Vergil who were their chosen heirs. In the early 1640s, however, when Milton wishes to urge the importance of the poet as the keystone for society, it is Pindar's—not Vergil's or Horace's—name he calls on. He cites in the sonnet "Captain or Colonel, or Knight in Arms," (composed when an assault was being leveled against London) the story of how the conqueror Alexander in reverence for Pindar's reputation spared his house and his descendants. In so doing, he enjoins that the

---

forward, hospitable to strangers and not devious in their dealing, summing up his praise by saying that they have not forgotten their service to the lovely arts of the Muses (*Olympian 11.15–19*). For Milton's association with views such as these with Pindar, see my article, "Milton's Muse and the Daughters of Memory," *ELR* 9.

Muses be respected even in time of war: "Lift not thy spear against the Muses Bowre" (9).[28]

As I have argued in Chapter 6, Pindar and Pindaric ode underlie "Lycidas" in concept and in form. In "Lycidas" Milton makes his shepherd-swain assume the voice of the poet-priest and, like Pindar, lay praise and scatter blame. The middle sections of the Rouse ode call to mind both the poetic voice heard in "Lycidas" and some of the questions raised about poetry's responsibilities in a troubled land. In calling for a new kind of poet to purge the land, Milton echoes the pleas that his own Phoebus and Peter first urged in the earlier poem. With the authority of the Apollonian bard and the conviction of the Christian pastor, he cries out:

> Modò quis deus, aut editus deo
> Pristinam gentis miseratus indolem
> (Si satis noxas luimus proiores
> Mollique luxu degener otium)
> Tollat nefandos civium tumultus,
> Almaque revocet studia sanctus
> Et relegatas sine sede Musas
> Jam penè totis finibus Angligenûm? (25–32)

> But what god or demigod,
> remembering with pity the ancient character of our race—
> If we have made enough atonement for our past sins,
> our degenerate idleness and effeminate luxury—
> will put an end to the wicked broils of civil war,
> and with his sacred power will bring back our nourishing
>   studies
> And the banished Muses who have been left
> with scarcely any refuge in all England?[29]

The words, "quis deus, aut editus deo" call to mind the beginning of Pindar's *Olympian 2*, Horace's 1.12, written in imitation of it, and also Horace's 1.2.[30] Pindar's ode is addressed to Theron, the tyrant-ruler of the Sicilian

28. Thomas Corns rebukes Milton for taking a pacifist position in this sonnet. See "The Plurality of Miltonic Ideology," in *Literature and the English Civil War*, 118–19. But the sonnet, like "Ad Joannem Rousium," does not adopt the pacifist quietism of the elegiac poet; Milton is arguing for preserving the treasures of a society—namely its poetry and its poets—especially in time of war.

29. Although most translators render line 25 as a question, it is possible to translate it as an optative: "Would that some god or demi-god might. . . ."

30. J. H. Finley Jr. cites a number of parallels in Horace to Milton's appeal to an unnamed hero or god. In ode 1.2 Horace calls on one of the gods to succor Rome: "quem vocet divum populus." He also chastises the people for their slackness and invokes the

city Acragas, and invokes god, demigod, and man to serve and save the Sicilian city, founded by the descendants of the Theban Oedipus.

> Ἀναξιφόρμιγγες ὕμνοι,
> τίνα θεόν, τίν' ἥρωα, τίνα ἄνδρα κελαδήσομεν: (*Olympian* 2.1–2)

> Lordly-lyred songs,
> What god, what hero, what man shall we celebrate?

The god is the highest god, Zeus; the hero, his son, Heracles; and the man the Sicilian ruler Theron, the descendant of Thersander, Oedipus's surviving grandson. The ode not only singles out for praise the ruler Theron and his illustrious forbears, but also recounts how he and his sons prevailed in spite of the adversities their ancestors suffered. A disastrous war destroyed Thebes and its civilization, but Thersander, the child of one of Oedipus's sons, survived. Thersander is the "saving" hero who turned his back on the ill fortune of his family and overcame the plagues, wars, and civil tumults that beset those who came before him. With the favor of the gods, Pindar concludes, a person, a family, a nation can be saved.

Olympian 2's celebration of the saving god, hero, and man has special application to Milton's ode that also appeals to a god or a hero—"deus, aut editus deo"—to succor the land, an England spoiled like Thebes with civil tumult and plague. Indolent and luxury-loving, the English have become degenerate and brought dissension and misery to their race. Unable to help themselves, they need a god or hero—a Heracles, a Thersander, or a Theron—to help put an end to war—perhaps even a Fairfax or a Cromwell, who had brought peace once more to Oxford. As the sonnets that Milton addressed to Fairfax and Cromwell in the late 1640s and early 1650s demonstrate, Milton casts his heroes of war in the role of bringers of peace. Peace will heal not only the people, the nation, but also poetry itself.

SON OF APOLLO

The appeal for a god-sprung or god-elected man need not be restricted, however, to military and political leaders—to the hero Heracles, begotten

---

return of peace. See John H. Finley Jr., "Milton and Horace," in *HSCP* 48:54n. Passages cited by Finley include Ode 1.2.25–52; Epode 7.17–20; and Odes 1.2.47; 1.35.33–40; 2.1.25–36; 4.15.9–20. Horace's Ode 1.12 is a special case since its opening line directly imitates Pindar's *Olympian 2*. Renaissance commentators frequently pointed out that Horace had reversed the Pindaric order and instead of appealing to god, hero, and man in descending order, he appeals to man, hero, and god in rising order ("Quem virum aut heroa lyra vel acri / Tibia sumis celebrare, Clio? / Quem deum?" (1.2.1–2). Milton, like Pindar, appeals to God first.

by Zeus, or to the ruler raised by the gods. It may include the poet, also a man appointed by god.[31] In a nation troubled by war the springs of poetry have been polluted by foul birds of prey. It is the responsibility of the poet elected by the god and armed with an Apollonian quiver to slay these foul birds; to castigate the unworthy and to restore the Muses to their places.

> Immundasque volucres
> Unguibus imminentes
> Figat Apollineâ pharetrâ,
> Phinéamque abigat pestem procul amne Pegaséo. (33–36)

> Who with the shafts of Apollo
> will transfix the foul birds that threaten us
> with their claws and drive
> the plague of Phineus from the Pegasean stream?

Milton has conflated several myths here: Zetes' and Calais's defeat of the Harpies that plagued Phineas; Apollo's slaying of the Python; and Hercules' transfixing of the Stymphalian birds with his powerful bow and arrows. Reworking the myth of Phineus, Milton assigns the role of avenger to Apollo; but he transfers to the poet the task of execution. The poet needs mastery not only over Apollo's lyre, but also (metaphorically) over his bow and quiver. As Apollo slew the Python with his arrows and consecrated the oracle at Delphi at the very place of his victory, so the poet must kill the pestilential birds that pollute the place sacred to poetry. In "Lycidas" Apollo appears in person to remind the poet of his divine appointment: to forsake sport with Amaryllis and to seek the higher approbation of Jove. In "Mansus" the poet takes on the person of Apollo to move toward the epic he would write. Now in "Ad Joannem Rousium" Apollo seems to urge the poet beyond mere poetic goals to be both the spokesman for truth and the oracle through which the god will purge the land.

Milton's portrait of the vatic poet resembles Pindar's. Pindar tells us in *Pythian 1* that the poet's golden lyre, his gift from Apollo and the Muses, has powers that transcend mere music-making. The lyre can soothe the eagle, Zeus's own bird, and it can also make the savage god Ares drop his arms. Poetry can bring peace and good government to the land. It can even justify the ways of God to men. In *Olympian 2,* in fact, Pindar compares the god-appointed poet to the eagle that soars above the ravens that vainly caw at him from below. He also describes himself as an archer

---

31. The Latin word *editus* (the participle of *edo*) signifies "sprung from" or "born from" and also "elevated" or "standing out," and by extension "published," "proclaimed," or "spread abroad."

with a quiver under his arm and his words as arrows that he directs to men of understanding.[32] Milton reworks Pindar's metaphor, giving the poet an Apollonian bow and quiver and urging that he with the god's assistance drive away the menacing birds that threaten the poet and poetry. The call for a "divine poet" is not new; Milton had been fitting himself for this role, putting on wings in hopes of flight, ever since he first sang with Muses and angels in the Nativity ode.

The appeal in strophe 2 for Apollonian power affirms not only the importance of poetry to the land, but also the importance of the "libellus," the little book once lost but now replaced by the volume sent to Rouse. The book even assumes a kind of heroic personality, as though it had survived its trial in the underworld (the cave or den alluded to) and had escaped Lethe to mount on high and join the gods.[33] In a sense it too is chosen and elected by Rouse, who in strophe 3 begs for it to complete the just number. Milton almost makes his book a saint—one of the "redeemed" in an Oxfordshire heaven. We might even apply the word "editus," used for the hero of strophe 2, to the book, which now is, as the Latin word implies, not only born, but published and disseminated in the world abroad, and about to be received into a library that has books more precious than the treasures at Delphi.

> Téque adytis etiam sacris
> Voluit reponi quibus et ipse praesidet
> AEternorum operum custos fidelis,
> Quaestorque gazae nobilioris,
> Quàm cui praefuit Iön
> Clarus Erechtheides
> Opulenta dei per templa parentis
> Fulvosque tripodas, donaque Delphica
> Iön Actaea genitus Creusâ. (52–60)

> You he desires to place in the hallowed
> sanctuaries over which he himself presides,
> the faithful custodian of immortal works,
> the guardian of treasure more illustrious
> than the golden tripods and Delphic offerings

32. Milton appears to share Pindar's conviction that the poet is a man with special powers that have been given him by God to use as God directs. In turn, God protects and guides the poet. In books 3, 7, and 9 of *Paradise Lost* Milton invokes the special protection that God confers on the poet through the Muse.

33. Milton deliberately conflates the two books—the lost volume (addressed in antistrophe 1 and strophe and antistrophe 2) and the replacement volume (addressed in antistrophe 3)—which completes the journey the lost book began and which redeems its unlucky fate.

which were entrusted to Ion
in the rich temple of his divine father—
Ion the son of Erechtheus' daughter, Actaean Creusa.

When Fairfax and the Parliamentarian army took Oxford in June 1646, one of Fairfax's first acts was to assign an armed guard to the Bodleian Library so that its books would not be looted. As a poet who aspires to set his volumes of verse side by side the poets of the past, Milton is attentive, like Fairfax, to the role that a university library plays in preserving the treasures of the past in order to guarantee learning and liberty to the future. Now held by the parliamentary forces, the library can welcome not only Milton's little book, but also those political tracts that Milton had sent to Rouse when he had first dispatched his poems. Oxford had been liberated intellectually as well as physically.

The comparison of the Bodleian Library to the oracle at Delphi and Rouse to Apollo's son Ion extends still further the Apollonian myth-making of this Pindaric ode.[34] Rouse is no longer merely the genial *doctus amicus* of the earlier strophe, but a priest that guards the sacred heritage at Oxford, itself described as a rich and holy sanctuary. Like "Lycidas," "Ad Joannem Rousium" also indulges in metaphoric transformation, making its central addressee take on now this role, now another. These allusions to Apollo and Delphi not only reaffirm the sacred nature of the poet and his book, but also call to mind some Pindaric associations. Delphi was renowned in antiquity for its Pythian games as well as for its oracle, and Pindar composed twelve odes commemorating Pythian victories, the most famous of which was *Pythian 1,* written in praise of Apollo and in honor of Hieron, ruler of Sicily, who presented many treasures to the temple at Delphi, among them the famous statue of the charioteer. Pindar was fond, particularly in his Pythian odes, of reminding his audience that Apollo was served by poet and athlete alike, both of whom strive in his honor and seek as their ultimate goal the approbation of the god.[35] The athlete consecrates gifts of gold and tripods as thank-offerings, the poet his odes. In comparing the book-treasures of the Bodleian, the monuments of poets, to the golden treasures and tripods of Delphi, given by kings and athletes, Milton is inviting, like Pindar, comparison between different kinds of "monuments." Like the Greek poet he assigns the advantage to poetry as the more enduring monument. In

---

34. See Gyraldus on the description of the oracle at Delphi and particularly on the account of its institution and restoration (*De Deis Gentium* [1560], 219–20).

35. For a discussion of Pindar's linking of poetic and athletic performance, see John H. Finley, Jr, *Pindar and Aeschylus;* Thomas Hoey, "Fusion in Pindar," 243; Charles Paul Segal, "Pindar's First and Third Olympian Odes," 224.

Nemean 5.1–2, for example, Pindar had affirmed the superiority of the living ode over statuary in stone and metal, opening his ode with a resounding disclaimer of the latter: "Οὐκ ἀνδριαντοποιός εἰμ', ὥστ' ἐλινύσοντα ἐργάζεσθαι ἀγάλματ' ἐπ' αὐτᾶς βαθμίδος / ἑσταότ'." (I am not a maker of statuary, one who works on a image standing quiet on its step).

Pindar's boast prompts later poets to similar assertions: Propertius to declare that his elegy is more lasting than the Pyramids and the house of Jove; Horace to proclaim his ode more durable than bronze; and Shakespeare, echoing them, to announce "Not marble nor the gilded monuments / Of Princes shall outlive this powerful rhyme" (Sonnet 55.1–2).[36] Milton's poem "On Shakespeare," written for the second Folio and reprinted in the 1645 *Poems*—also echoes these ancient boasts, reaffirming the permanence of Shakespeare's works as a "live-long Monument" (8) and the deep impression of Shakespeare's verses as Delphic lines. Like "On Shakespeare," the Rouse ode deals both with the monumental and the mantic aspects of poetry. The description of the Bodleian library as a Delphic temple and of Rouse as its priest offers a graceful compliment to the librarian while at the same time it makes a statement about the works contained in that library. In calling Rouse a faithful custodian of immortal works and in assuring his own book a place among these works, Milton is modulating the self-applause of "Mansus." If his book rests besides the most famous works of the Greek and Roman people ("inter alta nomina / Authorum, Graiae simul et Latinae / Antiqua gentis lumina, et verum decus," 70–72), he too, as its author, can fulfill the role his Italian friends imagined for him—the successor to Homer, Vergil, and Tasso. Yet he does not say this directly. By assigning an immortal place to his little book, not to himself, Milton subtly sidesteps the self-congratulation of the earlier poem. He keeps the focus on Rouse and his role as faithful custodian.

By implication, however, when he compares Rouse to Ion and the Bodleian to Delphi, Milton takes us once more into the realm of Pindaric poetics and his own Apollonian ambitions. He reinforces earlier allusions to Apollo, while he makes use of one of the most characteristic devices of Pindaric ode—the digression. Typically, Pindar compares the principal person of the ode either directly or indirectly to a hero celebrated in a brief or extended digression. In *Pythian 1,* for example, he directly compares Hieron to Philoctetes (50–52); in *Olympian 1,* however, he links Hieron to Pelops, the hero of the mythic digression, only indirectly when he alludes to the great favor the gods granted to both men. Milton's comparison of Rouse to Ion functions indirectly. At first Milton seems only to be comparing

36. See Propertius 3.2, 18–20, 22, 25–26; Horace, Odes 3.30.1–5; Vergil, *Georgics* 3.12–15; *Aeneid* 8.312. Milton's use of the word "monumenta" to apply to books probably follows the usage of these Latin writers.

the treasure-houses that Ion and Rouse guard—the splendid temple at Delphi, the splendid library in Oxford. Yet in alluding to Ion as the son of a god and in referring to his ancestry, Milton means for us to consider how Rouse too is a priest, ordained to guard Apollo's sacred possessions in a sacred place. Milton's primary mythic source is Euripides' drama *Ion* that recounts how the temple boy Ion is discovered to be the son of Apollo and Creusa and how, narrowly escaping death, he is reunited with his mother and assumes his rightful place as Apollo's son and a priest of Apollo's temple.[37] Milton was undoubtedly aware how close Euripides' account of Ion was to Pindar's of Iamus, another son of Apollo, who, as Pindar relates in *Olympian 6,* was reunited with his mortal mother Evadne and claimed in adulthood his right as Apollo's son, the guardian of his father's oracle at Olympia.[38] What is significant in both these myths is the theme of restoration. Both Ion and Iamus are true sons of Apollo, restored to their vocations as priests of Apollo's temple. Once displaced and unknown, they at last fulfill their destinies as sons of Apollo, just as Rouse with the liberation of Oxford reassumes once more the role of "priest" in a temple reconsecrated to the arts. In this temple, moreover, the priestly Rouse can receive the book of another Apollonian son—the poet Milton—a lost book restored to a restored sanctuary. With the liberation of Oxford, Charles is expelled from his refuge and thoroughly dispossessed of his Apollonian role, while Apollo's true sons—Rouse and Milton—take possession of their father's temple.

Returning in antistrophe 3 to his narrative of the little book's adventures, Milton forsakes the bantering tone of the opening strophes. The book assumes an epic *persona.* It is both, as it was in antistrophe 2, the mythic hero, who has endured trial—like Hercules—in the underworld and an athlete who is returning home victorious to the divine home ("diam domum") of Phoebus to celebrate its Pythian victory.

> Ergo tu visere lucos
> Musarum ibis amoenos,
> Diamque Phoebi rursus ibis in domum

37. Merritt Hughes has suggested that Milton alludes to Euripides' dramatic version of Ion because it includes a description of Apollo's magnificent temple at Delphi that in turn might evoke the medieval splendor of Oxford. *Complete Poems and Major Prose* (ed. Hughes), 148 n.

38. Pindaric ode would also support him here too, for *Olympian 6* begins with a striking figure that compares the building of a palace to the construction of splendid verse, a comparison implicit, of course, in Milton's likening of Delphi's golden temple to Oxford's poetical one. See *Olympian* 6.1–3: "Χρύσεας ὑποστάσαντες εὐτειχεῖ προθύρῳ θαλάμου / κίονας ὡς ὅτε θαητὸν μέγαρον / πάξομεν" (Like those who raise up golden pillars for the forecourt of a well-built chamber, let us construct a wondrous palace).

> Oxoniâ quam valle colit
> Delo posthabitâ,
> Bifidóque Parnassi jugo:
> Ibis honestus,
> Postquam egregiam tu quoque sortem
> Nactus abis . . . (61–69)

> So you shall go to see
> the lovely groves of the Muses,
> and shall go again to the noble home of Phoebus,
> where he dwells in Oxford's valley
> in preference to Delos
> or twin-peaked Parnassus.
> You shall go with honor,
> since you depart in assurance
> of a notable destiny.

In the formulaic style of epic Milton three times dismisses the book on its journey—"ibis" (you shall go); he addresses it gravely and affectionately, lightening somewhat the somber mood of the preceding two strophes. It is almost as though he too were accompanying the book to the rustic haunts of the Muses and revisiting the world of eclogue and elegy—of valley and stream—where he sported as a young poet, his foot scarce touching the ground. Now his book will visit the rural scenes of the Muses that produced so much of the poetry contained in it, will see the temple of Apollo in Oxford, and will confer with the god that the Milton of the 1645 *Poemata* had made his special patron and guide. Milton's connection of Apollo's "temple" in Oxford with the temple at his birthplace in Delos and at his oracle in Delphi has several implicit meanings. In transferring Pindar's Pythian god and his Muses to an English setting, he is following the example of Vergil, who in a famous passage in the *Georgics* (3.8–39) once announced that he would bring Apollo and the Muses to Italy and build a temple for them on the banks of his native river.[39] With the victory at Naseby in 1645, the Parliamentarian forces looked forward to the taking of the royalist stronghold at Oxford; in June 1646 they liberated Oxford; in January 1647 Milton, writing to Rouse, rejoiced that Oxford could be once more a safe dwelling place for the Muses. Milton has in mind the

---

39. This passage is an important one for Milton since it marks the moment that Vergil is declaring his aspirations to be an epic poet—to be for Rome what poets like Homer and Pindar were for Greece. In the description of the triumphal chariot there is even an allusion to Pindar and his odes. As noted earlier, Milton lifts some Latin phrases from this passage: "temptanda via est," "tollere humo," and "modo vita supersit," that he employs in this and earlier Latin poems.

chronology of the past year and a half as he sends his book on a journey that would not have been possible earlier. England may now once more become a Hyperborean land, safe for the Muses and free from care and battles—a land like Pindar's refuge that Milton alluded to in "Mansus."[40]

Milton bestows a benediction on his little book, as it reaches its destination in Oxford, hoping that it may attain quiet rest ("placidam . . . requiem," 75–76). For himself as the book's author he foresees not rest but renewed labor, hoping, however, that the labors that produced the book were not in vain. The Latin word "labores," as critics have recognized, carries with it Herculean associations.[41] It advances, I think, a view of himself as a poet toward which Milton had been moving since the late 1620s. It is not just the little book that moves from the character in an elegy to one in an epic. Milton takes upon himself as poet the stance of an active epic hero, perhaps even a poetic counterpart to the parliamentary generals who had liberated Oxford. He envisions for his book the rewards—the illustrious lot ("egregiam sortem," 68) and true glory ("verum decus," 72)—that come with heroic achievement, having drawn the words *sors* and *decus* from the epic vocabulary. His book will rest in the blessed seats ("sedesque beatas"), he affirms, alluding both to the happy seats saints occupy in a Christian heaven and to the blessed isles where classical heroes enjoy rest after toil, the very isles that Pindar described at the end of *Olympian 2*. The glory that the little book finally attains is not only that of the hero, but also of the athlete who has been victorious in that race "where that immortal garland is to be run for, not without dust and heat."[42] Milton's book, like Pindar's athlete-hero, enjoys Apollonian rewards. From his early funeral elegies to "Mansus" and "Epitaphium Damonis" Milton has conflated the blissful seats that the Christian looks forward to in heaven with the isles of the blessed that are the Homeric and the Pindaric reward. It is appropriate on the one hand for the little book to travel to a classical reward, since it is Rouse as Hermes who awards the hero-book the blissful seat. "Blissful seat," is, however, also the name for the recovered paradise that the "greater man" of *Paradise Lost* will regain. Even for books, Milton imagines a classical-Christian afterlife.

40. See *Pythian 10*.30–42 and *Olympian 3*.16 (Pindar's references to the land of the Hyperboreans). Horace also wishes in *Carmina 2*.1 for a sage retreat for poetry, where in the company of Dione and the light lyre, the poet may live free from danger and find safe harbor.

41. Merritt Hughes believes that "labores" refers to the production of those tracts that he had also sent along to Rouse (*Complete Poems and Major Prose* [ed. Hughes], 148 n). For more recent information about the books and pamphlets that Milton sent to Rouse, see Gwen Hampshire, "An Unusual Bodleian Purchase in 1645."

42. In this celebrated passage from *Areopagitica* (*Complete Poems and Major Prose* [ed. Hughes], 728), Milton describes, as Pindar had, the pursuit of virtue as an athletic contest, perhaps taking the metaphor of games and a race from Pindar's own poetry.

In the concluding epode Rouse assumes yet one more mythic personality, becoming Hermes, the escort of the souls of the dead to the blest abodes, who will guide the little book to its final home. Not only marshal of the shades, Hermes is also the patron of learning and the god of pastoral poetry. Milton makes Rouse as just such a tutelary guide and spirit of good favor:

> sedesque beatas
> Quas bonus Hermes
> Et tutela dabit solers Roüsi. (76–78)[43]

> and to the blessed abodes
> that good Hermes will provide,
> and the watchful protection of Rouse.

At the same time he consigns his book to a safe haven, Milton looks to the future where generations to come in wiser ages with impartial mind and sound judgment may come to know and to judge his poetry.[44] Although the tone of these lines seems at first almost a return to the graceful elegance of the opening strophe, the poet does not seek to escape the harsh realities of his own time. Tongues of the multitude are now and may still be in future times insolent ("procax," 70), the crowd wicked ("prava," 80), and envy or spite ("livore," 85), not yet buried. Nevertheless, perhaps this book of gentle elegies and pastorals will be appreciated by a sane and healthy posterity.[45] He himself —as a god-elected bard—must heed a different call. Like "Mansus" and "Epitaphium Damonis," "Ad Joannem Rousium" is a valedictory poem. Although Milton does not tell us specifically, as he had in his previous Latin poems, that he is ready to assume the role of the epic poet, he does bid farewell, yet once more, to the world of pastures and forest shades.

When he composed "Ad Joannem Rousium" in January 1647, Milton created a Janus-like ode that looks forward and backward. Part elegiac, part Pindaric, it incorporates the multifarious traditions—classical, Christian,

---

43. "[T]utela solers Roüsi" may echo "custodia sollers" in *Georgics* 4.327. I have adapted Bush's translation.

44. "Et tutela dabit solers Roüsi, / Quò neque lingua procax vulgi penetrabit, atque longè / Turba legentum prava facesset; / At ultimi nepotes, / Et cordatior aetas / Judicia rebus aequiora forsitan / Adhiberit integro sinu." (78–84) (And provided by the watchful protection of Rouse; there the babbling tongue of the populace will not penetrate and the crowd of vulgar readers will be far away. But our remote descendants in a wiser age will perhaps see things with impartial mind and juster judgment.) I have adapted Bush's translation.

45. The contrast of present England with an idealized sane posterity ("sana posteritas," 86) calls to mind Dante's contrast of the Florence he had left behind with the just and sane people of Paradiso ("popol guisto e sano," *Paradiso* 31.39). The hope for a sane posterity juxtaposes Miltonic millenarianism with a typical elegiac urbanity.

Latin, and neo-Latin—that had produced the poems of the "double" volume. Milton does not deny his identity as the elegiac or pastoral poet—he even suggests that these classical and neoclassical impulses produced a gentler, softer poetry than that he and the England of the 1640s could and would now produce. "Ad Joannem Rousium" is unique among Milton's lyrics in that it affectionately looks back on the world of Neaera's bard, echoing Ovid's *Amores* in the very last lines, while at the same time it lays claim to the Apollonian lyre that will rule his poetry from now on.[46]

"Ad Joannem Rousium" may also provide us the answer to that question: why Milton chose the year 1645/1646 in which to publish his youthful poems. *Poems, English and Latin* come at a crucial moment in his personal life and in the political life of England. The personal moment is the return of his wife and the establishment of a new household. The political moment is that space between Naseby and the taking of Oxford that marked the decisive conquest for the Parliamentarian forces. After Naseby, Milton could set aside (for the interim) his labors as England's political pamphleteer to claim his place as England's poet. "Ad Joannem Rousium" is concerned both with reclaiming the Muses' place in England's life (after civil disorder) and with the establishment of Milton's place in England's "musaeum." The timely gesture of dispatching the poems to Rouse is only the completion of that process that had begun when Milton had turned the poems over to Moseley for printing. Now, having been dispatched to Bodley's treasury, they can be preserved for that new society that parliament's victory seemed to promise, a society that would value them as it valued the other works of the Muses.[47] As "Ad Joannem Rousium" cannot be separated from the occasion of its composition, neither should the *Poems, English and Latin* be separated from the hopeful year that saw their birth. Pindar often spoke of the critical moment—the *kairos*—that produces an event—the athletic victory or the poetical composition. Milton had come in 1645/1646 to that *kairos* in his poetical career, to the moment when he was staking his claim to poetic fame, even as his nation staked its claim for liberty. This moment was made propitious both by Apollo, Milton's patron, and by Rouse, Apollo's other son.

46. See *The Latin and Greek Poems*, 1.331 n (cf. Ovid, *Amores* 1.15.39–40). The editors comment that "It is interesting that Milton's last formal piece of Latin verse should end with an apparent echo of the poet of his youthful idolatry." In this particular elegy, Ovid is answering the charges of "livor edax" (biting envy) that he has wasted his youth, maintaining that in spite of envy he will seek glory and his works will live on.

47. As *Areopagitica* and other pamphlets argue, there is a direct relationship between the freedom of the Muses and the freedom of society. In *Areopagitica* he had urged that learning's fountain be free-flowing, that parliament keep the sinews of society strong by keeping it and its institutions untrammeled with censorship. When Milton originally sent his book of poems to Rouse, he sent his political pamphlets at the same time, almost as though to declare that the work of the one protected the life of the other.

Epilogue

When Milton reprinted the augmented *Poems, English and Latin* in 1673, the *Poemata* (except for the addition of "Ad Joannem Rousium") had little changed. The English *Poems,* however, had been augmented substantially. The sonnets had doubled in number; the psalm translations had become a major section placed at the close of the English volume; "On the death of a Fair Infant" was added, representing a precocious experiment with the ode form and an early English funeral lament to place opposite the Latin funera. It is true that no major English poem had joined the ranks of the Nativity ode, "L'Allegro" and "Il Penseroso," the Ludlow *Mask,* and "Lycidas," but the English volume testifies that Milton continued to write shorter poems in English and even to develop his expertise in two genres—the sonnet and the psalm. Some of the sonnets adopt the familiar style of the earlier sonnets to Lady Margaret Ley and to the Young Lady; others, however, make manifest Milton's growing political concerns; and still others echo the tone of faith and personal resignation that characterize the group of psalm translations composed in the 1650s.

Yet despite these additions and modifications, the story that "Ad Joannem Rousium" and the 1645 volume recounts remains much the same. Milton's *Poems, English and Latin* are a testament to his poetic experimentation in classical and neoclassical genres and to his development as a poet who had won both an English and a Continental reputation. Further, by 1673 the prediction of the epigraph on the 1645 title page had come true. The gods had indeed spared the future vates; *Paradise Lost* and *Paradise Regained* were written—and *The History of Britain*—even if not composed in verse as the English epic—stood as a labor of love for the English people.

The 1673 reissue of the *Poems Both English and Latin* as an expanded volume tells us how important the poems of his youth were to Milton— and how important the format in which he first presented them in 1645. In the most essential ways that format remains unchanged in 1673; *Poems,*

&c. Upon Several Occasions English and Latin remains a double book. Although Milton adds to the poems, he does not regroup them. Hence we may be confident that the experience of reading the volume—with the Latin poems balancing the English, with certain groups of poems being read in consort with one another—remains to a degree unchanged. When he collected and arranged the *Poems* in 1645, Milton wished to present us with a portrait of a poet skilled in different Latin and English genres, but a poet who was resolutely moving forward toward different genres— to epic and drama, impelled by pressing national and religious concerns. By the time he published the 1645 volume and composed "Ad Joannem Rousium," he had probably already sketched out the plan for *Paradise Lost* and may well already have envisioned *Samson Agonistes* as a drama doctrinal for the nation. Both *Paradise Lost* and *Samson Agonistes* are works that look to the Continent and to the rich tradition of humanistic learning that had informed the odes, elegies, and pastorals of the first volume of poetry. Although Milton in his lifetime never returned to the Continent, he continued to look to Italy and to draw sustenance from those literary traditions that had so much influenced his first poetry. What he had learned about the neoclassical poetry of the Renaissance and had adapted to this first book of poetry continued to inform structurally and thematically his later poetry. In making the poems of the 1645 volume, Milton was setting down the principles that would guide him as an epic poet.

Bibliography

MILTON'S WORKS

Milton, John. *Complete Poems and Major Prose*. Ed. Merritt Y. Hughes. New York: Odyssey Press, 1957.

———. *Complete Prose Works of John Milton*. Ed. Don M. Wolfe, et al. 8 vols. New Haven, Conn.: Yale University Press, 1959–1980.

———. *The Complete Poetical Works of John Milton*. Ed. Douglas Bush. London: Oxford University Press, 1966.

———. *Complete Shorter Poems*. Ed. John Carey. Burnt Mill, Harlow, Essex: Longman, 1971.

———. "Lycidas," *Obsequies to the memorie of Mr. Edward King* (Cambridge 1638). In *Justa Edovardo King. Reproduced from the Original Edition, 1638*. New York: Columbia University Press, 1939.

———. *A Maske. The Earlier Versions*. Ed. S. E. Sprott. Toronto: University of Toronto Press, 1973.

———. *A Maske at Ludlow. Essays on Milton's Comus. With the Bridgewater Version of Comus*. Ed. John S. Diekhoff. Cleveland: Press of Case Western Reserve University, 1968.

———. *Milton's Sonnets*. Ed. E. A. J. Honigmann. London: St. Martins Press, 1966.

———. *Poems, & c, Upon Several Occasions. Both English and Latin, & c, composed at several Times. With a Small Tractate of Education*. London: Thomas Dring, 1673.

———. *Poems of Mr. John Milton, Both English and Latin, Compos'd at several times*. London: Humphrey Moseley, 1645.

———. *The Sonnets of Milton*. Ed. John S. Smart. Glasgow, 1921. Reprint, Oxford: Clarendon Press, 1966.

———. "The Trinity Manuscript." *John Milton, Complete Poetical Works*. Ed. Harris Francis Fletcher. Urbana: University of Illinois Press, 1943.

————. *The Works of John Milton*. Ed. Frank Allen Patterson et al. New York: Columbia University Press, 1931.

A VARIORUM COMMENTARY

————. *A Variorum Commentary on The Poems of John Milton. The Italian Poems*. Ed. J. E. Shaw and A. Bartlett Giamatti. New York: Columbia University Press, 1970.

————. *A Variorum Commentary on The Poems of John Milton. The Latin and Greek Poems*. Ed. Douglas Bush. New York: Columbia University Press, 1970.

————. *A Variorum Commentary on the Poems of John Milton. The Minor English Poems*. Ed. A. S. P. Woodhouse and Douglas Bush. 3 vols. New York: Columbia University Press, 1972.

PRIMARY WORKS

Alcman. *Greek Lyric Poetry*. Ed. David A. Campbell. London: Macmillan, 1979.

Amaltheus, Joannes Baptista. *Carmina*. Venice, 1550.

Anderson, Henry. "Musarum Querimonia." *Delitiae Poetarum Scotorum hujs aevi Illustrium*. Amsterdam, 1637.

Anthologia Palatina, The Greek Anthology. Ed. W. R. Paton. 5 vols. London: Heinemann, 1916.

Apuleius. *The Golden Ass, Being the Metamorphoses of Lucius Apuleius*. Trans. W. Aldington, rev. S. Gaselee. London: Heinemann, 1915.

Aretius, Benedictus. *Commentarii Absolutissimi in Pindari Olympia, Pythia, Nemea, Isthmia*. Geneva, 1587.

Barberini, Maffeo [Urban VIII]. *Poemata*. Paris, 1620.

Barclay, John. *Poematum Libri Duo*. London, 1615.

Baudoin, Joannes. *Mythologie ou Explication des Fables*. Paris, 1627.

Bembus, Petrus [Pietro Bembo]. *Le Rime di M. Pietro Bembo*. Vinegra, 1562.

————. *Carmina, Quinque Illustrium Poetarum*. Rome, 1753.

Berni, Francesco. *Tutte le Opere*. Vinegia, 1538.

Blount, Thomas Pope. *De Re Poetica*. London, 1694.

Boccacius, Joannes [Giovanni Boccaccio]. *Genealogiae deorum gentilium*. Venice, 1492.

————. *Genealogiae deorum Gentilium*. Venice, 1511.

Bocchius, Achilles. *Carmina Illustrium Poetarum Italorum*. Florence, 1719.

Britanniae Natalis. Oxford, 1630.

Buchanan, George. *Poemata.* Amsterdam, 1687.

———. *Miscellaneorum Liber.* Ed. Philip J. Ford. Aberdeen: Aberdeen University Press, 1982.

Caesarus, Iulianus. *In Regem Solem.* Madrid, 1625.

Calcagninus, Caelius. *Carmina.* In *Io Baptistae Pignae Carminum.* Venice, 1553.

Callimachus. *Hymns and Epigrams.* Ed. G. R. Mair. London: Heinemann, 1977.

Cantabrigiensium Dolor & Solamen: seu Successio Beatissimi Regis Jacobi Pacifici: et Successio Augustissimi Regis Caroli. Cambridge, 1625.

Capilupus, Hippolytus. *Capiluporum Carmina.* Rome, 1590.

Carolus Redux. Oxford, 1623.

Cartari, Vincenzo. *Le imagine de i dei de gli antichi.* Venice, 1571.

———. *Le Imagini de i Dei de gli Antichi.* Venice, 1587.

———. *The Fountaine of Ancient Fiction.* Trans. Richard Linche. London, 1599.

Casa, Giovanni Della. *Rime, et Prose di M. Giovanni della Casa.* Florence, 1564.

——— [Ioannes Casa]. *Ioannis Casae Latina Monumenta.* Florence, 1567.

———. *Trattato di M. Giovanni della Casa.* Venice, 1589.

——— [Joannes Casa]. *Carmina Quinque Illustrium Poetarum.* 1753.

———. *Opere.* Milan, 1937.

Castiglione, Balthazar. *Carmina Quinque Illustrium Poetarum.* Venice, 1558.

Catullus. *The Poems of Catullus.* Ed. W. B. McDaniel. New York, 1931.

Chapman, George. *The Memorable Masque.* 1613. In *The Plays of George Chapman. The Comedies.* Ed. Allan Holaday. Urbana: University of Illinois Press, 1970.

Claudian. Ed. Maurice Platnauer. London: Heinemann, 1922.

Clement of Alexandria. *Hymni in Christum.* Paris: Morel, 1598.

Comes, Natalis [Natale Conti]. *Mythologiae.* Venice, 1568.

———. *Mythologiae, sive explicationum fabularum. Libri decem.* Venice, 1581.

———. *Mythologiae.* Patavia, 1616.

———. *Mythologiae.* Padua, 1637.

Cornutus, Lucius Annaeus. *Natura deorum gentilium commentarius.* Venice, 1505.

Crashaw, Richard. *In Voces Votivae.* Cambridge, 1640.

Crinitus, Petrus. *Poematum Libri Duo.* Paris, 1508.

Dousa, Jan, Filius. *Poemata.* Ed. Gulielmus Rabus. Rotterdam, 1704.

Drayton, Michael. *Odes.* London, 1619.

———. *The Works of Michael Drayton.* Ed. J. William Hebel. 5 vols. Oxford: Shakespeare Head, 1931–1941.

Echlin, David. *Carolides ad Patrem Carolum.* London, 1630.

Eidyllia. In obitum Fulgentissimi Henrici Walliae Principis Duodecimi. Oxford: J. Barnes, 1612.

Elaiophoria, sive Ob Faedera, Auspiciis serenissimi Oliveri, Reipub. Ang. Scot. & Hiber. Domini Protectoris. Oxford, 1654.

Exequiae Illustrissimi Equitis, D. Philippi Sidnaei Gratissimae Memoriae ac Nomine Inpensae. Oxford: Joseph Barnes, 1587.

Ferro, Giovanni. *Teatro d'Imprese.* Venice, 1623.

Flaminius, Marcus Antonius. *Doctissimorum Nostra Aetate Italorum Epigrammata.* Paris, 1548.

———. *Carmina Quinque Illustrium Poetarum.* Venice, 1558.

Fulgentius, Fabius Planciades. *Mythologiarum libri tres.* Basel, 1556.

Gafurius, Franchinus. *Theorica Musice.* Milan, 1496.

Genethliacum Illustrissimorum Principum Caroli & Mariae. Cambridge, 1631.

Gherus, Ranutius, ed. *Delitiae CC. Italorum Poetarum.* Frankfurt, 1608.

Gil, Alexander, Jr. *Parerga Sive Poetici Conatus.* London, 1632.

Gyraldus, Lilius Gregorius [Giglio Gregorio Giraldi]. *De Deis Gentium.* Basel, 1548.

———. *De deis gentium varia et multiplex historia.* Basel, 1560.

———. "De Musis libellus." in Hyginus, *Fabularum liber.* Paris, 1577.

Habert, Isaac. *Les trois livres des Meteores avec que autres oeuvres poëtiques.* Paris, 1585.

Hesiod. *Hesiod, the Homeric Hymns, and Homerica.* Ed. Hugh G. Evelyn-White. London: Heinemann, 1914.

Horace. *Carmina.* Ed. T. E. Page. London, 1964.

———. *Odes and Epodes.* Ed. Charles E. Bennett. New Rochelle, N.Y.: Aristides D. Caratzas, 1984.

Hume, David. *Daphn-Amaryllis.* London, 1605.

———. *Poemata.* Paris, 1639.

Iacobi Ara. Deo Reduci. Oxford, 1617.

Jonson, Ben. *The Masque of Blackness.* 1605. In *The Works of Ben Jonson.* Ed. W. Gifford. London, 1875.

Justa Edovardo King. Reproduced from the Original Edition, 1638. New York: Columbia University Press, 1939.

Lactantius. *De Ave Phoenice.* Ed. and trans. Mary Cletus Carpenter. Philadelphia, 1933.

Lagausie, Sieur de. *Le Pindare Thebain: Traduction de grec en françois, meslée de vers et de prose.* Paris, 1626.

Lampridio, Benedetto. *Carmina.* Venice, 1550.

———. *Carmina Illustrium Poetarum Italorum.* Ed. J. M. Toscanus. Paris, 1576.

Landinus, Cristophorus. *Carmina Omnia*. Ed. Alexander Perosa. Florence: Leo S. Olschki, 1939.

Leochaeus, Joannes [John Leech]. *Musae Priores, sive Poematum*. London, 1620.

Linocerius, Geofredius. [Geoffroi Linocier]. *Mythologiae Musarum libellus*. Paris, 1583.

Lucretius. *De Rerum Natura*. Ed. W. H. D. Rouse. London: William Heinemann, 1924.

Macrobius. *Commentary on the Dream of Scipio*. Trans. William Harris Stahl. New York, 1952.

Manso, Giovanni Battista. *I Paradossi overo dell' Amore Dialogi Di Gio. Battista Manso*. Milan, 1608.

———. *Nomiche Poesie*. Venice, 1635.

Mantuanus, Baptista (Spagnuoli) [Baptista Mantuan]. *Aureum contra impudice scribentes opusculum*. Paris, 1508.

———. *Fastorum Libri Duodecim*. Strassburg, 1518.

———. *The Eclogues of Baptista Mantuan*. Ed. with introduction and notes by Wilfred P. Mustard. Baltimore: Johns Hopkins Press, 1911.

———. *Adulescentia, The Eclogues of Mantuan*. Ed. and trans. Lee Piepho. New York: Garland Publishing Inc., 1989.

Marullus, Michaelis [Michele Marullo]. *Hymni et Epigrammata Marulli*. Florence, 1497.

———. *Marulli Constantinopolitani Epigrammata & Hymni*. Paris: Andreas Wechelus, 1561.

———. *In Poetae Tres Elegantissimi*. Paris, 1582.

———. *Michaelis Marulli Carmina*. Ed. Alessandro Perosa. Zurich: Thesaurus Mundi, 1951.

Minturno, Antonio. *L'Arte Poetica*. Venice, 1563.

More, Henry. *The Complete Poems of Dr. Henry More*. Ed. Rev. Alexander B. Grosart. Edinburgh: Edinburgh University Press, 1878.

Musarum Oxoniensium. Ελαιοφορία, *sive Ob Faedera, Auspiciis serenissimi Oliveri, Reipub. Ang. Scot. & Hiber. Domini Protectoris*. Oxford, 1654.

Naugerius, Andreas. *Doctissimorum Nostra Aetate Italorum Epigrammata*. Paris, 1548.

———. *Carmina Quinque Illustrium Poetarum*. Venice, 1558.

Obsequies to the memorie of Mr. Edward King. Cambridge, 1638.

Observationum libellus. In *Mythologiam Natalis Comitis*. Padua, 1615.

Orpheus. *Orphei Hymni*. Ed. Guilelmus Quandt. Berlin: Weidmannos, 1955.

Ovid. Ed. and revised G. P. Goold. 6 vols. London: Heinemann, 1929–1938. [Includes *Metamorphoses, Tristia, Ars Amatoria (The Art of Love), Fasti, Heroides,* and *Amores.*]

———. *Amores*. Ed. E. J. Kinney. Oxford, 1961.

Ovide Moralisé en Prose. Ed. C. De Boer. Amsterdam: North-Holland Publishing Company, 1954.

Peacham, Henry. "Of Poetrie." *The Compleat Gentleman* (1622). In *Critical Essays of the Seventeenth Century*, ed. J. E. Spingarn. 2 vols. Bloomington: Indiana University Press, 1963.

Peplus Illustrissimi Viri D. Philippi Sidnaei Supremis Honoribus Dicatus. Oxford: Joseph Barnes, 1587.

Perosa, Alessandro and John Sparrow, eds. *Renaissance Latin Verse, An Anthology*. Chapel Hill: University of North Carolina Press, 1979.

Petrarca, Francesco. *Rime, Trionfi e Poesie Latine*. Milan: Riccardo Ricciardi, 1951.

Phillips, Edward. *Theatrum Poetarum*. London, 1675.

Pindarus [Pindar]. *Periodos*. Ed. Erasmus Schmidt. Wittenberg, 1616.

———. *Periodos*. Ed. Joannes Benedictus. Saumur, 1620.

———. *Odes of Pindar with Several Other Pieces in Prose and Verse*. Trans. Gilbert West. London, 1749.

———. *The Olympian and Pythian Odes*. Ed. Basil L. Gildersleeve. London: Macmillan, 1908.

———. *Carmina*. Ed. C. M. Bowra. Oxford: Oxford University Press, 1935.

———. *The Odes of Pindar*. Ed. and trans. Geoffrey S. Conway. London: Dent, 1972.

Plato. *Republic*. In *Platonis Opera*. Ed. John Burnet. Oxford: Clarendon Press, 1902.

Poetae Graeci Veteres. Ed. Petrus de la Roviere. Cologne, 1614.

Politianus, Angelus [Angelo Poliziano]. *Omnia Opera*. Venice: Aldus, 1498.

———. "Stanze per la Giostra Orfeo." In *Rime*. Ed. Bruno Maier. Novara: Instituto Geografico, 1968.

———. *The Stanze of Angelo Poliziano*. Trans. David Quint. Amherst, 1979.

Pontanus, Ioannes Iovianius [Giovanni Pontano]. *Pontani Opera. (Urania, Meteororum, De Hortis hesperidum, Lepidina, Meliseus, Maeon, Acon, Hendecasyllaborum, Neniae, Epigrammata.)* Venice: Aldus, 1505.

———. *Pontani Opera. (Urania, Meteororum, De Hortis hesperidum, Lepidina, Meliseus, Maeon, Acon, Hendecasyllaborum, Tumulorum* [liber unus], *Neniae, Epigrammata.)* Venice: Aldus, 1513.

———. *Opera Pontani. (Amorum libri II, De amore coniugali III, Tumulorum II, Lyrici I, Eridanorum II, Eclogae duae Coryle, Calpurnij Siculi Eclogae VII, Aurelij Nemesiani Eclogae IIII.)* Venice: Aldus, 1518.

———. *Carmina. Ecloghe, Elegie, Liriche*. Ed. Johannes Oeschger. Bari: Laterza & Figle, 1948.

Postlethwaite, Norman, and Gordon Campbell, eds. *Edward King, Milton's*

"Lycidas": Poems and Documents. In *Milton Quarterly* 28 (December 1994).

Proclus. *Poetae Graeci Veteres, Carminis Heroici Scriptores, qui extant, Omnes.* Geneva, 1606.

———. *Inni.* Florence, 1929.

Propertius. Ed. L. Richardson, Jr. Norman: University of Oklahoma Press, 1977.

Psalterium, Hebraeum, Graecum, Arabicum, & Chaldaeum, cum tribus latinibus interpretionibus & glossis. 1516.

Puttenham, George. *The Arte of English Poesie.* 1589. A facsimile reproduction. Kent, Ohio: Kent State University Press, 1970.

Rex Redux. Cambridge, 1633.

Ronsard, Pierre de. *Les Hymnes de Pierre de Ronsard.* Paris, 1555.

———. *Odes.* In *Oeuvres Complètes.* Ed. Gustave Cohen. Paris: Librairie Gallimard, 1950.

Ruscelli, Girolano. *Le Imprese Illustri con espositioni et discorsi.* Venice, 1566, 1572, 1580, 1584.

Sannazaro, Jacopo [Jacobo]. *Sonetti, e Canzoni del Sannazaro.* Venice: Aldus, 1534.

———. *Opera Omnia Latine Scripta.* Venice: Aldus, 1535.

———. *Arcadia & Piscatorial Eclogues.* Trans. Ralph Nash. Detroit: Wayne State University Press, 1966.

Sappho. *Poetarum Lesbiorum fragmenta.* Ed. E. Lobel and Denys Page. Oxford: Oxford University Press, 1955.

Sarbiewski, Casimire. *Lycorum, Libri Tres.* Cologne, 1625.

Scaliger, Julius Caesar. *Poetices Libri Septem.* Lyons, 1581.

Secundus, Joannes [Ioannes Secundus]. *Opera.* Utrecht, 1541.

———. *Opera nunc secundum edita.* Paris, 1561.

———. *In Poetae Tres Elegantissimi.* Paris, 1582.

———. *Opera quae reperiri potuerunt omnia.* Leiden, 1619.

Shakespeare, William. *The Riverside Shakespeare.* Ed. G. Blakemore Evans, et. al. Boston: Houghton Mifflin, 1974.

Sidney, Sir Philip. *The Defense of Poesie.* In *Complete Prose Works.* 4 vols. Ed. Albert Feuillerat. Cambridge: Cambridge University Press, 1923.

Solis Britannici Perigaeum. Oxford, 1633.

Soowthern, John. *Pandora.* London, 1584.

Sostra, sive, Ad Carolum II, reducem. Cambridge, 1660.

Spenser, Edmund. *Poetical Works.* Ed. J. C. Smith and E. de Selincourt. Oxford: Oxford University Press, 1970.

Statius. "Silvae." Ed. J. H. Mozley. London: Heinemann, 1928.

Stephanus, Carolus [Charles Estienne]. *Dictionarium historicum, geographicum, poeticum.* Geneva: Iacobus Stoer, 1596.

Synesius. *Hymni carmine.* Ed. Gulielmus Canterus. Basel: Oporinus, 1567.
———. *The Essays and Hymns of Synesius of Cyrene.* Trans. with introduction and notes by Augustine Fitzgerald. Oxford: Oxford University Press, 1930.

Tasso, Bernardo. *Ode di Messer Bernardo Tasso.* Vinegia, 1560.
———. *Rime di Messer Bernardo Tasso.* Vinegra, 1560.

Tasso, Torquato. *Poemi Minori di Torquato Tasso.* Ed. Angelo Solerti. 2 vols. Bologna, 1891.
———. *Creation of the World.* Trans. Joseph Tusiani. Binghamton: MRTS, 1982.

Theocritus. "The Poems of Theocritus." In *The Greek Bucolic Poets,* ed. J. M. Edmonds. London: Heinemann, 1950.
———. *Theocritus.* Ed and trans. A. S. F. Gow. Cambridge: Cambridge University Press, 1965.

Threno-thriambeuticon. Cambridge, 1603.

Toscanus, Ioannes Mathaeus, ed. *Carmina Illustrium Poetarum Italorum.* 2 vols. Paris, 1576.

Varchi, Benedetto. *Lettura di M. Benedetto Varchi, sopra un sonetto della Gelosia di Mons. Dalla Casa* [sic], *Edita nella celebratissima accademia de gl' Infiammati a Padova.* Mantua, 1545.
———. *I Sonetti di M. Benedetto Varchi.* Venice, 1551.

Vergili Maronis, P. *Opera.* Ed. R. A. B. Mynors. Oxford: Clarendon Press, 1969.

Voces Votivae. Cambridge, 1640.

SECONDARY WORKS

Allen, Don Cameron. "Milton as a Latin Poet." In *Neo-Latin Poetry of the Sixteenth and Seventeenth Centuries.* Los Angeles: University of California Press, 1965.

Alpers, Paul. *What is Pastoral?* Chicago: University of Chicago Press, 1996.

Archer, Stanley. "'Glutinous Heat': A Note on *Comus* 1.917." *Milton Quarterly* 7 (Dec. 1973): 99.

Arthos, John. *Milton and the Italian Cities.* New York: Barnes and Noble, 1968.
———. "Milton's Sabrina, Virgil and Porphyry." *Anglia* 79 (1962): 204–13.

Austin, Warren B. "Milton's Lycidas and Two Latin Elegies by Giles Fletcher the Elder." *Studies in Philology* 44 (1947): 41–55.

Behrendt, Stephen. "Blake's Illustrations to Milton's 'Nativity Ode.'" *PQ* 55 (1976): 65–95.

Benet, Diana Treviño. "The Escape from Rome: Milton's *Second Defense* and a Renaissance Genre." In *Milton in Italy,* ed. Mario Di Cesare, 31–49. Binghamton: Medieval and Renaissance Text and Studies, 1991.

Benet, Diana Treviño, and Michael Lieb, eds. *Literary Milton: Text, Pretext, Context.* Pittsburgh: Duquesne University Press, 1994.

Berley, Marc. "Milton's Earthly Grossness: Music and the Condition of the Poet in *L'Allegro* and *Il Penseroso.*" *Milton Studies* 30:149–161. Ed. Albert C. Labriola. Pittsburgh: University of Pittsburgh Press, 1993.

Binns, J. W. *Intellectual Culture in Elizabethan and Jacobean England: The Latin Writings of the Age.* Leeds: Francis Cairns, 1990.

———. "William Gager on the Death of Sir Philip Sidney." *Humanistica Lovaniensia* 21 (1972): 221–38.

Bober, Phyllis Pray, and Ruth Rubinstein. *Renaissance Artists and Antique Sculpture: A Handbook of Sources.* London: Harvey Miller Publishers, 1986.

Bowra, C. M. *Pindar.* Oxford, 1964.

Breasted, Barbara. "*Comus* and the Castelhaven Scandal." *Milton Studies* 3:201–24. Ed. James Simmonds. Pittsburgh: University of Pittsburgh Press, 1971.

Brooks, Cleanth, and John Edward Hardy. "Essay in Analysis: *Lycidas.*" In *Poems of Mr. John Milton,* New York: Harcourt, Brace & Co., 1951, 169–86. Reprinted in *Milton's Lycidas: The Tradition and the Poem,* ed. C. A. Patrides, 140–56. Columbia: University of Missouri Press, 1983.

Brown, Cedric C. *John Milton's Aristocratic Entertainments.* Cambridge: Cambridge University Press, 1985.

Brown, Deborah. "The Apollo Belvedere and the Garden of Giuliano della Rovere at SS. Apostoli." *Journal of the Warburg and Courtauld Institutes* 49 (1986): 235–38.

Brummer, Hans Henrik. *The Statue Court in the Vatican Belvedere.* Stockholm: Almqvist and Wildsell, 1970.

Butrica, James. *The Manuscript Tradition of Propertius.* Toronto: University of Toronto Press, 1984.

Calhoun, Thomas O. "On John Milton's Mask at Ludlow." *Milton Studies* 6:165–79. Ed. James D. Simmonds. Pittsburgh: University of Pittsburgh Press, 1974.

Campbell, Gordon. "Imitation in *Epitaphium Damonis,*" *Urbane Milton, The Latin Poems* in *Milton Studies* 19:165–77. Ed. James Freeman and Anthony Low. Pittsburgh: University of Pittsburgh Press, 1984.

Carey, John. "The Date of Milton's Italian Poems." *Review of English Studies,* n.s., 14 (1963): 383–86.

———. "Milton's Harmonious Sisters." In *The Well Enchanting Skill,* ed.

John Caldwell, Edward Olleson, and Susan Wollenberg, 245–57. Oxford: Clarendon Press, 1990.

Carrithers, Gale H., Jr. "*Poems* (1645): On Growing Up," *Milton Studies,* 15: 161–79. Ed. James D. Simmons. Pittsburgh: University of Pittsburgh Press, 1981.

Chaudhuri, Sukanta. *Renaissance Pastoral and Its English Development.* Oxford: Clarendon Press, 1989.

Ciceri, Pier Luigi. "Michele Marullo e i suoi 'Hymni Naturales,'" in *Giornale Storico della letteratura italiana,* 64 (1914): 289–357.

Coiro, Ann. "Herrick's Hesperides: The Name and the Frame." *ELH* 52 (1985): 311–36.

Condee, Ralph W. "The Latin Poetry of John Milton." In *The Latin Poetry of English Poets,* ed. J. W. Binns, 58–92. London: Routledge, 1974.

————. "'Mansus' and the Panegyric Tradition." *Studies in the Renaissance* 15 (1968): 174–92.

————. "The Structure of Milton's 'Epitaphium Damonis.'" *Studies in Philology* 62 (1965): 577–94.

Cook, A. S. "Two Notes on Milton." *Modern Language Review* 2 (1907): 121–24.

Cooper, Lane, ed. *A Concordance of the Latin, Greek, and Italian Poems of John Milton.* Halle: Max Niemeyer, 1923.

Corns, Thomas. "Ideology in the *Poemata* (1645)." *Urbane Milton, The Latin Poetry* in *Milton Studies,* 19:195–203. Ed. James A. Freeman and Anthony Low. Pittsburgh: University of Pittsburgh Press, 1984.

————. "The Plurality of Miltonic Ideology." In *Literature and the English Civil War,* ed. Thomas Healy and Jonathan Sawday. Cambridge: Cambridge University Press, 1990.

Creaser, John. "'The Present Aid of This Occasion': The Setting of *Comus.*" In *The Court Masque,* ed. David Lindley, 111–34. Manchester: Manchester University Press, 1984.

Curtius, Ernst Robert. *European Literature and the Latin Middle Ages.* Trans. Willard R. Trask. New York: Pantheon Books, 1953.

D'Amico, John. *Renaissance Humanism in Papal Rome.* Baltimore: Johns Hopkins Press, 1983.

Daniel, Clay. *Death in Milton's Poetry.* Lewisburg: Bucknell University Press, 1994.

De Filippis, Michele. "Milton and Manso: Cups or Books," *PMLA* 51 (1936): 745–56.

Demaray, John G. *Milton and the Masque Tradition.* Cambridge: Harvard University Press, 1968.

Dust, Philip. "Milton's *Epitaphium Damonis* and *Lycidas.*" *Humanista Lovaniensia* 32 (1983): 342–46.

Elledge, Scott. *Milton's "Lycidas."* New York: Harper and Row, 1966.

Evans, J. Martin. "Lycidas, Daphnis, and Gallus." In *English Renaissance Studies,* ed. John Carey, 228–44. Oxford: Clarendon Press, 1980.

————. "Lycidas and the Dolphins." *N & Q,* n.s., 25 (1978): 15–17.

————. *The Road from Horton: Looking Backwards in "Lycidas."* Victoria: University of Victoria Press, 1983.

Falco, Raphael. *Conceived Presences: Literary Genealogy in Renaissance England.* Amherst: University of Massachusetts Press, 1994.

Finley, John H., Jr. "Milton and Horace." *Harvard Studies in Classical Philology* 48 (1937), 29–73.

————. *Pindar and Aeschylus.* Cambridge, Mass., 1955.

Finley, M. I. *Ancient Sicily.* London, 1979.

Fletcher, Harris Francis. *The Intellectual Development of John Milton.* 2 vols. Urbana: University of Illinois Press, 1956, 1961.

Flosdorf, J. W. "'Gums of Glutinous Heat': A Query." *Milton Quarterly* 7 (March 1973): 4–5.

Ford, Philip J. *George Buchanan, Prince of Poets, Miscellaneorum Liber.* Aberdeen: Aberdeen University Press, 1982.

————. "The *Hymni Naturales* of Michael Marullus." In *Acta Conventus Neo-Latini Bononiensis,* ed. R. J. Schoeck, 475–82. Binghamton, N.Y.: Medieval and Renaissance Texts and Studies, 1985.

Freeman, James A. "Milton's Roman Connection: Giovanni Salzilli," *Urbane Milton, The Latin Poetry* in *Milton Studies,* 19:9, 87–104. Ed. James A. Freeman and Anthony Low. Pittsburgh: University of Pittsburgh Press, 1984.

French, J. Milton, ed. *The Life Records of John Milton.* New Brunswick, N.J.: Rutgers University Press, 1949.

Gaisser, Julia Haig. *Catullus and His Renaissance Readers.* Oxford: Clarendon Press, 1993.

Gottfried, Rudolf. "Milton, Lactantius, Claudian, Tasso." *Studies in Philology* 30 (1933): 497–503.

Grant, W. Leonard. *Neo-Latin Literature and the Pastoral.* Chapel Hill: University of North Carolina Press, 1965.

Graziani, René. "Philip II's Impresa and Spenser's Souldan." *Journal of the Warburg and Courtauld Institutes* 27 (1964): 322–24.

Griffin, Dustin. "Milton in Italy: The Making of a Man of Letters?" In *Milton in Italy,* ed. Mario Di Cesare, 19–27. Binghamton: Medieval and Renaissance Texts and Studies, 1991.

Haan, Estelle. "'Written Encomiums': Milton's Latin Poetry in Its Italian Context." In *Milton in Italy,* ed. Mario Di Cesare, 521–47. Binghamton: Medieval and Renaissance Texts and Studies, 1991.

Hale, John K. "Artistry and Originality in Milton's Latin Poems." *Milton Quarterly* 27 (Dec. 1993): 138–49.

———. "The Audiences of Milton's Italian Verse." *Renaissance Studies* 8 (1994): 76–88.

———. "Milton Playing with Ovid," *Milton Studies* 25:3–19. Ed. James D. Simmonds. Pittsburgh: University of Pittsburgh Press, 1990.

———. "The Pre-Criticism of Milton's Latin Verse, Illustrated from the Ode 'Ad Joannem Rousium.'" In *Of Poetry and Politics: New Essays on Milton and His World,* ed. P. G. Stanwood, 17–34. Binghamton: Medieval and Renaissance Texts and Studies, 1995.

———. "Sion's Bacchanalia: An Inquiry into Milton's Use of Latin in the *Epitaphium Damonis,*" *Milton Studies* 16:115–30. Ed. James Simmonds. Pittsburgh: University of Pittsburgh Press, 1982.

Halley, Janet E. "Female Autonomy in Milton's Sexual Poetics." In *Milton and the Idea of Woman,* ed. Julia M. Walker, 230–53. Urbana: University of Illinois Press, 1988.

Hamilton, Elizabeth. *Henrietta Maria*. London: Hamish Hamilton, 1976.

Hampshire, Gwen. "An Unusual Bodleian Purchase in 1645." *Bodleian Library Record* 10 (1982): 339–48.

Hanford, James Holly. *John Milton, Englishman*. New York: Crown Publishers, 1949.

———. "The Pastoral Elegy and Milton's *Lycidas*." *PMLA* 25 (1910): 403–47. Reprinted in *John Milton, Poet and Humanist: Essays by James Holly Hanford*. Cleveland: Press of Western Reserve University, 1966.

———. "The Youth of Milton." In *Studies in Shakespeare, Milton, Donne*. New York: Macmillan, 1925.

Harrison, William P., Jr. "The Latin Pastorals of Milton and Castiglione." PMLA 50 (1935): 480–93.

———. Thomas Perrin, and Harry Joshua Leon. *The Pastoral Eclogue, An Anthology*. Austin: University of Texas Press, 1939.

Hartwell, Kathleen Ellen. *Lactantius and Milton*. Cambridge: Harvard University Press, 1929.

Haskin, Dayton. *Milton's Burden of Interpretation*. Philadelphia: University of Pennsylvania Press, 1994.

Hoey, Thomas. "Fusion in Pindar." *Harvard Studies in Classical Philology,* 70 (1965): 235–58.

Hubbard, Margaret. *Propertius*. London: Duckworth, 1974.

Hunt, Clay. *Lycidas and the Italian Critics*. New Haven: Yale University Press, 1979.

Hunter, William B., Jr. *The Descent of Urania: Studies in Milton, 1946–1988*. Lewisburg: Bucknell University Press, 1989.

————. *Milton's Comus: A Family Piece*. Troy, N.Y.: Whitston Publishing, 1983.

Jayne, Sears. "The Subject of Milton's Ludlow *Mask*." *PMLA* 74 (1959): 533–43.

Kale, Margaret Hoffman. "Milton's 'Gums of Glutinous Heat': A Renaissance Theory of Movement." *Milton Quarterly* 29 (1995): 86–91.

Kelley, Maurice, and S. D. Atkins. "Milton and the Harvard Pindar." *Studies in Bibliography* 17 (1964): 77–82.

Kendrick, Christopher. "Milton and Sexuality: A Symptomatic Reading of *Comus*." In *Re-membering Milton: Essays on the texts and traditions*, ed. Mary Nyquist and Margaret W. Ferguson, 43–73. New York and London: Methuen, 1987.

Kennedy, William J. "The Audiences of *Ad Patrem*," *Urbane Milton, The Latin Poetry* in *Milton Studies*, 19: 73–86. Ed. James A. Freeman and Anthony Low. Pittsburgh: University of Pittsburgh Press, 1984.

————. *Sannazaro and the Use of Pastoral*. Hanover, N. H.: University Press of New England, 1983.

Kerrigan, William. *The Sacred Complex*. Harvard: Harvard University Press, 1983.

Kidwell, Carol. *Pontano*. London: Duckworth, 1991.

Kirkconnell, Watson, ed. *Awake the Courteous Echo*. Toronto: University of Toronto Press, 1973.

Knedlik, Janet Leslie. "High Pastoral Art in *Epitaphium Damonis*," *Urbane Milton, The Latin Poetry* in *Milton Studies* 19:149–63. Ed. James A. Freeman and Anthony Low. Pittsburgh: University of Pittsburgh Press, 1984.

Labriola, Albert C. "Portrait of an Artist: Milton's Changing Self-Image." *Milton Studies* 19:169–94. Ed. James D. Simmonds. Pittsburgh: University of Pittsburgh Press, 1984.

Le Comte, Edward. *Milton Re-viewed, Ten Essays*. New York: Garland, 1991.

Lees-Milne, James. *Saint Peter's: The Story of the Saint Peter's Basilica in Rome*. London: Hamish Hamilton, 1967.

Leonard, John. "'Trembling Ears': The Historical Moment of 'Lycidas,'" *Journal of Medieval and Renaissance Studies* 21 (1991): 59–81.

Lieb, Michael. *The Sinews of Ulysses: Form and Convention in Milton's Works*. Pittsburgh: Duquesne University Press, 1989.

Lindenbaum, Peter. "Authors and Publishers in the Late Seventeenth Century: New Evidence on their Relations." *The Library*, Sixth series. 17.3 (September 1995): 250–69.

————. "John Milton and the Republican Mode of Literary Production." *The Yearbook of English Studies* 21 (1991): 121–36.

————. "The Poet in the Marketplace: Milton and Samuel Simmons." In

Of Poetry and Politics: New Essays on Milton and His World, ed. P. G. Stanwood, 249–62. Binghamton, N.Y.: Medieval and Renaissance Texts and Studies, 1995.

Lipking, Lawrence. "The Genius of the Shore: Lycidas, Adamastor, and the Poetics of Nationalism," *PMLA* 111 (March 1996): 205–22.

Lister, Raymond. *The Painting of William Blake.* Cambridge: Cambridge University Press, 1986.

Lloyd, Christopher. *The Royal Collection.* London: Sinclair-Stevenson, 1992.

Lloyd, Michael. " 'Justa Edouardo King.' " *Notes and Queries* 203, n.s., 5 (1958): 432–34.

Low, Anthony. "Elegia Septima: The Poet and the Poem." *Urbane Milton, The Latin Poetry* in *Milton Studies,* 19:21–35. Ed. James A. Freeman and Anthony Low. Pittsburgh: University of Pittsburgh Press, 1984.

———. "*Mansus:* In its Context." *Urbane Milton, The Latin Poetry,* in *Milton Studies,* 19:105–26. Ed. James A. Freeman and Anthony Low. Pittsburgh: University of Pittsburgh Press, 1984.

MacKellar, Walter, ed. and trans. *The Latin Poems of John Milton.* New Haven: Yale University Press, 1930.

MacLaren, I. S. "Milton's Nativity Ode: The Function of Poetry and Structures of Response in 1629." *Milton Studies* 15:181–200. Ed. James D. Simmons. Pittsburgh: University of Pittsburgh Press, 1981.

Maddison, Carol. *Apollo and the Nine: A History of the Ode.* London: Routledge, 1960.

Maltzahn, Nicholas von. "Laureate, Republican, Calvinist: An Early Response to Milton and *Paradise Lost* (1667)." *Milton Studies* 29:181–198. Ed. Albert C. Labriola. Pittsburgh: University of Pittsburgh Press, 1992.

———. *Milton's History of Britain: Republican Historiography in the English Revolution.* Oxford: Clarendon Press, 1991.

Marcus, Leah S. "Justice for Margery Evans: A 'Local' Reading of *Comus.*" In *Milton and the Idea of Woman,* ed. Julia M. Walker, 66–85. Urbana: University of Illinois Press, 1988.

Martyn, John R. C. "Joannes Secundus: Orpheus and Eurydice." *Humanistica Lovaniensia* 35 (1986): 60–75.

———. "Milton's Elegia Septima." In *Acta Conventus Neo-Latini Lovaniensis,* ed. J. I. IJsewijn and E. Kessler, 383–87. Leuven: Wilhelm Fink Verlag München, 1973.

Martz, Louis L. *Poet of Exile: A Study of Milton's Poetry.* Reissued as *Milton: Poet of Exile.* New Haven: Yale University Press, 1980, 1986.

———. "The Rising Poet, 1645." In *The Lyric and Dramatic Milton,* ed. Joseph H. Summers. New York: English Institute Essays, 1965. Reworked in *Poet of Exile.* New Haven: Yale University Press, 1980.

Masson, David. *The Life of John Milton: Narrated in Connexion with the Political, Ecclesiastical, and Literary History of his Time.* London: MacMillan, 1873.

McColley, Diane Kelsey. "Tongues of Men and Angels: *Ad Leonoram Romae Canentem.*" *Urbane Milton, The Latin Poetry* in *Milton Studies* 19:127–48. Ed. James A Freeman and Anthony Low. Pittsburgh: University of Pittsburgh Press, 1984.

McGuire, Maryann Cale. *Milton's Puritan Masque.* Athens: University of Georgia Press, 1983.

Michaelis, A. "Geschichte des Statuenhofes im vatikanischen Belvedere." *Jahrbuch. Deutsches Archaeologische Institut* (1890): 5–72.

Miller, Leo. "John Milton's 'Lost' Sonnet to Mary Powell." *Milton Quarterly* 25 (Oct. 1991): 102–8.

Miller, William S. *The Mythology of Milton's Comus.* New York: Garland, 1988.

Morris, David B. "Drama and Stasis in Milton's 'Ode on the Morning of Christ's Nativity.'" *Studies in Philology* 68 (1971): 207–22.

Moseley, C. W. R. D. *The Poetic Birth: Milton's Poems of 1645.* Aldershot: Scolar Press, 1991.

Mustard, Wilfred P. *The Piscatory Eclogues of Jacopo Sannazaro.* Baltimore: Johns Hopkins Press, 1914.

Nardo, Anna K. "Academic Interludes in *Paradise Lost.*" *Milton Studies,* 27: 209–41. Ed. James A. Simmonds. Pittsburgh: University of Pittsburgh Press, 1991.

———. "Milton and the Academic Sonnet." In *Milton in Italy,* ed. Mario Di Cesare, 489–503. Binghamton, New York: Medieval and Renaissance Texts and Studies, 1991.

———. *Milton's Sonnets and the Ideal Community.* Lincoln: University of Nebraska Press, 1979.

Newman, J. K. "Empire of the Sun: Lelio Guidiccioni and Pope Urban VIII." *International Journal of the Classical Tradition* 1 (Summer 1994): 62–70.

Nichols, Fred J. "'Lycidas,' 'Epitaphium Damonis,' the Empty Dream and the Failed Song." In *Acta Conventus Neo-Latini Lovaniensis,* ed. J. I. IJsewijn and E. Kessler, 445–52. Leuven: Wilhelm Fink Verlag München, 1973.

———, ed. *An Anthology of Neo-Latin Poetry.* New Haven: Yale University Press, 1979.

Norbrook, David. *Poetry and Politics in the English Renaissance.* London: Routledge, 1984.

———. "The Reformation of the Masque." In *The Court Masque,* ed. David Lindley, 94–110. Manchester: Manchester University Press, 1984.

Nyquist, Mary, and Margaret W. Ferguson, eds. *Re-membering Milton: Essays on the Texts and Traditions*. New York: Methuen, 1987.

O'Malley, J. W., S.J. "Fulfillment of the Christian Golden Age under Pope Julius II: Text of a Discourse of Giles of Viterbo, 1505." *Traditio* 25 (1969): 265–338.

Oman, Carola. *Henrietta Maria*. London: Hodder and Stoughton, 1936.

Osgood, Charles Grosvenor. *The Classical Mythology of Milton's English Poems*. New York: Holt, 1900.

Parker, William Riley. *Milton: A Biography*. 2 vols. Oxford: Clarendon Press, 1968.

———. "Milton and the Marchioness of Winchester." *Modern Language Review* 44 (1949): 547–50.

———. Review of *The Miltonic Setting, Past and Present*. *Modern Language Notes* 55 (1940): 215–18.

Pastor, Ludwig. *The History of the Popes*. Ed. and trans. Ralph Francis Kerr. London: Routledge and Kegan Paul, 1925–1957.

Patrides, C. A., ed. *Milton's Lycidas: The Tradition and the Poem*. Columbia: University of Missouri Press, 1983.

Patterson, Annabel. "That Old Man Eloquent." In *Literary Milton: Text, Pretext, Context*, ed. Diana Treviño Benet and Michael Lieb, 22–44. Pittsburgh: Duquesne University Press, 1994.

Peacock, John. "The French Element in Inigo Jones's Masque Design." In *The Court Masque*, ed. David Lindley, 148–168. Manchester: Manchester University Press, 1984.

Postlethwaite, Norman, and Gordon Campbell, eds. "Edward King, Milton's 'Lycidas': Poems and Documents." *Milton Quarterly*, 28 (Dec. 1994).

Prince, F. T. *The Italian Element in Milton's Verse*. Oxford: Clarendon Press, 1954.

———. "*Lycidas* and the Tradition of the Italian Eclogue." *English Miscellany* 2 (1951): 95–105.

Quint, David. "Sannazaro: From Orpheus to Proteus." In *Origin and Originality in Renaissance Literature*, 43–80. New Haven: Yale University Press, 1983.

Rajan, B. "*Lycidas*." In *Milton Encyclopedia*, ed. William B. Hunter Jr., et al. Lewisburg: Bucknell University Press, 1978–1980.

Rand, Edward K. "Milton in Rustication." *Studies in Philology* 19 (1922): 109–35.

Reilein, Dean A. "Milton's *Comus* and Sabrina's Compliment." *Milton Quarterly* 5 (May 1971): 42–43.

Revard, Stella P. "Building the Foundations of the Good Commonwealth: Pindar, Marvell, and the Power of Music." In *"The Muses Commonweale": Poetry and Politics in the Seventeenth Century*, ed. Claude J.

Summers and Ted-Larry Pebworth. Columbia: University of Missouri Press, 1988.

———. "Milton's Gunpowder Poems and Satan's Conspiracy." *Milton Studies,* 4:63–77. Ed. James Simmonds. Pittsburgh: University of Pittsburgh Press, 1972.

———. "Milton's Muse and the Daughters of Memory." *English Literary Renaissance,* 9 (1979): 432–41.

———. "The Politics of Milton's Hercules." *Milton Studies* 32: 217–45. Ed. Albert C. Labriola. Pittsburgh: University of Pittsburgh Press, 1995.

———. "Vergil's *Georgics* and *Paradise Lost:* Nature and Human Nature in a Landscape." In *Vergil at 2000,* ed. John Bernard. New York: AMS, 1986.

Riddell, James A., and Stanley Stewart. *Jonson's Spenser: Evidence and Historical Criticism.* Pittsburgh: Duquesne University Press, 1995.

Rollinson, Philip. "Milton's Nativity Poem and the Decorum of Genre." *Milton Studies* 7:165–88 Ed. James A. Simmonds. Pittsburgh: University of Pittsburgh Press, 1975.

Røstvig, Maren-Sofie. *The Happy Man: Studies in the Metamorphosis of a Classical Ideal, 1600–1700.* Oslo: Oslo University Press; New York: Humanities, 1962.

Rumrich, John. *Milton Unbound.* Cambridge: Cambridge University Press, 1996.

Ryan, Lawrence V. "Milton's *Epitaphium Damonis* and B. Zanchi's Elegy on Baldassare Castiglione." *Humanisticia Lovaniensia* 30 (1981): 108–17.

Sandys, J. E. *Transactions. Royal Society of Literature.* 32 (1914): 233–64.

Schoeck, R. J. in *Notes & Queries* 101 (1956): 190–91.

Schröter, Elisabeth. "Der Vatikan als Hügel Apollons und der Musen. Kunst und Panegyric von Nikolaus V bis Julius II." *Römische Quartalschrift für christliche Altertums Kunde und Kirchengeschichte* 74 (1979): 208–40.

Scott, John Beldon. *Images of Nepotism: The Painted Ceiling of Palazzo Barberini.* Princeton: Princeton University Press, 1991.

Segal, Charles Paul. "Pindar's First and Third Olympian Odes." *Harvard Studies in Classical Philology,* 68 (1964): 211–67.

———. *Pindar's Mythmaking: The Fourth Pythian Ode.* Princeton: Princeton University Press, 1986.

Shafer, Robert. *The English Ode to 1660.* Princeton: Princeton University Press, 1918.

Shawcross, John T. "Form and Content in Milton's Latin Elegies." *Huntington Library Quarterly* 33 (1970): 331–50.

———. *John Milton, The Self and the World.* Lexington: University Press of Kentucky, 1993.

————. "Milton's Decision to Become a Poet." *Modern Language Quarterly* 24 (1963): 21–30.

————. "The Prosody of Milton's Translation of Horace's Fifth Ode." *Tennessee Studies in Literature* 13 (1968): 81–89.

————. "Two Comments." *Milton Quarterly* 7 (December 1973): 97–98.

Shumaker, Wayne. "Flowerets and Sounding Seas: A Study in the Affective Structure of *Lycidas*," *PMLA* 66 (1951): 485–94. Reprinted in *Milton's Lycidas: The Tradition and the Poem*, ed. C. A. Patrides, 129–39. Columbia: University of Missouri Press, 1983.

Shuster, George N. *The English Ode from Milton to Keats*. New York: Columbia University Press, 1940.

Skulsky, Harold. "Milton's Enrichment of Latin Love Poetry." In *Acta Conventus Neo-Latini Lovaniensis*, ed. J. I. IJsewijn and E. Kessler, 603–611. Leuven: Wilhelm Fink Verlag München, 1973.

Spiller, Michael R. G. " 'Per Chiamare e Per Destare': Apostrophe in Milton's Sonnets." In *Milton in Italy*, ed. Mario Di Cesare, 477–88. Binghamton: Medieval and Renaissance Texts and Studies, 1991.

Sprott, S. E. *Milton's Art of Prosody*. Oxford: Basil Blackwell, 1953.

Starnes, De Witt T., and Ernest William Talbert. *Classical Myth and Legend in Renaissance Dictionaries*. Chapel Hill: University of North Carolina Press, 1955.

Steadman, John M. *Milton's Biblical and Classical Imagery*. Pittsburgh: Duquesne University Press, 1984.

————. *Moral Fiction in Milton and Spenser*. Columbia: University of Missouri Press, 1995.

Striar, Brian. "Milton's Elegia Septima: The Poetics of Roman Elegy and a Verse Translation." *Milton Quarterly* 27 (Dec. 1993): 138–49.

Tayler, Edward W. "*Lycidas* in Christian Time." In *Milton's Poetry: Its Development in Time*, Pittsburgh: Duquesne University Press, 1979; reprinted from *Huntington Library Quarterly* 41 (1978): 103–17. Condensed and reprinted in *Milton's Lycidas: The Tradition and the Poem*, ed. C. A. Patrides, 303–18. Columbia: University of Missouri Press, 1983.

Tillyard, E. M. W. *Milton*. London: Chatto & Windus, 1930.

————. "Milton: 'L'Allegro' and 'Il Penseroso.' " *English Association Pamphlet* 82 (1932). Reprinted in *The Miltonic Setting, Past and Present*. Cambridge: Cambridge University Press, 1938.

————. *Studies in Milton*. London, 1951.

Turner, Alberta T. "Milton and the Conventions of the Academic Miscellanies." *The Yearbook of English Studies* 5 (1975): 86–93.

Tuve, Rosemund. *Images and Themes in Five Poems by Milton*. Cambridge: Harvard University Press, 1957.

Waddy, Patricia. *Seventeenth-Century Roman Palaces.* Cambridge: MIT Press, 1990.

Walker, Julia M. *Milton and the Idea of Woman.* Urbana: University of Illinois Press, 1988.

Watson, Sara R. "Milton's Ideal Day: Its Development as a Pastoral Theme." *PMLA* 57 (1942): 404–20.

Weismiller, Edward. "The 'Dry' and 'Rugged' Verse." In *The Lyric and Dramatic Milton,* ed. Joseph H. Summers. New York: English Institute Essays, 1965.

Wilding, Michael. *Dragons Teeth: Literature in the English Revolution.* Oxford: Clarendon Press, 1987.

Wilson, Gayle Edward. "Decorum and Milton's 'An Epitaph on the Marchioness of Winchester.'" *Milton Quarterly* 8 (March 1974): 11–14.

Wind, Edgar. *Pagan Mysteries in the Renaissance.* 1958. 2d ed., London: Faber, 1967.

Woodhouse, A. S. P. "*Comus* Once More," *University of Toronto Quarterly,* 19 (1949–1959): 218–23.

———. "Milton's Pastoral Monodies." In *Studies in Honour of Gilbert Norwood,* ed. Mary E. White, 263–72. Toronto: University of Toronto Press, 1952.

Index

287

Credits

Acknowledgment is made as follows for permission to quote from copyrighted material:

"The Tangles of Neaera's Hair: Milton and Neo-Latin Ode," by Stella P. Revard, in *Acta Conventus Neo-Latini Hafniensis: Paper from 1991,* ed. Rhoda Schnur, et al., Medieval & Renaissance Texts & Studies, vol. 120 (Binghamton: MRTS, 1994), pp. 75–96. Copyright, Center for Medieval and Early Renaissance Studies, SUNY Binghamton.

"Alpheus, Arethusa, and the Pindaric Pursuit in 'Lycidas,'" by Stella P. Revard, in *Of Poetry and Politics: Essays on Milton and His World,* ed. P. G. Stanwood, Medieval & Renaissance Texts & Studies, vol. 126 (Binghamton: MRTS, 1995), pp. 35–45. Copyright, Center for Medieval and Early Renaissance Studies, SUNY Binghamton.

A revision of the article "*Ad Joannem Rousium:* Elegiac Wit and Pindaric Mode" by Stella P. Revard from *Milton Studies: Volume XIX (Urbane Milton: The Latin Poetry),* James A. Freeman and Anthony Low, Guest Editors. © 1984 by the University of Pittsburgh Press. Reprinted by permission of the University of Pittsburgh Press.